Praise for Andrew Lawler's

UNDER JERUSALEM

"In *Under Jerusalem*, journalist Andrew Lawler directs our contemplation away from the heavenly city, and down into the roots of history and faith. . . . In a city where the winner takes all, Mr. Lawler does an admirable job of striving for the diplomats' ideal of 'evenhandedness.'"
—*The Wall Street Journal*

"A sweeping tale of archaeological exploits and their cultural and political consequences told with a historian's penchant for detail and a journalist's flair for narration. . . . Timely. . . . [Shows] how and why ordinary men and women, and great empires alike, continue to seek meaning in the dirt and debris beneath this magnetic, confounding city."
—*The Washington Post*

"Lawler's history tracks both the marvels found underground and the events unfolding above them. . . . Probing excavators' often partisan motivations, Lawler highlights archaeology's power to shape narratives and its development from a discipline 'not far removed from its far older cousin, tomb robbing,' into a modern tool of nationalist myth-making."
—*The New Yorker*

"Magisterial. . . . [A] fast-paced adventure-story account. . . . This is a spellbinding book—and a reminder that, just when one might have imagined that nothing new could be written about Jerusalem, there is still more to be found beneath its surface."
—*Moment*

"Lawler's prose and the spotlight he shines on the history of each era make his account read like an exciting adventure story."
—Jewish Book Council

"An impressively absorbing, admirably executed exploration of the labyrinthine layers of history, politics, religion, and science buried beneath one of the most religiously significant and politically volatile cities on earth. Painterly descriptions, engaging storytelling, and meticulous research turn what could be a yawning tale of endless bureaucratic permit wrangling and religious and political machinations into a surprisingly exciting page-turner."   —*Boing Boing*

"Lawler gives a comprehensive, evenhanded, clearheaded story about one of the most argued over pieces of land on the earth. But this is no dry treatise. It's more of an adventure story with the main characters being archaeologists and treasure seekers. Lovers of Indiana Jones and *Raiders of the Lost Ark* won't be disappointed."
                                                    —*New York Journal of Books*

"In *Under Jerusalem*, American author Andrew Lawler tells the story behind a century and a half of excavating the world's most contested city, paying as much attention to the aboveground politics as to the subterranean discoveries. Part history, part journalism, and part adventure story, the book is nearly as fun to read as exploring the underground passages it describes."   —*The Jerusalem Post*

"Richly detailed, sensitively argued, and entertainingly written, this immersive history casts Jerusalem in a new light and reveals the tensions that meet at the intersection of science, politics, religion, and history. This fascinating, evenhanded chronicle is a treasure."
                                                    —*Publishers Weekly* (starred review)

"At its heart, *Under Jerusalem* is a terrific story, bursting at the seams with dubiously legal digs and eccentric personalities."   —*Booklist*

"Lawler's writing is clear and engaging, whether detailing colorful characters seeking fame and fortune or recounting the history of the West Bank. . . . This archaeological exploration of Jerusalem will find a welcome audience among readers interested in or curious about the historic city."   —*Library Journal*

ANDREW LAWLER

UNDER JERUSALEM

Andrew Lawler is author of the bestselling *The Secret Token: Myth, Obsession, and the Search for the Lost Colony of Roanoke* and the acclaimed *Why Did the Chicken Cross the World?: The Epic Saga of the Bird That Powers Civilization*. His work has appeared in *The New York Times, The Washington Post, National Geographic,* and *Smithsonian.* He is a contributing writer for *Science* and a contributing editor for *Archaeology.* Lawler's work has appeared several times in *The Best of Science and Nature Writing.*

UNDER
JERUSALEM

UNDER JERUSALEM

The Buried History of the
World's Most Contested City

ANDREW LAWLER

ANCHOR BOOKS
A Division of Penguin Random House LLC
New York

FIRST ANCHOR BOOKS EDITION 2023

Copyright © 2021 by Andrew Lawler

All rights reserved. Published in the United States by Anchor Books,
a division of Penguin Random House LLC, New York, and distributed in
Canada by Penguin Random House Canada Limited, Toronto. Originally
published in hardcover in the United States by Doubleday, a division of
Penguin Random House LLC, New York, in 2021.

Anchor Books and colophon are registered trademarks of Penguin Random House LLC.

The Library of Congress has cataloged the Doubleday edition as follows:
Names: Lawler, Andrew, author.
Title: Under Jerusalem : the buried history of the world's most contested city /
Andrew Lawler.
Description: First edition. | New York : Doubleday, 2021.
Identifiers: LCCN 2021004655 (print) | LCCN 2021004656 (ebook)
Subjects: LCSH: Excavations (Archaeology)—Jerusalem. | Jerusalem—History. |
Jerusalem—Antiquities.
Classification: LCC DS109.9.L38 2021 (print) | LCC DS109.9 (ebook) |
DDC 956.94/42—dc23
LC record available at https://lccn.loc.gov/2021004655
LC ebook record available at https://lccn.loc.gov/2021004656

Anchor Books Trade Paperback ISBN: 978-0-593-31176-9
eBook ISBN: 978-0-385-54686-7

Author photograph © Samir Alsharif
Book design by Cassandra Pappas
Maps by Jeffrey L. Ward

anchorbooks.com

Printed in the United States of America
10 9 8 7 6 5 4 3 2

For JoAnn Clayton-Townsend
1935–2020

I will not cease from mental fight,
Nor shall my sword sleep in my hand
Till we have built Jerusalem
In England's green and pleasant land.

—WILLIAM BLAKE

Who has ever seen Jerusalem naked?
Not even archaeologists;
Jerusalem never gets completely undressed
But always puts on new houses over the shabby and broken ones.

—YEHUDA AMICHAI

Is it from a dimly lit stone that wars flare up?

—MAHMOUD DARWISH

Contents

Timeline

Circa 3000 BCE	The first homes and rock-cut tombs are constructed near Jerusalem's pulsating spring.
Circa 1700 BCE	Massive stone fortifications, pools, and channels are built around the spring.
Circa 950 BCE	Israelites conquer the city from Jebusites; Jerusalem becomes the capital of Judea.
586 BCE	After a prosperous era, a Babylonian army destroys Jerusalem and, with it, the temple attributed to Solomon.
516 BCE	The temple is rebuilt under Persian domination, but Jerusalem is slow to recover.
332 BCE	Captured by Alexander the Great's army, the city falls under Hellenistic rule.
141 BCE	Judeans expel the Seleucid Empire garrison, and local Hasmonean rule begins.
63 BCE	The Roman general Pompey the Great conquers Jerusalem; Roman rule begins.
37 BCE	Aided by Romans, Herod the Great ousts Parthian invaders and secures the throne.

20 BCE   Herod begins a major renovation of the temple complex.

Circa   Jesus is crucified under the rule of the Roman governor
34 CE   Pontius Pilate.

66 CE   Riots in Judea lead to rebellion against Rome; civil war
         envelops Jerusalem.

70 CE   A Roman army besieges and destroys the city.

130 CE   The Roman emperor Hadrian rebuilds and rebrands
         Jerusalem as Aelia Capitolina.

335 CE   The Holy Sepulchre, built at the order of the Roman
         emperor Constantine the Great, is consecrated.

637 CE   Following a brief Persian occupation, the city, now known as
         Aelia, is conquered by Muslim forces.

691 CE   Under Umayyad rulers, the Dome of the Rock is built on the
         city's ruined acropolis; soon after the nearby al-Aqsa Mosque
         is completed.

1099 CE At the urging of Pope Urban II, European Christian
         Crusaders seize Jerusalem.

1187 CE Saladin, the Ayyubid dynasty founder, defeats the Crusaders
         and returns the city, now known as al-Quds, to Muslim
         control.

1260 CE After Mongol raids, Egyptian Mamluks take charge.

1516 CE The Turkish-speaking Ottomans incorporate Jerusalem into
         their expanding empire, based in Istanbul.

1530s CE Suleiman the Magnificent rebuilds the city walls and creates
          a courtyard at the acropolis's western wall.

1831 CE Muhammad Ali Pasha's Egyptian forces capture Jerusalem;
         European travelers are welcomed.

1838 CE Britain appoints its first foreign consul in Jerusalem;
         Edward Robinson visits and launches the city's first biblical
         research effort.

1840 CE   Ottomans reconquer Jerusalem and permit the opening of additional consulates.

1863 CE   Louis-Félicien Joseph Caignart de Saulcy conducts the city's first archaeological dig, prompting Jewish outrage.

1865 CE   The Palestine Exploration Fund is founded in London; Charles Wilson completes his survey of the city.

1867 CE   Charles Warren begins his underground excavations; Mark Twain visits with an American tour group.

1883 CE   Conrad Schick conducts a Russian-sponsored Holy Sepulchre dig to confirm the site's authenticity.

1897 CE   Frederick J. Bliss's dig identifies the elusive City of David.

1911 CE   Montagu Brownlow Parker's effort to find the Ark of the Covenant under the Dome of the Rock leads to riots.

1913 CE   On the eve of World War I, Raymond Weill seeks both the Ark of the Covenant and David's tomb.

1917 CE   British forces, under General Edmund Allenby, oust the Ottomans from Jerusalem.

1929 CE   Tension at the Wailing/al-Buraq Wall sets off Jewish-Arab riots.

1935 CE   Amid increasing Jewish immigration, Arabs revolt against British rule in Palestine.

1948 CE   The British withdraw, Israel is created, and war breaks out between Arabs and the new state; the Jewish Quarter is damaged in fighting.

1949 CE   The battered city is partitioned between Jordan and Israel, which makes West Jerusalem its capital.

1967 CE   In the Six-Day War, Israel conquers East Jerusalem and then demolishes the Mughrabi Quarter.

1968 CE   Israeli excavations begin near the Temple Mount, in the Jewish Quarter, and, secretly, next to the Western Wall.

1981 CE   Yigal Shiloh's dig leads to Jewish riots; Rabbi Yehuda Getz hunts for the Ark of the Covenant under the Temple Mount.

1987 CE   The first Palestinian intifada breaks out; the Western Wall Tunnel is nearly complete.

1993 CE   As President Bill Clinton is inaugurated, the Oslo peace talks between Israelis and Palestinians begin.

1996 CE   The Western Wall Tunnel exit is opened, resulting in deadly violence; Ronny Reich and Eli Shukron begin Silwan/City of David dig.

1999 CE   Palestinian excavations on the Temple Mount/Noble Sanctuary cause Jewish outcry.

2001 CE   Israeli-Palestinian peace talks collapse; the al-Aqsa intifada begins.

2005 CE   Eilat Mazar digs for King David's palace; Reich and Shukron commence new excavations beneath Silwan/the City of David.

2013 CE   The tunneling effort beneath Silwan/the City of David resumes under Joe Uziel.

2018 CE   The United States moves its embassy from Tel Aviv to Jerusalem.

2019 CE   The City of David Foundation inaugurates the "Pilgrimage Road" tunnel; France sued over the Tomb of the Kings.

2021 CE   Clashes between Israeli forces and Palestinians rock Jerusalem.

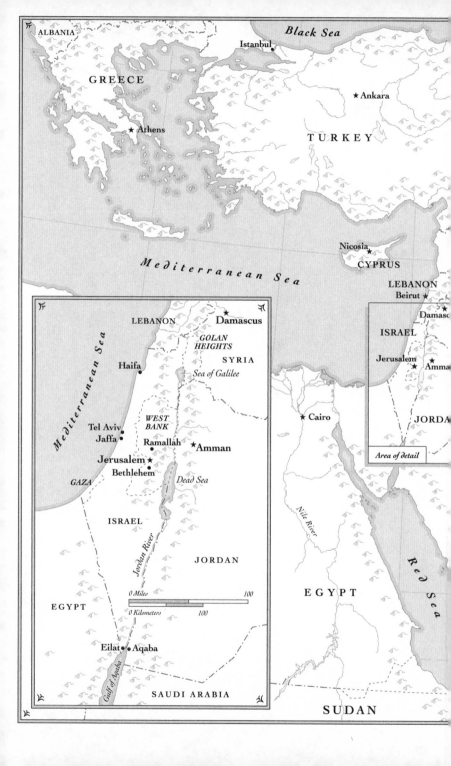

Author's Note

"Writing about Jerusalem was very stressful; every word counts," said author Simon Sebag Montefiore. Which word to select is part of that trial. The recording at a single light-rail stop announces your arrival at the Hebrew Shechem Gate, the Arabic Gate of the Column, and the English Damascus Gate. What one calls it says as much about the speaker as the place.

Naming is, of course, the ultimate power, as described in the biblical book of Genesis. Most of the names here, with a few exceptions, favor common usage in the West. I use the translated term Temple Mount when referring to the city's acropolis from a Jewish point of view and Noble Sanctuary from that of Muslims, though a quote might refer to the Arabic terms Haram al-Sharif or al-Aqsa. The traditional tomb of Jesus is in the Church of the Resurrection for Eastern Christians, but here I use Holy Sepulchre (not Sepulcher, as American readers might expect). Also, English transliterations of Arab and Hebrew proper names are rendered in their most typical modern-day English form: Qur'an instead of Koran, and Benjamin rather than Binyamin.

Even capitalizing requires care in this city of political hypervigilance. The Western Wall is uppercase when referred to in a Jewish context after 1967, and lowercase if not. I also go by the international convention that capitalizes the term East Jerusalem, the sector formerly occupied by Jordan and now by Israel, though Israel no longer recognizes the 1948 border dividing eastern and western sectors.

As for scripture, the terms "Bible" and "biblical" refer to either the

Hebrew or the Christian text, depending on context. There are, of course, many versions of each.

Since this book tracks the stories of Jerusalem's excavators, most of the individuals in this story are Christian and Jewish. This reflects, I hope, not a bias but the stark reality that Palestinian Arabs, for reasons explored, have overseen few excavations during the past century and a half compared with Europeans, Americans, and Jewish Israelis. This does not detract from the role played by Arabs—and, to a lesser extent, Jews—in doing much of the hard labor as well as in opposing digs many viewed as disrespectful, chauvinistic, and even blasphemous.

Finally, there are the many names of the city itself, each of which reflects a different time or culture from which to view it. For ancient Canaanites and Egyptians, it was Ursalim, which might refer to the city of Shalem, a Canaanite god of dusk. For ancient Judeans, it was variously Yerushayalem, Yerushalaim, the City of Jebus, or the City of David; Jewish scripture mentions more than seventy versions of the city's name. For ancient Greeks and Romans, it was Ierousal or Hierosolyma.

In the second century CE, in the wake of the Roman destruction, Emperor Hadrian combined his family name with a reference to the Roman god Jupiter Capitolinus to call the rebuilt city Aelia Capitolina. Byzantines shortened that to Aelia; medieval Christians revived the older term, which eventually was spelled Jerusalem in English. Early Muslims used Ilya as well as Bayt al-Maqdis—"the Holy House"—and, later, al-Quds, "the Holy One," which remains the city's Arabic name today.

Here, again, following the Western fashion, I use the name Jerusalem.

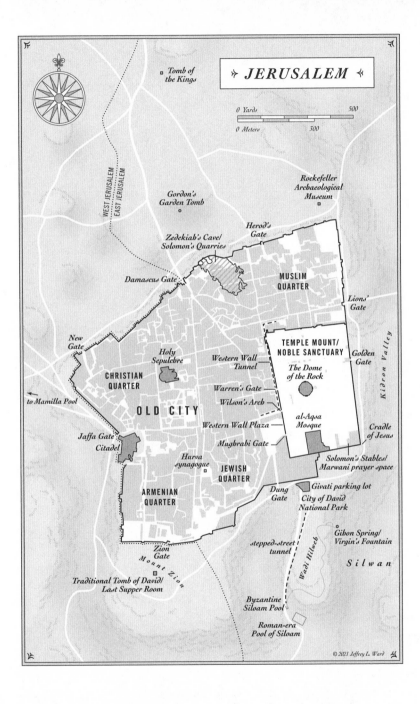

⚜ *JERUSALEM* ⚜

Tomb of
the Kings

0 Yards · 500
0 Meters · 300

WEST JERUSALEM
EAST JERUSALEM

Rockefeller
Archaeological
Museum

Gordon's
Garden Tomb

Herod's
Gate

Zedekiah's Cave/
Solomon's Quarries

MUSLIM
QUARTER

Damascus Gate

Lions'
Gate

New
Gate

Holy
Sepulchre

Western Wall
Tunnel

TEMPLE MOUNT/
NOBLE SANCTUARY

The Dome
of the Rock

Golden
Gate

CHRISTIAN
QUARTER

Warren's Gate

Wilson's Arch

to Mamilla Pool

OLD CITY

Western Wall Plaza

al-Aqsa
Mosque

Kidron Valley

Jaffa Gate
Citadel

Mughrabi Gate

Cradle
of Jesus

Hurva
synagogue

JEWISH
QUARTER

Solomon's Stables/
Marwani prayer space

ARMENIAN
QUARTER

Dung
Gate

Givati parking lot

City of David
National Park

Zion
Gate

stepped-street
tunnel

Gihon Spring/
Virgin's Fountain

Mount Zion

Wadi Hilweh

Silwan

Traditional Tomb of David/
Last Supper Room

Byzantine
Siloam Pool

Roman-era
Pool of Siloam

© 2021 Jeffrey L. Ward

Introduction

I see the Past, Present, & Future existing all at once.
—WILLIAM BLAKE

Sacred to three faiths and revered by more than half the people on the planet, Jerusalem conjures up powerful images of the celestial. According to Christians, Jesus ascended into its skies; many believe he was followed by his mother, Mary. For two billion Muslims, this is where Muhammad climbed through the seven heavens on his mystical night journey. Jewish folklore places here the angel-filled ladder that Jacob dreamed rose into the firmament. And in many traditions, God's final judgment will descend from the clouds hovering above the city.

"Jerusalem is the gateway to heaven; all the nations of the world agree on this," noted the twelfth-century Spanish Jewish poet and scholar Judah Halevi. A century later, the Muslim author Fakhr ad-Din al-Fazari reported that "angels descend every night unto Jerusalem."

Yet the Holy City conceals a secret subterranean self. Below the ground is a labyrinthine three-dimensional time capsule recording five millennia of bustling prosperity, brutal war, and remarkable religious innovation that altered the course of human history. A twentieth-century Israeli poet compared Jerusalem to a terrestrial Atlantis where everything "is submerged and sunken."

That observation is grounded as much in geology as poetry. Water and stone define this landscape. During the age of the dinosaurs, the entire Middle East was covered with a shallow sea. When the marine organisms that made it their home died and collected on the bottom, the mass eventually hardened into limestone. Each block of Jerusalem's famed building material is, in essence, a congealed cemetery.

Forty million years of folding and lifting combined with the tenacious trickle of water rolling down slopes and seeping underground created the rugged Judean hills above and an intricate world of cracks, crevices, and caves below. One of those rivulets eventually burst out of the flank of a steep and stony ridge, creating a mysteriously pulsating but reliable spring. That water source drew permanent settlers about the time that neighboring Egyptians and Mesopotamians were building the earliest cities and writing the first stories some five thousand years ago.

Another draw was a local rock with almost magical qualities; soft when extracted, it became tougher when exposed to the elements, and it turns the color of honey in the slanted rays of day's end. Along with quarries, residents dug underground passages to funnel water and waste. As the city above rose, they punctured the surface to insert cisterns, lay foundations, and carve out tombs.

Over millennia the Jerusalem above waxed and waned, its walls swelling, contracting, or vanishing as its fortunes rose and fell. Yet the territory beneath relentlessly expanded. An earthquake or an invasion might suddenly cast whole neighborhoods onto the subterrestrial shore, but most of the accretion came with the mundane actions of urban life; a first floor filled with debris became a basement, an old cistern turned into a convenient septic tank.

"Jerusalem is lifted on the carnage of its own centuries, layer upon layer of destruction and daily waste," wrote British author Colin Thubron. "Age upon age, the city grows and is buried."

Like the marine organisms that created the limestone, succeeding generations created new strata. But Jerusalem is not like the abandoned towns, such as nearby ancient Jericho, dotting the Middle East that left behind high mounds resembling layer cakes, with the old neatly stacked beneath the more recent. Constant human activities jumbled the past; a Roman column might be repurposed for a Byzantine church, and stones cut by Jewish masons two thousand years ago could adorn a medieval mosque. Jerusalem is an old puzzle that reassembles itself in fresh ways, like the faiths that grew from it.

A lack of wood on the barren hillsides also shaped the growing underground terrain. Without the luxury of cheap and sturdy beams, architects learned early to span distances with stone vaults and domes. "The knobbiest town in the world," said Mark Twain, the itinerant newspaper reporter who arrived in 1867 as part of one of the first American tour groups. He added that it "looks as if it might be roofed, from center to circumference, with inverted saucers."

As a result, a succession of invisible arches came to undergird much of the city. "There is an old Indian saying, that the arch never sleeps," noted British archaeologist Charles Warren, who began his excavations the same year Twain visited. "And as Jerusalem is a system of arches (every house being built of vaulted rooms), it may be said that the Holy City never sleeps."

Jerusalem is perched ever more precariously on a succession of ruins, built vault upon vault, bathed in sewage while mounting slowly to heaven.

◆ ◆ ◆

EVER SINCE ABRAHAM LINCOLN was in the White House, when a French explorer broke into an ancient Jewish tomb, this subterranean realm has sparked riots, threatened to trigger regional war, and set the entire world on edge.

Adventurers seeking the Ark of the Covenant nearly plunged two empires into chaos in 1911. They rattled the Middle East six decades after that. When the mayor opened a new exit to a tunnel along the Western Wall in 1996, more than one hundred people lost their lives. Five years later, a bitter dispute over who would control Jerusalem's underground territory led to the collapse of peace talks between Palestinians and Israelis.

Jerusalem "ignites heat in the human breast, a viral fever of zealotry and true belief that lodged in the DNA of Western civilization," said American author James Carroll. The search under its streets during the past century and a half has played a central role in creating the embattled city of today.

This book is about the hunt for the Holy City's past by a strange and colorful mix of treasure hunters, scholarly clerics, religious extremists, and secular archaeologists. They were looking for many things—the Ark, King David's palace, King Solomon's treasure, and even ancient garbage that might reveal something of everyday life. In so doing, they helped spawn Zionism, create the state of Israel, and undermine efforts to secure peace between two warring peoples. By digging for the past, they continue to alter the city's future.

Yet while the compulsion to dig has triggered discord and violence, it may, paradoxically, provide the way to dissolve the stony tribal rancor that has for so long frustrated the earthly city's aspirations for heavenly harmony.

⋅ ⋅ ⋅

TWAIN AND WARREN WERE in the vanguard of a novel kind of pilgrim in what is the world's oldest tourist town. Far from any major trade route and lacking a fertile hinterland, Jerusalem had long welcomed religious believers eager to pray at its myriad shrines and tombs, seek food and lodging, and buy souvenirs to take home. Faith was and remains the city's primary industry.

The city was already a thousand years old when a dancing king is said to have brought the gilded Ark containing the Ten Commandments through its streets amid a fanfare of lyres, castanets, cymbals, and timbrels. According to the story, David's coup provided the centerpiece for a temple—later ruined, rebuilt, and ruined again—that crowned the city's acropolis and attracted worshippers from around the region.

A dozen centuries after that, a Roman empress declared that she had found the rock upon which Jesus was crucified, the cross that bore him up, and the tomb in which he was laid. These discoveries, barely a third of a mile from the Temple Mount, transformed the site into the holiest place in Christendom. Nearly four centuries later, a Muslim caliph ordered a magnificent dome built over another rock, this one on the city's ruined acropolis, to mark the spot where the prophet Muhammad was said to have risen into heaven. Even the memory of a holy place has proved a draw; Jews have long journeyed to the city to lament a vanished temple that once stood on that same sacred esplanade.

The pilgrims who converged on Jerusalem came from six continents and brought their own distinct languages and traditions, but until the nineteenth century nearly all shared the goal of praying in a place deemed to be a living link to the divine. Westerners like Twain and Warren were different. Their goal was less to pray than to find a bygone Jerusalem, a pious quest that would fashion the city's future in profound and often violent ways.

Given Jerusalem's capacity to ignite "heat in the human breast," it is easy to forget that Westerners had all but forgotten the earthly city for more than five centuries. That process began when Arab warriors expelled the last of the European Crusaders—a motley collection of feuding knights, fortune seekers, and devout Christian wanderers—from their Kingdom of Jerusalem in 1291, ending nearly two centuries of Holy Land occupation.

After that date, the long trek east, always arduous and expensive, became more dangerous as well. Political upheavals and Arab memories of Crusader atrocities made Western European Christians, aside from a few monks and adventurers, scarce in Jerusalem. Medieval mapmakers still placed it at the center of the world, but in Europe the physical place receded into a metaphor for the human longing to fuse heaven and earth.

At the end of 1516, the guns and artillery of Ottomans triumphed over the scimitars and lances of Arab cavalry, and Jerusalem fell to a fast-growing empire ruled from Istanbul by Turkish-speaking Muslims. Less than a year later, a Catholic monk in a distant German town launched what became the Protestant Reformation.

Both the Ottoman victory and Martin Luther's challenge to the Catholic Church made Jerusalem slip even more in the Western mind from city to symbol. The Ottomans spent the next century warring with Catholic Spain and its allies for control of the Mediterranean Sea, disrupting pilgrimage routes. And among the growing numbers of Protestants, pilgrimages, like relics and indulgences, quickly fell out of fashion.

"Come let us declare in Zion the word of God," said the English Puritan William Bradford as he stepped off the *Mayflower* in 1620. But it was on the shore of North America rather than Palestine that he landed. "Jerusalem was, New England is," wrote the Reverend Samuel Wakeman succinctly in 1685. Protestants sought to build a New Jerusalem in the New World rather than conquer that of the Old World. Zions, Mount Zions, and Jerusalems proliferated across the North American map.

As one historian put it, "The Puritans did not need to visit the Holy Land; they brought Palestine with them."

This lack of ardor for the real Ottoman city held true for European Jews as well; while the Talmud admonished the Jewish people not to forget Jerusalem, few actually paid a visit, much less settled there prior to the nineteenth century. When the Christian monarchs Ferdinand and Isabella expelled Jews from Spain in 1492, far more relocated to the thriving hubs of Rome and Istanbul than to the more remote Holy City. Even smaller towns like Safed, north of Jerusalem, attracted larger numbers of Jewish scholars.

The Western enchantment with Jerusalem only revived in 1831, after a progressive Egyptian regime briefly seized Jerusalem from the Ottomans. The new rulers eased restrictions on non-Muslims and encouraged visits by foreign Jews and Christians, including Protestant missionaries. The British government, fearful of growing Russian influence in the region, took advantage of the opening to appoint the first foreign consul to Jerusalem in 1838. The same year, a New England theologian and classical scholar named Edward Robinson arrived in the city. "Obeying an impulse from on High," he sought to marry scripture with science, and is often credited with founding the field of biblical archaeology.

Robinson's novel goal was to map biblical Jerusalem, with the Good Book serving as his guidebook and a telescope and a compass as his instruments of discovery. He waded through underground tunnels and studied the aboveground stones along what was known as the Temple Mount to Jews and the Noble Sanctuary to Muslims. "Here then we have indisputable remains of Jewish antiquity, consisting of an important portion of the western wall of the ancient temple area," he wrote.

His claims fired the imaginations of other Westerners. Robinson's sojourn coincided with an evangelical revival in Britain, Canada, and the United States called the Second Great Awakening, when Jesus's return was thought to be near. Millions of Christians were swept up in a religious fervor that saw Jerusalem as the main stage for the impending drama of the End Times; the catalyst, many believed, would be the immigration of Jews to the land of the Bible.

For these Protestant evangelicals, the Jews were necessary tools for redemption, a view that went hand in hand with entrenched anti-Semitism. Once returned to their ancient homeland, they would cast off their antique and misguided notions and accept Jesus as their savior, setting the wheels in motion for the Day of Judgment. Anthony Ashley Cooper, Seventh Earl of Shaftesbury and a leading British evangelical, viewed the Jews as "not a people, but a mass Error" waiting to be corrected, according to historian Barbara Tuchman. In July 1840, he wrote that "everything seems ripe for their return to Palestine."

Three months later, a British fleet bombarded the Mediterranean coast, expelling the Egyptians from the region. The Ottoman sultan subsequently permitted other Europeans to open consulates in Jerusalem to serve the growing trickle of visitors and pilgrims from their nations. Russia, Britain, France, Prussia, and Austria-Hungary at the time were busy absorbing peoples and territories across Africa and Asia. Ottoman lands represented the century's most coveted colonial prize, and Jerusalem lay at its heart.

Amid these religious and political developments, radical scientific ideas were beginning to sweep Europe and North America. The same month that the Egyptians conquered Jerusalem, a young naturalist named Charles Darwin set out on his round-the-world expedition on the HMS *Beagle*. He took with him the first volume of British geologist Charles Lyell's work challenging the biblical claim that the world was six thousand years old and that Noah's flood had covered the whole planet. The journey would lead to his theory of biological evolution contradicting scripture's version of human origins.

The new discipline of archaeology also had begun to gnaw away at long-held beliefs. Excavators unearthed ancient civilizations in the Middle East that seemed to predate the biblical patriarchs and translated clay tablets that told familiar stories—such as that of Noah's flood—heretically suggesting the biblical authors cribbed from older sources. For devout and conservative scholars like Robinson, however, the tools of science could be used to counter religious skepticism among American and European academics that was rapidly spreading to the public.

In the 1850s, a Christian missionary from Virginia heard "the citizens of Jerusalem tell marvelous tales about its subterranean passages, galleries, and halls." An Ottoman official explained to him that "ancient Jerusalem was several strata below the superficies of the present city; and that it would be interesting to explore the magnificent subterranean remains of the gorgeous palaces of King David, Solomon, and various other monarchs of former times—could an entrance but be effected."

Finding such remains might do more than verify biblical accounts and push back the tide of scriptural skepticism; they might also make one famous and rich. Ancient texts and persistent legends suggested that hoards of gold, silver, and gems were still hidden in Jerusalem's depths, including objects as famous as the Ark. These dual dreams of discovering objects of spiritual significance as well as material wealth would power Jerusalem excavations into the twenty-first century.

It wasn't until the fall of 1863, just months after Robinson died, that the first official archaeological expedition arrived in Jerusalem. Led by a French senator and devout Catholic who was a former artillery officer, the dig created a worldwide sensation and an international scandal. Britons, Germans, Russians, and Americans followed in his wake. The race was on to uncover biblical Jerusalem; the Holy City was no longer a pious metaphor but an enticing destination promising spiritual as well as earthly adventure.

"There is no place I so much desire to see as Jerusalem," Lincoln told his wife a year after the first excavation took place in the city, and moments before an assassin's bullet left him mortally wounded on Good Friday in 1865.

◆   ◆   ◆

THE FIRST SIGHT of the city that Lincoln, had he lived, would have encountered often drove even cynics and skeptics to their knees. "It was indeed Jerusalem," related the nineteenth-century Irish writer Eliot Warburton when he laid eyes on its distant domes and steeples. "And had the Holy City risen before us in its palmiest days of magnificence and glory, it could not have created deeper emotion, or been gazed at more earnestly or with intense interest."

Upon entering the gates, however, visitors found a warren of winding alleys, steep stairs, and uneven pavement smelling of garlic and spices with strong notes of human and animal waste, all encircled by a wall enclosing an area only a quarter of the size of New York's Central Park. Jerusalem was essentially an Arab medieval town far removed from the Sunday-school city of Jewish prophets and palaces.

Ecstatic enthusiasm invariably was followed by disappointment and even revulsion. "How false it all is!" exclaimed the French novelist Gustave Flaubert during his 1850 visit. "How crudely painted it is, how cheap looking, how varnished, made for exploitation, for propaganda, and for displaying merchandise! The Holy City of three religions is rotting away from boredom, dejection, and neglect."

Seven years later, a disenchanted Herman Melville found "the color of the whole city is grey and looks at you like a cold grey eye in a cold old man." A decade after that, Mark Twain described a feeling just short of contempt. "Rags, poverty, and dirt" was how he summed up the place. "Jerusalem is mournful, dreary, and lifeless." One of the most progressive Americans of his day, Twain scorned the Holy Land's populace as "ignorant, depraved, superstitious, dirty, lousy, thieving vagabonds," adding memorably, "Christ been once—never come again."

Such harsh assessments by perceptive writers reflect more than disdain for a dusty city lacking sewers, streetlights, and nightlife. Jerusalem's unforgivable sin was that it failed to live up to its legendary role as the sacred abode of wise kings, ascetic prophets, and robed priests tending to animal sacrifices. It certainly didn't seem a worthy setting for the Second Coming or Last Judgment.

In his 1876 travel guide, the German publisher Karl Baedeker tried to prepare tourists for the inevitable letdown. "It would seem at first as though little were left of the ancient city of Zion and Moriah, the far-famed capital of the Jewish empire; and little of it indeed is to be discovered in the narrow, crooked, ill-paved, and dirty streets of the modern town."

This view had the peculiar effect of making the actual city an obstacle to rather than a source of religious inspiration. While traditional pilgrims engaged with the living city packed with ancient shrines, the European and American newcomers were primarily concerned with that which was dead and buried. Melville was put off by what he observed above, but he was intrigued by the "strata of cities buried under the present surface of Jerusalem." Baedeker explained that "only by patiently penetrating beneath the modern crust of rubbish and rottenness which shrouds the sacred places from view" would travelers reach "the Jerusalem of antiquity."

The goal of the typical European traveler was, after all, not to visit the actual Ottoman city called al-Quds, Jerusalem's Arabic name, which means "the Holy One." It was, instead, to find "a timeless place in which events of the biblical past continued to be taking place despite the passage of centuries," concluded the historian Issam Nassar. "It was as if the journey to the city was a voyage to the past." What lay aboveground could therefore be dismissed as counterfeit, and the city's longtime residents—Muslim, Christian, or Jewish—could be brushed off as modern-day interlopers.

Twain had a Bible inscribed with "Jerusalem" in Hebrew for his mother, but he never returned. The city of the present might not be worth a second visit, but that of scripture was eternal. If, as Baedeker said, "the far-famed capital of the Jewish empire" was not to be found along the "dirty streets of the modern town," then perhaps it could be found beneath them.

PART I

"You see, it's like this. They own the land, just the mere land, and that's all they *do* own; but it was our folks, our Jews and Christians, that made it holy, and so they haven't any business to be there defiling it. It's a shame, and we ought not to stand it a minute. We ought to march against them and take it away from them."

—MARK TWAIN, *Tom Sawyer Abroad*

1

A Moment of Insanity

Henceforth we will approach the Holy Land not by brandishing our sword, but with Bible and pen in hand.

—ERNEST VINET

On the bright morning of December 8, 1863, a dapper fifty-six-year-old European stood nervously smoking in a vast sunken courtyard that faced Jerusalem's grandest tomb. In his well-tailored waistcoat, high-collared shirt, and silk cravat, Louis-Félicien Joseph Caignart de Saulcy would not have looked out of place at a Parisian gallery or court soiree.

The French senator and confidant of Emperor Napoleon III anxiously waited for word of a momentous discovery that he believed would rock the world, and make the former soldier from a provincial town both rich and famous.

When his assistant emerged covered in dust from the small square hole leading into the tomb, de Saulcy knew with a glance that the news was good. "An intact sarcophagus! And an inscription!" the man exclaimed, trying to keep his voice low to avoid attracting the attention of the Arab workers lounging nearby. "This is the most beautiful jewel in your crown!"

Earlier that morning, while de Saulcy was still asleep inside the city walls, an Arab worker named Antoun Abou-Saouin had been examining the deepest part of the ancient catacombs. He traced a seam in the rock that revealed the outline of a hidden door. A member of the excavation team rushed through the olive groves and into the city to roust de Saulcy from his hotel bed with the electrifying news. The senator had dressed quickly but punctiliously in a room littered with crates of ancient pottery and glass vessels, then made his way along crooked alleys to Damascus Gate.

De Saulcy had walked briskly through the crenellated portal and followed a dusty path to a broad set of worn stone stairs his workers had cleared the week before. These led to an open square plaza dug out of the rock that was large enough to contain two tennis courts. At one end stood a battered but graceful portico bathed in the golden morning light, finely decorated in intricately carved grape bunches and wreaths, towering over one end of the empty space. The sole entrance into the tomb was a small door on the left side of the portico. In antiquity it had been closed with an enormous rolling stone operated using an ingenious system of weights.

In a city thick with graves, this was Jerusalem's most magnificent burial complex. A second-century CE Greek geographer rated it the world's most beautiful tomb after that of Mausolus, the eastern Anatolia monument that was one of the seven wonders of the ancient world and bequeathed us the term "mausoleum." At least since medieval times, the Jerusalem site had been revered as the Tomb of the Kings, though which kings was a matter of dispute.

The French senator believed he had solved the mystery.

As he had entered the courtyard, de Saulcy assumed a nonchalant air. The Arab landowner and local workers were there, and he didn't want to raise their suspicions. If word leaked of the discovery, there might be unwelcome complications; the landowner certainly would want the third of the treasure that he would be owed by local tradition. So the Frenchman had loitered casually, ostensibly to have a smoke, while three French members of the team went below. They used iron pliers to wrench open the door exposed by Abou-Saouin.

De Saulcy was tall, with a high forehead framed by swept-back graying hair and a meticulously groomed Vandyke. When his assistant emerged from the tomb with the news that the secret chamber was accessible, he maintained his composure, strolling casually to the entrance before bending low to duck through the small entrance. Once out of sight, he quickly threaded his way through a maze of rock-cut rooms while his assistant scrambled to keep up.

Large arched niches designed to hold shrouded corpses lined the dark labyrinth, along with smaller triangular alcoves that once held flickering oil lamps. Bits of stone littered the floor, remains from Arab, Ottoman, British, and French tomb raiders who had smashed stone coffins in their search for treasure. Breathing hard from his sprint through the stuffy space, the senator stepped through the newly opened door. It led into a square rough-hewn space dominated by a pale-white limestone casket.

"We finally had found our burial chamber," de Saulcy later wrote. "How joyful I was!"

◆ ◆ ◆

IT WAS A DEATH that led him to the tomb. A military officer from the northeastern city of Metz, de Saulcy studied engineering and eventually was transferred to Paris to serve as curator of the nation's artillery museum. This left him time to pursue his passion for old coins, which led him to archaeology and the history of the Holy Land.

When his young wife died suddenly in 1850, de Saulcy left Paris to tour the eastern Mediterranean and busy himself with the ancient past. "It would be no advantage to science were we to tread again the beaten paths already traced by hundreds of tourists," he wrote a friend as he left Paris that fall. "Mystery and danger sufficed to fix my resolution, and I determined to proceed at once to Jerusalem."

During de Saulcy's first visit to Palestine, he had explored the passages of the Tomb of the Kings and recovered a few broken pieces of a sarcophagus lid, which he donated to the Louvre. In subsequent years, the amateur scholar grew ever more certain that this subterranean realm hid the final resting place of the early monarchs of Judah, including King David and his son Solomon. It was widely believed that they had lived some three thousand years ago.

In the Bible, the Israelite leader David was credited with conquering Jerusalem from a people called the Jebusites. David united the tribes of Judea in the south with those of Israel to the north, establishing Jerusalem, which lay on the northern end of Judea, as his capital. Solomon then built a short-lived but mighty empire that channeled enormous riches to the city and drew distinguished visitors, such as the queen of Sheba.

At its heart was an elaborate temple built by foreign artisans to house the Ark of the Covenant. When these early kings were laid to rest, the scripture said it was within "the City of David"—presumably, inside the walls of Jerusalem. The site apparently survived at least until the first century CE. "Fellow Israelites," Jesus's apostle Peter said in the Christian New Testament, "I can tell you confidently that the patriarch David died and was buried, and his tomb is here to this day."

Legends of fantastic treasure secreted in the tombs had circulated for millennia. In the time of Jesus, the Roman Jewish historian Josephus wrote of the "great and immense wealth" buried with Solomon. He reported that when the city was besieged by a Greek army centuries earlier, a Judean high priest had plundered three thousand talents—a king's ransom—from just one room of the sepulcher to buy off the invaders.

Josephus also said that Herod the Great, who ruled Judea a generation before Jesus, was desperate for cash to finance his renovation of the city's temple, so he "opened another room, and took away a great deal of money." The king did not disturb the coffins of his predecessors, however, "for their bodies were buried under the earth so artfully, that they did not appear to even those that entered into their monuments."

Tales of divine retribution went hand in hand with those describing fabulous riches. Elsewhere, Josephus related that when two of Herod's grave robbers approached the coffins, they were slain when "a flame burst out upon those that went in." A similar story was popular in medieval times. A Christian cleric hired two Jewish workers to fix a damaged building in the city, and they stumbled on a secret passage that led to a hall with marble columns and a golden crown and scepter on a table. When a strong wind and loud voices arose, they fled and vowed never to return.

By contrast, de Saulcy longed for a dozen years to probe the Tomb of the Kings more thoroughly. His public goal was to discredit the theory put forward by the American biblical explorer Edward Robinson, who argued that the early Judean leaders were buried on the opposite side of the city on what was called Mount Zion. His private passion was to find the long-lost wealth of Solomon. Lacking the connections and resources required for such an ambitious project, however, he had to bide his time.

De Saulcy's luck changed when he met and married the daughter of a French diplomat, a woman who also was a close friend of Empress Eugénie. This vaulted him into the midst of the reconstituted French court. Soon he was spending hours discussing the Roman Empire with the empress's husband, the Caesar-obsessed emperor Napoleon III, a nephew of Napoleon Bonaparte. De Saulcy accompanied the French ruler on trips as far afield as Iceland, and convinced him to support excavations in France to link the glory of the Roman past to the present-day regime.

In 1859, as Darwin published *On the Origin of Species* in Britain, the emperor appointed de Saulcy senator; three years later he awarded him the Legion of Honor. The same year, he traveled with the emperor to the site of a decisive battle between Romans and Gauls outside Paris; Napoleon III ordered an elaborate monument built to commemorate the event, and personally cleaned a gold-and-silver Roman vase recently unearthed there. In France, as was later true in the Holy Land, politics and archaeology were intimately intertwined.

The senator used his newfound influence to launch an expedition to the Middle East that included a military mapmaker, a skilled photographer, and several distinguished French scholars. With "the appreciation of the emperor," the mission was funded with 20,000 francs, roughly the equivalent of about $100,000 today, drawn from the Ministry of Public Education. That was nearly a quarter of the ministry's annual budget.

Since the sixteenth century, the Ottoman Empire had granted France the role of protector of Christian holy places in the Holy Land, largely to annoy its Spanish and Italian enemies. The French embassy in the empire's capital of Istanbul—the conquered Byzantine center of Constantinople—secured written approval from Sultan Abdulaziz allowing de Saulcy to conduct excavations. It was the first official dig permit issued for Jerusalem, and by a man whose titles included Caesar of the Roman Empire.

Now, standing in the dim light of candles held by his assistant, de Saulcy caught his breath as he took in the burial chamber. He saw two inscriptions cut into the side of the stone casket. He hurriedly copied the letters, which seemed to be Hebrew, into his notebook and was stunned to recognize one word repeated twice—*melek,* an ancient word for king. "I clung with all my strength to the hope that I had my hand on the tomb of a king of Judah," he recalled.

When de Saulcy glanced up from his scribbling, he noticed that the cover of the sarcophagus was still sealed irregularly with what appeared to be ancient cement. It was rare to find a Holy Land casket that had not been plundered. He backed out of the chamber and made his way up to the courtyard, using the time to come up with a plan. His immediate goal was to convince the Arab landowner, who was still in the dark about the find, to leave the scene so that he could complete his historic discovery free of interference.

De Saulcy asked the man to personally take a note to two of his colleagues within the walled city. The message—written in French and not comprehensible to the messenger—begged them to come with all haste to the tomb. Along with the note, he handed the delighted landowner a five-franc coin emblazoned with the profile of the emperor. This guaranteed at least a half hour for the team to examine the contents of the sarcophagus without being disturbed.

To ensure that no one hindered the operation, he gave a pocket pistol to Captain Charles Gelis, the team's cartographer. De Saulcy ordered him to use it on the first intruder. "I had a moment of insanity," he later admitted. Gelis laughed but stashed the weapon in his coat. Then they rushed back down to the chamber, which was now crowded with a dozen people and heavy with heat and humidity.

The men gathered wood and hay bales on one side of the sarcophagus, unsealed the lid with pocket knives, and flipped the heavy stone top onto the pile "without making a scratch." Within the casket lay a "well-preserved skeleton, the head resting on a cushion." The skull had collapsed into itself and the bones of the feet had fallen to the side "as a result of the decomposition of the flesh." But the arms were still crossed over the pubic bone. The deceased proved to be a diminutive five-foot-three-inch female.

De Saulcy directed Gelis to recover what was left of the head. "He slid his hands delicately as he could under the skull, and instantly everything caved in and disappeared as if by magic, leaving at the bottom of the casket nothing but a long patch of brownish soil mixed with splinters of bone." As the men watched, "everything else vanished in the blink of an eye."

The French explorer was devastated. "That was all! Not a piece of jewelry, not a ring, not a necklace," he wrote. "Nothing, absolutely nothing."

That is when he spotted the gold, though not in the form or quantity de Saulcy might have wished. Thousands of thin and twisted gold threads lay at the bottom of the casket, presumably part of a gold band lining the shroud that had been made of a coarse linen fabric, "of which some stitches survived on a small fragment of flat bone." He had the team collect the threads as well as all the human remains—mostly a brown soil in the lower half of the casket—for detailed study back in France.

De Saulcy then dispatched one of his assistants to bring the French consul, Edmond de Barrère, to the tomb so he could authenticate "the importance of my discovery." By the time the consul arrived around noon, "the whole world was assembled." Despite the senator's attempts to keep his secret, word of the find spread like wildfire across town. Within an hour, "all Jerusalem was informed." The Frenchman sent a message to the Ottoman governor of the city, alerting him to the news and informing him imperiously that he planned to "take my sarcophagus to Paris."

Barrère descended to the chamber to examine the find. After the inspection, de Saulcy ordered the tomb closed, and the consul went back to his office to draw up an affidavit confirming the discovery. The next day, the ten French members of the team gathered at the consulate to sign the document, which became Jerusalem's first formal archaeological report.

De Saulcy's brief dig failed to find treasure, but it would spark a religious revolt that quickly turned into a media tempest reaching as far as North America. The uproar would launch a European race to recover the biblical secrets locked beneath the Holy City.

· · ·

IN THE 1860s, archaeology was a novel discipline not far removed from its far older cousin, tomb robbing. Digging for treasure had long been a profession in the Ottoman region known as Palestine. In a harsh land where animals and plants had to be carefully tended, the buried past offered an alluringly quick and lucrative harvest.

"There are certain men who spend nearly all their lives in seeking for kanûz—hidden treasures," wrote the English traveler Mary Eliza Rogers the year before de Saulcy's excavation. "Some of them become maniacs, desert their families, and though they are often so poor that they beg their way from door to door, and from village to village, they believe themselves to be rich." She also encountered treasure necromancers, often women, credited with the ability to see what lay concealed beneath the earth. But such activities typically took place in remote areas or under cover of darkness.

The sight of a haughty Christian foreigner disturbing a venerated grave in broad daylight scandalized Jerusalem's Jewish community, which made up roughly half of the city's population of less than twenty thousand. On November 19, three weeks before he found the sarcophagus and the same day that Lincoln gave his Gettysburg Address, the city's Hebrew-language newspaper, *Halebanon,* reported on de Saulcy's initial rummaging in the tomb: "This month, an important Frenchman, de Saulcy, came to Jerusalem with a letter from the sultan that allowed him to dig everywhere he wants and take whatever he finds, and no one can stand up to him." The article complained that "he did not respect the dignity of the bones. He took them out and threw them away. He could not care less. He cleared the entire cave without leaving anything inside."

The outrage extended across religious lines. "Even the Muslims are upset because of this wickedness, for they respect the dead just like Jews and they sanctify Jewish cemeteries," the report noted. Several Arab families were angry for an additional reason: they claimed ownership of parts of the site and demanded payment. When one man confronted de Saulcy and insisted on a thousand piasters for the work to proceed, the offended senator offered instead "a hundred whacks with my walking stick."

This was not out of character. One contemporary scholar described de Saulcy as someone who lived "in an atmosphere of perpetual dispute." The senator also derided the city's Jewish residents as "the most idle population of all those on earth," noting that they gathered in small groups each day to watch the excavation from above. They watched his workers dump baskets of bones in the open courtyard. He insisted these were not Jewish at all, but the partially cremated remains of Roman soldiers. This did little to ease the onlookers' distress.

"I did not want my research to be hampered at any cost, so in agreement with the owners of the land, I forbade access to everyone, including Christians, Muslims and Jews," he said. Two of the fierce Sudanese who guarded the city's most sacred Muslim site, the Noble Sanctuary—what Jews called the Temple Mount—were assigned to bar entry to anyone without de Saulcy's authorization.

The growing antipathy toward the French dig put the governor, Mehmed Khurshid, in a bind. Though a modest-sized town of little economic consequence, Jerusalem was fast becoming one of the empire's most sensitive posts. Khurshid had been personally appointed by Sultan Abdulaziz, who controlled an empire that stretched from the Adriatic Sea to the Persian Gulf. An experienced diplomat, he had been on the job as the district's pasha, or governor, for only six months.

His primary task was to keep peace in a city split among its three main religious communities, and in particular to maintain comity among the unruly Christian sects. A second and increasingly important goal was to maintain cordial relations with the European nations and the United States that had recently established consulates to serve visitors from their respective nations. These consulates also provided convenient bases for spying on the Ottomans and each other.

At first, the pasha had brushed aside the complaints. De Saulcy, after all, had the ear of an emperor and the decree of a sultan. He was a personal favorite of Napoleon III, a vital Ottoman ally and a devout Catholic. A few years before, the sultan had presented the French leader with the Crusader church of Saint Anne in Jerusalem as a gift for his assistance in fending off Russian advances in the Crimean Peninsula.

But the December discovery of the sarcophagus set off a new and more vehement round of protests that was difficult to ignore. Members of the dominant Jewish community made up of what were called Sephardim, originally from Spain and Arab-speaking countries, bribed a guard so they could inspect the tomb site and verify the rumors. "They saw how human bones were tossed on the ground," according to a newspaper account. The horrified men rushed back to Jerusalem to complain to their chief rabbi, who took the grievance to the pasha.

Khurshid immediately set out for the tomb with a retinue that included the rabbi. According to the report, de Saulcy was infuriated by the Jewish opposition. "If he saw a Jew after that, he would throw stones and dust at him," the report claimed. But "all the difficulties seemed to have been ironed out," the senator noted confidently in his journal after the meeting. "What is certain," he added, "is that I will not leave Jerusalem until my sarcophagus is in a safe place."

Violence flared briefly when Ashkenazi Jews, more recent immigrants from Germany and Russia, tried to enter the site by force but were driven off by the Sudanese guards and workers. *Halebanon* stated that the pasha had stationed his own servants outside the tomb "to stone any Jew who gets close to the site."

Meanwhile, the governor politely evaded de Saulcy's demand for permission to export the artifact. "What tribulations, to be denied possession of what I already own by right!" the senator sulked in his journal entry from December 10. The comment underscored his unshakable conviction that Jerusalem's ancient heritage belonged not to those who lived in and ruled there, but to foreigners like himself.

That afternoon, de Saulcy went to the tomb to oversee his workers' removal of the heavy stone box from its small chamber. "It's a diabolical job," he noted.

• • •

ON DECEMBER 14, de Saulcy's mood was as foul as the cold and rainy weather that had set in. He had planned to leave Jerusalem two days earlier, but still had no word from the Ottoman governor. At 1:00 p.m. he received a note that Khurshid was on his way to the hotel. "I barely had time to prepare the lemonade, coffee, and cigars," de Saulcy groused. But it proved worth the trouble. "Our interview concluded well," he wrote later. The Ottoman pasha had reassured his prickly visitor that "tomorrow everything definitely would be settled."

A few hours later, however, Jewish rabbis presented Khurshid with a formal petition opposing de Saulcy's activities and warned that they intended to complain in writing to Istanbul's chief rabbi. While de Saulcy was an important representative of a strategic ally, the pasha could ill afford to alienate several thousand Jewish residents, who now made up roughly half of Jerusalem's citizens. Nor could he anger their influential supporters in Istanbul and European capitals. The delicate situation required careful statecraft.

Khurshid was all too familiar with the way minor incidents could explode into sectarian violence. A former general, he had been in Lebanon in 1860 when simmering tensions among ethnic groups erupted into a bloody civil war that drew the armed intervention of Europeans to protect the Christian population. Later he was part of the delegation led by the Ottoman foreign minister that brokered a fragile peace. This gave him useful experience. Caught between the rabbis and the French courtier, the pasha played for time. Once again he postponed his decision on the export of the sarcophagus.

The senator was also a military man, though of a far different temper. "Monsieur de Saulcy seemed made to live and die a soldier," one colleague later said. "Everything about his exterior, his demeanor, his way of acting and speaking, was military." Khurshid's delay moved him to fury. He delivered a written ultimatum to the governor demanding a final decision by 10:00 a.m. the next day.

There was no telegraph office in Jerusalem, and correspondence was delivered only once a week. "As tomorrow is mail day for France, I want the pasha to know that I will write to the emperor if necessary if he doesn't reply in my favor," he confided to his journal.

That afternoon he huddled with the consul and his staff to discuss options. "I am ready to remove my find by force," he told Barrère. It was no bluff. De Saulcy "always had the sword close to his pen," a colleague once said of him. The alarmed diplomat tried to dissuade him from rash action. Less than a decade earlier, a dispute among Christian clerics in Bethlehem had drawn the attention of Napoleon III and his bitter opponent, the Russian czar. Soon after, Russia invaded the Ottoman Empire, igniting the vicious Crimean War. British and French troops joined Ottoman forces to defeat a Russian invasion, but at a terrible cost. The consul had no interest in sparking an international conflict over an old casket.

When word came that the pasha required until noon the following day to "reflect" on the matter, a furious de Saulcy decamped to his hotel and "prepared to write directly to the Emperor, to the Minister of Public Education, and to the Marquis de Moustier, our Ambassador in Constantinople."

De Saulcy attended Catholic mass the next morning at the Franciscan monastery. After lunch, shivering in his hotel room on another cold and wet day, he finally received the pasha's answer. The senator's threats had proved effective. Khurshid agreed to let him depart with the sarcophagus, but he asked the Frenchman to provide three thousand piasters to the Arab landowners to quiet their concerns. De Saulcy agreed, then fretted over how to get the heavy object to the Mediterranean port of Jaffa, which was a long day's journey to the west. "Will we have to cut it into pieces?" he wondered.

After a week, the dreary weather gave way to warm sun, and on December 19, de Saulcy paid a farewell visit to the pasha, who was no doubt relieved to see the last of this troublesome excavator. Two days later, the disassembled sarcophagus, sawed into sections, was loaded onto a half-dozen camels and sent to Jaffa, the first step in its journey to the Louvre. De Saulcy departed the following day, paying a last visit to the Tomb of the Kings on his way out of town.

Just outside Jerusalem, he encountered five horsemen sent by a "learned society in England." Led by an English clergyman and ornithologist named Henry Baker Tristram, an early supporter of Darwin's theory of evolution, the group had the twin goals of cataloging the area's natural history and pinpointing the location of biblical sites. They seemed, he said, "a little disappointed" to learn that de Saulcy's team had beat them to the punch. "I comforted them as best I could, assuring them that there was still good work to be done."

Making topographical maps and charting resources were the opening act by competing European powers like France and Britain in their campaigns to expand colonial possessions across Africa and Asia. The strange twist in the Holy Land was that the new tools of science would be turned to study and then claim the biblical past as well.

As the city's domes vanished behind him, de Saulcy could not know he had launched a new era in which the search for that past would define a European struggle to gain Jerusalem as a central jewel in various colonial crowns. From that moment until the present, excavations would be an essential component in that effort to control the city, and the threat of protests, violence, and even war would haunt each dig.

Not long after the sarcophagus and the senator sailed from Jaffa on a steamship, a German-born Protestant missionary named Conrad Schick rode past the Tomb of the Kings; he would soon emerge as one of Jerusalem's leading archaeologists. Schick reported that he saw "a number of Jews—men and women, old and young—busy carrying buckets of earth etc. taken out by M. De Saulcy into the chambers where it had been before." He stopped to ask them why they were doing this. "The Messiah will now come," one man explained, adding that "it was their duty to bring the dust of former bodies into the tomb again."

◆　◆　◆

JERUSALEM'S GOVERNOR HAD MANAGED to rid himself of de Saulcy and to assuage the concerns of Arab landowners, but the Frenchman's departure did not satisfy the outraged Jewish community. Its leading rabbis immediately turned to their allies in Istanbul as well as Europe, shrewdly targeting Napoleon III's two primary foes—Britain and Russia.

On December 25, as Western Christians celebrated Christmas, the rabbis delivered an impassioned letter to the British consul, "throwing ourselves at your feet" to protest "French subjects, who have dared to unearth the bones of our ancestors . . . in one of our most respected places." They complained that a sarcophagus inscribed with what they believed were Hebrew letters had been cut to pieces and human remains were thrown away as if so much trash.

"It is an operation that we have never before heard of, in any part of the world, to dig up the bones of the dead in a city considered holy by all nations and powers," the rabbis wrote. They pleaded, "in the name of H.M. Queen Victoria," for help in protecting their burials and halting the export of the casket, which was then at Jaffa. The same day, the rabbis delivered a similar request for help to Jerusalem's Russian consul, asking for the intervention of the French emperor's other foe, Czar Alexander II.

A courier also was sent to Beirut with a letter that was then telegraphed to the president of the Universal Israelite Alliance in Paris, as well as to the French capital's chief rabbi. "We beg you to intervene with all your influence and intercede with the sultan in order that a stop may be put to this desecration," read the message. European Jews expressed their concern to the Ottoman grand vizier, who served as the sultan's prime minister. He promptly ordered the Jerusalem governor to forbid "further profanation of the remains of the saints." The sultan himself pledged that "no one in the future would be able to dig Jewish graves without the permission of the chief rabbi," according to *Halebanon*.

The British consul forwarded the rabbis' complaint to the British foreign secretary on January 6, 1864. He dismissed the Jewish claims as lacking "validity," noting that the site was owned by a Muslim family and "no Jewish shrine of any description existed on the spot." The consul was more alarmed by a French discovery of "high interest and importance." The Middle East was a source of tension between the French and British; a French company was digging the Suez Canal in nearby Egypt, and politicians in London feared it would allow Napoleon III to dominate the region and threaten the fragile new British Raj in India.

The British press, always eager to highlight what it deemed French perfidy, fanned a local controversy into a global scandal. The same day that the letters were sent to the consuls in Jerusalem, London's *Jewish Chronicle* published a disturbing report from Rabbi Chaim Zvi Schneersohn of Jerusalem. He wrote "with trembling hands and broken loins" to proclaim "evil tidings" of "the misdeed wrought in the Holy Land."

The rabbi said residents had learned that "a great and distinguished man" from France "was routing out everything" in the Tomb of the Kings. "Woe, woe, that such things should occur in our days," he added. The bodies of the "righteous dead kings and princes who have peaceably slept in the ground for 2000 years . . . were thrown forth from their graves like abominated offal. Alas, alas, the despoiler has entered our borders and carried off the bones of our fathers."

The governor had explained to the city's Jews that de Saulcy had full approval from the sultan in Istanbul to conduct the excavation, a fact that Schneersohn found "incredible." He didn't claim that the tomb held the kings of ancient Judah; instead, he said the tombs were those of later Jewish judges, holy men, and wealthy patricians. He noted bitterly that Muslims had mocked the Christian desecration of Jewish bones, saying, "Look how the uncircumcised make sport of the remains of your fathers."

On January 21, 1864, the influential London *Times* published an extract from the telegram under the ironic headline "French Protection of the Holy Places," a play on the ancient French claim as defender of sacred Christian sites in Jerusalem. The damning report stunned European scholars.

There was no love lost between de Saulcy and his academic colleagues, who considered him, at best, an amateur. His assertions that the walls around the Noble Sanctuary dated to the time of Solomon and that Damascus Gate was "a superbly Jewish construction" were dismissed by many scholars as wholly inaccurate. Even de Saulcy's grasp of his specialty, ancient coins, was suspect.

"A credulous enthusiast, a shallow scholar, a questionable quoter, a perverter of holy writ to suit his own mistaken views, never even right by accident, and always wrong through ignorance or design" was how one merciless colleague viewed him. His frequent bouts of obstinance, he added, led to "a lavish expenditure of ink, argument, and temper."

Nevertheless, public attacks on a distinguished archaeologist, no matter how incompetent, prompted academics to leap to his defense. A Cambridge University professor wrote to the *Times* "to refute the charge of rifling the sarcophagus and scattering the bones." He added in his January 26 letter that his French friend was "utterly incapable of such sacrilegious vandalism."

The well-meaning apologia only gave legs to the debate. The *Times* published a rebuttal to the professor's claim on February 1 under the eye-catching headline "Desecrations at Jerusalem," quoting Schneersohn's letter. Two days later, an Italian engineer who had worked for years in Jerusalem rejected the rabbi's "unjust attack upon a distinguished antiquary."

But public opinion turned against de Saulcy. "A shameless profanation," thundered one letter to the *Times*. Other British, Canadian, and American newspapers gleefully spread the story that a senior member of Napoleon III's court was guilty of robbing the tombs of the Bible's most famous kings.

This withering criticism earned only scorn from the senator, who accused the British of rank hypocrisy. After all, they had ripped the frieze from Athens's Parthenon and extracted massive statues from Iraq's Nineveh "to enrich" the "splendid British Museum." He complained that "there have been no invectives, no insults, no curses not lavished on me in the newspapers of England," angrily adding that "I am denounced as a tomb violator, a shameless defiler."

◆ ◆ ◆

IN PARIS, de Saulcy was warmly received by the court and by Louvre curators on his January 28, 1864, return. Napoleon III ruthlessly suppressed information; he had shut down hundreds of newspapers and journals and censored those few that remained. There would be no hint of dishonor attached to a man married to one of the empress's attendants who had become a personal favorite of the emperor. The empress herself described de Saulcy as a "well-known antiquarian," and he had brought back a spectacular find for public display. British criticism was dismissed as envy.

De Saulcy quickly set to work translating the inscriptions. What he assumed was the word for "king" turned out instead to mean "queen." This last fitted with the results of the bone analysis, which determined the tomb's occupant was a "young Semitic female." With no other evidence, de Saulcy declared her to be the consort of a Judean ruler from the seventh century BCE.

It was a controversial conclusion. "There are people who would be frightened to find themselves alone holding an opinion on so important a matter," a French colleague noted sardonically. "This did not bother Mr. de Saulcy."

Scholars of Semitic languages scoffed at the senator's analysis. They agreed that the word "queen" was used twice, but the proper name given was enigmatic. They also noted that the script was not in Hebrew but in Aramaic, a cousin tongue that only came into wide use in Jerusalem much later. In addition, they dated the architecture of the tomb and the sarcophagus to the era of Jesus. By then, de Saulcy's biblical queen would have been dead for at least six centuries.

Most of the academics who studied de Saulcy's discoveries concluded that the casket and bones belonged to Queen Helena of Adiabene, a royal Jewish convert from a small kingdom in today's Iraq who settled in Jerusalem in the first century CE. According to the Roman Jewish historian

Josephus, she fed the city's poor during a famine and eventually was buried in a tomb three furlongs from Jerusalem. His description seemed to fit the complex.

Eventually, de Saulcy grudgingly accepted that he was wrong; Queen Helena might have been royal, but she was not Judean and had lived long after the demise of the Davidic line of kings.

By then, however, his initial and sensational claim had captured the European, Canadian, and American imagination even as it had sparked outrage. For the first time, an object that a scholar had claimed to be associated with the biblical past was on public display. The British Museum might boast of its elegant marbles from the pagan Parthenon, but to see physical evidence from the days of scripture, you had to go to the French capital. Visitors flocked to the new exhibit.

"The monument, unique in its kind, has arrived at the Louvre, together with other antiquities found during the expedition," a Scottish journal noted in April 1864. "The whole is destined to form a Hebrew museum, on the interest of which we need not enlarge." The same month, London's *Morning Chronicle* ridiculed de Saulcy's "pseudo-discoveries" and the exhibit's "marvelous assumption" that the casket on display was "nothing less than the identical sarcophagus of King David himself."

Though the identification of the casket's occupant might be questioned, the discovery opened the possibility that archaeology could yield concrete proof of scripture's accuracy at a moment when advances in geology and biology had put Christianity on the defensive. De Saulcy's coup also startled France's political rivals. The lavishly funded expedition suggested a growing Gallic influence over the Ottoman Empire, and spurred an unusual coalition of clerics, scholars, and politicians in Britain to launch their own scientific effort.

The scramble was on among European Christians to unearth that which lay below Jerusalem. The furor over de Saulcy's expedition demonstrated that excavations could be met with vehement opposition and even violence from locals and draw criticism from others around the globe. But these concerns paled before the beguiling chance to resurrect the famous lost city of the Bible.

Squeezed between the European powers and local residents was the city's pasha. His attempt to placate de Saulcy had succeeded only in encouraging the Jewish community to go over his head. Amid the unrest and international uproar, Khurshid lost the confidence of the sultan. As the sarcophagus was being unboxed at the Louvre in February 1864, the unlucky governor was removed from his post. He was only the first in a long line of leaders to learn that the inevitable mix of politics, religion, and archaeology in Jerusalem created a volatile brew.

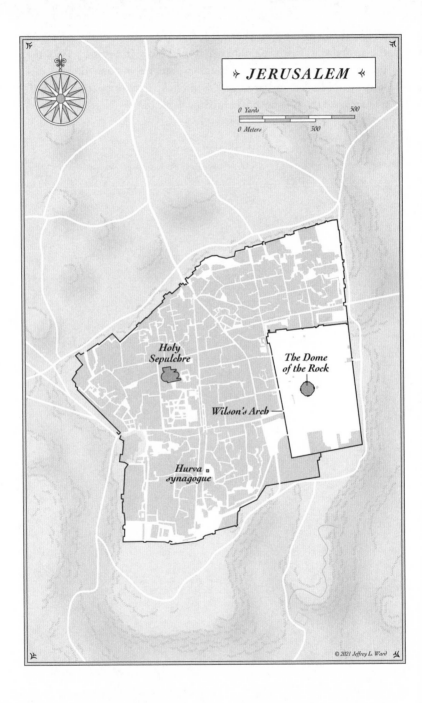

2

A Fool's Errand

Palestine, when dug and harrowed by enterprising travelers,
must exhibit the past with all the vividness of the present.
—SEVENTH EARL OF SHAFTESBURY

A few months after de Saulcy's departure, Jewish leaders gathered
to dedicate a rebuilt synagogue that had lain in ruins for more
than a century. Funded by a Baghdad merchant, the Prussian
king, and Jewish philanthropists from Britain and France, the house of
worship called the Hurva boasted a massive dome that rose eighty feet in
the air. The enormous vault joined the Christian Holy Sepulchre and the
Muslim Dome of the Rock as one of Jerusalem's dominant landmarks.

"It rises higher than all the towers," boasted Rabbi Yosef Rivlin, who
attended the event. "A person standing on one of the mountains around
Jerusalem will see the dome of the synagogue . . . like a moon among
stars."

The ceremony was a harbinger of dramatic change. In 1864, the city
was poised between the old and the new. The Jerusalem that de Saulcy left
behind still huddled behind locked gates at night. Surrounded by shabby
villages, lonely cemeteries, and religious sites holy to three monotheisms,
it hugged stony hills between the fertile Mediterranean coast to the west
and the burning desert surrounding the earth's lowest point, the Dead
Sea, to the east.

Within its sixteenth-century walls was a typical midsize Middle Eastern town of its day, riven with narrow alleys crowded with loaded donkeys
and lined with small shops selling spices, fruits, and housewares. Homes

often rose three or four stories high, facing onto a central courtyard that covered a water cistern fed from the roofs that also served as light-filled terraces. Ten families might share a compound. Charcoal brought by camel was the usual fuel for cooking and heating during the chilly and wet Jerusalem winters, while lamps filled with sesame or olive oil burned as they had millennia before.

Residents took a practical approach to their surroundings. Ancient stones belowground might be reused to add a new floor on a house or above a shop. One British visitor recorded barbers conducting their trade within the crumbling remains of a Crusader hospice, herdsmen making their home in a Roman-era tomb, and a blacksmith lodged against an ancient palace wall that might have once housed a Judean potentate. De Saulcy noted less romantically that "the houses of this famous city" were, "without exception, conceived with impossible layouts."

Today, Jerusalem's Old City is divided neatly into four quarters—Muslim, Jewish, Christian, and Armenian. Before the twentieth century, however, neighbors might share a family, tribe, religion, or ethnicity, or some combination of these. Arabs rented homes to Jews, and Christians bought their vegetables from a nearby stall owned by Muslims. On his map of Jerusalem from that era, the German missionary Conrad Schick labeled the central area of the city as "mixed quarters."

What set Jerusalem apart from other Middle Eastern towns were the myriad shrines that filled the city and spilled outside the walls. This made for an astonishingly diverse if volatile community. "For in Jerusalem, there is always sufficient variety of religion, language, costume, incident, nationality, and character to be met with," the British consul noted.

The area between the Mediterranean Sea and the Jordan River had long been called the Holy Land by Jews, Christians, and Muslims. At that time it consisted of some four hundred thousand souls, overwhelmingly Arabic-speaking Sunni Muslims, and old Sunni families dominated regional as well as local politics under the watchful eye of Ottoman authorities. Within the city, only a quarter of the city's roughly eighteen thousand people—about the size of contemporary Columbus, Ohio—were Muslim. Those included Shiites and Ismailis, as well as Sunnis from North Africa and Central Asia with dialects and traditions quite different from those of local Arabs. There were Muslim offshoots, such as the Druze, and various orders of the mystical Sufis, with devotees drawn to the Holy City from around the Islamic world.

No group was more fractious than the Christians, who accounted for another quarter of Jerusalem's residents. The majority were Greek Orthodox Arabs. There were also Ethiopian and Egyptian Copts, Orthodox Georgians, Syrian Jacobites, Orthodox Armenians, Greek Catholics, Roman Catholics, Eastern Orthodox Greeks and Russians, Syriac Maronites, and Melchites. Each sect constantly maneuvered for influence in Christian shrines and in the pasha's palace. A few Western European and American Protestants—mostly diplomats and missionaries—were the latest arrivals. Ensuring that sectarian squabbling among Christians did not disturb Jerusalem's peace was a major task of the governor.

Until the mid-nineteenth century, the community of Jews under Ottoman rule had been relatively small and poor. Many came from abroad to study or to die in the Holy City—or both. Some traced their ancestors back to refugees from Ferdinand and Isabella's Spain; they identified as Sephardim, a word derived from a Hebrew term for their former homeland, and many spoke Judeo-Spanish, also called Ladino. Other Jews had emigrated over the centuries from various Arab lands, spoke exclusively Arabic, and shared many of the traditions of their Arab neighbors.

The Hurva synagogue was rebuilt to serve a new kind of Jewish settler, Yiddish-speaking European Jews, who began to arrive in numbers at the same time as Western Protestants. Called Ashkenazi, a term from a biblical figure said to have lived north of the Middle East, they came primarily from the German states and Russia. By 1864, the combined influx of Sephardim and Ashkenazim made Jews the single largest community in the Holy City for the first time in nearly two thousand years.

Though Arabic was the town's primary language, one European archaeologist in that day marveled at the city's Babel of tongues: "The hotel-keeper talks Greek, his cook, Amharic; one waiter, Polish-Hebrew; another, Italian, another, Arabic; the barber speaks French; the washerwoman, Spanish; the carpenter, German; the dragoman, English: and the Pasha, Turkish; Sepoys from India mutter English oaths." Along the steep and narrow streets, lined with coffee shops, bakeries, and pipe makers, armed Bedouin sheikhs brushed by robed Moroccan Sufis as black-hatted Russian Jews passed Syrian merchants in tasseled red fezzes.

Ottoman forces had squelched the bloody rivalries of rural sheikhs that had long made travel to and from the city dangerous. After a new quay was completed in 1864 at Jaffa, the port that lay forty miles to the west, steamship lines began to make regular stops there. The road to Jerusalem was still rough, but there was even talk of a railroad that could link the city to Istanbul. These changes encouraged the first wave of Western tourists as well as a revival of pilgrimages by people of all three faiths.

The sultan in Istanbul recognized Jerusalem's growing importance that same year, when he expanded Jerusalem's district to include major towns in the area like Gaza and Hebron, and granted the city's noble Arab families the power to appoint their own city council. But the court in Istanbul was ambivalent about making Jerusalem more accessible to Westerners. "I shall never concede to these crazy Christians any road improvements in Palestine," said the sultan's grand vizier in 1865, "as they would then transform Jerusalem into a Christian madhouse."

He did not realize that it was too late. "And now, so many Franks, what a wealth of spiritual activity!" declared Swiss Protestant scholar Titus Tobler the same year. "The peaceful crusade has begun. Jerusalem must be ours!"

Ashkenazi Jews were not the only newcomers altering the city's skyline. Construction of an Austrian hospice, a British sanitarium, a Greek hospital, and a German refuge for lepers were in the works. Just outside the walls, the Russian government was putting the finishing touches on a sprawling complex complete with a cathedral, consulate, hospital, and dormitories, while residents of the first Jewish suburb had just settled into their new homes. It was all part of the architectural one-upmanship among competing European powers to demonstrate their commitment to the Holy City.

The frenzy of construction by Westerners led to a demand for clean water and indoor plumbing. Like most cities of its day, Jerusalem lacked a safe and reliable municipal water supply. There were no springs within the city walls, and private cisterns filled during winter rains remained the primary source of water. By the end of summer, these had often turned foul, and they required constant maintenance. The sole nearby spring—the one that drew the city's first residents thousands of years earlier—flowed directly beneath the close-packed city, making it a source of last resort.

This glaring gap in infrastructure drew the attention of the future British king's private chaplain. In 1862, the Prince of Wales visited Jerusalem with the dean of Westminster, the royal's personal priest. While a Christian Arab adorned the prince's arm with a tattoo of five crosses and three crowns, the Anglican cleric inquired about the city's grim sanitation situation. He returned to London to organize the Jerusalem Water

Relief Society, and the following year a British engineer conducted a brief survey.

"In its present and degraded state, [the city] is subject to much disease and general unhealthiness," concluded the 1864 report. What was needed was a new aqueduct that would mimic the ancient systems that had in Roman times brought clean and plentiful water from the hills around Bethlehem. The result would be "a monument of English enterprise and sympathy."

It was a philanthropic idea that anyone, no matter their religious belief, could get behind. The medical reformer and heroine of the Crimean War, Florence Nightingale, was among those who supported a modern water system that would benefit the health of Jerusalem's residents and visitors. So did the Seventh Earl of Shaftesbury, Britain's most influential evangelical. He promised to "aid to the utmost of my power so good a cause."

The British government, however, held a large public debt and was ill-disposed to pump money into a land that it didn't—yet—control, however holy. The estimated 22,000-pound cost, the equivalent today to some $3.6 million, was an enormous sum to raise privately, so the Fund's board turned to the wealthiest woman in Britain after Queen Victoria.

Angela Burdett-Coutts had inherited a banking fortune, and she was a well-known philanthropist. The Prince of Wales called her "the most remarkable woman in the kingdom" after his mother, the queen. A devoted Anglican and friend to Charles Dickens and London's dogs—she'd had drinking fountains built for them across the city—she also was close to the dean of Westminster. With his encouragement, Burdett-Coutts provided 500 pounds, or about $84,000, to get the charitable effort underway.

The dean then used his connections to win the secretary of state for war's approval to assign the Ordnance Survey to conduct the required topographical study. Among the world's best mapmakers, the members of this military organization were typically Royal Engineers rigorously trained in the precision science of surveying. Their origin went back to England's effort to pacify Scotland in the Jacobite rebellion of the mid-eighteenth century, and, later, to dominate Ireland.

The military's sole condition was that the Burdett-Coutts fund cover the expedition costs. Though billed as a private philanthropic endeavor, this would be a sanctioned government project, with a team made up of enlisted men under the direction of a British officer using government-owned equipment.

Finding that officer, however, was no easy matter. Jerusalem might have quickened the hearts of Christian Zionist earls and Anglican heiresses, but it was a career killer for any ambitious military man. India, Southeast Asia, and Africa were where promotions were to be had. To make the position even less appealing, the officer would have to take unpaid leave. Months passed as several candidates turned down the job. Finally, an obscure twenty-eight-year-old captain and cartographer named Charles Wilson accepted.

⋅ ⋅ ⋅

WILSON WAS an introverted bachelor who provided a marked contrast to de Saulcy's abrasive arrogance. He was "not what could be called a society man," according to a biographer. The officer came from a privileged family—he grew up in a medieval Welsh castle and his uncle founded Philadelphia's entomological society—but Wilson had endured the rigor of an English boarding school. His schoolmaster "began the morning lessons by striking all the pupils on their hands with his cane, not for any offense committed, but as a general means of inculcating obedience."

By the time he joined the military he had missed the Crimean War and the Indian rebellion of 1857. Peace reigned, so Wilson took a position charting the boundary between Canada and the United States in the far West. For the next four years, he trudged with bulky equipment through thick forests and up seven-thousand-foot-high mountains, often in subfreezing temperatures. He also dodged bullets in a steamboat brawl and watched a rattlesnake drop onto the lapels of a coat he had just hung on a tree. Lean and sporting a thin mustache, Wilson returned to Britain in 1862 but quickly grew bored at his post defending England from an unlikely invasion by Napoleon III.

One day he happened to be present in the barracks when one of his fellow officers received a letter with the offer of the Jerusalem job. The man immediately decided to decline. "The conditions were so hard, and the possibility of doing the work within the estimate considered to be so remote, they all refused," Wilson recalled. Without hesitation, he asked the officer to propose his name instead. "I was generally considered to be going on a fool's errand."

At the end of September in 1864, just nine months after de Saulcy left Jaffa, Wilson landed there with a lieutenant who had been with him in North America, along with combat engineers, miners, and a photographer. They loaded donkeys with their spirit levels, sextants, artificial horizons, theodolites, chronometers, "and other weapons of their peculiar warfare," as one contemporary described the ordnance trade. After making their way across what Wilson called the "wild desolation" of stony hills, they arrived in Jerusalem.

He approached the Ottoman governor's compound the next day in his finest uniform, and the Ottoman guards snapped to attention and saluted the red coat. Khurshid's replacement, Izzet Pasha, had only recently arrived. He greeted his guest with a European-style handshake. "I found the pasha very civil and liberal-minded," Wilson said. "He is well-educated, seemed to take a great interest in what I was going to do, and promised to give me all the help he could."

This was fortunate, since Wilson in his haste had not obtained the vital decree from the sultan approving his mission. Unlike de Saulcy, who was an emperor's friend with the proper paperwork, the British officer had to depend entirely on the discretion of the pasha, who no doubt was aware of the debacle that had taken place less than a year before. Giving a European free rein in the city was a dangerous business, but Izzet proved surprisingly willing to take the risk.

Jerusalem's residents soon began to notice strange horizontal marks chiseled into the corners of Jerusalem's city walls, gates, churches, and other notable buildings. These benchmarks, critical for surveying, helped the team produce an astonishingly accurate topographical map of Jerusalem and its environs. Wilson also traced the remains of the ancient aqueducts that snaked through the Bethlehem hills and once provided abundant clean water for the thirsty city. Within a few months and with remarkable precision, he had gathered exactly the data needed for Britain's philanthropists to launch their project.

Unknown to the pasha, however, Wilson had two secret missions. The first was to provide the secretary of state for war with intelligence on a waterway completely unrelated to an ancient aqueduct. The Suez Canal, then under construction by a French company, posed a threat to Britain's interest in the Middle East and its colonial government in India.

The philanthropic work in Jerusalem was the perfect cover to explore the Jordan Valley to the west. This led south to the Sinai Peninsula, where the canal work was underway. There was also British interest in a possible railroad to India via Palestine, bypassing the canal altogether. What was needed were accurate maps of a region little known to Westerners.

The officer's second secret mission was to gather evidence to prove a controversial theory proposed by a wealthy Scottish historian. A few weeks after Wilson's October 3 arrival in Jerusalem, he was joined by James Fergusson, who had made a fortune on an Indian indigo plantation but was made famous by his architectural study of Indian temples. He also harbored a deep fascination with the Bible and Jerusalem.

At the city's eastern edge stood the huge rectangular platform that Muslims call the Noble Sanctuary. Near its center was the famous Dome of the Rock, an eight-sided building that scholars agreed was built by an early Islamic caliph in the seventh century CE after Muhammad's followers conquered Jerusalem. The shrine covers a rough stone Muslims believed to be the spot from which the prophet Muhammad made a nighttime journey to heaven.

Fergusson, however, was convinced that it was constructed by the Roman emperor Constantine the Great over the true tomb of Jesus three centuries before. The Holy Sepulchre, which stood five hundred yards to the west, was, he maintained, a medieval fabrication.

This assertion was a shocking idea. The platform already was home to Islam's third-holiest site. It also stood over the very spot that many Jews claimed as the place where the Ark had rested in Solomon's temple, and in the so-called Holy of Holies in the sanctuary renovated by Herod the Great and destroyed in 70 CE by the Romans. If the Scottish historian was correct, then the city's famous acropolis was sacred to not just two but three of the world's great monotheisms.

Like de Saulcy, Fergusson was seen as a dangerous dilettante by many contemporary academics, who mocked his idea as absurd. Fergusson intended to use Wilson to prove his critics wrong. Bald and bearded, the fifty-four-year-old Scotsman strolled with the young officer around the platform's massive walls to discuss his plan. He wanted Wilson to pursue excavations on the platform itself, but this was strictly forbidden by the sultan. He settled instead on paying Wilson to produce the first fully detailed survey of the Noble Sanctuary.

When Fergusson returned to Britain, he wrote in a November 29 letter to the *Times* that the cartographer's work was proceeding "most satisfactorily" given that the pasha provided "complete protection and he gives them every facility they require." The result, he noted, in a nod to Wilson's official job, would be "the means by which [Jerusalem's] sanitary condition may be improved."

He neglected to mention he was sponsoring a separate project to prove his theory. But after his "totally exhaustive" investigations of the ancient city, Fergusson added, "I have come back more confirmed than before in the correctness of all I have written or said with regard to the Holy Places." That implied reference to the Dome of the Rock as the true Holy Sepulchre was lost on no one.

Wilson's boss, Colonel Henry James, apparently was well aware of his subordinate's multiple masters. In a December 30 letter to the *Times,* he revealed that the team had "made some important discoveries to elucidate [Jerusalem's] ancient topography." This hinted at more than data gathering to bring clean water to thirsty residents. But in the clubby world of Victorian Britain, there was little risk that this diversion of an officer of the Royal Engineers to bolster a peculiar theory would ruffle feathers. The prime minister had tapped Fergusson to design coastal forts to defend Britain from attacks by Napoleon III; before taking the Jerusalem assignment, Wilson had been stationed near one.

The British captain had to tread carefully in approaching the Noble Sanctuary. In centuries past, Jews or Christians who wandered into the sacred enclosure had suffered injury and even death. A band of well-muscled, well-armed Sudanese kept a close eye on who came and went from its gates. Only in the preceding three decades had it been possible for non-Muslims to set foot at all within the sacred complex, and then only under careful guard. Aside from an Italian engineer, few Westerners had examined the site in any detail.

Wilson's quiet manner allowed him to cultivate a friendship with the pasha as well as with the sheikh who oversaw the sanctuary. Eventually he was permitted not just to examine its surface but to briefly explore what lay below. James reported in the *Times* that Wilson found the ground beneath the platform "perfectly honeycombed with passages and cisterns."

His most dramatic find, made with the assistance of the German missionary Conrad Schick, was a massive buried arch that sprang from the platform's western wall. He called it "one of the most perfect and magnificent remains in Jerusalem." The structure appeared to have once been a bridge or aqueduct leading from the western hill to the Temple Mount in the time of Jesus. Though it had been noted by a previous explorer, Wilson was able to determine that while it now served as the vault for an underground cistern, it had once soared seventy-three feet above the ancient pavement.

If his dating was correct, then what became known as Wilson's Arch confirmed that the platform renovated by Herod the Great starting in the first century BCE had been a monumental project, as ancient writers contended.

The captain worked in a half-dozen locations both inside and outside the city walls, and dug one shaft that dropped eighty feet below the surface before hitting bedrock. "I have been doing a good deal of underground work lately, and have been rewarded with several discoveries," he wrote a day after Fergusson's letter was published. "It is rather dirty work, crawling about in the middle of the earth, but very interesting." In one tunnel south of the Old City, he and his men were forced to "wriggle along like eels, not a comfortable sort of locomotion at any time, but when it has to be done in six inches of water and mud, dreadfully unpleasant."

A burrowing Englishman at first was a curiosity to Jerusalem's residents, but "the inhabitants are now quite accustomed to see my head suddenly appearing out of wells and cisterns. The greatest difficulty I have is in getting into the interior of private houses, especially amongst the Jews, and they live just in the place where I want to work."

Little wonder, given de Saulcy's controversial visit only a few months earlier. That problem was solved with help from the British Jewish financier Moses Montefiore, who sent letters of introduction intended for the city's Jewish leaders to Colonel James, who in turn forwarded them to the captain. Montefiore, who had helped fund the Hurva reconstruction, clearly was sympathetic to the new archaeological investigations; he also sent James ten pounds and ten shillings "towards the expense of Captain Wilson's underground explorations, the expense of which Captain Wilson has been defraying from his private purse," James noted in a January 28, 1865, letter to the London *Times*.

Though Wilson conducted his Noble Sanctuary work with financial support from Fergusson, the officer was careful to gather data but avoid conclusions. This set him apart from his patron and de Saulcy, who used their wealth and influence to peddle pet theories. He also declined to address the fierce dispute in Europe over the location of the temple attributed to King Solomon or the rebuilt version renovated by Herod. Nor did he get involved with the arguments over the date of the platform's walls.

Wilson's discreet approach was revolutionary. He gathered accurate data and left speculation to others. "The ancient past of Jerusalem was no longer a matter for armchair scholarly discourse, turning upon the credibility and background of a given scholar, but had now become a matter for clear-cut scientific rigor," wrote the modern archaeologist Shimon Gibson.

Dispatches by Wilson and visitors to Jerusalem spread news of the finds around the world. On January 2, 1865, for example, the *New York Herald* reported on his progress. Lincoln was a regular reader of the publication, and word of the discoveries may have been on his mind when he told his wife, moments before his death three months later, that he longed to see the Holy City.

◆　◆　◆

"IT HAS BEEN PROPHESIED to me many years I should not die but in Jerusalem," said King Henry IV in William Shakespeare's play by the same name. During a convocation of Parliament at Westminster Abbey on March 20, 1413, the monarch fell ill. Clerics carried him to a nearby room in the abbot's residence, where he passed away. In an eerie fulfillment of the prophecy, the room where he died was known as the Jerusalem Chamber.

At 5:00 p.m. on May 12, 1865, as Confederates and Union forces on the other side of the Atlantic fought their last battle of the American Civil War along the Rio Grande, two dozen men crowded into the small medieval hall, with its oak beams and sturdy stone fireplace. Hosted by the dean of Westminster, who had initiated the water project, the gathering included politicians, newspaper publishers, and scientists along with senior clergy. They were the cream of Victorian society as the British Empire was emerging as the world's most formidable military, political, and economic power. Its only true rival was Napoleon III's France.

Wilson was then packing to return to Britain, but James Fergusson was there; his new book expounding on his theory about Jesus's entombment below the Dome of the Rock was being advertised that week in London newspapers for seven shillings and sixpence.

The men resolved to launch a fund to promote the exploration of Jerusalem and the surrounding area, with a goal "to throw much light on the archaeology of the Jewish people." In a prospectus published in the *Guardian,* they declared that "what is above ground will be accurately known when the present survey is completed; but below the surface hardly anything has yet been discovered." A host of research questions were waiting to be answered. "It is not too much to anticipate that every foot in the depth of the 60 feet of rubbish on which the city stands will yield most interesting and important matter for the archaeologist and numismatist."

There was pushback. A day after the Westminster meeting, a devout *Guardian* reader gave a blistering critique of the "dangerous fallacy" that science could be used to verify or deny biblical veracity. While research might end "vehement controversies" such as the location of the true tomb of Christ, geographical surveys and relic hunting could never prove whether David was introduced to Saul for the first time on two occasions, one of the Bible's many troubling contradictions. The endeavor, he warned, was as foolish as the search for El Dorado or the philosopher's stone. "Such schemes are not worthy of those who profess to believe in a righteous Father."

But there were more powerful forces at work. Progress on the Suez Canal coupled with fears—however overblown—of a French invasion had the British government on edge. De Saulcy's discovery posed a new political challenge by Napoleon III, and one that had to be answered.

◆ ◆ ◆

FIVE WEEKS LATER, as Wilson was steaming back home from Jerusalem, the Palestine Exploration Fund was created at a public meeting in the assembly rooms of a former Westminster tavern in London. The elegant ballroom capable of accommodating nearly one thousand people was crowded. The bishop of London opened with a prayer and went on to say, "We feel confident that such an effort must strengthen the faith of our people." The crowd responded, "Hear, Hear!"

But the chair, the archbishop of York, hastened to set the more secularly minded at ease. "We mean to lay down and vigorously adhere to . . . strictly inductive inquiry," the cleric said emphatically. "We are not to be a religious society."

This was the moment when the dispute between those upholding traditional values and those pushing new ideas was at its fiercest, when "the controversy between 'science' and 'religion' took fire," as one historian put it. The previous year, Britain's last heresy trial ended with the government dismissing the charge. The move had infuriated many devout Christians, while more liberal churchmen, such as Dean Stanley of Westminster, had defended the rights of religious naysayers even if they opposed their views.

It was in this charged environment that the Victorian elite, scientists as well as clerics, gathered under the ballroom chandeliers to discuss the

Holy Land. Among them was the naturalist Richard Owen, one of Britain's leading researchers, and a man credited with coining the word "dinosaur." The glue that held this disparate group together was their belief in the inevitability of Britain's imperial expansion and a conviction that the Holy Land and its artifacts were by rights theirs.

As the meeting began, the archbishop explained that "Palestine belongs to you and to me, it is essentially ours." The territory controlled by the Ottomans, he added, was "the land from which comes the news of our Redemption . . . to which we may look with as true a patriotism as we do to this dear old England." He called for "a new crusade to rescue from darkness and oblivion much of the history of that country in which we all take so dear an interest." The crowd cheered.

Amid the enthusiasm, Britain's most distinguished archaeologist sounded a note of caution. Austen Henry Layard was born in Paris to French Protestant parents, and as a young British diplomat he had filled the British Museum with massive statues of bearded Assyrian kings and winged animals—the very ones that led de Saulcy to cry hypocrisy when his methods in Jerusalem were criticized.

Layard had gone on to become a prominent politician and was then serving as undersecretary of state for foreign affairs. He rose to warn the gathering that Palestine, which lay between the empires of Egypt in the west and Babylonia and Assyria in the east, had always been a relative backwater. He predicted that excavators might find small artifacts that "throw light upon the history, manners, and civilization of the Jews," but added that the Jewish prohibitions on graven images made the discovery of statues or other impressive art to be unlikely.

At a later meeting, he was more blunt. While "some interesting fragments might be discovered, no series of sculptures such as those at Nineveh or Babylon could be hoped for," Layard said. This, in turn, might make it difficult to raise money for what inevitably would be costly and time-consuming excavations. "You must remember, as we go on we have to dig a bit; and when you begin digging, greater expenses will be necessary."

It proved a prescient warning, in more ways than he could have imagined.

At the inaugural gathering, Layard cited another obstacle that was rarely an issue in Egypt or Mesopotamia. "There will of course be considerable difficulties in the way of obtaining permission to excavate in Jerusalem," he said. Layard also reminded the audience that the French had already launched ambitious excavations around the Near East. Unlike Britain, they "were always more ready than our own government to undertake researches of this character."

The resources pumped into the recent French expedition had dwarfed the small amount spent by Wilson. But Layard made a point to dismiss de Saulcy's artifacts, then drawing crowds at the Louvre. These were, he said, poor-quality Roman work that had nothing to do with ancient Jewish kings or queens.

The reminder of French competition had an obvious political dimension. Napoleon III was a Catholic emperor and nephew of the man who had fought long and hard against the British. Firing up anxieties among pious Anglicans and excitable evangelicals that French Catholics were pillaging biblical treasures served a pragmatic purpose.

When Layard was seated, a thirty-six-year-old Frenchman rose to speak. Charles-Jean-Melchior, Marquis de Vogüé, had abandoned a promising diplomatic career to dig in Palestine. He had just published a scholarly book on Jerusalem's Jewish temples and Hebrew inscriptions. "The best way of conducting this business," he advised, "is to put aside all exaggerated, or national, or ecclesiastical feeling—to collect facts and leave others to come to a conclusion." It was sound advice that later archaeologists would struggle to follow. Had he been present, Wilson certainly would have applauded.

Jerusalem's history covered five thousand years, but the focus of the archaeological investigations would be squarely on the single millennium between the time King David was said to have danced through the city's newly conquered streets to the Roman destruction of the city in 70 CE. This research effort would be centered on the era when the Judeans, who would later emerge as the Jewish people, had dominated the city.

Science would provide the tools, but the research guide would be scripture itself. "The Bible was transformed from an instrument of faith into a tool for scientific inquiry," wrote Ashley Irizarry, a historian who studied the era. "What made this transformation possible however, was the explorers' faith that the Bible was a trustworthy source of information on the natural world as well as in spiritual matters." This assumption of infallibility, she added, "was important for Protestants who believed that contemporary beliefs threatened traditional views of the Bible."

Before adjourning, the members chose a friend of Fergusson's, George Grove, as honorary secretary of the new organization; Grove was the man who had worked tirelessly behind the scenes to assemble the impressive list of supporters spanning the divide between scientists and clergy. Darwin himself, at the urging of his friend and colleague Joseph Dalton Hooker, pledged eight guineas—though with the hope that the goal was "not merely to map the Temple." A few British Catholics contributed, as did distinguished British Jews such as Montefiore and Baron Lionel de Rothschild. Queen Victoria provided the royal sum of one hundred pounds.

Grove's job now was to turn the financial pledges into a coherent mission to gather scientific data.

Lost in the fervor of the moment, however, was the very reason that Wilson had gone to Jerusalem in the first place. In the rush to unearth biblical remains, the philanthropic project to provide clean water for the city's residents was forgotten. For the enthusiastic Victorians, it was clearly Jerusalem's past, not its present, that mattered most.

3

A Masonic Mission

Moles, that would undermine the rooted oak!
—SAMUEL TAYLOR COLERIDGE

Wilson disembarked in Britain on July 10, 1865, and was met with good news. Flush with pledges of 2,500 pounds— worth some $420,000 today—the managers of the new Palestine Exploration Fund asked him to return "to carry out explorations, and to make such excavations as would be possible at Jerusalem." Colonel James from the Royal Engineers agreed once again to provide men and equipment.

So in October of that year, Wilson set out again, this time by way of Beirut and Damascus, a roundabout route that likely involved gathering intelligence on French and Russian activities in that region. Wilson was not technically a spy—he wore a uniform and didn't hide his identity—but he would go on to help found the British military intelligence apparatus.

As Layard had warned, however, Jerusalem would provide few of the dramatic finds expected of archaeologists in those days, such as museum-ready statues and sarcophagi. Wilson made accurate measurements critical for researchers, but he failed to duplicate discoveries such as the massive underground arch. Public interest waned. Partly as a result, contributions to the Fund lagged; its supporters were reduced to selling copies of expedition photographs, though they didn't even own these: the originals belonged to the Royal Engineers.

When Wilson returned to England in the summer of 1866, the honorary secretary, Grove, criticized him for busting his budget. A disgusted

Wilson went back to full-time military work, though he agreed to serve on the organization's board. Meanwhile, Grove was locked in battles with any and all who opposed his friend Fergusson's controversial theory that the Dome of the Rock commemorated the true tomb of Jesus. The Fund, which had begun with such fanfare, suddenly seemed on the verge of collapse.

Wilson's boss came to its rescue. The War Office needed maps of a region that was increasingly strategic, and the Fund was the least conspicuous method to obtain them. James had grown impatient with the Fund's fixation on what he dismissed as the "absurdities" of Fergusson's theory, and he saw limited value in further work within Jerusalem itself. He agreed to support a third expedition with men and materials, but this time insisted that "military reconnaissance" be the first priority, with excavations second. With no alternative, Grove agreed.

The new venture required a skilled cartographer with digging experience and a taste for adventure. The man who eventually agreed to take the assignment shared Wilson's first name and an upbringing in Wales. The two men also shared remarkable mathematical skills and deeply held beliefs in the virtue of the British Empire. Yet Wilson's personality was diametrically opposite to that of his successor, Charles Warren.

A maverick twenty-five-year-old artillery officer, Warren was self-confident to the point of cockiness, and he was addicted to what we would today call extreme sports. As it happened, as Wilson's steamer docked at the British naval base at Gibraltar to refuel on his 1865 trip back to Britain, Warren was packing to leave his station on the Rock. For the previous six years, his job had been to conduct a trigonometrical survey of the fourteen-hundred-foot-high limestone promontory jutting out of the Spanish shore just inside the Mediterranean. He was the first to climb its treacherous face.

Warren also was tasked with blowing up crags on the eastern cliff face that might serve as enemy footholds. In his spare time, he explored the caves and tunnels that riddled the immense outcrop. He even assisted in an excavation of prehistoric remains; some of the first Neanderthal skulls to be unearthed were discovered in Gibraltar's caves. All these skills would prove useful in his next post.

One day Warren dared three friends to climb the Rock from the sea to its peak, with no rope or safety apparatus—and this was after he had blown up all footholds. They were only halfway up when night fell; Warren managed to return to the base and organize a rescue party, a remarkable feat of stamina and courage. He had his share of close calls. Shortly before he left Gibraltar in July 1865, he suffered a fall from a high scarp that injured one arm. But he remained confident of his abilities. "I used to spend much spare time in jumping down steep places with soft landings, and I was rather expert at it," he recalled of his childhood in Wales.

Warren was from a military family; his elder brother died fighting in the Crimean War and his father was a major general at the Battle of Waterloo who was later injured in the Opium Wars with China. The family had a devout Anglican streak. His grandfather had been the dean of a small Welsh cathedral, and Warren knew the Psalms by heart. And like his father and grandfather, Warren was a member of the Freemasons, that fraternal organization embraced by many elite European men of the day as a circle of fellowship that was also a useful ladder for social climbing.

Soon after his arrival in Gibraltar, Warren had joined the Masonic lodge and within three years, though he was barely past twenty, was made its master. "Many of the best soldiers of all ranks are to be found among the Masons," he later said. It was a meeting at the Masonic lodge with an Anglo-Irish military engineer named Francis George Irwin that likely fired Warren's interest in Jerusalem. According to the Masonic historian Colin Macdonald, Irwin proved "one of the most influential Masons of all time." Irwin was a "sapper"—that is, a Royal Engineer trained to demolish structures—who was fascinated by ancient construction. While in Gibraltar, he expounded at length on the "reconstruction of the Solomonic Temple in Freemasonic thought."

In Masonic lore, King Solomon was said to have assembled eighty thousand masons to build his temple. These were organized into guilds, or degrees, with increasing levels of knowledge, and the first lodge, with the king as their leader, was on the Temple Mount. English Freemason tradition held that ancient Jews passed along Masonic knowledge to the first English Christian martyr, Saint Alban. They also told stories of the warrior-monks called the Knights Templars, headquartered on the sacred platform during the Crusades, who were said to have discovered— and later, perhaps, hid—a vast Solomonic treasure beneath Jerusalem's acropolis.

Irwin called the temple built under Solomon's direction "the greatest achievement of architecture in ancient society." But it was also a symbol of virtue and a mystical metaphor. "The Temple became a moral edifice as an example of what was noble and splendid and true," he said. This was why every lodge contained a representation of the two columns, Boaz and Jachin, that the Bible said framed the entrance to Solomon's sanctuary.

The sapper was intensely interested in Jerusalem's ruins. He speculated on the "still visible foundations of King Solomon's Temple." That was likely a reference to de Saulcy's questionable contention that the walls of the platform built by the early Judean monarch remained intact. As a young Freemason, Warren looked to Irwin as a mentor. "There is no doubt that Warren, as an active Mason, would have been eager to discover anything that would corroborate any part of the Masonic legend and ritual," wrote the historian Macdonald.

In 1863, as de Saulcy was on his way to Jerusalem to make his fateful discovery, Warren was following in Irwin's footsteps, donning a white robe bearing a red cross to be initiated as a member of the Masonic Knights Templar, an order within Freemasonry that bound him to defend Christianity. The Knights Templars viewed themselves as successors to the medieval martial organization, which was abolished in the fourteenth century.

When Warren returned to Britain from Gibraltar in the summer of 1865, steeped in Irwin's fascination with Jerusalem's ruins, he received mild acclaim for his surveying work and was elected a fellow of the Royal Geographical Society. Then he settled down with his new wife to teach military engineering in the southeastern town of Chatham.

Within eighteen months, however, he would be packing for Palestine. His grandson later said that he had gone to Jerusalem "somewhat in the role of a Crusader" who was "stirred by the longing to reveal to the Christian world those sacred places hidden by the debris of many a siege, and jealously guarded by the Turkish Mussulmans."

It is here that the difference between the two Charleses becomes most salient: while Wilson had been happy to accept the Jerusalem task for the sake of adventure and a technical challenge, Warren was primed for the position for closely guarded spiritual reasons.

◆ ◆ ◆

AS 1867 DAWNED, the second lieutenant left Britain with three enlisted men on the Palestine Exploration Fund's third expedition. He was given a nearly impossible job. The Fund ordered him to dig on and around the Noble Sanctuary, identify the biblical City of David, and explore important Christian sites. Any one of these was a tall order, given the sensitivity of the holy places. He also had not received a decree from the sultan permitting a dig. And he was to do the work for next to nothing.

At a London hotel the night before the team's departure, Grove handed Warren a check for 300 pounds, the equivalent today of $45,000. The expedition leader assumed it was a down payment for what would be a far costlier mission, but the Fund's honorary secretary neglected to tell him there was no more money. The surveyor later recalled bitterly that he was "kept in happy ignorance" of the dire financial situation.

Warren's arrival during a fierce February gale didn't augur well for the expedition. Customs officials at Jaffa were suspicious of red-coated British soldiers carrying sophisticated instruments and explosive material. They impounded baggage they declared "warlike." After the team managed to extract and pack up their equipment for the trek to Jerusalem, they encountered winds so strong that some of their eight mules, with heavy loads tied to their backs, toppled over.

Upon reaching the city, Warren was met cordially by Izzet Pasha. Despite the Englishman's lack of a permit, the governor agreed to let him excavate until the document arrived from Istanbul. The sole restriction was that he not disturb the Noble Sanctuary. He also was required to request permission for each excavation and pay an Ottoman guard to watch over the proceedings.

The British officer wasted no time showing his contempt for such restrictions. The guard, he wrote, turned out to be "such a nuisance, always stopping the work" and he "found it took so many days to get through the necessary forms." Warren simply dispensed with asking permission, and immediately dug as close to the Noble Sanctuary's walls as possible. "He was already displaying something of an imperial mentality," noted his biographer, Kevin Shillington.

To add insult to injury, Warren hired dozens of armed men and boys from the nearby village of Silwan, just south of the walled city, to begin the first major excavations around the sacred platform. He described them as "a lawless set, credited with being the most unscrupulous ruffians in Palestine." They would make the governor think twice about interfering with his work. Warren found them "industrious, willing, and good tempered, easily made to laugh." When it was chilly they dressed in leather slippers, cotton shirts, and woolen waistcoats, but in extreme heat they didn't hesitate to work naked. The residents of this village would serve as the backbone for Jerusalem archaeological excavations for more than a century, laboring under European, American, and then Israeli archaeologists.

Warren was accomplished at mining techniques as well as surveying, and he set his workers digging next to the southern walls of the Noble Sanctuary. The team hit rubble as far down as 130 feet, and the ground proved dangerously unstable. Warren, however, felt driven to discovery. The message the Fund sent, he later explained, was "For heaven's sake, find the Tomb of David or we shall be bankrupt!" He was told that he "must get results, not to go where I thought best for the work, but to go where every basketful unearthed would give information. I had to choose."

He quickly was given no choice but to stop. The team broke through a wall and entered a tunnel that led beneath the Noble Sanctuary. "Our progress through these passages had been rapid, but unhappily the hammer-blows, resounding through the hollow walls in so unwonted a manner, alarmed the modern representative of the High Priest," he wrote.

The Muslim sheikh in charge of the site, infuriated to find heretics burrowing without permission within the sacred precinct, climbed to the top of the sanctuary wall. "With full turban and long flowing robes, edges tipped with fur" he stood "stamping his feet with rage and bellowing imprecations." He aimed his anger not at the infidels but at the sheikh of Silwan for allowing the villagers to assist in the desecration. That sheikh, in turn, shouted back insults across the rocky valley. "Soon the whole world might have heard a very distorted account of our doings, echoing among the ruins and rocks of Jerusalem," said an amused Warren.

The consequences, however, were not so comical. The city's military commander ordered all work halted. The governor remained gracious as he explained that the Englishman had violated a sacred area without the proper authority. An extra guard was posted to maintain the platform's sanctity. "I was told by Izzet Pacha not to work near it," Warren groused, "but that I could work elsewhere." He left to conduct surveying work outside of town, but returned to find the governor had been replaced with a man less amenable to Europeans digging up the Holy City.

Warren's only prior contact with the Arab world had been a visit or two to Morocco while in Gibraltar and a childhood fascination with *The Arabian Nights*. He spoke neither Turkish nor Arabic and lacked the cultural skills to overcome the suspicion of the new governor, Nazif Pasha. Unlike the more introverted Wilson, he didn't have a quiet and diplomatic touch. And unlike de Saulcy, he was not a high-ranking official with the blessing of the sultan.

The new governor was not going to risk his career for a brash low-level British engineer. He immediately rescinded his predecessor's permission to dig until written approval arrived from Istanbul. The disdain was mutual. Warren dismissed Nazif as "a bigoted Moslem, without any French polish; he was of the sterner class of Turk, so inflated with his religious notions, that he considered all Christians of an inferior class of human nature." On top of that, he declared him "guided by a few illiterate dervishes"—Sufi holy men—"and the more fanatic of his citizens." This faction "could only see in the Franks rival nations of unclean barbarians."

In a huff, Warren set off again, this time to survey the Dead Sea. On his return, the governor slighted him during their interminable negotiations in subtle ways at first lost on the Englishman. For example, he gave Warren a cigarette rather than offering to share a pipe with him, as he would have with a high-ranking official. He contemptuously dismissed the young lieutenant as "the mole."

When a letter from the grand vizier in Istanbul finally came, it was, Warren wrote, "worse than useless." He was granted "permission and every possible facility to dig and inspect places, after satisfying the owners, with the exception of the Noble Sanctuary and the various Moslem and Christian shrines." That left few places in shrine-filled Jerusalem to excavate. Warren contrived to flash around the document without revealing its actual contents, but the pasha wasn't fooled.

As precious time elapsed, the Englishman found himself with few options. He rejected the idea of distributing bribes to get his way, since this "spoilt the market"—that is, it would only increase the appetite of the bribed. Nor would he descend to "wheedling and coaxing," methods, he explained, that were "quite foreign to the habits of our countrymen."

Instead, he launched a cat-and-mouse game that lasted for the next three years. When Warren began the dig near the Holy Sepulchre, the pasha's soldiers shut down the dig. Unperturbed, the Englishman simply chose another site next to the Noble Sanctuary walls. His strategy was to wear down the opposition.

The annoyed pasha insisted that Warren could not dig within forty feet of the platform. So the dogged excavator hit on a bold tactic of deceit. He rented land that was just beyond the forty-foot limit and ordered vertical shafts dug. At a sufficient depth, the men then tunneled horizontally in the direction of the ancient walls. From the surface, it appeared Warren was abiding by the rule. There was the added advantage that the team could then dig in any direction without having to pay the residents who lived above.

This required a full-scale mining operation. Nothing like it had ever been done in Palestine. The Royal Engineer needed vast amounts of timber to support shafts as deep as 150 feet, with even longer tunnels. But timber was expensive and rare—he had to import some from as far away as Malta—and he sometimes resorted to flimsy brushwood instead to brace the passages. Wood rotted quickly in the extreme heat and humidity of the tunnels. Each foot dug required more labor and materials while increasing the chance for disaster.

The Silwan workers labored from sunrise to sunset summer and winter, digging into the unstable rock-laden soil and filling baskets. Each one, heavy with debris, required a long climb up a rickety ladder to the surface to be dumped. Their fearlessness was a particular asset given the danger of the work. Warren knew the tricky nature of limestone, which is porous and can easily crumble, from his years spent clambering over and through the Rock of Gibraltar. Here it was still more treacherous. Jerusalem's underground was filled with small chips left over from millennia of demolished buildings that formed a solid that could quickly turn liquid with devastating results.

"The shingle would suddenly burst in like water, burying our tools and sometimes partially our workmen," he noted. The falling chips might then expose a large rock that would "descend with a crash, dragging tons of debris with it, smashing one side of the shaft flat against the other, and breaking up the boards like so many sticks." There were formidable solid obstacles as well, such as thick-walled cisterns and sheer solid rock.

It is a testament to the safety measures that Warren and his excavation manager, Corporal Henry Birtles, insisted upon, as well as the nimbleness of the Silwan workers, that there were no deaths and only a few injuries during two years of excavations. One man ignored the rules and broke his back, while another Arab workman was buried, dug out of the rubble, and carried away unconscious, though both recovered. A less dramatic but more deadly threat was "tetanus and other infections from the poisoned soil, impregnated with sewage of many past ages."

Their safety record was more than a credit to careful work; it was also vital for the project to continue. Warren was well aware that an underground disaster would have turned the citizens and governor against the expedition. "The strain on the nerves during this work was intense, and required of the men the greatest amount of fortitude and self-control," he recalled later. He paid "about a penny a day more than the market price, so as to secure our men, and soon found that a tight hold could be kept on them." When some of the men went on strike, Warren responded by reducing their wages, which put a halt to collective action.

Each day, the Englishman marveled that his employees "come to the work cool and collected." For his part, Warren suffered from "intense anxiety" as well as bouts of intestinal illness during the nonstop digs, though he also made frequent military surveying trips to the Dead Sea region, leaving Birtles in charge. A rangy man with hair cut short and face framed by a dark beard, Warren kept a hotel room but slept in a tent outside of town in the heat of summer, returning in the morning to dress in a loose tweed jacket, baggy trousers, Spanish leather shoes, and a sun helmet. He didn't vary his outfit, he explained, "so that natives who did not know me by sight would recognize my dress."

By 7:00 a.m. he was breakfasting on bread, grapes, honey, boiled milk, "and the diminutive leg of a chicken." Warren hated the goat, deplored the mutton, found pigeon meat disgusting, and complained that the soup invariably was served with "half an inch of oil floating on its surface." The absence of beef, he added, was "a great drawback." Were it not for "quince jam, tomatoes, and peaches, I should say generally that no eatables in this country have any taste."

Warren's underground odysseys often bordered on the absurd. Beneath the convent of the French Sisters of Zion, close to the northwest corner of the Noble Sanctuary, he and Birtles set out to chart a tunnel noted by Wilson but still unexplored. It was filled six feet deep with sewage that "was not water and was not mud." This was not unusual; Jerusalem lacked working sewers, and human and animal waste collected in pockets and passages below the streets. What was unique was their method of transport.

The two men laid planks from old doors and made "a perilous voyage" by taking the plank from behind and placing it ahead. "The sewage in some places was more liquid than in others, but in every case it sucked in the doors so that we had much difficulty in getting the hinder ones up, while those we were on sunk down, first on one side and then on the other as we tried to keep our balance."

As they proceeded, "everything had now become so slippery with sewage that we had to exercise the greatest caution in lowering the doors and ourselves down, lest an unlucky false step might cause a header into the murky liquid." One false move meant "dying like a rat in a pool of sewage." Finally, the goo became firm enough to tread upon, and they moved south, parallel to the western wall of the sanctuary as the tunnel grew narrower until it ended at a stone wall. The men found themselves beneath the administrative headquarters of the pasha; they could hear voices and footsteps from above. "On this account we did not venture to break through the masonry," he noted drolly.

In another instance, Warren crawled through an ancient water tunnel beneath the narrow ridge that extended south of the Old City, "one hand necessarily wet and dirty, the other holding a pencil, compass and field-book; the candle for the most part in my mouth." Nearby Warren encountered a steep fifty-two-foot-deep chasm that he deduced must be the passage mentioned in the Bible that King David's soldiers used to infiltrate and conquer Jebusite Jerusalem. Warren clambered up the nearly vertical shaft that now bears his name, a difficult feat few later archaeologists managed. More important, he believed he had found what might be the long-lost City of David mentioned in the Bible.

While exploring a series of cisterns on the north end of the Noble Sanctuary, Warren and Birtles stripped off their clothes to wade through murky water to access a narrow shaft, wriggling through the tight space and into a pitch-black chamber. "On lighting up the magnesium wire and looking about me, I was astonished, my first impression being that I had got into a church similar to that of the cathedral (formerly a mosque) at Cordova," he wrote. "I could see arch upon arch to north and east, apparently rows of them." For the next three hours, waist-deep in cold water, they measured every inch of the abandoned hall.

The team's indefatigable burrowing led to rumors that Warren's "very sinister mission" was to plant gunpowder to "destroy the grand old walls" of the Noble Sanctuary. He suspected the military commander of starting the story "to cause dislike among the people to our excavations."

Whatever the source, the concern was real; Warren occasionally used bags and even barrels of black powder to clear underground obstacles that would not give way to hammering. Alfred Nobel had patented dynamite that May, but it was not yet in commercial use. Had it been, there is little question that the British officer would have made frequent use of it.

◆ ◆ ◆

IT WAS WARREN'S EXPLORATIONS around Wilson's Arch, the soaring ancient structure his predecessor had noted, that led to his most stunning discovery.

The arch that had once supported a massive bridge onto the Temple Mount now served as the roof of an underground cistern providing water for residents above. Locals called it the Pool of al-Buraq, for the magical steed that the Qur'an says carried Muhammad from Mecca to "the farthest mosque," long identified as the Noble Sanctuary. According to a legend dating to early medieval times, the prophet tied his steed to this section of the platform's western wall before he climbed a celestial ladder to the seventh heaven to meet Adam, Abraham, Moses, Jesus, and other prophets—a tale of spiritual ascent that may have inspired Dante's *Divine Comedy*.

Just south of the pool was a small and narrow courtyard facing the huge stones of the exposed platform wall, with a footprint no bigger than a suburban home's, built by the Ottoman ruler Suleiman the Magnificent in the early 1500s. For Muslims it faced the wall of al-Buraq, but for Jews it was the Wailing Wall, where they gathered to mourn the loss of their temple. "It is a most remarkable sight," Warren reported, "these people all thronging the pavement, and wailing so intensely, that often the tears roll down their faces."

Warren suspected that beneath this area he would find remains from the days of Herod the Great or even Solomon. Since digging in a courtyard owned by Muslims and sacred to Jews was out of the question, he instead directed his team to cut through the concrete floor of the underground reservoir below Wilson's Arch, which was at that moment dry. They struggled down through boulders and broken masonry coated in reeking mud and sewage, using the occasional round of black powder to clear a path. This not only was dangerous for the workers, but must have proved deeply disturbing to worshippers in the courtyard as well as those in the city's courthouse, which was above the excavation.

The team's effort was rewarded with access to a series of long-lost chambers, including a large room with elegant pilasters with a single pillar in its center. "This hall is probably of the time of the Kings of Judah," he wrote. Later archaeologists pegged it to the days of Herod the Great nearly a millennium later, but this presumed connection to Solomon and his immediate successors may be why Warren dubbed it the Masonic Hall. Beyond, the British excavator found a series of high vaults and followed a 250-foot-long causeway he named the Secret Passage. The series of massive piers and arches had once led to the sacred platform.

The bewildering collection of ancient structures left Warren overwhelmed. "What a chaos of ruin upon ruin is here to be found, so confusing and perplexing, that I fear it baffles my powers of description," he wrote. The team then attempted to tunnel north along the buried stones at the base of the western wall of the platform, but the formidable foundations of medieval Islamic religious schools and hospices forced a halt to their progress.

The underground complex of "arches upon arches, aqueducts and shafts" provided Warren with the first extensive evidence that large swaths of ancient Jerusalem remained intact beneath the modern city. Excited, he approached Jewish leaders to offer a tour. As a Mason seeking to uncover that tradition's link to Solomon, Warren felt a kinship with the city's Jews, and he cultivated friendships with several Sephardic and Ashkenazi rabbis. Still traumatized by de Saulcy's actions, however, many were not inclined to look favorably on Warren's work. "These Jews are constantly awaiting the advent of their Messiah, and looked upon my work at Jerusalem as assisting in bringing about the end"—that is, the end of the world.

But many Ashkenazim, with their European backgrounds, were intrigued by this Christian seemingly obsessed with Jewish heritage. The British officer, in turn, could not help but admire what he called "an irrepressible pride and presumption about this fragile wayward people." Though they dressed in "greasy rags, they stalk about the Holy City with as much dignity as though they were dressed in the richest garments, and give way to no one; years of oppression have in no way quelled their ancient spirit."

Decades before Jewish Zionism took shape, Warren called for "gradually introducing the Jew, pure and simple, who is eventually to occupy and govern this country." He supported "a Jewish principality" in the Holy Land "guaranteed by the Great Powers." Yet he also was wary of what he called the Ashkenazi "bursts of fanatical zeal," and presciently warned that they would "cause trouble in Jerusalem in future days."

A group that included the chief rabbi met Warren beside the Wailing Wall one morning to question him closely before setting off on their subterranean journey. "Was I quite sure we were not going under the Temple area? This was their great fear, for they have a tradition that the volume of the Sacred Law is buried somewhere within the enclosure," he recalled. "Having been reassured on this point, they trooped down after me."

Passing through a door at the north end of the Wailing Wall, they entered the courthouse, ignoring protests by the Muslim guards, and made their way into a cellar to reach Wilson's Arch. "I had lighted up magnesium wire, and they could view its vast proportions, and see the mouths of the shafts sunk below the springing of the arch at each end. We now descended the ladder under the arch itself, into the void place which of late years has been used as a tank."

He guided them through the hole that led fifty feet below the surface, past treacherous pits and open cisterns. "I was very much afraid I should lose a few rabbis; but fortune favored us." While in the Masonic Hall, some rubble collapsed on the party, but the visitors didn't complain. "We had come for sightseeing, so they did not mind a few bruises."

The rabbis were so enthusiastic about Warren's discoveries that "they had prayers in their synagogues for the welfare of our undertaking, and at last had a grand ceremony at the synagogue, to which I was invited." Even better than prayers, a rabbinical committee suggested a subscription to raise money to publish Warren's scientific reports in Hebrew, a move they said "would do much towards promoting the interests of the work."

Nothing came of the proposal, but it was an early sign of Jewish enthusiasm for the budding work of archaeology launched by European Christians.

Jerusalem's Arab residents did not share this passion. Soon after the rabbis' tour, the city council sent a committee to investigate complaints from homeowners who claimed the digs were undermining their foundations. The committee members descended into the passages, and noted with alarm that Warren's team had demolished a sturdy supporting arch and replaced it with timber. They feared its collapse might send portions of the courthouse crashing down.

"There is danger of great injury occurring therefrom to the places above, which neither the Almighty nor his Majesty the Sultan would sanction," they concluded in a February 1868 letter to the governor. "We recommend that your Excellency be pleased to take measures to prevent them from doing this."

The pasha waited until Warren was out of town on a surveying expedition to block the entrance to the complex. When the Englishman returned, he complained bitterly that "we were prevented continuing our excavations there, and were thus stopped in the midst of the solution of a most intricate problem." He blamed the closure on Ottoman jealousy in the wake of the tour he had given the Jewish notables.

"It may be many years before anyone is able to resume the excavations," his colleague Wilson later wrote. In fact, it would be a full century. And when excavators did return, they would not be Christians or even archaeologists. They would be rabbis.

◆ ◆ ◆

THE SUCCESS OF the Jewish tour demonstrated that the digs might generate desperately needed donations as well as data. Warren's work in the late 1860s also drew media attention that encouraged Western tourists to make the long trek to the Holy City. "The main result of these excavations is the discovery that ancient Jerusalem lies buried beneath enormous masses of debris," the *New York Times* reported. "Underneath the pavements of the modern streets lies the old sacred City of Zion."

Begun as a covert way to avoid the limits placed on him by the Ottomans, the tunnels proved popular attractions. European ladies in bell sleeves and bustles were gently lowered into the depths on a special chair rigged with pulleys. Upon reaching the bottom, they trod on carpets laid on the rough stone while incense burned, "for in one of the vaults a great amount of sewage had accumulated." These precautions were not always sufficient; occasionally visitors fell faint, "and they had to be dragged up with the rope."

The Englishman took as many as two or three parties a day into the subterranean world. "Of course, it made us lose time, much time," he explained later, but "I thought, as it was a public Fund, that all visitors should have facilities for seeing what was going on." As archaeologists working ever since in Jerusalem have learned, serving as a tour guide for the curious is an essential part of their job. "We did not lose in the end," Warren noted. "For each party went back full of interest in the subject, and prepared to push it through on arrival in England."

American missionaries, German barons, and artists for the *Illustrated London News* lined up for their chance to see Jerusalem's underground wonders. "It is hoped that the Marquis of Bute will go down the shaft this week," one tourist remarked. The marquis did, and on the spot gave Warren a check for 250 pounds.

The Scottish adventurer John MacGregor left a particularly vivid account of his journey below Robinson's Arch, the remnant of the span attached to the Noble Sanctuary. Warren and Birtles met him one morning at the site, the former in "a blouse of genuine mud color" and the latter bearing "long tapers for our dark promenade." They lowered a rope ladder down the square shaft and the visitor descended.

"The hole we are in is like a well, but it is lined with strong planks, and at the dark bottom our passage is through an opening as if into a kitchen grate, where we grope on all fours, with a hard knock on the head now and then, bending sideways too, as well as up and down, until suddenly the roof becomes rugged and crooked, indescribably contorted by angles, all of them the corners of well-cut stones," he recalled. "For here we are in the confused heap of huge voussoirs or arch-stones, which, once high in the air, spanned gracefully the rocky vale between Zion and the Temple."

As they made their way through the tunnel, "tanks, cisterns, aqueducts, pavements, here open to us underground. Once we have got down we can scan by the magnesium light a subterranean city, the real city of Jerusalem. The labour of building this, and of now mining into it when buried, is forgotten in wonder as we gaze on the silent relics or wander about the caverns echoing a hollow voice. But for this we must be agile, like cats or monkeys, and follow Mr. Warren complacently crawling on his back through a dark crevice."

The vast majority of the visitors were Western Protestants, and descending into the earth allowed them to step into the days of Solomon and Jesus. Climb down a ladder or settle into a chair, and you could touch the familiar biblical past.

"The Jerusalem we see today is not the real Jerusalem," MacGregor went on to explain. "That is buried under fifty feet of wreck and confusion, but in its forced silence somehow it speaks eloquently, bidding the Christian and the Jew to heave its burdens off, to open the dark to light and air, and to read in the covered relics the story of past times."

For Jerusalem's residents, of course, the aboveground city was quite real. Life for them was lived not in some long-ago era but in the busy markets, crowded compounds, and sacred shrines covering the surface. Western Christians rooting around in sewage-choked cellars and musty tunnels were an oddity; for locals of all faiths, the only sane reason to dig was to locate water or find treasure. Warren claimed to be doing neither of these, and his use of explosives close to Islam's third-holiest site kept people on edge.

This menace was offset in part by the opportunity to make extra income by renting a plot of land to Warren's team or lending a hand at the excavation itself. But when the work threatened the home of one distinguished Arab family, it sparked a bitter battle that would help sour Ottoman authorities on the Western penchant for burrowing, and was a factor in placing Jerusalem's depths largely off-limits for the next quarter century.

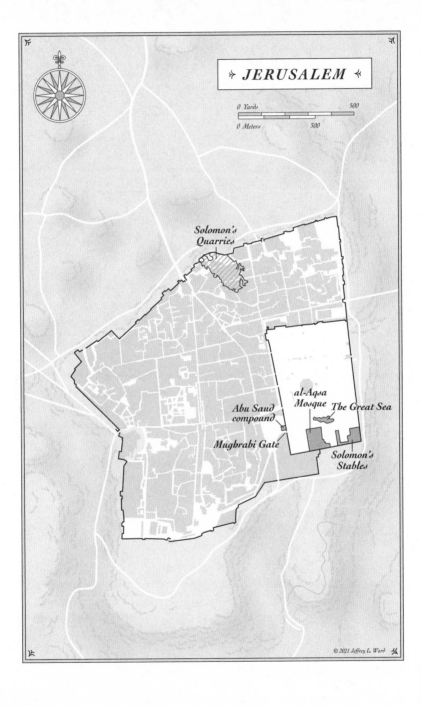

JERUSALEM

0 Yards 500

0 Meters 500

Solomon's
Quarries

al-Aqsa
Mosque   The Great Sea

Abu Saud
compound

Mughrabi Gate

Solomon's
Stables

© 2021 Jeffrey L. Ward

4

The Roots of Our Problem

It remains for us to institute a new crusade for the peaceful conquests at which science aims.

—RICHARD OWEN

By November 1867, Warren's team had dug twenty-seven shafts. Each led to a tunnel or tunnels snaking hundreds of yards beneath the homes, mosques, and businesses of Jerusalem residents. This impressive engineering feat, conducted with speed and under strict safety conditions, all the while producing prodigious and precise measurements, leaves archaeologists in awe even today.

Warren devoted most of his excavations to boring along the perimeter of the Noble Sanctuary. Like scree covering the base of a mountain, later construction hid the base of these impressive walls. At the northern end, he encountered an underground passage next to the wall that led to a secret chamber. "Here was an exciting discovery: what might not be in this chamber in the wall?" he wrote. "The ark and utensils secreted at the destruction of the Temple might here be hidden away."

But his dreams, like de Saulcy's, were shattered by reality. Instead of the temple treasures, he found that "nothing was observable of value."

At another spot, Warren's tunneling intersected with the course of stones that had once lain on the surface. He estimated that the wall extended an astonishing 180 feet to the top course—higher than Nelson's Column in London. This demonstrated that the platform was indeed a wonder of the ancient world.

But how ancient? Most scholars believed the walls were built at the order of Herod the Great in the first century BCE, as detailed by contemporary Roman and Jewish writers. Yet while probing the southern corner of the platform's west wall, the excavators came across letters and numbers made in red paint on the buried stones. A visiting Jewish scholar declared them Phoenician. Warren concluded they must be the masons' marks from the Phoenicians that the Bible said had built the *first* temple, fully a millennium earlier.

This theory surely appealed to Warren's Masonic orientation. He wrote that the find "proves that the foundations of this great wall are indeed part of the original Temple of Solomon." The Bible's frequent mentions of the early grandeur of early Jerusalem were vindicated. The team also uncovered a fragment of clay that read "*Haggai*" in Hebrew and was declared to refer to the biblical prophet of that name—a find Warren considered as confirmation of the holy book's veracity.

At a time when a growing number of Europeans and Americans dismissed the scripture as more legend than history, archaeology appeared to be living up to its promise of lending scientific credence to the holy text. Warren assured his benefactor Grove in a November letter that "you may safely boast that in these nine month's work you have discovered more than all previous travelers in a thousand years." He added that "many of the merest conjectures are now certainties."

This public success, proclaimed in newspapers from Singapore to San Francisco, masked a grim financial reality. "I had supported the excavations entirely out of my own pocket, a most cruel position to be placed in, when there were so many rich people who could afford so much better than I could," Warren later wrote. His situation was in fact not so dire; the British officer had married the daughter of a wealthy British banker. Nevertheless, for eight months Grove had ignored his increasingly frantic requests for money. Expenses mounted. The Fund, he added sarcastically, had become "The Debt."

The artifacts unearthed by Warren did little to attract donations. Roman and Byzantine oil lamps, some coins, and jar handles with Hebrew lettering would barely fill a single case in the British Museum, much less rival de Saulcy's sarcophagus in the Louvre. Grove was forced to send a stream of correspondence to British newspapers extolling Warren's progress—and begging for money. In October, the *New York Times* published his desperate letter to Americans, including those "who have been down his shafts, and felt their way along his passages and galleries," requesting funds.

Pledges arrived, but not enough to pay for the large sums Warren required for his ever-expanding subterranean world. By the end of 1867, Grove had sent only half as much as Warren had spent, and the excavator was on the verge of quitting. Meanwhile, Warren's relationship with the local governor took a turn for the worse. Nazif Pasha's closure of the area around Wilson's Arch was followed by his insistence in early 1868 that Warren request permission for any future dig. Then Birtles fell ill and had to be sent home, a major setback for the project. Two replacements arrived, but they lacked the corporal's calm competence.

To make matters worse, while Warren had succeeded in largely neutralizing Nazif's opposition, he faced growing criticism from Jerusalem's leading families. These local Arab aristocrats—called "notables"—served as important intermediaries between the Ottoman governor and the populace. They already had succeeded in shutting down the digs below the Pool of al-Buraq that threatened the courthouse, but residents continued to complain that new British excavations were damaging their homes.

In a January 22, 1868, letter to the Fund, Warren had explained that "our system in excavating . . . is to give the landlord presents for the privilege of digging in their soil." For the most part, he reported, the negotiations had only taken at most a day or two to complete. "The problem," he added, "is the Government, not the people."

That was before he tangled with a landowner named Abd-es-Salam Abu Saud. This patriarch of an old and wealthy Arab family lived in a cluster of buildings constructed against the western wall, just south of the Wailing Wall. The area was part of the Mughrabi Quarter, which was settled in medieval times by North Africans ("Mughrab" means Westerner in Arabic). The Abu Sauds had long been notables, serving as Muslim scholars, Sufi sheikhs, and city administrators through the centuries.

By Warren's day, their elaborate compound had grown to include forty separate apartments housing some eighty people. Its proximity to al-Aqsa Mosque on the southwestern end of the Noble Sanctuary made it prime Muslim real estate. It also was prime archaeological real estate, given that it lay adjacent to Robinson's Arch, named for the American biblical scholar. What lay beneath held the promise of clues to biblical times.

Wilson had tried without success to gain access to Abu Saud's property in 1865. Two years later, Warren also was rebuffed. The Arab was, he asserted, "too greedy to listen to any moderate terms." Abu Saud, however, seemed less interested in money than in keeping the Europeans off his family's land.

The enterprising Warren found a way around the problem by paying "a fair rental" to the sheikh of the Mughrabi Quarter, who lived next door. That sheikh was in charge of what is called in Arabic a *waqf,* a cross between a religious commune and a nonprofit organization that holds land for the benefit of a community. (To this day, waqfs control a large portion of the land in and around the Old City.) The subsequent excavations gave the archaeologist access to a rich assortment of ancient ruins below; this was the passage visited by MacGregor.

For Abu Saud's family, however, the constant noise of digging was exasperating. Warren himself confirmed that his team was "working night and day, and Abu Saud complained that he could not sleep at night for fear his house should tumble around his ears." The archaeologist insisted that the men were merely cleaning out a drain and an aqueduct they had encountered paralleling the western wall of the platform, and that the work posed no threat to the structure of his home.

Later, Warren conceded that his efforts in the area constituted "a very dangerous proceeding, as the stones are all lying piled upon each other, with vacant places between, and our gallery frames were quite unfit for supporting stones that weighed several tons each." He clearly did far more than clear existing drains, and he did not refrain from using explosives.

Abu Saud protested to the governor, which Warren, without elaborating, characterized as "blackmail." Nazif dismissed the complaint, and the Englishman claimed that he and Abu Saud then "became firm friends." In exchange for a tour of a cistern the team had found beneath his property, "he wanted to teach me astrology: we did not go very deep into the matter."

The reconciliation was brief. Not long after, a four-foot-deep hole opened on the surface when the excavators hit a trench dug by Wilson two years before. "Abu Saud was indignant, and said we were bringing down the Sanctuary wall," Warren wrote. The disgruntled resident invited the Jerusalem city council—the Mejelis—to inspect the hole, but by the time the councilors arrived the next morning, Warren had already filled it in. "He was very much perplexed about it, as the Mejelis thought he was playing a joke on them, and did not pay much attention to him after that."

Following that prank, Warren proceeded to sink a new shaft along the wall that was "immediately outside my friend Abu Saud's house," no doubt further irritating the homeowner. In his second complaint to the pasha, Abu Saud claimed the British were digging under his compound. Warren maintained that they were "still several feet distant from it."

Faced with repeated accusations from a distinguished citizen, Nazif began to lose patience with Warren. He reiterated that the officer must first request permission for all digs and hire a guard. "Certainly the Pasha has the letter of the law on his side," Warren admitted. But he added that "all the more important excavations" had been done by ignoring these constraints. The search for the biblical past, in other words, trumped the objections of current-day residents.

Frustrated by Warren's intransigence, Nazif went over his head. He wrote British consul Noel Moore that the expedition had to live within the constraints of the sultan's decree. When Moore confronted the excavator, Warren was defiant. "I told the Consul that I could not deviate from my course of procedure without the consent of the Palestine Exploration Fund Committee, unless he compelled me to do so." He warned that if there were any attempt to interfere with the excavations, he would abandon the digs and leave the safety issues for the governor and consul to sort out. The officer was, in effect, thumbing his nose at the senior Ottoman as well as British authorities.

A cascade of complaints from other residents further soured the governor on his prickly British guest. One Arab citizen asserted that Warren had damaged several tombs "and that our shafts were dangerous to wayfarers." Another homeowner demanded thirty pounds so he could fix cracks in his home, but Warren "refused to give anything, as the damage was not our doing."

In March 1869, the Jerusalem city council demanded payment from Warren to repair fissures in a building owned by a religious foundation. He dismissed the cracks as "all of ancient date" and the whole matter as "an iniquitous attempt at extortion." An effort to resolve the dispute ended in a bitter stalemate. The German missionary Conrad Schick, who was an architect as well, was later brought in as an "umpire." He concluded Warren was not responsible for the damage.

The British officer blamed Abu Saud for turning both the pasha and the residents against him, claiming that he "appeared to think he could pull the wires to his own advantage." He insisted that the real issue was the city's shoddy construction. "The houses were so insecure, that if we came even within a hundred yards of them, the people were inclined to call out and ask for compensation; yet we never did any damage, and took the greatest care—they were as safe from our operations as they were from fire."

Warren would be plagued by Abu Saud long after he returned to Britain. The mutual suspicion and distrust between residents and archaeologists that began with de Saulcy was amplified during Warren's tenure. Westerners tended to discount the grievances of locals as attempts to wheedle money out of them, but the clash between the two groups would grow more bitter, and even violent, in the century to come.

• • •

ONE OF THE FEW bright spots for Warren that spring came on May 13, 1868, when he entered an enormous quarry that extended deep below the northern part of the Old City. He was accompanied by the Ottoman governor of Jaffa, the Prussian consul, a Kentucky poet, and several British naval officers. In a remote corner of the man-made cave, they performed Jerusalem's first recorded Masonic rite.

Though he avoided mention of his Freemason membership in his professional writings, Warren would go on to found a London lodge devoted to research into Masonic origins and to publish a paper in its journal on the orientation of ancient temples that revealed the esoteric beliefs behind his data-driven efforts. "For if we cannot trace our descent from the Phoenician craftsmen who worked on the Temple of Solomon," he said in an address to his fellow Masons, "and if it be only an allegory, then our position descends from the sublime to the ridiculous."

The day after the ritual, Warren departed for Britain to attend the Fund's annual meeting and make a personal plea for support. He was back in London by May 26 with a full report on his finds. "For the first time the actual streets of the ancient city have been reached—underground passages, which have been hidden for centuries by the mass of incumbent ruins, have been brought to light, a complicated network of drains and reservoirs is being laid bare," stated the document that he presented to members. He insisted that he needed 350 pounds a month—about $53,000 today—paid in advance.

The pleas by Grove and media reports of Warren's exploits had eventually brought in enough money to ease the crisis, and the delighted members assured Warren adequate funding and an organizational shakeup. A new full-time secretary replaced Grove, who remained on the board but outside daily operations. Satisfied with a promise of 300 pounds per month, Warren was back in Jerusalem by July, and confident enough of his position to bring along his wife and infant daughter.

His return brought tragedy. Within weeks of their arrival, one of the new recruits died in an agony of fever; he was buried beneath a column extracted from the Robinson's Arch excavation. A second man fell ill and had to be evacuated to Britain. Birtles soon returned, however, and four more men arrived in September.

By then, the lieutenant felt he had the upper hand in his struggle with the Nazif Pasha. What might be termed gunboat archaeology had had an impact. The presence of a British fleet off the coast, and the influx of British sailors and officers in the streets of Jerusalem, "not only had their effect upon the people, but to a certain extent influenced the pasha himself," Warren noted. "After two years' warfare we were able to work all round the walls of the Noble Sanctuary with his cognizance and tacit consent," he wrote, describing his efforts in starkly military terms.

The pasha, in fact, seemed to have been worn down by the young man's tenaciousness. "By degrees I have been able to get nearer and nearer to the Noble Sanctuary," Warren noted with satisfaction. But he had yet to conquer that most alluring and contentious ground in Jerusalem. The city's military commander assured the Englishman that there was nothing new to discover there. The Ottoman official patiently explained that it lay "on the top of a palm tree, from the roots of which spring all the rivers of the world." Understandably, any attempt to dig "would only be followed by some catastrophe."

Using a combination of lunacy and cunning, Warren launched a patient campaign to access the carefully guarded gates of the sacred enclosure.

◆ ◆ ◆

THE NOBLE SANCTUARY, or the Temple Mount as it is known to Jews, was more like an unkempt park than a religious complex. Anchored by the octagonal Dome of the Rock near its center, with the low-slung al-Aqsa Mosque dominating its southern end, it sprawled over the equivalent of nearly thirty football fields. The site was dotted with elaborate stone kiosks and flashing fountains amid olive groves and shaded lawns littered in ancient marble columns.

To the west, the city blanketed a steep hill crowned with the citadel and its two-thousand-year-old towers. To the east were sweeping vistas of the white stones of the cemetery that clung to the steep slope of the Mount of Olives; beyond and below lay the wild and tawny landscape that dropped to the shores of the distant Dead Sea.

What interested Warren was the subterranean interior that Wilson found "perfectly honeycombed with passages and cisterns." Aside from survey work by Wilson and an Italian engineer, no one had conducted systematic mapping of this hidden terrain. Warren hoped to find evidence of the temple complex built by Solomon and the compound renovated a thousand years later by order of Herod the Great.

The British officer argued with local Muslim officials that "there is nothing contrary to their law in a Frank"—the old Crusader-era term for a Westerner—"working inside, and that there would be no harm in our excavations." Despite Nazif's continued opposition, Warren eventually won the guarded friendship of the elderly sheikh who served, in Anglican terms, as "a sort of Moslem Dean and Chapter in one man." Provided Warren was chaperoned, the sheikh agreed to allow the Englishman to explore.

The best-known area beneath the platform was a vast vaulted space that filled the entire southeast corner of the compound. "Down in the hollow ground, underneath the olives and the orange-trees that flourish in the court of the great Mosque, is a wilderness of pillars," wrote Mark Twain, who beat Warren to the site during his brief 1867 visit. The space covered an entire acre adjacent to al-Aqsa Mosque. His guide called it Solomon's Stables and said it had undergirded that famous king's sanctuary.

This had impressed even the famously cynical Twain, who was initiated as a Mason a year after Warren; when the writer returned home, he presented a gavel made of Jerusalem cedar to his St. Louis lodge. "We never dreamed we might see portions of the actual Temple of Solomon," Twain noted, hinting at something close to awe. He wandered among nine barrel-vaulted aisles with a larger central nave soaring nearly thirty feet high, all supported by ninety-four massive stone piers. Even more impressive than the space was the fact that these ancient remains could be enjoyed without "shadow or suspicion that they were a monkish humbug and a fraud."

Yet Warren knew that the age of the stables—which received their name from Crusader Knights Templars who kept their horses there—"has been the subject of much dispute." He was eager to resolve a debate of foremost interest to Masons. But when he sought entry a year after Twain's visit, he found the Ottomans had sealed the subterranean space. While Warren assumed that this was to deprive their soldiers of a hiding place at prayer times, the Palestinian historian Ehab Jallad said it more likely was shut to exclude tourists like Twain. "They were interested in these underground vaults, and the Ottomans were afraid that it would become a popular place for Christian pilgrims and Western explorers," he added.

The closure forced the resourceful Warren to improvise. He found a hole above the stables that was nine inches wide and nineteen inches high, through which he squeezed his lean body. Then he rappelled forty feet down into darkness, past "an overhanging mass of crumbling masonry." Though he managed to accomplish the task, even the daring Warren said, "I would not wish to try again."

Using a magnesium torch to illuminate the cavernous halls, Warren quickly saw they were made up of weather-worn stone and old lintels that clearly had spent a good deal of time exposed to the elements outside the windowless space. The joke was on Twain. The "ponderous archways" he so admired were not Solomonic, but made up of the odds and ends from later buildings.

Even more imposing was the Great Sea, an enormous reservoir that could hold enough water to fill two Goodyear blimps. There were dozens of other cisterns, as well as innumerable drains, tunnels, and secret passages. MacGregor, the Scottish explorer, left a memorable portrait of an afternoon spent with Warren and his minder, the sheikh, as the explorer examined what lay under the platform. One moment, the British officer was lounging on the grass, chatting, and the next he would disappear into a cistern to swing on a rope and take measurements by the light of a magnesium torch. Twenty minutes later, he would reappear, grinning, a hundred yards away. Both his disappearance and his return were accompanied by loud groans from the old sheikh who was responsible for the curious foreigner.

One day Warren told the Noble Sanctuary's Sudanese guards that he had spotted a giant lizard of a type they were fond of eating (later dubbed Warren's girdled lizard in honor of an unrelated naturalist). The men rushed off in the direction he pointed, leaving Warren and his Arab workers free to probe behind a promising wall that lay in the opposite direction. "It was very exciting; we had visions of wonderful vaults beyond us with sculptures and what not; but, when we had got through the wall, we only found earth." He acknowledged later that "we had put our lives in the greatest peril for these negative results."

Warren's tenacity ultimately produced a detailed study of the Noble

Sanctuary, with its forty-three cisterns, dozens of passages, and innumerable hidden vaults, that remains the primary source for archaeologists more than a century later.

Like many of his Western contemporaries, however, the British officer never seemed to grasp the reluctance of Muslim authorities to approve excavations within their cherished shrine. He dismissed this obstinance as superstition and willful ignorance. MacGregor saw it differently: "Even the Dean of Westminster, so valuable a co-operator of the Palestine Exploration Fund, would be reluctant to allow a Turkish officer of Engineers to dig by the east buttresses of Westminster Abbey."

Warren's measurements were precise, but he lacked many of the methods that archaeologists today take for granted, such as the careful plotting of stratigraphy and the dating of finds based on changes in pottery types. As a result, a host of his conclusions proved wrong. The red letters were not Phoenician, nor were the stones Solomonic. Even the name Haggai had nothing to do with the biblical prophet. The sole artifacts that might date to the early Judean kings later proved to be two small and broken jar handles stamped with the image of a sun disc and the Hebrew words "belonging to the king," what one historian called "the first genuine Biblical artifacts ever scientifically excavated in the Holy City."

These finds, even if their significance had been recognized at the time, proved too arcane to justify his expensive excavations. By the end of 1868, the focus of the Fund and its essential partner, the British military, had shifted to the Sinai Peninsula, where work on the French-sponsored Suez Canal was nearing completion. Warren's predecessor, Wilson, was tasked with leading a Sinai expedition at the end of that year that included Grove, an Anglican minister, and other supporters. Ostensibly the goal was to trace the route of the Israelites through the desert after their flight from Egypt.

Warren, meanwhile, continued to work on his maps and measurements, but time was running out. The Fund had less than two hundred pounds left in its till, and he was spending nearly twice that each month. In a desperate gambit, the board asked the Ottoman ambassador in London whether his government would be willing to chip in to cover the expedition's expenses. Unsurprisingly, it was not. In June, the sultan sent a decree to Nazif Pasha forbidding excavations near any important religious site in Jerusalem.

Ill with rheumatism, sciatica, and neuralgia, plagued by recurrent fevers, and no doubt poisoned by the toxic earth, a disheartened Warren left for Lebanon at the end of that month to rest. Though he returned for nine months, his digging days were over. At the end of March 1870, he departed with his wife and young daughter to catch a steamer home. He had just turned thirty, and he would never see Jerusalem again.

◆ ◆ ◆

BACK IN LONDON, the British officer was hailed as "Jerusalem Warren" and treated like a celebrity. Queen Victoria made him a knight and he joined the prestigious Royal Geographical Society.

"It was Warren who restored the ancient city to the world," gushed the Fund's secretary. "He it was who stripped the rubbish from the rocks, and showed the glorious Temple standing within its walls, 1000 feet long and 200 feet high, of mighty masonry; he it was who laid open the valleys now covered up and hidden; he who opened the secret passages, the aqueducts, the bridge connecting temple and town. Whatever else may be done in the future, his name will always be associated with the Holy City which he first recovered." This was, in part, hyperbole; Warren may have found evidence of the Jewish temple complex, but not of the temple itself.

But the years of arduous work had taken their toll. He had only begun to recover in 1874 when disaster struck the Abu Saud household.

"Most of our buildings have cracked and split," Abu Saud and four of his relatives wrote in a signed affidavit. The immediate cause was heavy winter rains, but the family blamed Warren. "On account of the excavation most of our property is ruined; only a few rooms remained undamaged." The residents "feared that the damaged rooms will fall on us, and therefore we were obliged to abandon the house and to seek lodgings outside the city, some in rooms and some in tents."

The detailed legal document presented to the British consul asserted that the family had refused Warren permission to dig precisely because they "feared that such underground excavations might damage our houses." They accused the officer of ignoring their concerns and tunneling beneath their property without permission, and added that they didn't suspect that the work had seriously weakened their foundations until the downpours of 1874.

The Abu Sauds added that an examination of Warren's drawings compared with the damaged buildings would provide "convincing proof" of their claim by demonstrating that the collapse matched the places the British had excavated. They concluded their petition by praising the "just"

British government and asking that their complaint be sent to the Fund, "whose integrity and uprightness are well known, and would not let the weak suffer."

The consul asked Conrad Schick, who had served as umpire in a previous dispute involving Warren, to conduct an investigation of the claim. The German missionary and architect paid a visit to the family in April 1875. He examined the damage and made drawings, concluding that Warren's dig was at least in part to blame for the damage. The consul sent the report to Britain's foreign secretary; a dispute between a British officer and a distinguished Jerusalem family merited attention of the highest order. He noted that a lack of maintenance combined with winter rains were common causes of house collapses in Jerusalem.

The Foreign Office in London nevertheless determined that there was "some foundation" to the complaint and the Abu Saud family had "a good claim to be compensated." The documents were then forwarded to the Fund—a private organization not officially linked to the government—with the request that it handle the delicate situation.

Warren responded with the same level of diplomacy he had displayed while excavating. In a blistering response, he first attacked the investigator. "Mr. Schick did not possess my confidence at Jerusalem and knew very little about the work as practically carried on," he wrote in early 1876, adding that his "lack of structural knowledge and his relation to the Turkish government should preclude him giving an opinion."

He went on to insist that all the "operations were carried on with the full sanction of Abu Saud's family, who were paid periodically during the occupation of their premises." Warren reiterated that all the digs in the area were simple operations of cleaning an existing drain and aqueduct, an activity that posed no structural threat.

These statements seemed at odds with his previous claims that Abu Saud refused Warren all access to his property. The archaeologist's assertion that he was merely cleaning a drain also contradicted his writing of the "dangerous" work done in the area. Certainly he had constructed a network of tunnels in the area, passages visited by hundreds of European and American visitors like MacGregor.

The Fund set up a special committee to address the complaint, and appointed Warren as one of its members. That made him simultaneously a defendant and a juror in the dispute. Not surprisingly, the committee report echoed much of the language used in his letter. The document also noted that the cracks cited by Schick were 150 feet from the nearest dig site, "or twice the breadth of the street of Pall Mall East," where the Fund's headquarters were located. The panel concluded that the organization should inform the Foreign Office of "their inability to entertain Abu Saud's claims on the above grounds."

For Warren, that was the end of the irritating matter. He went on to serve as London's police chief in the 1880s, only to resign in disgrace when he was blamed for not capturing the notorious serial murderer Jack the Ripper (some speculated, with little evidence, that the crime spree was instigated by Freemasons). His youthful intransigence seems to have hardened into middle-aged obstinacy. During the 1899 Boer War, Warren quarreled with his superiors and was accused of having a "disagreeable temper." One of his fellow officers called him a "duffer" and another dismissed him as "preposterous." He left the military to help found the Boy Scouts.

Yet the apparently minor skirmish with the Abu Saud family, which rates barely a footnote in his busy life serving imperial Britain, had major repercussions in Jerusalem. Both Ottoman authorities and local Arabs felt burned, and Warren's dismissal of the claim "prejudiced the chances of any further excavations" on or near the Noble Sanctuary, one historian concluded.

No amount of political pull could reverse this policy. "It is a pity that excavations are not being carried out at this important site," Kaiser Wilhelm II hinted to his Muslim guide when he visited the site three decades after Warren's departure. "A man should direct his eyes and his thoughts upward, at the skies," the cleric replied tactfully, "instead of downward to the depths."

After Warren, the only Westerner granted regular access to the Noble Sanctuary for research purposes was the very man the British officer so despised. Conrad Schick would rival Warren in his contributions below Jerusalem and outstrip him in his contributions above. But his most important legacy would be resolving an escalating debate over Christianity's most sacred site.

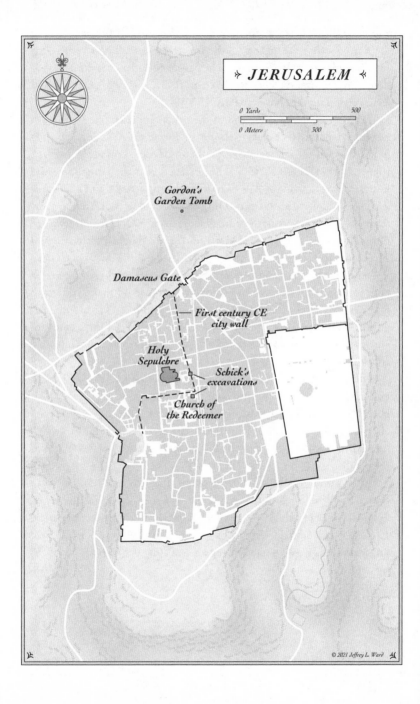

JERUSALEM

0 Yards 500
0 Meters 300

Gordon's
Garden Tomb

Damascus Gate

First century CE
city wall

Holy
Sepulchre

Schick's
excavations

Church of
the Redeemer

© 2021 Jeffrey L. Ward

5

A Faithful Watchman

"I am the great Rock, the everlasting; but what is Golgotha?
I am what I am—no one can be in doubt where to find me;
but where is Golgotha?"

—SELMA LAGERLÖF

In the race to stake a claim to Jerusalem's past, Warren's work seemed to secure a firm lead for Britain. Prussia's invasion of France a few months after his return to London knocked its leading rival out of the competition. Revolutionaries rose up at the war's end to oust the French emperor and his court. The deposed Napoleon III, with de Saulcy and wife in tow, fled to a country estate outside the British capital.

The former senator and pioneer of archaeology in Jerusalem was reduced to helping organize the ancient coin collection of the British Museum, an institution at which he had once scoffed. There would be no more lavishly funded government missions to the Holy Land. In 1871, working-class opponents to the monarchy set a fire that nearly consumed the Louvre and the sarcophagus de Saulcy had brought back to Paris in triumph.

That year, soon after Warren's departure, another Frenchman made one of Jerusalem's most important archaeological discoveries. The young scholar and diplomat Charles Clermont-Ganneau dug up a battered fragment of stone with a Greek inscription just outside a gate leading into the Noble Sanctuary. It was a warning forbidding non-Jews from entering the sacred area within the Temple compound: "Whoever is caught will be himself responsible for his ensuing death."

The sign found a mere fifty yards from the platform's entrance was mentioned in contemporary accounts, and provided what remains—aside from the massive walls—one of the few undisputed pieces of physical evidence from within the complex renovated under Herod the Great and destroyed by the Romans in 70 CE. "It is remarkable that this stone that . . . comes from the ancient Jewish Temple [compound] hasn't been carried away far from its original location," Clermont-Ganneau wrote.

Back in England, Warren's successor, a fellow lieutenant in the Royal Engineers, set out for Jerusalem the following year. Grandson of a famous evangelical abolitionist, Claude Reignier Conder was only twenty-four when he rode into Jerusalem. One of his first stops was the home of Conrad Schick. "After a long talk," the baby-faced officer left confident there were "still more decisive discoveries" to be made in Jerusalem.

Evidence for the temple built by Solomon was still lacking, and the location of the City of David, with its palaces and tombs of the early Judean kings, remained a matter of debate. There was also the issue of whether the Holy Sepulchre truly covered the site of Jesus's crucifixion, death, and burial, or whether it was, as Robinson had asserted three decades earlier, "a mere fancy." Conder called this "the most interesting question connected with the topography of Jerusalem."

His job description, however, precluded major excavations in Jerusalem. The officer's task was to map western Palestine for the Fund, whose diminished coffers had benefited from the quiet backing of a British War Office that cared little for biblical disputes. He would later be joined by another young Royal Engineer, Horatio Herbert Kitchener, who went on to become one of Britain's most prominent imperial military leaders. Before leaving Jerusalem on his mission, Conder wrote wistfully that he hoped the Fund would supply "men, materials, and money" to solve the "vexed" issue of the authenticity of the Holy Sepulchre. "These opportunities should not be lost."

Even had that support been forthcoming—which it was not—Ottoman authorities for the next decade refused most requests for dig permits in Jerusalem. They were suspicious of Western intentions and fearful that such excavations, after the de Saulcy and Warren debacles, might spark unrest. Protecting Islam's holy places, including Mecca, Medina, and Jerusalem, was an important Ottoman responsibility. Its rulers could ill afford to alienate Arab Muslims, who formed a central piece of their vulnerable empire.

Despite the restriction, the Fund's work spawned copycat organizations such as the American Palestine Exploration Society and the German Society for the Exploration of Palestine. Largely shut out of the Holy City, they focused their attention on the hundreds of ancient mounds and ruins dotting the region's hills and plains. Explorers arriving from the United States and Europe, Bibles in hand, came to Jerusalem only to scatter across the countryside. But first, like Conder, they invariably made their way to Schick's kitchen table.

◆ ◆ ◆

HE WAS THE ZELIG of Jerusalem's first era of archaeology. Conrad Schick assisted the engineer who conducted the 1863 water survey that led to creation of the Palestine Exploration Fund. He monitored de Saulcy's dig, assisted Wilson, and earned Warren's contempt for suggesting that his excavations had undermined the Abu Saud home. He also earned the trust of local Jews, Christians, and Muslims, as well as Ottoman officials— a rare accomplishment in this conflicted city.

With his blunt features, rumpled clothes, and coarse beard, this former cuckoo-clock repairman served as the unlikely Pied Piper for Western excavators. Growing up in a southern German village, he had been a sickly child who spent his days reading, and then apprenticed in carpentry and watch repair. When he turned twenty, he joined a sect of celibate evangelical Swiss Protestants in Basel and put his woodworking skills to use building a model of Solomon's temple.

In 1846, as Jerusalem was first opening up to Protestant missionaries, the sect leader sent him to the Holy City to convert Jews to Christianity. His only way to earn an income was to assemble and repair cuckoo clocks, then popular among well-to-do Arab families, and he scratched out a predictably precarious existence.

Celibacy and poverty didn't suit Schick, who four years later broke with his Basel pastor to marry a German woman and join the London Society for Promoting Christianity amongst the Jews. With its headquarters in the gleaming new Gothic-style Christ Church just inside the Old City's Jaffa Gate, the organization offered greater financial security. By then fluent in Arabic, he was tasked with teaching carpentry skills to converts. Since these proved scarce, he found himself with time on his skilled hands.

Schick began to build and sell precise models of the Church of the Holy Sepulchre. Although Schick was a Protestant missionary, the Greeks and Catholics who dominated Christianity's most sacred site granted him full access to measure the ramshackle complex. Likewise, Muslim clerics on the Noble Sanctuary allowed him to roam its thirty-seven acres in order to make miniatures of the platform, both in its present form and how he imagined it during the days of Solomon and Herod the Great. In subsequent decades, his models would be seen by tens of thousands of people at exhibitions and world's fairs across Europe, inspiring many to travel to the Holy City.

In the 1850s, the demand for European-style structures grew along with the Western community, so Schick taught himself how to construct full-scale buildings. Overseeing work on a German hospital annex in 1858, he was fascinated by the ancient vaults and drains uncovered while the workers were digging the foundations.

"I think this was the moment he became enchanted with the real deep history of Jerusalem," said the German historian Holger Siegel.

When Wilson arrived in 1865, he made good use of the German's familiarity with Jerusalem and his fluency in Arabic. He "frequently accompanied me in my subterranean explorations," the British surveyor noted. "I found his local knowledge of great assistance." In fact, Schick was with Wilson when he examined the arch that came to bear his name, and even made the first drawing of the famous vault. It's quite likely he led Wilson to it in the first place, though he never claimed credit.

Before leaving Jerusalem, Wilson had advised his collaborator to closely examine the trenches dug for the foundations for new buildings and record what he found. The construction boom, the officer warned, threatened to destroy the very heritage that drew Westerners to the city in the first place. The German took this message to heart. "He was always on the spot, recording what could be seen, and making plans of all that was discovered underground," a contemporary archaeologist later noted.

No one was in a better position, since Schick was responsible for the construction of dozens of private residences and public structures. All the while, he continued to record what lay beneath the city's surface. One contemporary likened him to "a faithful watchman" who "carefully surveyed, sketched, and recorded everything that came under his notice." Conder declared him to be "better acquainted than anyone else with the depth of the rock at various points throughout the city." One historian noted that "everybody—except the great archaeologist Charles Warren—asked Schick for help."

One of those was a local Greek landowner. In 1867, he appeared at Schick's door to ask him for advice. He explained that while digging a cistern on his hillside property just outside Damascus Gate he had encountered a cave containing a carved cross. He wanted the architect's opinion about what to do. Schick followed him up the steep hill. The landowner pointed out an opening beneath a rock scarp that led into a shallow cave. It was filled nearly to its roof with skulls and other bones covered in mold. On the eastern wall was a red-painted cross with Greek letters.

"I would leave things as they are, and stop up the hole and fill in the trench again," Schick told the man. He made some notes at the time; it was not an unusual find in a city surrounded by cemeteries. Schick later learned that the owner cleared the cave in an apparent search for treasure, also not unusual. In 1874, Schick published a brief paper in Germany describing the site. It was mentioned in the Palestine Exploration Fund journal the following year.

By then, Schick was churning out a steady stream of reports about his finds and submitting them to scholarly journals in both German and English. This particular paper likely would have remained one of his more obscure contributions had a famous British military mystic not stumbled on this very tomb nearly a decade later and decided that it was the authentic grave of Jesus.

This serendipitous event sparked a fierce competition, this time pitting Britain against Russia rather than France. Each power sought to ascertain the accurate location of Christianity's most sacred site. Schick, of course, would be intimately involved with both efforts.

•   •   •

IF THE NOBLE SANCTUARY resembled a scruffy public garden, the Holy Sepulchre, which lay on a slope a third of a mile west of the platform, was a gloomy and cluttered basement. According to legend, it was born in the dirt of an empress's excavation.

The Christian gospels say that Jesus was executed just outside Jerusalem's walls at Golgotha, Aramaic for "the place of the skulls," and buried nearby in a newly cut rock tomb. Scholars guess this occurred in 34 or 35 CE. A century later, in the aftermath of a second Jewish revolt during the reign of Emperor Hadrian, the Romans built a temple over a site that likely was already sacred to the worrisome new Jewish sect that proclaimed Jesus as the Messiah. Saint Jerome later wrote that the Romans set up a statue of Venus on the rock of Golgotha and a statue of Jupiter over the grave in which the crucified Jew was laid.

If the Romans hoped to co-opt the site, they simply preserved its sanctity. Two centuries later, after on-and-off-again persecution by Roman leaders, Emperor Constantine the Great legalized Christianity. In 327 CE, after the offending pagan temple had been demolished, his mother, Empress Helena, paid a visit to Jerusalem. One account has the elderly royal gamely jumping into the open trench. "She opened up the earth, scattered the dust, and found three crosses in disarray." Helena declared one to be the cross on which Jesus was crucified; this became the first of thousands of relics that would shape Christian worship for centuries to come.

A contemporary bishop, who may have been an eyewitness, added that Helena went on to identify a burial cave a few dozen yards away that she maintained had held the body of the dead Jesus. "After lying buried in darkness, it again emerged to light."

With his mother's stamp of approval, Constantine ordered a lavish sanctuary constructed on the site of Christ's alleged entombment. When it was completed in 335 CE, Christian pilgrims could enter a grand court off the city's main street that opened into a massive basilica. Just beyond was a courtyard featuring the rock of Golgotha that rose twenty feet into the open air, surrounded by a metal screen and topped with a cross. That led to a circular building, also open to the sky, surrounding the tomb that was Christianity's holiest place. It was hallowed as the site of Jesus's resurrection.

Earthquakes and a Persian invasion took their toll on the structure. When Muslims seized control of Jerusalem in the seventh century CE, they left the building intact, but three centuries later a mad Egyptian caliph ordered the building demolished. It was rebuilt, but the memory of this violation added to Christian fervor to reconquer the Holy City. When European Crusaders arrived in 1099, they found a crumbling complex shared by Christian Greeks, Armenians, Georgians, Syrians, Egyptians, and Nestorians, members of the Church of the East. The invading Roman Catholics initially expelled the Greeks, who were seen as too cozy with the former Muslim rulers, and rebuilt the complex in a late Romanesque style then fashionable in northern France. Though an 1808 fire wreaked havoc, today's decaying structure remains essentially that of the Crusaders.

Another enduring aspect of the church was the relentless feuding among sects for control of its every nook and cranny. This competition extended beneath the compound, which includes subterranean networks of quarries and tombs and an ancient water cistern the size of an Olympic swimming pool. The squabbles prompted the twelfth-century Muslim ruler Saladin to assign the door key to the safekeeping of a Muslim family to prevent arguments over which sect had the right to open the building in the morning and close it at night. The key is still in their possession.

By the time Protestants began to trickle into Jerusalem in the mid-nineteenth century, a fragile peace imposed by Ottoman authorities more than a century earlier was keeping disputes in check. No changes, no matter how minor, could be made in ownership or usage at Christian sites in the Holy Land—and particularly in the Holy Sepulchre—without a formal decree by the sultan in Istanbul. Even a homely wooden ladder perched on a lintel above the main entrance remains, since removing it would break what was called the status quo. One of Schick's first tasks in Jerusalem had been to draw a map showing the intricate territorial divisions of each sect.

When Napoleon III challenged the system in the 1850s on behalf of Roman Catholics, the result was the Crimean War. Needless to say, neither the sultan nor the existing sects wished to make room for Protestants, who returned the favor. In 1841, Robinson declared that "Golgotha and the Tomb shown in the Church of the Holy Sepulcher are not upon the real places of the Crucifixion and Resurrection." The place was, he decided, "a pious fraud."

The clouds of incense, strange tongues, and even stranger rituals on shadowy altars disturbed Protestants accustomed to bare sanctuaries and plain preaching. The candlelit processions past dusty paintings seemed distressingly removed from the sunny Easter morning garden described from their pulpits. "I should be loath to think that the Sacred Tomb had been a witness for so many years of so much human ignorance, folly, and crime," wrote Conder. The devout Protestant was disgusted by what he saw as "fierce emotions of sectarian hate and blind fanaticism" and dismissed it as a "grim and wicked old building."

There was more than a little sour grapes involved. "The Protestants alone have no part or parcel in the sacred inheritance," bemoaned Lady Mary Elizabeth Herbert in *Harper's Magazine* in 1868. "Ordinary Protestants take refuge in a comfortable kind of skepticism as regards to every spot and every tradition in the church." Mark Twain, who had visited the previous year, took a slightly more charitable view. "With all its clap-trap side-shows and unseemly impostures of every kind," he wrote, "it is still grand, revered, venerable."

Yet, as one British scholar noted, there was good reason that many educated people "entertained grave and serious doubts" as to the legitimacy of the ancient site. The gospels described the crucifixion and the resurrection taking place outside the city walls, yet the church lay squarely at the heart of the walled city. Tradition was no longer enough; only archaeology combined with the biblical accounts could provide a convincing answer. Identifying the correct location had become, one historian noted, "a geopolitical contest."

◆　◆　◆

BY THE 1870S, steamships and a growing rail network had brought the first big wave of European and American tourists—most of them Protestant—to Jerusalem. They demanded to know the authentic place of Jesus's death and resurrection. What had been an esoteric academic discussion suddenly emerged as a burning public question.

"The whole Christian world has naturally a deep anxiety to know the exact truth," London's *Daily News* noted, presumably referring only to the Protestant world. "A great many people believe that the Holy Sepulchre does not stand on Golgotha."

There were two main alternatives. James Fergusson had continued to insist that the Dome of the Rock was Constantine's original church, which lay above Jesus's actual burial cave. In the aftermath of Warren's expedition, however, the Scottish historian found himself increasingly isolated in his view. Warren published a whole book in 1880 listing Fergusson's "numberless errors" and dismissing his theory as untenable. The death knell to the argument came after 1884, when workers in today's Jordan uncovered a sixth-century CE mosaic map of Jerusalem that showed the Holy Sepulchre in its present position. That put the lie to the idea that it was a medieval fabrication.

A more likely prospect was a rocky scarp that lay just north of Damascus Gate, not far from the Tomb of the Kings excavated by de Saulcy. The promontory was made up of two hills about five hundred feet apart. In the 1840s, a German theologian had imagined one of the hills looked like a skull, complete with eyeless sockets. This suggested to him that it was the true "place of the skulls." He was not alone; in the following decade the president of the Brooklyn White Lead Company also remarked on the shape. In the 1870s, the American consul and a British bishop revived the idea.

Conder weighed in on the controversy after completing an exhausting five years surveying in the field. In an 1878 book, he cited early Christian accounts suggesting Golgotha referred either to the shape of a hill or a place of execution, while the gospels pointed to a site near a cemetery. He expanded on this proposal in a February 1883 scientific report, when he admitted that the skull shape idea was "rather fanciful" but added that the area around the knoll was "well-fitted for a place of public execution," since it could accommodate "the whole population of the city." He asserted that Jesus's tomb was a three-chambered Jewish grave on the hillside that he had examined, though his reasoning was vague.

Just weeks before Conder's article was published, one of Britain's most famous generals—nearly twenty years senior to Kitchener and in the prime of his career—had arrived in Jerusalem. Renowned for fighting in the Crimea and China, Charles Gordon was also a zealous and celibate evangelical, albeit one who subscribed to unconventional Protestant beliefs, such as reincarnation. The blue-eyed and fair-haired military commander came to the Holy Land for a year of religious study. He shared the view of his friend, the author Laurence Oliphant, who excoriated Jerusalem as the source of "more sacred shams and impostures than any other city in the world." The general set out on a military-style campaign to find the *true* Golgotha.

By his own account, he solved the matter the morning after his arrival. The officer lodged with an American missionary family in a compound in the Old City overlooking Damascus Gate and the rock scarp to its north. It was the same hill that so many predecessors had viewed as skull shaped. "It is very nice to see it so plain and simple, instead of having a huge church built on it," he wrote.

He marched out to the gate and up the slope to find what he declared the rock-cut tomb of the Christian Messiah. It was the same bone-filled tomb that the Greek landowner had shown to Schick more than a decade before. Gordon spent the following months elaborating on his discovery, poring over Palestine Exploration Fund maps. "He rose at seven, read and prayed till eleven or twelve, worked at his biblical researches till four," a friend wrote. After taking a ride, "he read and wrote again until ten or eleven."

The result was a thesis so eccentric that it made Fergusson's theories

seem tame by comparison. The skull-shaped hill was more than just Golgotha, he averred. It was, in fact, the actual "head" of the body of Jerusalem
itself. That left the Noble Sanctuary as the city's buttocks—a neat assumption that in one stroke denigrated Fergusson as well as Islam's third-holiest
site. One French scholar called the theory "wonderfully weird."

Gordon had had professional help developing this peculiar idea. He
wrote an acquaintance that while he struggled to put together his case, "I
deluge a poor old German, Mr. Schick, with papers and plans."

◆ ◆ ◆

IN 1881, Czar Alexander II unwisely stepped out of his bulletproof car-
riage a mile away from the Winter Palace in Saint Petersburg after an ineffective bomb attack on the vehicle. A waiting anarchist tossed a second
bomb that fatally injured the Russian leader, an event that launched a
bloody round of pogroms against Jews. It also, in an oblique way, thrust
Russia into the Holy City's archaeological race.

Russia held greater sway in mid-nineteenth century Jerusalem than
any other European nation, even after its 1856 defeat in the Crimean War.
Britain and France were distant lands and increasingly secular, but the
czar's fast-expanding empire lay just north of the Ottoman domains, and
eight out of ten Christian pilgrims who came to the city were Russian
Orthodox peasants. When Warren visited the Holy Sepulchre before its
Easter celebration one year, he was astonished to see that "Russian women
lined the wooden beams of a scaffolding high above us to our left; and
even the projecting cornices might boast of statuary drawn [from] life."

The czarist government considered itself the protector of the Greek
Orthodox Church, which dominated the city's Christian community in
numbers and influence. Russian rulers had taken to styling their realm as
the "Second Jerusalem" or the "Third Rome" after the Italian capital and
its successor, Constantinople, which had fallen to the Ottomans.

Two months after the royal tragedy, Alexander II's son, Grand Duke
Sergei, visited Jerusalem to pray at the Holy Sepulchre for the soul of his
dead father. Tall, handsome, and a lover of antiquities as well as a hater
of Jews, he was fascinated by the possibility of conducting excavations in
the city.

The grand duke almost certainly was aware of a report written by
Jerusalem's Russian consul a few years before noting archaeological discoveries made on Russian property just east of the Holy Sepulchre. These

seemed to be the remains of Constantine's original grand fourth-century structure that extended outside the smaller medieval church. The consul had suggested building a hospice and a church on "the ruins of the ancient basilica" for the use of Russian pilgrims visiting the neighboring shrine.

Sergei returned to Saint Petersburg to expand an existing scholarly committee into the Imperial Orthodox Palestine Society. The duke made himself president of an organization devoted to researching a land that was, as one society official put it, "a huge museum, a catalog of already collected knowledge that needs to be put in order." This organization would avoid the focus on "apocryphal texts and legends" favored by Catholics and give a wide berth as well to the "cold skepticism" of Protestants. In a novel approach, clerics and scholars would work collaboratively.

Sergei provided 1,000 gold rubles—worth about $100,000 today—to kick off excavations. The first dig was at the property adjoining the Holy Sepulchre, with the senior Russian Orthodox cleric and Schick as co-directors of the excavation. In March 1883, two months after General Gordon arrived in Jerusalem, Schick went to work at the Russian site. Whether he told the British general of his activities isn't known; Schick was sworn "to maintain confidentiality about any discoveries made." But rumors quickly swirled that the team had uncovered the original entrance to the Holy Sepulchre, one that would allow them direct access into the church from their property.

If true, it was an important scientific find as well as an ominous political development. The Russian ambassador in Istanbul feared this could upset the delicate status quo among the quarreling Christian sects and potentially spark an international crisis. This was no idle concern; after all, the Crimean War had begun over an even less important matter. The diplomat advised the excavation team to keep a low profile until the work was finished. Only then, he added, should Russia take advantage of the discoveries, "whether political, scholarly, or religious."

The grand duke kept abreast of the dig's progress, noting at the end of 1883 that "although the excavations are not yet completed, they have been highly successful. Not only have traces of the Second Wall of Second Temple Jerusalem been found, which confirms the authenticity of the place of Jesus's burial, but there has even been discovered on the Russian domain the gate that led from the City to Golgotha."

This second temple referred to Herod's renovated sanctuary, and the second wall was known to be part of the city's fortification that stood at the time of Jesus. Its location was key to the debate about the Holy Sepulchre's authenticity. If the wall lay west of the building, then it contradicted the gospel account of the crucifixion and burial taking place outside of town, casting serious doubt on the shrine's authenticity. But if it lay to the east, the sacred complex indeed had been beyond the city walls at Jesus's death. That would give credence to the traditional site identified by Roman empress Helena.

In a December 27, 1883, letter from the city's Russian Orthodox leader to Clermont-Ganneau, the French archaeologist, the cleric revealed the discovery of the "threshold of a large antique door and a fragment of a Roman inscription" at the excavation. The news was leaked to the London *Times* in April. Six months later, the imperial society published a scholarly volume claiming that Schick had identified "the threshold of the Gate through which Christ climbed to Calvary." The historian Elena Astafieva said the archaeological coup, which was "widely publicized in Russia and other countries," gave Russia "symbolic ownership of two of the places most sacred to Christianity, the Way of the Cross (Via Dolorosa) and the Holy Sepulchre." It was, in other words, a political, scholarly, and religious triumph.

Schick later reported that the Russian dig uncovered stones used in the east end of Constantine's basilica that were "Jewish masonry" dating to the era of Herod. They apparently had been reused. He also found the remains of an arch that he believed likely marked "the passing of our Lord to Calvary" commemorated in the entrance to the Byzantine church, as well as enormous marble columns and a stairway that were part of the original basilica. Below these he found evidence of quarries. Such industrial operations almost certainly would have been located outside the city.

Just east of these discoveries, Schick uncovered the remains of a thick band of cut stones that seemed part of a city wall that he dated to the era just before the time of Jesus. If he was correct, then the Holy Sepulchre was indeed outside Jerusalem then, matching the gospel accounts of the crucifixion. For Schick, the wall offered compelling evidence that Empress Helena had been right in choosing the demolished Roman temple as the site of Jesus's death, burial, and resurrection.

Not everyone was convinced. A senior Russian official was skeptical that the finds "produced irrefutable evidence that the historic traces it has discovered date to the period before Jesus Christ." He feared that the results had been skewed by clerics, and warned that the dramatic claim required enough evidence "to leave no room for debate and doubt, because it is a matter of recognizing the authenticity of the Christian Holy of Holies."

His concern proved well founded. Protestant scholars pounced. Some accused Schick of misinterpreting his finds or, worse, twisting them to suit his Russian bosses. Even Wilson, his archaeological mentor, expressed skepticism about his methods—though not until after the German's death nearly two decades later. He wrote that "Dr Schick, whose accuracy as regards measurements is well known, rarely made any distinction either in his writings or in his drawings between existing and assumed remains."

There was a whiff of British snobbishness in the critiques. Schick certainly lacked the professional training of a Royal Engineer or formal university education, and his use of terms like "presumed wall" raised questions about his accuracy. Yet he also produced more than one hundred archaeological reports and dozens of maps as well as intricate wooden models of the city and its key religious sites. Quick to acknowledge his errors, he was also known for freely sharing his time and his data with people of all nationalities while showing little interest in personal credit.

A devout Protestant himself, Schick sided with the evidence rather than his beliefs. Until 1883, he said that he had maintained "the private conviction that the Church of the Holy Sepulchre is standing on the wrong place, although I could not prove this." The data from the Russian dig changed his mind, even if it provoked the ire of those who shared his faith. Over time, his results won over most skeptics. The *Guardian* noted in 1887 that the Russian dig marked the end of a controversy "which has raged for so many years over the so-called Church of the Holy Sepulchre."

◆ ◆ ◆

BY THEN, General Gordon had found his own martyrdom, though by a spear thrust rather than stoning or crucifixion. Imprisoned in the Sudanese city of Khartoum, he was killed in 1885 by the guards of Muhammad Ahmad bin Abd Allah, who claimed to be Islam's messianic redeemer. Wilson had attempted, without success, to rescue the beleaguered officer. Gordon quickly morphed into a kind of imperial Christian saint.

Schick was left with some three hundred pages of the dead man's papers and letters. Though he put no stock in Gordon's theory, he was a loyal friend. In 1891, he published a lengthy paper detailing the general's tortured ideas, including drawings, photographs, and a plan of "the rock-cut tomb suggested by the late General Gordon to be the Sepulchre of Christ."

While Gordon was alive, his eccentric proposal had attracted little attention, but his dramatic death in the name of empire—brought to the screen by Charlton Heston three-quarters of a century later—made it immortal. Schick's publication inspired a group of wealthy British Protestants. They formed the Garden Tomb Association to raise money in order to purchase the area and make it a site of devotion in memory of the general as well as Jesus.

Wilson scoffed at the idea, suggesting the money would be better spent on proper archaeology. Even Conder was skeptical; he believed the tomb Schick had first studied dated not to the Roman era but to the ninth century CE. A fellow member of the Palestine Exploration Fund expressed the hope that English Protestantism would "rid itself of the incubus with which it has thus burdened itself." The tomb's advocates, he warned, had fallen into the same trap as medieval Christians who declared a place sacred through mere hearsay. The protestations by the cantankerous scholars had little impact on the earnest believers.

Soon after, Schick seized a new opportunity to test his theory about the Holy Sepulchre's authenticity. In thanks for the Prussian crown prince's participation in the 1869 inauguration of the Suez Canal, Ottoman sultan Abdulhamid II had granted the royal a piece of land across the street from the Russian parcel that Schick had excavated. In 1893, construction began at the site on a Lutheran church that would be Jerusalem's largest Protestant place of worship. Schick was put in charge of the excavations of its foundations, under the auspices of the German Society for the Exploration of Palestine.

His team quickly uncovered a thick ancient wall, still nearly ten feet high, running from east to west. This seemed incontrovertible proof of his contention that the fortifications around Jerusalem in the time of Jesus lay east of today's Holy Sepulchre. To underscore the find's importance, the church builders placed the foundation stone directly on the ancient wall. Later archaeologists dated the wall to a century or so after the death of Jesus. But other evidence, including the extensive quarries beneath the Holy Sepulchre, continues to uphold Schick's conclusion.

The German's results impressed other scholars, but they had no impact on Gordon's British supporters. In 1894, a savvy German speculator sold the land on the hill to the Garden Tomb Association for five times its value just a few years previous. The site was then tastefully landscaped with winding pathways and shaded benches that evoked a feeling more akin to Sunday-school memories than the Holy Sepulchre's clouds of incense and weeping Russians. It was an instant hit among visiting Victorians, and it remains so today among American and British Protestants, as well as Mormons. It is located, in an irony that he might have appreciated, just off Conrad Schick Street.

Archaeology emerged in the late-nineteenth-century race not just as a tool to verify the Bible or unearth biblical artifacts, but to identify and in essence "certify" holy sites. A measure of scientific credibility, no matter how flimsy, was essential. For example, in 1864, the same year de Saulcy finished his dig at the Tomb of the Kings, French nuns excavated flagstones etched with a Roman-era board game beneath their convent on the Via Dolorosa. They interpreted this as the site where Roman soldiers gambled over Jesus's robe, at what the gospels called "the stone pavement." A century later, the stones were determined to date from a century after Jesus, but by then the site's popularity with pilgrims was assured.

The push to identify new sacred sites appealed to Western Christians who felt ill at ease amid Eastern traditions and excluded from Jerusalem's choicest sacred places. They wanted to secure what was, in effect, a new spiritual beachhead in the Holy City. The popularity of the Garden Tomb demonstrated that faith could subordinate science, even among those Protestants who prided themselves in giving reason precedent over superstition. Archaeological finds that bolstered a particular belief were welcome; those that did not could be dismissed or even attacked as false.

Not everyone adopted archaeology as an essential new tool in the struggle for power and influence in Jerusalem. Orthodox Greeks, Sephardic Jews, and Muslim Arabs remained largely oblivious to this competitive race to uncover, and claim, buried sanctity. For those with deeper roots in the city, there was no need to dig tunnels or unearth ancient foundations. They already were secure in their shrines and status.

But as the nineteenth century drew to a close, another group of Europeans would turn to the discipline of archaeology in order to establish and reinforce their own bastions of sanctity. Their efforts would reshape Jerusalem and Palestine, rock the Middle East, and create an international struggle that, more than a century later, remains unresolved.

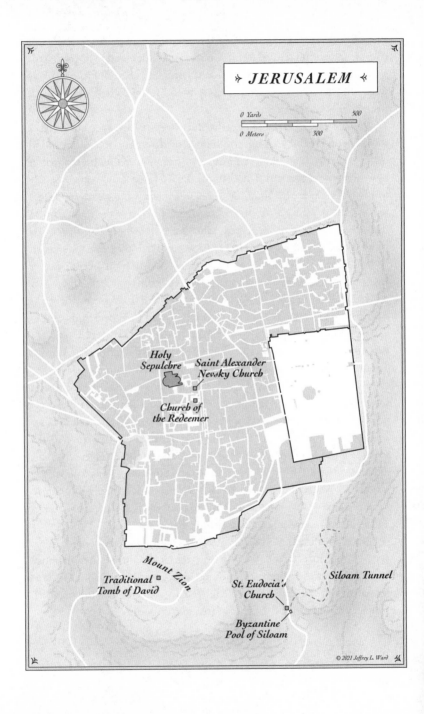

JERUSALEM

0 Yards   500

0 Meters   300

Holy
Sepulchre

Saint Alexander
Nevsky Church

Church of
the Redeemer

Mount Zion

Traditional
Tomb of David

St. Eudocia's
Church

Siloam Tunnel

Byzantine
Pool of Siloam

© 2021 Jeffrey L. Ward

6

A Great and Potent Force

Jerusalem—center of pilgrimage to three great religions—unholiest city under the sun! . . . The swarming of sects around the corpse of religion . . . A center through which pass all the great threads of history, ancient and medieval, and now at last quivering with the telegraphic thread of the modern.

—ISRAEL ZANGWILL

At the start of 1896, the British archaeologist Flinders Petrie was despondent. Amid the glories of the ancient Egyptian city of Luxor, the particular site he had chosen to excavate seemed filled with nothing more than "worn bits of sandstone" and had proved "disastrously dull." Petrie was pondering halting the effort entirely when his workers uncovered a ten-by-five-foot slab of black granite covered with hieroglyphics.

It was too big to move easily, so he had the Egyptian crew shovel out the sand beneath it and brace either end with stones. A young German philologist then crawled below the slab and spent the better part of the afternoon copying the inscription that lay just inches from his nose. He emerged dusty and sweaty with news that the stele, or inscribed stone, described Pharaoh Merneptah's victories over various cities in Palestine and Syria around 1200 BCE. There was one name, however, that he did not recognize. It read as Isiriar.

"Why that is Israel," declared the self-taught Petrie.

"So it is, and won't the reverends be pleased," quipped the philologist. At dinner that night, the accomplished archaeologist astonished his team by announcing that "this stele will be better known in the world than anything else I have found."

His prediction proved correct. The Merneptah inscription gave the world its earliest mention of Israel in the archaeological record, a full two centuries before King David was thought to have conquered Jerusalem. After Petrie gave a lecture in Britain that April, the *Yorkshire Post* decreed his stone to be "one of the most notable monuments ever found."

The evidence was incontrovertible: ancient Israel was no biblical fiction, as some scholars had maintained, but an actual people or place. The reverends were indeed pleased that archaeology confirmed their belief. The finding coincided with another important discovery, made by Petrie's protégé, that would answer one of Jerusalem's most perplexing questions.

Drawing solely on scripture, scholars had long believed that King David and his Israelites conquered the city from the Jebusites—likely a Canaanite people—around 1000 BCE and made it his capital. His son Solomon then turned it into the wealthy capital of a powerful empire.

The story was well known to most Jews and Christians, but despite three decades of excavations, archaeologists had yet to uncover any decisive evidence to pinpoint what was referred to as the City of David. There were several competing theories. Some believed the ancient settlement lay concealed under the Old City or north of the walled town, beyond Damascus Gate and the Garden Tomb.

A more popular candidate was Mount Zion, the high hill that lay just beyond the southwest corner of the Old City's walls, not far from the citadel. Muslims prayed at a tomb in this neighborhood said to be that of David, who in his Islamic form was a prophet and poet. The building and the stone sarcophagus appeared to be of medieval construction, but a brief dig by Conder uncovered nearby remains of what seemed an ancient city wall. It was a promising lead.

Another contender was the narrow ridge jutting south from the Noble Sanctuary. An apron of land sloped away from the southern wall of the sacred platform, ending in a narrow ridge less than five hundred feet wide and not quite a half mile long. On either side lay steep slopes, and at the base of the narrow spine of land was a pool of water fed by a spring.

While exploring beneath this limestone outcrop in the 1830s, Robinson had found a large water tunnel that channeled water from an underground spring located near the hill's eastern flank to its base. Thirty years later, Warren had discovered this was just one of a network of subterranean spaces, including a steep shaft that he believed David's warriors used in their surprise attack on the Jebusite city as described in the Bible. But there was little data to back up his colorful theory.

Two decades after Warren's departure, the Palestine Exploration Fund made a bid to resume its Jerusalem excavations in order to locate the missing City of David.

◆ ◆ ◆

THE BRITISH EMPIRE IN the early 1890s was nearing its global zenith, covering a quarter of the globe and dominating a quarter of the world's population. The threat posed by Russia had faded as Czar Alexander III sought to avoid major international conflicts while grappling with growing domestic challenges. Britain's purchase of the Suez Canal, meanwhile, had undermined French influence in the Middle East; Egypt was now out of the Ottoman orbit and under British sway.

Nevertheless, an 1891 alliance between France and Russia unsettled London, while a reformed and modernized Ottoman Empire was building up a formidable military. Sultan Abdulhamid II, celebrated as the Sublime Khan, looked to the rising power of Kaiser Wilhelm II's Germany to offset British ambitions. German companies were constructing railroads across Anatolia financed by Deutsche Bank, and there was talk of a Berlin-to-Baghdad link in the future.

Though Jerusalem remained under Ottoman control, European nations flaunted their growing status by competing to create elaborate compounds. Just outside the city's walls, an Italian hospital modeled on Florence's Renaissance city hall went up, and work was underway on a French complex designed to house sixteen hundred Catholic pilgrims. Its massive stone chapel was topped with a large statue of Mary holding aloft the baby Jesus that was sure to irritate those Jews, Muslims, and Protestants who deplored religious sculpture.

Not to be outdone, the British began work on the Anglican Saint George's Cathedral down the street from the Garden Tomb. The central courtyard of the Gothic-style structure was dominated by a Byzantine column. On top was a cross and a large Roman catapult stone ball excavated nearby. French Dominicans established a formidable research institute, the École Biblique, just down the street. With lush gardens surrounding a Byzantine-style church, library, and monastery, it served as headquarters for French biblical scholars and archaeologists.

Inside what was now known as the Old City, the sites dug by Schick near the Holy Sepulchre were busy construction sites. The huge German Protestant church was rising on one side of the street, its foundation perched over the presumed second wall, while on the opposite side, Russia put up the Saint Alexander Nevsky Church to enshrine some of the ancient columns and gates found by the German excavator.

In 1894, the Fund secured a coveted license allowing for a two-year dig to tackle "some of the problems having reference to Ancient Jerusalem." John Wodehouse, the First Earl of Kimberley and the British foreign secretary, had intervened personally with the sultan to obtain the document, a clear sign of the high political value that Britain placed on restarting archaeological digs in the Holy City. "It is to be hoped that these excavations will soon determine definitely the disputed question as to the site of the City of David," one British pastor wrote.

According to the Bible, David conquered a city that his son Solomon transformed into the prosperous capital of an impressive empire. Phoenician craftsmen arrived to construct a renowned temple with a gilded interior and a crystal floor, while his beautiful palace took thirteen years to complete. That complex alone housed four thousand horses and chariots ridden by twelve thousand warriors, as well as the king's seven hundred wives and three hundred concubines. Royalty, such as the queen of Sheba, came from afar to marvel at Jerusalem's magnificence. Jesus had hailed "Solomon in all his splendor," while in the Qur'an he commanded spirits to help build everything from arches to ritual basins.

British scholars were determined to uncover remains from this glorious but elusive era.

The Fund's choice to lead the expedition was a promising researcher named Frederick J. Bliss, who had trained under Petrie, discoverer of the Merneptah inscription. Bliss was fascinated by the older British excavator, who ate dinner from a can, worked in his underwear, and never wore socks, all the time managing his men "like a good despot." The American said "his knowledge is marvelous." Petrie at the time also was providing ancient skeletons to Darwin's cousin, Francis Galton, who was developing the racist theory of eugenics later used by the Nazis to justify the Holocaust.

For a few weeks in 1890, Petrie had left Egypt at the Fund's request to excavate a mound thirty-five miles southwest of Jerusalem. There he had pioneered what he called "sequence-dating." Rather than simply digging a hole and searching for interesting architecture and artifacts, Petrie closely examined each layer of soil and learned to identify the successive periods laid down over time. Pottery, he realized, evolved, and by mapping the location of broken bits of ceramics and other material objects, an archaeologist could chart a detailed chronology.

Thomas Jefferson had experimented with this stratigraphic technique in an excavation into a Native American mound near his Virginia home of Monticello in the 1780s, but the method had not caught on. Petrie's work at Tell el-Hesi marked the beginning of modern archaeology. Bliss brought the new technique to Jerusalem.

Wilson, Warren, and Conder had been young and pious British military engineers as concerned with expanding empire as with digging up ancient ruins. Bliss, already in his mid-thirties, wasn't even British. He was born in Lebanon to American missionary parents; his mother had been childhood friends with Emily Dickinson, and his father helped found what became the American University of Beirut, a center of learning that helped fertilize Arab nationalist aspirations. The first American to dig in Jerusalem, he backed Arab self-rule.

Whereas his British predecessors prided themselves on their toughness in the field, Bliss was frail and bookish, a lifelong bachelor who struggled with physical and mental ills. He also was steeped in Ottoman culture as well as Arab traditions and the Arabic language. These qualities, so lacking in British archaeologists of the day, would serve him well in the coming years. But what truly set Bliss apart from his predecessors was his lack of religious fervor. "He did not allow preconceived religious notions to interfere with his archaeological conclusions," one biographer noted.

The Fund's London managers sent Bliss an assistant who also had trained with Petrie, a man named Archibald Dickie. In a photograph taken in Jerusalem, both men are in Arab headgear and appear almost identical with their pale complexions and drooping mustaches.

Bliss was pleasantly surprised to discover that the city's foreign community did not spend afternoon teas and Sunday picnics gossiping about society scandals, as they did in Beirut. Instead, they debated "the site of the Holy Sepulchre, the direction of the Second Wall, the date of this and that bit of masonry." Many of the clergy, from French monks to Greek Catholics, regularly published about the city's past, and Ottoman officials expressed curiosity about the latest finds and theories.

Fund managers told Bliss to begin his search for the City of David along the "Rock Scarp of Zion." This lay on the edge of Mount Zion, just outside the city walls and close to the traditional tomb of David, and close to Conder's trenches from a decade before. The contours of the steep hill made it an obvious place to trace the ancient city's walls, which had proved so critical for understanding Jerusalem's growth and contractions over time. When the excavations began, the American turned to the ever-helpful Schick, now a septuagenarian but still vigorous. The two men walked through a garbage dump on the edge of the hill and discussed the best places to sink shafts. His suggestions, the young excavator said, "have been of much profit to me."

Bliss was well aware of just how daunting the project would be. "When I . . . remember how few interesting antiques and inscriptions the turned-over soil of Jerusalem has yielded," he wrote, "then I confess to a feeling of discouragement." He also knew that anyone tackling the city's past "must combine the qualities of a geographer, a geologist, an ethnologist, an historian, an epigraphist, a Biblical student, a painter, a mystic, and a poet," Bliss wrote. "If he is an excavator as well he must also include the attainments of an engineer and a miner."

Unlike his Royal Engineer predecessors, he had neither of the last two qualifications. He did, however, have the experienced workers of Silwan, the locals who had been so indispensable to Warren's digs. Under Bliss and Dickie's direction, they begin to excavate an ambitious network of tunnels unmatched in the annals of Jerusalem archaeology. Two or three workers had even worked with Warren, a quarter century prior. They showed the archaeologists the best methods for bracing the passages in the crumbly soil. Their first tunnel alone would stretch three hundred feet beneath the rock and rubble of Mount Zion.

What Bliss didn't know about engineering he made up for with his easy familiarity with Ottoman etiquette, which helped smooth relations with senior officials. "We are especially fortunate in having Ibrahim Pasha for Governor," he wrote soon after his arrival. "He is a man of great intelligence and unquestioned integrity." The two became fast friends, a relationship Warren could not have imagined, much less developed.

The American also worked his charms on the Arab-speaking residents, a critical factor in ensuring local cooperation and something Warren had failed to do. "Landowners do not trouble us, in fact have hardly been near us since the first novelty wore off," Bliss asserted. When his team uncovered a large cistern, the previously suspicious sheiks in charge of the traditional tomb of David were delighted with the practical discovery that they could put to use.

Bliss's success was due in no small part to the tact and negotiating skill of his accomplished foreman and longtime personal servant, Yusif Abu Selim, a Lebanese Christian. Abu Selim gained the "confidence and affection" of the tough Silwan workers, who labored from 5:00 a.m. until 6:30 p.m. within the growing network of tunnels while the aged Schick drew up the plans. "The eight hours' movement has not yet been inaugurated in Jerusalem," Bliss wrote sardonically. Neither had wage increases. The going rate was the same as it had been under Warren. And, of course, no child-labor rules were on the books; the digs always involved boys of school age as well as men.

As Warren had, the expedition leader found himself busy entertaining curious guests while Dickie—who also spoke fluent Arabic—oversaw the day-to-day operations. These visitors included consuls from Britain, Russia, and Austria, along with the pasha and various clergy.

While the expedition found ancient walls and masses of pottery beneath Mount Zion, most of the remains proved to be Roman and Byzantine rather than from the earlier Judean era the men sought. Bliss was hampered by an inability to date the walls, since masonry techniques didn't change as quickly or as obviously as pottery. There were other setbacks. Both excavators were attacked one night in a dark alley and Dickie's arm was broken in the struggle, while the death of Abu Selim in March 1896 was a major blow. The equally abrupt passing of Bliss's friend the pasha also came as a shock.

With time running out on his permit, Bliss moved camp to the eastern hill, the ridge that extended south from the Noble Sanctuary, just across a valley from the village of Silwan. This required a patient round of negotiations with the cauliflower and cabbage farmers in the area, as well as those who actually owned the land, who were not always one and the same. But he accepted their insistence on adequate compensation. "As to the Jerusalem landowners, I think they were no more difficult to satisfy than would the inhabitants of any English city," Bliss noted.

His good relations with the Ottomans and locals won him a rare extension on his permit to continue the work for another year, and the team's pace of discovery picked up. One visiting reverend in August 1896 was impressed by the lack of friction at the dig and the respect the workers accorded Bliss. But he was appalled by the raw sewage that passed the excavation site at that time, which he found "most pungent, especially when reinforced by the carcasses of mules and donkeys which find there a resting place." This made entering the tunnels a relief.

Even there, however, Bliss reported that "an inky fluid" of sewage leaked into the underground passages. "The oozing galleries had to be sprinkled with carbolic acid, to the discomfiture of the long line of basket-boys, who declared a preference for the more natural conditions." Another deep shaft was cut to follow an ancient wall that turned out to be "impregnated with sewage." One time Bliss nearly asphyxiated while taking measurements. At all times, the passages were akin to Turkish baths, thick with humidity. "Artistic work undertaken underground is distinctly trying," he mordantly observed.

Bliss and Dickie's team tunneled directly into a nearly intact Byzantine church and pinpointed what they believed was the Pool of Siloam, fed by a water tunnel originating in the spring uphill. This was the presumed site of a miracle by Jesus mentioned in the gospels. They also uncovered a series of monumental steps from the same era that they speculated had once reached all the way to the Temple Mount. But these discoveries, which would make headlines a century later when rediscovered, were all frustratingly late in date. Gradually, however, the team began to collect pottery and uncover walls predating Greek and Roman times.

They found no monumental remains from the days of David and Solomon, but they did eventually gather enough ceramics and other artifacts to clinch the case. "The City of David was clearly on the eastern hill," Bliss concluded. Early Jerusalem was confined to the narrow ridge. Much of the confusion about its location was due to the moving target of Zion. "David captured the fortress of Zion—which is the City of David," stated the biblical account. Yet the same name was later used to denote the Temple Mount, to the north. Still later, it meant the western hill that was home to the traditional tomb of David.

Bliss's conclusion was corroborated by another key piece of evidence. In 1880, two Arab boys playing hooky had dared each other to crawl through a dank tunnel that pierced the hill and found something Robinson and Warren had missed. They encountered words carved into the wall and immediately alerted their teacher.

When later deciphered, the inscription turned out to be an early form of Hebrew dating to the eighth century BCE, just three centuries after King David was presumed to have arrived with his Israelites. It commem-

orated the dramatic moment when the men digging from two sides met—
"axe against axe and there flowed the waters from the source to the pool."

The chance find proved to be Jerusalem's most important known
inscription and one of Palestine's most sensational archaeological discoveries. The boys' teacher, naturally, was Conrad Schick.

◆   ◆   ◆

NEAR THE END of his excavations in the spring of 1897, Bliss dined with
a visiting delegation of twenty-one British Jewish leaders organized by
a member of the Palestine Exploration Fund board, a London lawyer
named Herbert Bentwich. Their goal was to encourage European Jewish
tourists to visit the Holy Land, as Christians had been doing for decades.
But the lawyer had a personal mission as well.

Bentwich was the first prominent British follower of Theodor Herzl,
the Viennese journalist who months before had published a book calling for a Jewish state. Herzl had asked him to report back on whether
Palestine was the best site for that homeland. There were other options.
Some Jews considered the United States, which at that time was accepting nearly a million immigrants a year, to be the modern promised land.
Others hoped that the Jewish-dominated regions of Eastern Europe could
be turned into a Jewish state. Later, the British would offer to make their
African colony of Uganda a Jewish refuge.

After his trip, Bentwich insisted to Herzl that Palestine was the best
choice. The black-bearded thirty-seven-year-old Herzl, who had yet
to visit the Holy Land himself, agreed with the lawyer's appraisal. The
pogroms and prejudice endured by European Jews might be enough to
push them to leave, but they needed something to pull them as well. "The
very name of Palestine would attract our people with a force of marvelous potency," he wrote, noting that the new state would be "a rampart
of Europe against Asia." He added that Christian sanctuaries "would be
safeguarded by assigning them an extra-territorial status."

That August, more than two hundred people gathered for the first
Zionist Congress in the Swiss town of Basel, the same city where, a half
century before, Schick had built his first model of the temple of Solomon.
"In Basel I founded the Jewish state," Herzl wrote in his diary on September 3. "If I said that aloud today, it would be met with universal laughter.
Perhaps in five years, certainly in fifty, everyone will see it." His latter
prediction proved remarkably accurate.

A year later, he made his first visit to Jerusalem to coincide with that of Kaiser Wilhelm II, whom he hoped to make an ally in creating a Jewish homeland. In their brief audience, the kaiser—who was busy cementing a fateful alliance with the Ottomans—refused to make any promises. Three days later, the German leader dedicated the Lutheran Church of the Redeemer, the site of Schick's excavation.

The onetime cuckoo-clock repairman stood in a place of honor outside the sanctuary to greet the kaiser, who arrived in a white pith helmet with a spike that gleamed in the September sun. "From Jerusalem came the light in splendor from which the German nation became great and glorious," the kaiser told the crowd. Schick was later photographed giving him a tour of the Tomb of the Kings.

The same week, Herzl also was photographed visiting the site of de Saulcy's excavation. Like many educated Westerners, he was mildly interested in archaeology and had attended lectures on the topic while visiting Egypt. And like many Western visitors, his romantic image of the ancient city clashed with the reality that he found. "The musty deposits of two thousand years of inhumanity, intolerance, and foulness lie in your reeking alleys," he wrote. "If Jerusalem is ever ours," he added, "I would clear out anything that is not something sacred." Herzl envisioned tearing down and burning the "secular ruins" and moving the bazaars outside the city walls.

Even without such drastic urban renewal, Jerusalem in the 1890s was undergoing rapid change. Most was due to the influx of European Christians, who set a precedent for Jewish settlement. It was all part of a campaign conducted not by "the loud clinking of weapons," as one German scholar who dug with Schick put it, "but with the quiet ways of Christian love, with the eyes of the researcher and the fruits of peaceful work."

German Protestants who styled themselves as spiritual descendants of the medieval order of the Knights Templar began to build a community outside the city's walls in 1878, complete with its own bakeries, cafés, and a cemetery. "The Templars were able to demonstrate that Palestine could be penetrated through colonies of the European style," noted one historian. An American colony formed in 1881, followed by one devoted to French Catholics the year after.

Other immigrants, usually less well off, included a rapidly growing number of European Jewish refugees. Alarmed by the influx of these foreigners, the sultan banned both Jewish immigration and land purchases in 1882. These restrictions, however, proved easy to circumvent through bribery and other means.

The newcomers found an advocate in Baron Edmond de Rothschild, a Parisian from the famous banking family. Tall and thin, with a small round beard and blue eyes set in a pale face, he disdained Herzl's ideas as too radical. But a year after Herzl's visit he partnered with the Jewish Colonization Association to organize large-scale settlement across the Holy Land, including around Jerusalem.

By the turn of the century, Jerusalem's fast-expanding suburbs had doubled the size of the city since de Saulcy's day. Nearly a quarter of the population of some 45,000 lived in these modern neighborhoods that catered to foreign communities. Schick was responsible for a good deal of this change. While hailed by one acquaintance as "the greatest living authority on underground Jerusalem," he remade the city above by designing and building dozens of prominent structures, including the new train station that linked the city in 1892 with the wider world. He laid out Mea Shearim, the first Jewish Orthodox neighborhood outside the city walls, and his eclectic style still defines that era of Jerusalem architecture.

When he died in 1901, just days shy of age eighty, people of all faiths joined the solemn procession to his grave on Mount Zion to show respect for one of the rare individuals to earn the universal admiration of Jerusalem's quarrelsome tribes. "He was beloved and desirable to all the inhabitants of his city, without distinction of religion, Jewish, Muslim, and Christian," noted one Hebrew-language newspaper.

Schick's death marked the dawn of an ominous era. Jerusalem's outward prosperity—elegant hotels, paved streets, and gaslit alleys—masked growing fractures within the foreign and local communities. Those rifts would soon shatter the fragile peace and plunge Jerusalem into a cycle of violence that continues today. Archaeology would play no small role in intensifying that conflict.

◆ ◆ ◆

ROTHSCHILD'S ENTHUSIASM FOR Jewish settlement was matched by his passion for collecting art and supporting science. He sponsored archaeological excavations in Syria and Egypt, including an Egyptian project conducted by Clermont-Ganneau, the French scholar and diplomat who in 1871 had discovered the Greek inscription belonging to Herod the Great's temple complex.

In the 1880s, Clermont-Ganneau had suggested that a pronounced bend in the water tunnel with the inscription discovered by Schick's students could have been a conscious detour around the tombs of the ancient Judean kings. "Baron Edmond de Rothschild became interested in this theory," wrote the Columbia University scholar and Zionist Richard Gottheil. "He wished that the grave of the kings should be in Jewish hands if found." Bliss's conclusion that the City of David had been sited on the ridge with the tunnel gave new credence to Clermont-Ganneau's theory.

The Frenchman had an academic position in Paris he could not leave, so he recommended that a French Jewish Egyptologist named Raymond Weill, who had worked with Petrie, lead the charge. Weill would manage the dig with Clermont-Ganneau providing long-distance supervision.

The excavations of the previous half century had been conducted and almost solely funded by Christians. The apparent lack of Jewish interest in Jerusalem's past had long been a puzzle to some, including the Scottish explorer John MacGregor, who had visited Warren in 1869. "One wonders how, with all their love of their people and their land, they leave it to us Christians to search for their records among the rubbish of their ruined cities."

Rothschild set out to change that. But before he and Weill could organize their expedition, unexpected competitors entered the field. They made up Jerusalem's most bizarre excavation team, one that would bring thousands into the streets, nearly overturn the Ottoman government, and raise fears in Britain of a Muslim rebellion in their empire.

The expedition included a Scandinavian poet, a rich and young English aristocrat, a Swiss psychic, a French monk, and a Swede who piloted a steamboat on the Congo. Fueled by wealthy investors, including American hot-dog makers and British nobility, they set out to beat their competition in locating the ancient kings of Judea.

Both teams—one Jewish and one Christian—had another common goal that they kept strictly under wraps. A clandestine race was on to recover the world's most famous and valuable lost treasure.

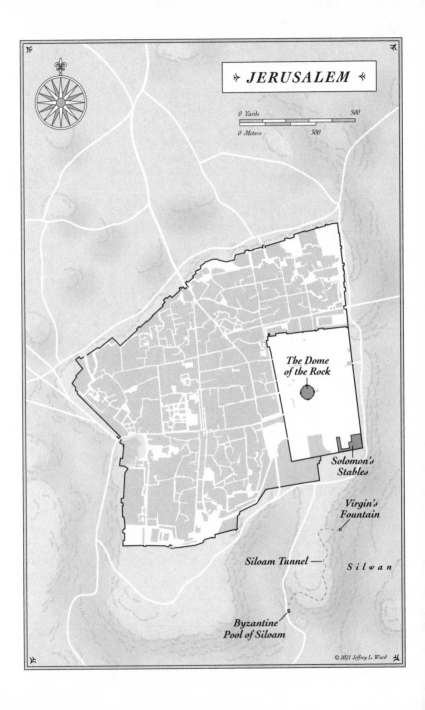

JERUSALEM

0 Yards 500
0 Meters 300

The Dome
of the Rock

Solomon's
Stables

Virgin's
Fountain

Siloam Tunnel —

S i l w a n

Byzantine
Pool of Siloam

© 2021 Jeffrey L. Ward

7

Gone with the Treasures of Solomon

"A scientist has no value in Jerusalem. There is always reason
to suspect he belongs to the devil's gang."
—VALTER JUVELIUS, *The White Camel*

A s Schick was laid to rest in Jerusalem, Protestant and Freemason
excavators were digging among the tombs of the ancient kings
of Ireland. To the accompaniment of a harpist, members of the
British-Israel Association of London searched for an artifact they suspected had been deposited in Éire's green hills by the lost tribes of Israel,
who were said to have vanished during an Assyrian invasion in the eighth
century BCE.

They believed that the Anglo-Saxon race descended from those tribes,
and that their long wanderings ended at a site called Tara, which fig-
ured prominently in Irish mythology and history. The association members considered this to be their "resuscitated" Jerusalem. The object they
sought was the Ark of the Covenant.

The Ark is described in the biblical book of Exodus as a rectangular wooden chest made of acacia wood covered in gold leaf and topped
with two winged figures on its gold lid. Scripture maintains it was built
soon after the Israelites departed Egypt to hold the two tablets inscribed
with the Ten Commandments. "There, above the cover between the two
cherubim that are over the Ark of the Covenant law, I will meet with you
and give you all my commands for the Israelites," God is recorded telling
Moses while providing detailed instructions on the design of the portable
object that could be carried with two wooden staves.

Such shrines were common in the ancient Near East. A similarly sized wooden chest was discovered in King Tut's tomb, while others in Egypt have been found topped with deities and used as sarcophagi. Some were ceremonial boats carried by priests on poles. The cherubim from the Bible were likely derived from Babylonian tradition.

What set the Ark apart from its Near Eastern cousins was the biblical claim that it served as a powerful spiritual weapon, capable of parting the Jordan River, bringing down the walls of Jericho, and generally routing any enemy of the Israelites. King David was said to have brought it to Jerusalem; he danced ecstatically before the sacred object as it entered the city. Eventually it came to rest in Solomon's temple within what was known as the Holy of Holies, the central sanctuary accessible only to the high priest, and then only once a year. Its presence would have given the city a new and powerful religious potency, yet it is never again mentioned in the Bible.

In 586 BCE, the Babylonian army attacked Jerusalem and "carried to Babylon all the articles from the temple of God, both large and small, and the treasures of the Lord's temple and the treasures of the king and his officials." If the Ark itself was among these is not clear; the invaders were, in any case, the third army mentioned in the Bible that had looted the temple. Whether taken, hidden, or destroyed, its fate has spawned innumerable legends, hundreds of books, and one Steven Spielberg blockbuster.

Some Jewish traditions maintain that the Ark remains hidden in Jerusalem, but other candidate locations include an Ethiopian church, a Vatican basement, a Jordanian mountaintop, and a Dead Sea cave. Tara appears to be off the list; in 1902, the British-Israel Association failed to find the artifact and gave up its dig, not least because of outrage from Irish nationalists at what they viewed as desecration of their heritage by British imperialists.

The widely publicized Irish excavation likely caught the attention of a scholar who was then working on his doctoral dissertation at a Helsinki university. Valter Juvelius was born in rural Finland when it was still under Russian control. Trained as a surveyor, he also wrote romantic poetry and translated foreign literature into Swedish and Finnish.

Juvelius developed a fascination with the medieval Jewish mystical tradition of Kabbalah, often expressed in secret codes and numerology. His dissertation drew on Egyptian inscriptions, astronomical events, and biblical texts to explain the ancient Judean concept of time, which he argued began with the inauguration of Solomon's temple.

After he was made a doctor of philosophy in 1906, Juvelius took a job directing a Finnish workers' education center. By the following year, however, he had more ambitious designs. He grew certain that he had cracked the code that would lead him to the true location of the Ark.

Theories involving secret codes in religious texts were popular at the turn of the last century; Petrie had spent a good deal of time overturning mystical mathematical formulas proposed to explain the shape and location of the Giza pyramids. Juvelius's fascination with Solomon's temples and Kabbalah, combined with news of the Irish dig, presumably drew him to the mystery of the Ark's disappearance.

According to some accounts, he came across an ancient manuscript with clues to its fate; others claimed he analyzed the writings of the prophets Ezekiel or Jeremiah and devised a new solution to the old mystery. The surviving pages of his notes are a mass of scribbled numbers, obscure phrases, and biblical references. Whatever his source, Juvelius believed he had a "cipher" that could lead to the Ark as well as other temple treasures.

Those objects included the hundreds of gold and silver basins, platters, and bowls mentioned in the biblical text. According to one estimate that he and his later cohorts made, the trove could net $200 million on the open market, or about $5.7 billion today. This was not simply a religious quest, but a search for valuable treasure of incredible proportions.

The first stop in Juvelius's campaign was Berlin, where he found government officials interested in his theory, though they declined to cut a deal. Then he traveled to London, where he wrangled an introduction to Captain Montagu Brownlow Parker, the thirty-year-old brother of the Fourth Earl of Morley. Educated at Eton, Parker was wounded and decorated during the Boer War but apparently was bored with his subsequent desk job.

Won over by Juvelius's idea, the tall and dashing Parker, who had a reputation as a feckless socialite, set out to raise the necessary funds. One American newspaper later claimed he was motivated less by piety or riches than by his desire to court a wealthy divorcée, Ava Willing Astor. "Well, bring back the Ark of the Covenant and I will talk to you again," she is alleged to have said.

With the help of other aristocratic friends, he set up a syndicate in

October 1908 to sell 60,000 one-pound shares in the venture. Parker's connections and charm opened the wallets of an array of wealthy Britons and Americans eager to find righteous fame as well as additional fortune. Consuelo Spencer-Churchill, a New York–born Vanderbilt who was then Duchess of Marlborough, and J. Ogden Armour, the Chicago meat-packing millionaire, were among those who contributed at least 20,000 pounds—about $2.4 million today—to the effort, "and [we] could have had double if we had needed it," said Parker's army friend, the cricket star Cyril Foley, who joined the adventure. The two men even rebuffed would-be investors; one American arrived at New York City's Ritz hotel with his checkbook, only to be firmly turned down. "He had to have two cocktails before he could believe it," wrote a tickled Foley.

◆ ◆ ◆

TO KICK OFF their expedition, Juvelius and Parker visited Jerusalem in late 1908 to examine potential dig sites; the Finn's surveying background would have served him well in the planning. Accompanying them was a Swedish steamboat captain named A. W. Hoppenrath. With his upturned mustache and shadowy past, he seemed right out of a novel by Joseph Conrad. In fact, he had served in the Belgian navy in the Congo at the very time Conrad was sailing up that river in the journey that served as the basis for his chilling 1902 novel, *Heart of Darkness.*

According to Foley, Juvelius "declared that his rendering of the Hebrew text denoted that the Ark of the Covenant could be found by working up the hill through underground passages" beneath the narrow ridge that Bliss had recently identified as the City of David. These tunnels, he added, "would lead us up to the mosque" atop the Noble Sanctuary. The artifacts were secreted somewhere in the vicinity.

The party then went to Istanbul, where Parker remained to negotiate for a dig license with Ottoman officials. "This was easily done," Foley wrote. "England had befriended the Young Turks." Just months before, these youthful politicians had staged a coup, declaring a constitutional system that sidelined the sultan and led to parliamentary elections. Members of the new government asked for 500 pounds—about $80,000 today—as well as half the treasure in exchange for the permit. Parker readily agreed; indeed, he may have even proposed the terms.

Grand Vizier Mehmed Kamil Pasha and his finance minister personally signed the agreement in November 1908. They also helped Parker navigate the fiendishly complex matter of purchasing land on the ridge between the Noble Sanctuary and the spring. The government's cover story was that the Ottomans intended to construct a hospital on the site.

At first, the landowners were unwilling to sell, and they had the backing of the Jerusalem governor. Under pressure from Istanbul, however, the deal was completed, and at a price that was advantageous to the Europeans. To keep an eye on their activities, the Ottoman government sent two parliamentarians with a hefty stipend. The historian Louis Fishman noted that Parker's remarkable success in Istanbul "should be seen as a clear sign of corruption and payoffs."

Hoppenrath stayed in Jerusalem to secure the property and buy materials like steel ladders. Crates of equipment, including electric lamps, arrived at Jaffa in the summer of 1909. The rest of the team—made up primarily of Parker's army buddies—arrived on the private yacht *Water Lily* in August, but were delayed in embarking because of an outbreak of bubonic plague. Forced to remain on the boat amid rising swells, the passengers grew increasingly seasick.

Among those who suffered the most was Otto von Bourg, a thirty-eight-year-old Swiss psychic then living in London. He had made a name investigating murders, and "became distinguished for fine and accurate Mediumship," according to one newspaper report. He then turned to using his gift in the search for archaeological treasures. Von Bourg would go on to lead the First Spiritualist Church of Minneapolis and serve as president of the State Spiritualist Association. While on the boat in Jaffa harbor, he fell into a different kind of trance when he passed out from the relentless motion.

Eventually the team put up at a "particularly dirty hotel, the cleanest in Jerusalem," Foley wrote. They spent two days preparing the dig, "and trying to avoid listening to Von Bourg, who told us that he knew exactly where the Ark was, much to the annoyance of Juvelius." The English war veterans rented a luxurious villa just outside the city walls, complete with Persian rugs and long-hosed hookahs, with one room dedicated to the valuable finds they were certain they would soon collect.

Juvelius spent time sightseeing and had his photo taken in a Jerusalem studio in a striped robe and turban, with two daggers tucked into his belt. With his neatly clipped mustache and pale complexion, he made an unconvincing Arab sheikh.

"They were certainly the oddest archaeologists to visit Jerusalem," remarked Bertha Spafford Vester, an American missionary who grew up in the city. She had been a child when General Charles Gordon stayed at the family home three decades before, and she was a keen observer of the social scene and knowledgeable about archaeology. "We heard of gay dinners given by the Englishmen, once with the Turkish Pasha as guest, and of their using oranges for target practice." She once recalled seeing the men "running alongside the donkeys and imitating the yelling, only much louder, usually made by the Arab boys, who were mounted in the Englishmen's places."

Vester's amusement turned to anger when she learned the team intended to dig on the historic slope south of the Noble Sanctuary. She was appalled "by their complete lack of archaeological knowledge." This was no exaggeration; one of the expedition members, Foley revealed, insisted that the Ark must be found on Mount Ararat, apparently having confused Noah's Ark with that of King David.

Trespassers were strictly forbidden on the parcel of land that had been secured with the help of the Ottoman government. Such secrecy only heightened local suspicions, as it had in the case of de Saulcy and Warren. "Soon the rumors were about that we are looking for Solomon's treasures," wrote Juvelius in a fictional account of the effort that was published in 1916.

Their cover was blown; "Nothing more was said about a hospital," Vester archly noted. She convinced her brother to speak with a leading Jerusalem dignitary. He explained to the Arab "the harm it would do to the whole archaeological world if they carried on excavations on the most historical spot in Palestine and left no scientific records." The notable, in turn, prevailed on the pasha to pressure Parker into involving Louis-Hugues Vincent, a thirty-seven-year-old Dominican monk who headed the city's École Biblique, the French biblical research center.

Vincent seemed the best possible choice to keep an eye on the English-led dig. He embraced Petrie's revolutionary use of pottery and stratigraphy to better contextualize finds, and he was one of the most respected biblical archaeologists of his day. Though thin and frail, "he didn't suffer fools gladly and could be extremely severe" in criticizing any dig that smacked of "sloppy workmanship," according to one colleague.

Vincent later wrote that his participation was allowed on the condition "that nothing should be divulged of what was going on until a time fixed by the leader of the expedition." The monk also wouldn't be permitted to interfere with the excavation, and his visits were limited to three days a week. "My sole task has been to examine and check the actual results," he later wrote. His presence, however constrained, eased the worries of the foreign community.

The team further allayed the suspicions of Arab residents by hiring nearly 180 workers for an excavation on a scale Jerusalem had never seen. When the difficult work of shaft digging and tunneling began beneath the ridge, it continued twenty-four hours a day, in four-hour shifts. Each bucket of earth had to be filled, then carried through a narrow passage only four and a half feet high, with air supplied by mechanical pumps.

Eventually they encountered the water channel explored by Warren, which contained the inscription publicized by Schick. This large tunnel, which began at the spring on the ridge's eastern flank and emptied into the Pool of Siloam at the southern base of the hill, was by then so clogged that only a trickle of muddy water emerged.

The team built a temporary dam inside to clear the mud-choked passage. Weeks of back-breaking labor clearing the tunnel produced no treasure, but the effort was celebrated by the villagers of nearby Silwan—with the exception of its mayor. When completed, the dam was breached, sending a wave of fresh water into the valley that swept the village leader off his feet and deposited him some distance away.

Meanwhile, Juvelius feuded with Von Bourg and set out in a pique for the countryside to search for the tomb of Moses. Neither he nor the Swiss psychic was successful in pinpointing a passage that led north, in the direction of the Noble Sanctuary.

"We lived underground nearly the whole time it was daylight," Vincent later wrote. "The work went on at nightfall without stopping, by the light of torches and to the sound of songs chanted by the workmen." He recalled "dark mysterious tunnels which seemed to stretch endlessly into the very entrails of the rock." But the only artifacts the team found were "some old Jewish flat lamps made of baked clay, some red pottery jars, [and] a few metal sling balls." The workers grew impatient. When the bucket brigade went on strike for higher wages, they were jailed by the local court. Foley reported, "Our hopes of finding the Ark had by this time diminished almost to vanishing point." When the weather turned cold and rainy that autumn, Parker and his team left for Britain.

They returned in August 1910, this time with the chief engineer of London's tube system. During the second season the team identified four other tunnels, but none that connected with the Noble Sanctuary. Soon Parker's friends began to desert him, and Juvelius departed after falling ill with malaria. Worse, the Ottoman parliamentarians left in disgust. The team's dig permit would expire in November 1911. Parker had managed to have it renewed twice, but a third chance seemed increasingly unlikely.

Time was running out, so Parker continued work through an unusually rainy winter. By spring, he was desperate, and he made a dangerous gamble.

♦ ♦ ♦

IN APRIL 1911, Passover, Eastern Orthodox Easter, and a local Muslim celebration of Moses coincided. The Islamic rite took place for more than a week far outside the city, so the Englishman bribed Sheikh Khalil al-Zanaf, the man in charge of the Noble Sanctuary, with, according to the *New York Times,* 5,000 British pounds (worth more than $800,000 today). The sheikh paid the platform's guards to attend the festival. Islam's third-holiest site was suddenly vulnerable to non-Muslim trespassers. In the past, such interlopers had faced injury and even death.

During nine subsequent nights, Parker led a select team to surreptitiously dig in the southeast corner of the platform, the site of what was known as Solomon's Stables. But after failing to find any treasure, the Englishman turned his attention to the Dome of the Rock.

This shrine marking the place where Muhammad was believed to have begun his visit to heaven covered a rough stone with a shallow cave beneath. An influx of Christian tourists in recent years had upset many Islamic fundamentalists. A year before, an Afghan Muslim had shot and wounded two American women while they were touring the building; he had just been sentenced to eight years in prison.

Parker was certain the treasure-filled tunnel he sought could be accessed through a secret tunnel that began inside the Dome of the Rock. Some accounts have the Englishmen dressed in robes and wearing fezzes as they hacked away at the sacred stone that lay beneath the ancient octagon.

The particulars of what took place on the night of April 12 are a matter of dispute. A sleepless Muslim wandering across the platform stumbled on the foreigners and raised an alarm. A guard at one of the gates wasn't satisfied with his bribe and made the desecration known. A caretaker who was not in on the secret noticed an open gate and investigated. One newspaper insisted the team had by then abandoned the search and left. Parker himself denied the whole story, though his friend Foley later confirmed widespread press reports that he dug on the platform. There is no doubt, however, that the residents of Jerusalem, of all religions, believed the Englishmen had committed an outrageous act of sacrilegious vandalism.

By the time alarmed Muslims rushed to the site, Parker and his friends were hurrying to their yacht anchored off Jaffa. The Jerusalem pasha, Azmi Bey, telegraphed the port to order their baggage searched but stopped short of ordering Parker's arrest. Parker was, after all, an aristocrat of the world's most powerful empire. According to one account, the Englishman—after coolly pausing at a Jaffa hotel for tea—offered to fete the officials on the yacht, which he welcomed them to search. He and his colleagues were rowed to the boat to prepare for their guests, only to sail away.

Rumors swirled around the globe that the foreigners had made off with the staff of Moses, the tablets of the Ten Commandments, or any number of other possible relics. "Gone with the Treasure That Was Solomon's," read the May 4 banner headline in the *New York Times,* followed by "English Party Vanishes on Yacht after Digging Under the Mosque of Omar." Three days later, the same newspaper published a long feature titled "Have Englishmen Found the Ark of the Covenant?" stating that "it is believed that the explorers found Solomon's crown, his sword, and his ring, and an ancient manuscript of the Bible."

Protests, strikes, and riots broke out across Jerusalem. In Juvelius's fictional account, the furious crowds in Jerusalem smashed the doors and windows of the villa where the English had been staying, ransacking the interior in their search for stolen sacred objects. That event is wholly plausible. "Jerusalem has been in a terror because of the buried treasures of the sacred mosque," reported an Arab newspaper in the city. The team had dug at night "under the sacred rock itself." The report concluded that "in truth, our loss is great."

Some two thousand demonstrators took to the city's streets demanding justice. "There was an awful row, which required both battalions of Turkish Infantry, quartered in Jerusalem, to quell," wrote Foley. With Parker gone, the Arab throngs returning from the Muslim festival turned on the Ottoman governor. They cursed him when he made a brief appearance. Other protests on the sacred platform targeted the Noble Sanctuary's Sheikh Khalil for allowing the desecration. He was cursed and spit upon, and according to the *New York Times,* a mob publicly shaved off the "beard and mustache" of the platform's caretaker.

At one point, shots fired by Ottoman soldiers set off a stampede, and frightened merchants shut their shops. Terrified foreigners barricaded themselves into their homes and hotels, and hundreds of Russian pilgrims visiting for the Easter season sought the protection of their government's walled compound. Muslims, in turn, suspected the Russians were armed and planned a massacre. To defuse the crisis, the governor had Khalil and two gendarmes imprisoned, but this did little to halt a situation spiraling out of control.

Newspapers around the world followed the rising tempest. "Moslems in a Rage: Recent Sensation from Jerusalem," read the headline of Washington, DC's *Evening Star* on May 11, 1911. The sacrilege, according to the newspaper's breathless account, nearly led to a massacre of the city's Christians. But in fact the ire of Muslims seemed directed squarely at the Ottoman leadership for failing to protect the Noble Sanctuary. Jerusalem's Greek Orthodox patriarch said that "this deplorable act could have caused a great disaster for our State." He expressed solidarity with Muslim demonstrators and demanded an investigation to "save everyone from grief and anxiety."

The British consul, meanwhile, assured a nervous London that "Moslem irritation so far has been directed against the Governor."

Azmi Bey had tried to calm the situation on April 16 by ordering an investigation by high-ranking Arab and Ottoman officials. He also had two of Khalil's sons and Parker's Armenian translator arrested. But the city's leading Arab families responded much as Jewish leaders had in the wake of de Saulcy's excavations: They telegrammed their protests to the Ottoman prime minister and other senior government officials. They also sent letters to their counterparts across the empire, addressed to "the Islamic people," warning of the danger posed by archaeologists.

This uneasiness with excavations extended beyond Jerusalem and was linked to Jewish colonization. A petition from Gaza, bordering Egypt, complained that their "ancient relics" were at risk from "Zionist ambitions." Plans for a British-sponsored colony of Jewish immigrants in Gaza were canceled three months later. Another complaint from Gaza charged that "the stealing of antiquities from Palestine does not end with the al-Aqsa Mosque," noting one site where the medieval Kurdish conqueror Saladin once ruled was being "raided by foreigners."

Archaeology in Palestine was seen by a growing number of Arabs as a threat to their homes and their heritage, a radically different perspective from that of Westerners who viewed digging as simply a search for knowledge. The controversy helped make archaeology an unappealing profession for the growing numbers of educated Palestinian Arabs.

Meanwhile, protests in Jerusalem continued. The Ottoman military commander of the region reported to Istanbul on April 21 that he had soldiers on duty "night and day" to maintain "public security." He also suggested that the central government set up its own investigation to supersede that of the governor. The demonstrations had taken on a nationalist flavor at a time when Arab dissatisfaction with Ottoman rule was on the rise. Alarmed, the cabinet in Istanbul ordered a high-level team sent from the capital to Jerusalem. News reports in the European press even suggested that Parker's debacle might lead to the overthrow of the government in Istanbul.

On May 8, the Ottoman parliament met in a special session. Palestinian Arab representatives intimated that leading members of the government had sought to profit from the Parker expedition. They noted that the grand vizier and finance minister had signed the agreement with the Englishman, an arrangement that properly should have been made with the Education Ministry, which oversaw excavation permits. The lawmakers also presented evidence that the Jerusalem pasha and the local military commander were bribed by Parker.

"The government covers everything up," concluded a scandalized representative from the Black Sea region.

In response, the interior minister confirmed many of the allegations but blamed the incident at the Noble Sanctuary on an unnamed spy and draft dodger. Parker, he added, had not fled out of guilt but had merely left on a previously scheduled vacation. These claims drew derisive hoots from the chamber. Another member of the government acknowledged the scheme but explained that had Parker been successful, it would have brought "great profit for the nation." It was claimed that the government's share of Parker's treasure would have totaled 100 million Turkish liras, the equivalent of many millions of dollars and nearly as much as the entire national debt.

The investigation completed on May 13 was widely seen as a whitewash. Parker's Armenian interpreter was blamed for bribing the guards at the Noble Sanctuary, but all senior government officials were cleared of wrongdoing. The report did acknowledge that the governor and the military commander had been on the take from Parker, and the governor was recalled and later dismissed from his post, along with the military commander. Only the smaller fish involved in the incident were punished; the Armenian and platform caretakers were jailed in Beirut, though later released. The investigators determined that despite media reports fueled by wild rumors, the expedition had found nothing of value.

The governor's removal calmed Jerusalem. But the events in the Holy City continued to stir anger across the Muslim world. One Ottoman parliamentarian reported it "caused profound animosity in India and Afghanistan." In fact, Indian Muslims sent their own team to Jerusalem to investigate the incident. This may explain why the London *Times,* which tended to espouse the government's views, resolutely stood by Parker, praising his scientific efforts and attributing the fuss to "the flamboyant imagination of the Orient," while newspapers in Germany, America, and France sharply criticized the expedition; the *El Paso Herald* called it "extraordinarily sacrilegious."

A half century before, Britain had nearly lost its hold on the subcontinent when rumors that gun cartridges contained pork products helped spark a bloody rebellion. It could hardly afford another such disaster. Fortunately for the British, the Indian committee also determined that there was no theft or damage involved in the digs on the Noble Sanctuary. But it had been a close call. One American newspaper warned that the treasure hunt by the Christian adventurers "might have provoked a holy war throughout the world."

◆ ◆ ◆

PARKER RETURNED TO Britain without grasping the impact of his actions, and the British Foreign Office did not appear to rein in the rogue aristocrat. In September 1911, he launched a new expedition to search for the treasure while also seeking the release of his jailed Armenian interpreter. Advised by Ottoman friends not to land at Jaffa, Parker boldly sailed instead to Istanbul.

It proved poor timing. The new government was in turmoil after war broke out between the empire and Italy, a conflict that saw the first bomb dropped from an aircraft on enemies. No amount of bribery could attract the attention of senior officials, and Parker never returned to Jerusalem. Members of the expedition remained silent about what had taken place, except for Juvelius's 1916 novel and Foley's later recollections.

Vincent was the only conspicuous figure to rise to the Englishman's defense. On October 14, 1911, he published a long article in London's *Field* newspaper clearly intended to counter the widely held impression that the expedition was conducted by inept and greedy bumblers. He simultaneously published a volume—available, he noted, for seven shillings—with maps and plans of the excavation, which he almost certainly made public with Parker's approval and financial assistance.

The cleric blamed rural Muslims for promulgating the idea that Parker's team was involved with sacrilegious pillage. The "villagers' crude suspicions of the explorers' motives" had infected "a higher level of society." But he reserved his most scathing criticism for the "grossly exaggerated reports hastily telegraphed to London by correspondents who preferred sensation to accuracy." These journalists, he added mockingly, apparently received their information from "the inner council of the gods."

The truth, he asserted, was that the excavators had worked for a total of twelve months, "not only with the most conscientious thoroughness, but with scholarly scruples that were sometimes almost excessive." While they had succeeded in uncovering "a vast tangle" of underground tunnels and chambers choked with rock and mud, the men had found "not a single object of great artistic value." But the team had revealed, among other discoveries, constructions of an ancient Canaanite city dating to a millennium before the arrival of the Israelites, or some four thousand years ago.

Vincent may have been correct that the bulk of the work had been done in a professional manner and that the finds were indeed significant. Yet the monk would have been fully aware of the Englishmen's desperate trespass on the Noble Sanctuary, an event that numerous journalists, government panels, and diplomats agreed took place and only Parker denied. A longtime Jerusalem resident, Vincent would have understood the serious implications of that act. He also would have been an eyewitness to the tumultuous events that resulted.

The puzzle is why such a distinguished scholar stood alone in publicly defending a team that included a treasure-hunting poet and psychic and was led by a patrician socialite. He may simply have wanted to protect his own reputation, now entangled in the fiasco. It may have been part of the initial agreement he had made with Parker. A more convincing explanation is that the Dominican monk preferred to turn a blind eye to the global repercussions of the expedition for the sake of immediate scientific gain. It would not be the first or last time that a Jerusalem excavator ignored the political consequences of excavations in order to collect data.

Whatever his motives, Vincent never wrote publicly about the expedition again, despite a career in Jerusalem that continued for another half century. His volume on the dig does not mention Parker by name. The monk even failed to put his own full name on the book, using initials instead, an unmistakable sign of his ambivalence about the effort.

Other scholars were unequivocal. "The treasure hunt by Captain Parker has checked scientific research in Palestine, and it is not probable that the results of his discoveries will compensate for this loss," warned the German theologian Gustaf Dalman. The secretary of the Palestine Exploration Fund dashed off a letter, which was published in the London *Times* on May 9, insisting that "Captain Parker's expedition and works are in no way connected with this society." He noted that "we seek to obey the law of the land while acquiring knowledge of its history, and we are not 'treasure-seekers.'"

It was a distinction lost on many Jerusalem residents. Since the days of de Saulcy, Western excavators had often wrapped their work in a shroud of secrecy that encouraged suspicion. Archaeologists had long claimed that they were not crass treasure hunters, an assertion shaken by the Parker expedition. Neither the British nor the Ottoman government officially denounced the desecration.

In the West, the sordid episode came to be seen as a minor comic opera. Yet the peculiar expedition had three lasting impacts. First, it inspired later generations to seek the Ark and other long-lost treasures beneath the city. Second, it increased mistrust between local Arabs and foreign excavators, and, fatefully, linked the rising tide of Jewish colonists with the search for the ancient past.

Finally, Parker's violation of the Noble Sanctuary demonstrated that Muslims as far away as India felt strongly about the sacred platform—and that the Ottomans were untrustworthy caretakers of their third-holiest site. Louis Fishman concluded that the Parker imbroglio awakened within Palestinian Muslims their special duty to protect the Noble Sanctuary. This sense of responsibility would emerge as a central tenet in Palestinian nationalism, and it would clash with the growing desire by Jewish immigrants to assert control over what to them was the revered Temple Mount. This escalating feud would propel the violent events in the turbulent century to come.

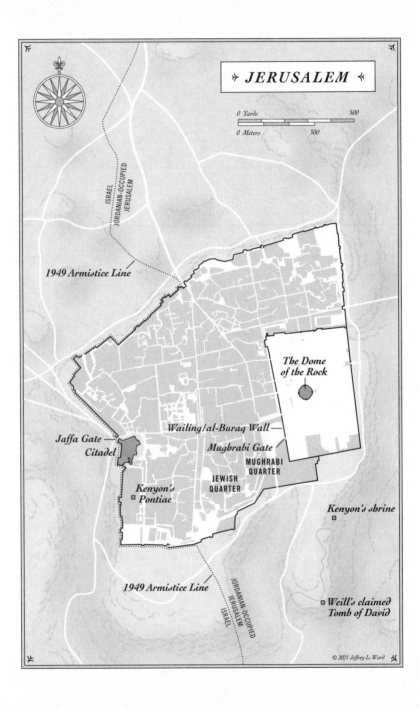

JERUSALEM

0 Yards   500

0 Meters   300

ISRAEL
JORDANIAN-OCCUPIED JERUSALEM

1949 Armistice Line

The Dome
of the Rock

Wailing/al-Buraq Wall

Jaffa Gate
Citadel

Mughrabi Gate

MUGHRABI
QUARTER

JEWISH
QUARTER

Kenyon's
Pontiac

Kenyon's shrine

1949 Armistice Line

JORDANIAN-OCCUPIED
JERUSALEM
ISRAEL

Weill's claimed
Tomb of David

© 2021 Jeffrey L. Ward

8

A Dangerous Fantasy

> We, who should be the most interested party in these archaeo-
> logical excavations, do almost nothing in this field and leave to
> whomever else wants it: Germans, Americans, British.
> —DAVID SMILANSKI, in a 1912 Russian Jewish newspaper

When he learned in 1909 that Parker's expedition was underway, Rothschild sped up plans for his own archaeological
project, led by the thirty-five-year-old French Jewish scholar
Raymond Weill.

Like so many of his predecessors, the short and muscular Weill had
been trained as a military engineer. He abruptly resigned his position as
captain in 1902, in the midst of a national scandal over a charge of treason
brought against another Jewish army captain, Alfred Dreyfus, who was
also a friend of his family.

Disgusted by what was later exposed as an anti-Semitic witch hunt,
Weill switched to archaeology when he was not quite thirty. Weill was
confident that "no ideological or political struggles were to be feared . . .
in this research on distant civilizations," one colleague wrote after his
death. But if he imagined that archaeology would insulate him from religion or politics, he was wrong.

Weill went to Egypt and worked under Petrie before Rothschild put
him in charge of the dig on the Jerusalem ridge. As the city's first Jewish
archaeologist, he felt the full weight of history on his shoulders. "Merely
the gesture of taking a pickaxe to the slope of the unforgettable hill is

moving," he wrote. "One dreams, even before obtaining any results, of vast buried evidence."

His ostensible goal was to test Clermont-Ganneau's theory that the tombs of the early Judean kings were hidden beneath the ridge identified by Bliss as the City of David. Like Parker, however, he and Rothschild secretly were hunting treasure. When Chaim Weizmann, who later became Israel's first president, questioned Rothschild on the effort, his response was blunt. "Excavations be damned, it's possession that counts," the baron retorted, adding that "his purpose was to uncover the Ark of the Covenant, which he believed was buried there."

Apparently fearing that the world's most sacred and valuable Jewish object might fall into the hands of Christians, Rothschild had an agent for his colonization society quietly purchase land on the ridge. A swath of property covering the equivalent of nearly two Manhattan blocks "was acquired and walled up by the Jews," wrote Bertha Spafford Vester, who had watched Parker's team with a jaundiced eye. "It appeared that Baron Rothschild had furnished the money for the Jews' purchase, and was trying to get a concession for them to ascertain whether it was possible to locate the royal tombs," she noted.

Weill did not receive a dig permit until 1913, two years after Parker left, but he apparently spent time in Jerusalem while the Englishman's dig was underway. European newspapers reported that Weill was in Jerusalem in late 1910. In early 1911, they mentioned that the baron was "about to visit Palestine in order to have excavations made in the locality where it is believed the tombs of the Jewish kings are situated."

That particular visit never took place, and known documents on Weill's activities are few, but the team clearly monitored Parker's progress closely. Vester heard that the Ottoman government had warned Parker that the concession would be turned over to the Rothschild-sponsored dig at the end of 1911. If this was the case, it must have added to Parker's desperation during his last season.

The fierce but covert competition between the French Jewish and English Christian teams may be reflected in the later novel published by Juvelius, a story he claimed was told by a "strange hermit who had taken over a fishing sauna." How much is fact versus fantasy can't be known, and he weaves a tale of anti-Semitic-tinged treachery. In the book, a character resembling Captain Hoppenrath—the Swedish steamboat captain who had served in the Congo—steals Parker's confidential documents in order to cut a better deal with the Rothschild expedition.

Juvelius also introduces a mysterious Frenchman working for Rothschild who throws up obstacles to halt the British dig; his ultimate goal is to prevent the sacred treasures from being found and studied by the Christians. "If the Jewish expedition is successful, they will forever hide these important finds from Western science," the character based on Juvelius warns. He may have modeled the Frenchman on Weill, an unlikely candidate in real life to hide away a prize artifact.

Weill's excavation did not officially begin until November 1913. Yet a short notice in Britain's obscure *Sunderland Daily Echo and Shipping Gazette* on July 20, 1912, suggested otherwise: "French savants engaged in extensive excavations in Jerusalem on the southeastern slope of the temple hill" had uncovered "a number of very early tombs containing pottery" dating to before the time of King David, as well as broken figures of Canaanite goddesses. "Inscriptions either in Babylonian or Phoenician were brought to light."

Whether Weill undertook digs before receiving his permit is unclear, but it was a moment of warming ties between the Young Turks and Jewish leaders. A report presented to the September 1913 Zionist Congress in Vienna cited "archaeological digging under way in Jerusalem" that was producing Jewish antiquities. "A museum should be set up in Jerusalem to house these tangible reminders of Jewish power in the past and its continuing presence in the city," it concluded.

When Weill detailed his discoveries in early 1914, he reported uncovering eight burial caves cut deep into the hill and filled with promising artifacts, just where Clermont-Ganneau had predicted. One of the chambers was an astonishing fifty-four feet long and eight feet wide, and high enough for a person to walk through without stooping. "These funerary deposits are certainly from the Judean royal period," Weill asserted. But the caves were crudely cut and appeared to have been altered by later Romans who quarried the site. There certainly was no sign of the Ark or other valuable artifacts from the era of David and Solomon.

Predictably, Weill's dramatic claims were met with skepticism from his colleagues. A German scholar reported that the dig had found "some graves and cisterns, but the Tomb of David expected to be found in this neighborhood, was not discovered: but extensive quarrying was found to have gone on." The French archaeologist continued to insist that the largest tomb was in fact that of King David himself. When he left Jerusalem in the spring of 1914, he intended to return that fall to gather more evidence to counter the skeptics.

Before departing, Weill made one discovery that proved important, though it was unrelated to the Ark or the early Judean kings. While excavating a cistern, he uncovered a Greek inscription from the early centuries BCE proclaiming that a Jewish priest's son named Theodotus had built a synagogue there. It was the oldest known evidence of a synagogue in Palestine.

Weill's return was postponed by a full decade. That June, a Serbian nationalist shot the Austrian archduke, and in August, war spread across Europe. By November, the Ottoman Empire had sided with Germany and Austria, largely to foil Russian designs on its northern lands. Suddenly, British, Russian, and French residents of Jerusalem were citizens of enemy powers. An exodus of foreigners followed.

Before war fever descended on Jerusalem, a group of Jewish Europeans—geographers, historians, and politicians—gathered to found the Society for the Reclamation of Antiquities. They were inspired by both Zionism and Weill's dig. Though short-lived, it would later be reborn as the Jewish Palestine Exploration Society, the Jewish answer to the Christian question of why they had failed to pursue their own heritage.

◆ ◆ ◆

THE GREAT WAR BLED Europe and starved Jerusalem. The impact on the city, with its economy heavily tied to European tourists, pilgrims, and the diplomatic corps, was swift and severe. Banks closed, hotels shut down, and newspapers were forced to halt publication. A naval blockade prevented export of the region's grain, cotton, and fruits while halting imports of flour and other necessities. Needless to say, all archaeological work ground to a halt.

Famine quickly took hold among the population of some seventy thousand, made worse by a plague of locusts across Palestine and Syria in 1915. By the end of that year, even flour had disappeared from the city's shops. Soon cholera, typhus, and other diseases were easier to find than fresh food.

As the war years dragged on, Ottoman officials increasingly feared an Arab uprising or a foreign fifth column among Jews and Christians.

Thousands of non-Ottoman citizens, mainly Russian Jews, were expelled from the city. A soup kitchen organized by Bertha Spafford Vester and supported by American aid from both Jewish and Christian organizations helped prevent outright starvation within the walls, but even that vital assistance came under increasing Ottoman scrutiny. "Starvation in Jerusalem: Bread Eleven Times as High as at the War's Beginning," read a headline in the *New York Times.*

By early 1917, facing an agonizing stalemate on the western front in France, British politicians looked beyond Europe to Jerusalem. Though it lacked any real strategic value, its capture was sure to boost flagging public morale. Some even saw an opportunity to transform Jerusalem into the Christian-dominated city it had been more than eight centuries before. Jerusalem's exiled Anglican bishop suggested it was an exciting chance to take "official possession of every building erected originally as a Christian church which is now used as a Mohammedan mosque."

The British government tamped down such inflammatory rhetoric, wary of alienating its one hundred million Muslim subjects. The sultan had declared the war a jihad, or religious struggle, in order to spread unrest in British dominions like Egypt and India. The highly censored British press was warned by the Foreign Office to avoid any reference to "a modern Crusade," adding that it was "obviously mischievous to suggest that our quarrel with Turkey is one between Islam and Christianity."

In April 1917, the British general Edmund Allenby was given command of the Jerusalem campaign. He launched a series of attacks from Egypt and pushed Ottoman armies and their German allies north. Detailed maps showing watering holes, ridges, and roads proved invaluable; many of them had been created for just such an opportunity by Wilson, Warren, Conder, and other Royal Engineers who had worked for the Palestine Exploration Fund in previous decades. Fifty years of intelligence investment paid off.

With Allenby closing in on Jerusalem, the British foreign secretary Arthur Balfour wrote a letter to the leader of the British Jewish community, Lord Walter Rothschild, cousin to the French baron of the same family. Weizmann had worked through Lord Walter, who had close contacts with senior British officials, to hammer out the precise language. That famous missive, the Balfour Declaration, declared that Britain viewed "with favour the establishment in Palestine of a national home for the Jewish people."

The declaration was the result of decades of advocacy that began not with Jews but with evangelical Christian Zionists like the Seventh Earl of Shaftesbury, who had pushed the water relief society that laid the foundation for the Palestine Exploration Fund. At the Fund's annual meeting in 1875, he proclaimed the Holy Land as "teeming with fertility and rich in history, but almost without an inhabitant—a country without a people, and look! scattered over the world, a people without a country." This formula, often repeated, managed to overlook a half-million Palestinian Arab inhabitants ruled by a five-centuries-old empire.

Influential archaeologists like Warren emerged as outspoken supporters of a Jewish homeland in the Holy Land. "The Turk can never govern Palestine well," he had concluded, adding that the Arabs could not govern themselves after "centuries of mismanagement and ill-treatment have made them incapable of knowing what self-government means." Jewish immigration, he had argued, offered a way to ensure Palestine's prosperity. Such arguments, picked up and amplified by Weizmann, won the day in London.

Many American politicians cheered the decision. "It seems to me that it is entirely proper to start a Zionist state around Jerusalem," said former U.S. president Theodore Roosevelt, who, like Warren, was an enthusiastic Protestant as well as a Freemason.

With British forces approaching the Holy City, the Ottoman governor fled, delegating the job of immediate surrender to the Arab mayor "for fear that these deadly bombs will hit the holy places." In fact, Allenby had been careful to avoid just that. On December 11, he dismounted to walk through Jaffa Gate, in carefully orchestrated contrast to Kaiser Wilhelm II's grand entrance on horseback two decades before. The British officer T. E. Lawrence, fresh from Arabia and wearing a borrowed brass hat, said that Allenby's stroll on foot into Jerusalem was "for me the supreme moment of the war."

The British Army marched into a hungry and destitute city of fewer than sixty thousand residents, though there was enough food for one British officer to notice that "the indescribable smell of Jerusalem rose up to meet us, a mixture of spices and sweet herbs, strange eastern cooking and dried fruits, camels and native garments and open drains."

Allenby made a brief statement to assembled dignitaries, declaring martial law but promising to protect all religious sites and "the existing customs and beliefs of those to whose faiths they are sacred." With this assurance, he went to lunch with French, Italian, and American diplomats, including François Georges-Picot.

The French negotiator, together with his British colleague Mark Sykes, had helped draft a secret British-French agreement to divide up the Middle East between the two European powers, placing Jerusalem under an international administration. "Tomorrow my dear general, I will take the necessary steps to set up civil government in this town," Georges-Picot told Allenby as the meal was served.

"Salad and chicken mayonnaise and foie gras sandwiches hung in our mouths unmunched while we turned our round eyes on Allenby and waited," recalled Lawrence.

The general, known for his quick temper, turned red with anger. He made it clear to the French diplomat that Jerusalem was now under his control until such time as it became a civilian government. "The City Placed Under British Rule" read that day's London *Times*. It would remain that way for precisely four decades, a colonial possession under the fig leaf of a League of Nations mandate. The long European scramble for the jewel of the Holy Land was over. Jerusalem—above- and belowground, for better and for worse—belonged to Britain now.

But the long-sought prize would prove a poison pill. The same day that Allenby hosted the luncheon, Sykes gave a talk in Manchester as church bells rang with news that the Holy City was in British hands. The Balfour Declaration made amends for two millennia of Christian persecution of Jews, he said. But he added that the forces unleashed by the decision could be "the beginning of bitterer strife than ever the world has known." And that strife, he cautioned, would be sparked in Jerusalem, which he called "inflammable ground where a careless word or gesture might set half a continent aflame."

• • •

THE NEW MILITARY GOVERNOR, an Arabic-speaking bureaucrat named Ronald Storrs, was the son of an Anglican priest. After halting a typhus outbreak and providing adequate food for the suffering populace, he moved quickly to protect a city of "invincible and unutterable attraction" by imposing strict building standards, reviving traditional crafts, and ordering conservation efforts at important sites.

Storrs had worked closely with Lawrence—a trained archaeologist—

during the war, and one of his roommates had been Howard Carter, who soon would become world-famous for finding King Tutankhamen's tomb. With the governor's encouragement, a group of academicians met in London in May 1918 to create the British School of Archaeology in Jerusalem. Unlike the Palestine Exploration Fund, this organization would seek more than biblical remains. A subsequent notice declared that "in addition to Hebrew and Jewish sites and antiquities, the school would include within its scope the Canaanite, Graeco-Roman, Byzantine, Arab, and Medieval periods." They also agreed that "no modern religious or political question nor any personal matter of religious persuasion will be allowed to affect the policy of the School."

Yet there was no keeping politics and religion out of the Holy Land. Both Allenby and the archbishop of Canterbury, as well as Sir Herbert Samuel, the high commissioner for Palestine and a well-known Zionist leader, were on the new board, while a British Jewish historian served as secretary. No Palestinian Arabs, Christian or Muslim, were part of the leadership, although Storrs created the Pro-Jerusalem Society as a "committee of the three races" to preserve antiquities and improve infrastructure.

French and American academics would be allies in peace as their nations had been in the preceding war, and the school would work closely with the new Palestine Department of Antiquities, also founded by Storrs, who became civil governor in 1920. Germans were not welcome, and with the czar assassinated and Lenin in charge in Moscow, Russian interest in Jerusalem had ceased abruptly.

Expectations were high that with the collapse of the Ottoman Empire and the arrival of the British, Jerusalem and the Holy Land would become an archaeological hotspot. "When the conditions which at present rule us relax their hold, we may hope to see the veil withdrawn from that mysterious past which has ever tantalized and fascinated the world," the new school's vice president, an Anglican cleric and archaeologist with the memorable name of W. J. Phythian-Adams, told the *New York Times* in 1921.

There was no more tantalizing place than the Noble Sanctuary, which now was fully under British authority. "Excellent minds demand that, once the war has finished and Palestine has been placed under the aegis of a civilized protectorate, science should have access to the Haram," Weill had written to Rothschild, referring to the platform's Arabic name, Haram al-Sharif. He relished "cutting into the old paving, hewing galleries and trenches, and thus finally discovering the depths of the thousand-year-old fill" containing uncounted biblical secrets. Evidence for Solomon's temple was still to be found, as well as the sanctuary destroyed in 70 CE.

Weill was quick to add that this dream was "a dangerous fantasy." This was no abandoned ruin but a vital sacred site. "One excavates a dead city, a place abandoned by humans," he added. "For as one dissects a corpse, one uncovers a skeleton, and the Haram of Jerusalem, whether one exalts it or deplores it, is a living person."

Apart from a brief Masonic ritual performed in the cave under the Dome of the Rock by New Zealand soldiers at the start of the occupation, the British were careful not to disturb the site's sanctity. Indian Muslim soldiers were posted to guard the platform. Storrs convinced Muslim clerics to allow architects and conservationists to study and restore its buildings, which in the last decades of Ottoman rule had fallen into disrepair. Excavations, however, remained off-limits.

"Any proved Christian or Jewish encroachment upon the Precincts of the Haram al-Sharif in Jerusalem would still kindle a fire which might blaze from Alexandria to Aswan," Storrs warned, referring to British-controlled Egypt. Even without such a dig, the situation was explosive. On the fourth anniversary of the Balfour Declaration, in November 1921, four Jews and one Arab were killed in a vicious riot.

In 1922, news of King Tut's tomb and the Royal Graves of Ur in Mesopotamia—also under Britain's suzerainty—generated a media frenzy. Jerusalem, however, remained on the sidelines. With the Noble Sanctuary off-limits, the possibility of dramatic discoveries receded. Finding the Ark or a stash of valuable temple artifacts no longer seemed plausible. The chairman of the Palestine Exploration Fund found it necessary to explain that "it was not expected" that a planned dig on the ridge south of the platform would yield "treasures of gold."

Weill returned the following year to continue his work on what he still believed was the tomb of David, but found little to back up his assertion of a decade prior. "One cannot know for sure for which prince—David himself, or one of his first Judean successors—this narrow opening with its funerary bed was cut into the mountain," he concluded. There was still no direct evidence outside of the Bible for the existence of either David or Solomon, much less their treasure-filled tombs. He prophetically predicted, however, that excavators had "only lifted a corner of the veil that covers the Davidic hill."

Two British archaeologists excavated in that area in 1925, further confirming Bliss's identification of the area as that of ancient Zion. A second major dig within the citadel near Jaffa Gate revealed parts of what appeared to be King Herod's palace from the first century BCE. These were only 2 of 140 recorded excavations that took place in Jerusalem before World War II broke out in 1939. Most, however, preceded new construction and were small in scale.

In 1925, the first courses in archaeology were offered at the city's new Jewish institute of higher learning, Hebrew University, that was funded in part by Rothschild; a full department was created three years later. Many of the early Jewish archaeologists arrived in Palestine with advanced degrees from European universities, but soon there was a rising generation of homegrown excavators schooled in biblical archaeology.

There was no comparable Arab institute. Christian and Muslim Palestinians educated within the old empire or in Europe typically chose professions like law or medicine. Excavations from de Saulcy to Parker had done little to inspire local Arab confidence in the profession, and digging was associated with lower-status blue-collar labor. Despite this, half of the six inspectors employed by Palestine's Department of Antiquities in the 1920s and '30s were Arabs. Only two had university degrees, but Arab scholars contributed roughly the same number of articles to the department's quarterly publication as did those who were Jewish.

Tellingly, most of the Arab research focused on aboveground cultural heritage rather than belowground archaeology. This reflected another, more subtle barrier that kept Arabs from pursuing archaeology with the same passion as Christian and Jewish Westerners. Sari Nusseibeh, a former president of al-Quds University as well as a philosopher and modern-day Palestinian activist, said that barrier remains largely in place. He explained that for the Arabs of Jerusalem—whether in the nineteenth, twentieth, or twenty-first century—one's heritage exists within, not below.

"Look around here, and you see people who build their houses on top of ancient remains," added Nusseibeh, whose Muslim family retains the keys to the Holy Sepulchre. "They know something is underneath, but they look upon themselves as a natural stage of evolution of that long history. You will become another layer, so they have no interest in digging into that history; you are an outgrowth of what came before, but your interest is in yourself and your time."

In other words, excavating a cistern or searching for treasure might make sense to Jerusalem's Arabs, but excavating to find your heritage did not. You *were* your heritage, and there was no need to find that which you had not lost. This profound cultural divide between Westerners and Arabs—and, later, between Israeli Jews and Palestinian Arabs—would grow wider in generations to come, with devastating consequences for all those involved.

• • •

THE BALFOUR DECLARATION WAS a major victory for both Jewish and Christian Zionists. Weizmann exulted that "Palestine should become as Jewish as England is English." But it came as a rude shock to Arabs, whom the British had encouraged to break from the Ottomans during the war with the promise of future independence. These two policies encouraging a homeland for two peoples in one place lit a fuse that would explode a half century later in war.

Relations between Jerusalem's Jewish and Muslim communities had a complicated past that had seesawed between tolerance and oppression. Not until well into the nineteenth century could Jewish residents claim most of the rights of their Muslim neighbors. Yet Islamic rule had proved more beneficent than that of Christians, who continued to blame Jews for the death of Jesus. The Byzantines and, later, the Crusaders persecuted and expelled them from Jerusalem.

Each time Muslims gained power, they had allowed Jews to return. In a telling rite performed at the death of an Ottoman sultan in the mid-nineteenth century, they even gave them control of the city. An Italian resident described the chief rabbi requesting the keys to the city from the governor when word of the sultan's passing reached Jerusalem. The pasha duly delivered them publicly at the door of the rabbi's residence. The two men shared refreshments for an hour, and the rabbi then restored the keys to the pasha. "So, in 1861," the Italian wrote, "the Jewish nation possessed for one hour the keys of Jerusalem, which were delivered over to them by the Arabs in consequence of the unvarying tradition which they had preserved."

By the end of World War I, the majority of Jews in the Holy City were no longer the Arabic- or Ladino-speaking Sephardim familiar to local Arabs. Yiddish-speaking Europeans were now dominant, and in many ways they had more in common with European Christian colonizers than with the Jews who had lived in Jerusalem for generations. "All of a sudden, a Jew in Arab Palestinian eyes became the European, the intruder from a different ethnic community which was contesting [ownership of] the land," one historian wrote.

Tension between the two peoples centered on the Wailing Wall. The courtyard was located in the heart of the Mughrabi Quarter, founded by Saladin, the sultan and liberator of Jerusalem from the Christian Crusaders in 1187. He awarded the area to his North African veterans who had fought in the campaign. Muslim pilgrims and immigrants from North Africa and Spain flocked to the neighborhood, where they could feel at home with the dialects, foods, and traditions of their distant homelands. The area was owned by one of the city's first waqfs, or religious endowments.

When the Ottomans conquered Jerusalem three centuries later, Sultan Suleiman the Magnificent ordered construction of the courtyard facing the high platform wall, though whether this was to accommodate Jewish or Muslim prayer—or both—is uncertain. It was a small space, only a quarter the size of a tennis court, with different meanings for the two religions. For Muslims, it celebrated the wall where Muhammad's steed, al-Buraq, had been tethered. It also became the preferred place for Jews to mourn the temple's 70 CE destruction. As they subsequently arrived in larger numbers, many settled just to the west of the Mughrabi neighborhood in what became known as the Jewish Quarter.

To reach what they called the Wailing Wall, Jewish worshippers had to thread their way through an area that was home to two mosques and a few elegant buildings, like those of the Abu Saud compound. Most of the neighborhood, however, retained the rural air of a Moroccan village, with chickens and goats foraging among low-slung houses. Local residents grew to resent what they saw as noisy intruders and sometimes resorted to harassment.

"While I was praying, I had an idea," said Baron Rothschild during an 1887 visit. He found "the squalid surroundings" to be "heart-rending and insulting," so he tried to buy the entire quarter for a million francs—roughly $10 million today—and relocate its Arab inhabitants in better accommodations. "Let us raze these hovels to the ground" and replace them with a plaza or "beautiful park." After lengthy negotiations, Rothschild's proposal, like a similar one made by Montefiore a decade before, failed.

In 1911, soon after the upheaval caused by Parker's excavation, Jewish worshippers at the wall brought a few chairs into the small courtyard. Anywhere else in the world, this would have been less than a trifling detail. But in Jerusalem, it was a grave and weighty matter. The head of the Muslim waqf that owned the site complained to Ottoman authorities that this was "contrary to usage," and an administrative council agreed that allowing chairs might suggest Jewish ownership.

The limitation rankled Ashkenazi Jews in particular. They had begun to see the huge stones of the Wailing Wall as a national as well as religious symbol. "When your feet enter the courtyard of the Wall, here you feel and experience the re-weaving of your soul into the eternal fabric of two thousand years," wrote the Russian Jewish author Zalman Shazar of his first visit to the site the same year. "The tears have all flowed from the hearts of one people, they have all come from one source and they will all pray to One."

In April 1918, Weizmann tried to broker another deal to buy the Mughrabi Quarter, this time for 70,000 British pounds, or about $5 million today. He was no more successful than Rothschild had been, so Weizmann turned to British foreign secretary Balfour. Places of worship were all in the hands of Christians and Muslims, and "even the Wailing Wall is not really ours," he wrote, adding that "our most sacred site, in our most sacred city, is in the hands of some doubtful Mogrhreb religious community" and "surrounded by a group of miserable, dirty cottages and derelict buildings, which make the whole place from a hygienic point of view a positive danger."

But the British were unwilling to alter the status quo, fearing that violence would result.

Muslim Arabs took to driving donkeys through the court to harass Jewish worshippers. In 1929, on the day when Jews lament the destruction of both Solomon's and Herod's temples, angry Zionists demonstrated in large numbers in the courtyard, waving Zionist flags and singing Zionist anthems. Muslims responded to what they saw as provocation with violence. Subsequent riots left more than 250 Jews and Arabs dead.

This bloody incident prompted the League of Nations to order Britain to appoint an international commission to investigate. The Jewish delegation recommended that the entire Mughrabi Quarter be vacated, a suggestion that the outraged Muslim delegation claimed revealed Jewish intentions to "lay hands by degrees on the Holy Places of the Muslims and to become the masters of the country." The panel ultimately concluded that while Jews owned neither the wall nor the area at its base, they were free to access it "for the purpose of devotions at all times."

Restrictions applied to both sides. Jews were forbidden from blowing their ceremonial ram's horn trumpet, called the shofar; Muslims were ordered to stop all harassment of the worshippers and forbidden from praying at the site. These findings were adopted by the British government, but the conflict only intensified. The wall was no longer simply another Jerusalem holy site. It was the stony symbol of the national ambitions of two peoples.

It was also a stalking horse for a bigger prize: the sacred platform itself. "The Temple Mount is Israel's eternal holy place, and even should it be under the hand of others for long days and periods of time, it will finally come to our hands," said the chief Ashkenazi rabbi, Avraham Kook, in 1920. Such talk prompted Jerusalem's grand mufti, Hajj Amin al-Husseini, to assert that the tears of Jewish worshippers "do not arise from their love of the Wall itself, but from their concealed aspirations to take control of the Noble Sanctuary."

When the British killed an anti-Zionist Muslim imam in 1935, Palestinian Arabs revolted against both British control and the growing influx of Jews and the rise of Jewish militias. "An irrepressible conflict has arisen between two national communities within the narrow bounds of one small country," stated a 1937 British commission that investigated the cause of the rebellion. "About 1,000,000 Arabs are in strife, open or latent, with some 400,000 Jews. There is no common ground between them."

The grand mufti sought assistance from Nazi Germany in the hope that Hitler would help rid them of their common foes, the British and the Jews. German attempts to capture the Holy Land during World War II failed, even as Jewish militants continued their efforts to secure a permanent foothold in Palestine and Jerusalem through a campaign of shootings and bombings.

Yet for some secular Zionists, Jerusalem was a historical ball and chain they would have readily traded for Palestinian land to create a socialist paradise of collective farms. "I would not accept the Old City even if they gave it to me for free," said Weizmann. But he also noted that "there are now two sorts of countries in the world, those that want to expel the Jews and those that don't want to admit them."

The Holocaust, which began in earnest four years later, would intensify both the conflict and Jewish attitudes toward Jerusalem and its past.

· · ·

BY 1945, the devastation wrought by Nazi Germany had created millions of Jewish refugees on top of the six million killed, increasing Jewish demands for their own state. Britain's hold on Palestine and the city became increasingly untenable. Two years later, Britain relinquished the jewel it had worked so hard to obtain.

The United Nations approved creation of a Jewish and an Arab state in Palestine, with Jerusalem to be administered by an international regime. As it had in the wake of World War I, such a regime proved chimerical. When British forces withdrew in May 1948, Israel announced its independence. Arab armies from around the region immediately attacked; some ten thousand Jews and some seven hundred thousand Palestinians fled or were forced to leave their homes during the fighting.

Jordanian forces besieged and bombed Jerusalem's Jewish Quarter and evicted its residents, while Jewish forces moved quickly to secure land both inside and outside the boundary set by the United Nations. The bitter battle made Jerusalem nonnegotiable. "It is the City of God, the seat of our ancient sanctuary," declared Weizmann, now the provisional president of the Israeli state, in December 1948. "But it is also the capital of David and Solomon, the City of the Great King, the metropolis of our ancient commonwealth." While Christians and Muslims held it sacred, "to us it is that and more than that. It is the centre of our ancient national glory."

A 1949 armistice drew a line through Jerusalem. The western section, in the more modern part of the city where most Jews had lived, became the capital of Israel, while the Jordanians occupied the Old City and eastern neighborhoods, which contained the bulk of the city's Arab population as well as religious shrines and archaeologically rich territory. Barbed wire, mines, and guardhouses lined the new border, which passed along a section of the Ottoman-era walls. A dozen years before the Soviets built the Berlin Wall, Jerusalem became the world's most divided city.

The war and the wall also put an end to the Palestine Department of Antiquities, which briefly had united both Arab and Jewish scholars in the search for understanding Jerusalem's history. The Hashemite kingdom of Jordan, ruled from its capital of Amman, less than fifty miles east of the Holy City, was now in charge of the most ancient parts of the fractured town. The only excavations that took place in the first dozen years of Jordanian control, however, were military trenches. That changed in 1961, when a fifty-five-year-old British excavator launched "one of the last great imperial digs" to celebrate the centennial of the Palestine Exploration Fund.

Kathleen Kenyon is now considered the most influential woman archaeologist of the twentieth century—and, by some, the century's greatest field excavator. The pious Anglican daughter of a British Museum director, she embraced a new method of digging small trenches and carefully mapping layers of soil that allowed for more precise dating.

Confident that she could use this approach to find the still-missing City of David, she set to work with a team of Silwan workers on the slopes of the ridge extending south of the Noble Sanctuary. Jerusalem's subterranean scramble, however, frustrated even the savvy Kenyon. Like Parker and Vincent, she found plenty of walls and fortifications dating to the millennium before the Israelite arrival. But Kenyon uncovered nothing clearly tied to the days of David and Solomon.

Her last excavation season came to a temporary halt on June 5, 1967, when tensions between Israel and its Arab neighbors suddenly exploded into war. Israel knocked out Egypt's air force and, when Jordan attacked, Israeli forces rapidly captured East Jerusalem as well as the territory as far east as the Jordan River, an area known as the West Bank. It was all over in six days, giving the war its name.

Though Kenyon bitterly protested the Israeli occupation, Israeli authorities allowed her to resume her work. (She was, however, careful to get permission as well from Jordan's government, which still claimed the territory as its own.) Two weeks before she wrapped up the dig, she unearthed a cave near the underground spring crammed with fragments of more than thirteen hundred pottery vessels, including incense burners and figurines of animals, clothed women, and male riders; all had been smashed around the eighth century BCE. The remains—apparently from a popular sacred site—were from a century or two after the presumed arrival of the Israelites, but no dig in the area had ever produced such large numbers of artifacts. The surprising find demonstrated that the heavily explored ridge still contained unplumbed secrets.

Kenyon's departure in the fall of 1967 marked the end of a century of archaeology dominated by Western Christians. The era's formal burial was held in a garden not far from Jaffa Gate that had marked the tense border between East and West Jerusalem, and between Jew and Arab. It is a tradition among archaeologists to leave something contemporary behind—a coin, a wine bottle—so later excavators would know they were there, and when. As Kenyon watched, tears in her eyes, workers pushed her beloved but battered old wood-paneled Pontiac station wagon into one of her archaeological trenches. A bulldozer then covered it with earth.

Now it was the Israelis' turn.

PART II

The Doorkeepers of Zion,
They do not always stand
In helmet and whole armour,
With halberds in their hand;
But, being sure of Zion,
And all her mysteries,
They rest awhile in Zion,
Sit down and smile in Zion;
Ay, even jest in Zion;
In Zion, at their ease.

—RUDYARD KIPLING

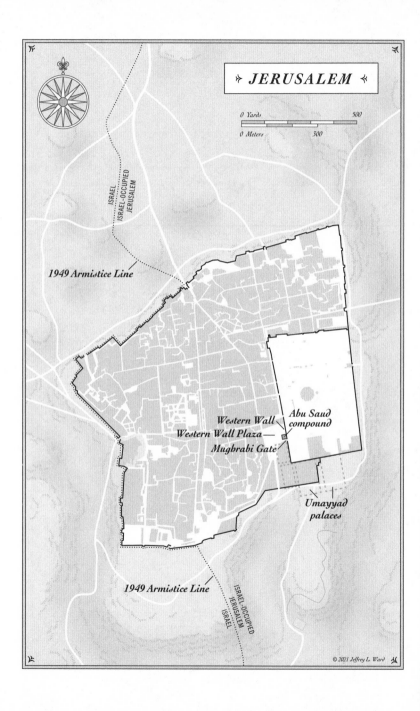

JERUSALEM

0 Yards   500
0 Meters   300

ISRAEL
ISRAEL-OCCUPIED JERUSALEM

1949 Armistice Line

Western Wall
Western Wall Plaza —
Mughrabi Gate

Abu Saud
compound

Umayyad
palaces

1949 Armistice Line

ISRAEL-OCCUPIED JERUSALEM
ISRAEL

© 2021 Jeffrey L. Ward

9

Exalting the Walls

The stone's alive with what's invisible.
—SEAMUS HEANEY

W e entered the Old City and headed straight for the Western Wall," wrote Israel's first prime minister, David Ben-Gurion, in his diary on June 8, 1967. The day before, Israeli troops had captured East Jerusalem, including the ridge where Kenyon had been digging. For the first time since a Persian invasion more than fourteen centuries earlier, the keys to the Holy City were truly in Jewish hands.

When he arrived, Ben-Gurion recoiled at the presence of a latrine against the sacred stones. "Aren't you ashamed? Look, a toilet next to the Wall!" he barked at National Parks Authority chief Yaakov Yanai. Then he spotted a plaque in colorful Armenian tile identifying the street as "Al Buraq Road" in Arabic and English. The Wailing Wall was mentioned, but only in English, and then only in parentheses.

"I said that first of all this sign should be removed," the former prime minister recalled. A soldier used his bayonet (Ben-Gurion said it was a stick) to dislodge the offending ceramic marker, but he was told to stop when it seemed likely to damage the ancient stones. Another soldier brought an axe and completed the job. It was, Ben-Gurion said later, "the greatest moment of my life since I came to Israel."

That evening, West Jerusalem's mayor, Teddy Kollek, convened a meeting at his home with political, academic, and military officials to determine the fate of the surrounding quarter that had offended Jews for so many decades. In his 1978 autobiography, Kollek wrote that "something had to be done about the small slum houses that crowded close to the Western Wall—the Moghrabi Quarter. The one area that should have been spacious and bright was cramped and dark." Israeli authorities, he added, were encouraging the public to come to the site on the upcoming June 14 Jewish holiday of Shavuot. Hundreds of thousands of celebrants were expected from all over Israel.

"My overpowering feeling was: do it now; it may be impossible to do it later, and it must be done." After a century of foiled Jewish attempts to buy the area from its Arab inhabitants and demolish their homes, Kollek saw a narrow window in which he could sweep away an entire neighborhood in a single night.

One of those present at Kollek's home that evening was the architect Arieh Sharon (not to be confused with the later prime minister, Ariel Sharon), who had designed the Israeli Pavilion at the 1967 World's Fair in Montreal. As the others watched, he sketched on a loose piece of paper the boundaries of a large plaza that would replace the medieval quarter. Sharon then signed the sketch—the only official document of the decision—as did Yanai and several others.

Among the signatories was the lone archaeologist present, sixty-two-year-old Michael Avi-Yonah. A respected academic who taught at Hebrew University of Jerusalem, he had excavated near the Mughrabi Quarter in the 1930s and was deeply familiar with the city's history. Neither he nor any of the others are recorded as having opposed the destruction of a long-established urban area dotted with significant religious buildings, some of which dated back nearly a thousand years.

Israel had signed the Geneva Conventions, which prohibits demolition in occupied territory unless "such destruction is rendered necessary by military operations." Kollek's intention was plainly to bulldoze the area to allow for greater ease of religious worship. He was aware the move could spark a worldwide outcry, so he asked Jerusalem's local association of Jewish building contractors to conduct the operation swiftly and secretly at night.

"Tell the workers that they should stop the work only on the direct order of Teddy Kollek," the mayor recalled saying, "and I will make sure that I am unavailable until the work is finished."

On the evening of Saturday, June 10, after the Sabbath was over, some fifteen workmen made their way through the quarter's narrow alleys to the Wailing Wall. Their first task was to rip out the toilets. "I was sky-high,"

Sasson Levy, one of their number, told a reporter later. "It was a pleasure." The team attacked the structure "with a sense of historic mission and mystical feelings," noted the historian Shmuel Bahat. But their tools proved ineffective on the hard stone. One of the contractors brought in a tractor to speed up the process, and then two Israeli military bulldozers arrived to assist in the effort.

Using megaphones, military officials told the quarter's residents—numbering 650 people by some estimates—that they had fifteen minutes to leave their homes. One Israeli contractor said the refugees were herded out of the Old City through Zion Gate, rather than nearby Dung Gate. This has symbolic importance, he added, "because through this gate they took out the refugees of the Jewish Quarter" in the 1948 war.

The forced relocation and the quarter's demolition marked "the settling of historic accounts," concluded Meron Benvenisti, who later served as Kollek's deputy mayor. Israelis had been outraged to find the Jewish Quarter's three dozen religious schools and places of worship nearly all destroyed. Jordan maintained the damage took place during the 1948 conflict, while Israel insisted the quarter's Jewish heritage was systematically targeted in the aftermath.

A 1972 report by the Ministry of Religions provides a vivid account of the midnight destruction that Kollek ordered: "Bulldozers pounded with a deafening roar upon the Mughrabi neighborhood" with "their fangs extended and their steel teeth taking bites of the small, meager, densely packed houses and the fences of courtyards and alleys." Clouds of dust rose in the night "as houses, domes, arches, and the vaults of alleyways collapsed and crashed to the ground."

By 3:00 a.m., four hours after the work began, the rubble of 135 buildings lay in heaps. Among the demolished structures was the twelfth-century al-Madrasa al-Afdaliyya, the religious law school funded by Saladin's son, later transformed into a Sufi tomb, that had formed the historic core of the quarter.

A small mosque near the wall dedicated to al-Buraq also was destroyed. "Why shouldn't the mosque be sent to heaven, just as the magic horse did?" said Major Eitan Ben-Moshe, the Israeli military engineer who led the demolition effort. He was mocking the Islamic tradition, though inaccurately, since in the legend the steed had remained tethered to the wall.

At least one person—an elderly woman identified as Rasmiyyah Ali Taba'aki—died from injuries sustained when her home was bulldozed.

In a 1999 interview, Ben-Moshe revealed that a total of three bodies were recovered from the rubble, which he said he took to a West Jerusalem hospital. He claimed that other corpses were buried close to the Wall in unmarked graves; these were later excavated by archaeologists. Ben-Moshe added that he was ordered by his military superiors to take responsibility for the destruction in case of international outrage, but was assured that any prison sentence he incurred as a result would be commuted.

Their work complete, the jubilant contractors agreed to found the "Order of the Kotel"—the Hebrew name of the wall as it is often abbreviated—to celebrate their unofficial role in having "purified the Kotel plaza for the people of Israel."

On June 12, the *Jerusalem Post* reported that "yesterday afternoon a bulldozer was overturning the last of the houses. Protruding from the rubble were beds and bedding, other items of furniture and kitchen utensils, food and shoes, presumably abandoned by those who had fled the area during the fighting for the city. When the general public is admitted to the area sometime later this week they will find that the slum buildings which had cluttered the place for more than a century have been razed."

The article also noted that Baron Edmond de Rothschild, a grandson of the man who had tried to buy the quarter decades before, was "among those who came to see the demolition work."

Later that day, Kollek reported to Ben-Gurion "that he had the buildings removed that the Arabs constructed next to the Western Wall." But the Israeli leader neglected to mention in his corresponding diary entry that the demolition involved the *entire* quarter, a striking omission. In subsequent days, other workers arrived to create a level space for the new plaza, first envisioned by nineteenth-century Jews. Mughrabi residents meanwhile snuck back to the ruins to retrieve what personal items they could find.

The sole surviving buildings were clustered around Mughrabi Gate, which led from the neighborhood onto the sacred platform. These included elaborate structures dating to the Mamluk era, which lasted from 1260 to 1516. They were spared not because of their architectural and historical significance but to avoid disrupting the structural stability of the gate itself, the sole entrance to the Noble Sanctuary for non-Muslims. The complex also happened to be the family compound of the Abu Sauds, descendants of those who had tangled with Charles Warren a century before.

Like Checkpoint Charlie in then–Cold War Berlin, Mughrabi Gate now marked a tense border between two warring worlds. One was centered on the sacred Islamic site of the Noble Sanctuary and the other was the Wailing Wall, now transformed from a narrow corridor into a vast space nearly two football fields in size. It was dubbed the Western Wall Plaza, since the time for mourning was over, and it became an open-air synagogue as well as the heart of the Israeli state.

After the fact, Israel's justice minister deemed the demolition of the Mughrabi Quarter to be illegal, but he let the matter drop. By Shavuot in June, more than two hundred thousand euphoric Israeli Jews had crowded into the new space, which was still strewn around the edges with heaps of rubble.

The following year, the government sent formal eviction notices to each displaced family and offered to pay a sum amounting to a few hundred dollars; some agreed to take the money and even thanked Kollek, while others refused. In response to an international outcry, the government provided the United Nations with documents from East Jerusalem's municipal files showing the Mughrabi Quarter had been a threat to public health; they blamed the Jordanian government for allowing the area to deteriorate. Critics were not convinced.

By the time the eviction notices were sent, however, a new conflict had engulfed the Western Wall area. This bitter struggle would rage for two decades, yet it involved neither Christians nor Muslims.

◆ ◆ ◆

THE BULLDOZING OF the Mughrabi Quarter had provided archaeologists with a once-in-a-millennium opportunity to unearth an enormous area in the heart of the Old City. Despite a century of excavations, researchers had glimpsed only a tiny fraction of what lay under the walled town. Benjamin Mazar leapt at the unique chance.

The sixty-one-year-old archaeologist was by then a famous figure in Israel. The Polish-born academic had conducted the first official digs by a Jewish organization in Palestine and received the first Israeli dig license, in 1948. Later he was president of Hebrew University; his late brother-in-law Yitzhak Ben-Zvi had served as the nation's only three-term president.

Mayor Kollek backed Mazar's idea of investigating beneath the Old City, promising to provide a modest 50,000 Israeli pounds—about $15,000 today—to get the work started. Securing a dig permit from Israel's small

Department of Archaeology seemed a simple matter. "The dream of every archaeologist is within reach!" Mazar jubilantly told his young colleague Meir Ben-Dov, just days after the Six-Day War's end. Ben-Dov replied without hesitation, "When do we start?" Mazar smiled. "Yesterday!"

In fact it would be nine months before they could put a spade into the soil. Both the Jordanians and the United Nations opposed any excavations. But it wasn't these opponents who mattered. Mazar's true foes were his own country's religious leaders.

Israel had two preeminent Jewish clerics: Rabbi Yitzhak Nissim represented the Sephardic community and Rabbi Isser Yehuda Unterman led the Ashkenazi community. The religious men and the secular archaeologists each had their own competing designs on the Old City. The rabbis wanted the Ministry of Religions to gain jurisdiction over the coveted Western Wall site; officials like Kollek argued in favor of the National Parks Authority, which controlled West Jerusalem's ancient sites. If the rabbis won, then archaeologists like Mazar would face an uphill fight in pursuing excavations.

To Mazar's dismay, the Israeli prime minister in July granted the rabbis full control over the Western Wall area. By September, workers from the Ministry of Religions were digging along the base of the wall, exposing two levels of stone long hidden underground and creating a more dramatic impression for visitors.

Despite the obvious scientific value of the site, archaeologists were forbidden from taking part in the work. A protest by Israel's antiquities department succeeded in securing only a temporary halt to the effort. Mazar was told he had to obtain approval from Nissim and Unterman to pursue his dream of excavating beneath what had been the Mughrabi Quarter.

Mazar launched a charm campaign to win them over, shuttling between their homes and "drinking steaming Turkish coffee and quaffing glasses of hot tea with home-baked cakes," recalled Ben-Dov, who became his deputy. According to him, Nissim told Mazar that he feared archaeological discoveries might contradict Jewish texts, and even threatened to organize mass demonstrations to prevent any digs. Unterman's concerns were quite different. The Ashkenazi leader worried the team would uncover temple treasures, including the Ark of the Covenant. This, he explained to a thoroughly puzzled Mazar, could not happen until the arrival of the Messiah.

The rabbis, meanwhile, pressed their advantage. In an October 7 letter to the Ministerial Committee on the Holy Places, Nissim argued that the Abu Saud compound by the Mughrabi Gate should be demolished. The religions minister, Zerah Wahrhaftig, concurred, arguing that evicting the twenty or so Arab families still living in the Abu Saud complex was a humanitarian act, since they were "suffering in their homes along the Wall" and that "children could not grow properly under such conditions."

Kollek and Mazar protested, though not out of empathy for the residents. They feared the demolition was part of a strategy by the rabbis to extend their control far beyond the plaza. They had reason to worry. In November 1967, Nissim and Unterman backed a prohibition on any archaeological digs until the surviving Mughrabi buildings were demolished and a long-term plan for the Western Wall Plaza was in place.

The clerics ordered a new round of excavations, this time to expose the lower courses of the southern wall, around the corner from the Western Wall Plaza. Nissim wrote that his goal was not archaeology but to "glorify and exalt the walls" by exposing their full height. He explained that this would ensure the area "would remain in its sublime sanctity and that its primary purpose as a place of worship would be preserved."

His goal, in effect, was to maintain the ban on scientific research imposed by the Ottomans, even though there was no Jewish tradition that the southern wall itself was sacred. Only grudgingly did the rabbis allow limited archaeological supervision of the dig. But they agreed to this only on the condition that the archaeologists not interfere with their project.

By the start of 1968, the rabbis appeared to have won the struggle to keep some of the city's most prime ancient real estate beyond the reach of archaeologists. "Each day I made a habit of touring around the Temple Mount," said Ben-Dov, "both to plan our own excavation and to keep an eye on what was going on there." He and Mazar continued to lobby government officials, and the antiquities department eventually relented: It agreed to lift its insistence that the archaeologists first obtain rabbinical permission to dig. Elated, the men began to plan an excavation south of the platform's southern wall.

When the chief rabbis heard this alarming news, they convened an emergency meeting. In a memo prepared for the gathering, Nissim said he opposed "turning the place into an archaeological site, with professionals whose sole interest is their research and historical curiosity." The best he would offer them was the chance to "observe" digging conducted by the

Ministry of Religions. Sanctity, he added, trumped science. "A license for archaeological excavations at a holy place cannot be granted without the consent of the relevant religious authorities," concluded a senior ministry official.

On February 23, 1968, Jordan's UN representative, Muhammad El-Farra, tried to halt any and all excavations. He wrote to the UN secretary-general that the demolition of the Mughrabi Quarter and creation of a square facing the Western Wall amounted to "naked aggression" against Muslims that violated the Geneva Conventions. He also complained that it contradicted a UN resolution ordering Israel to "desist forthwith from taking any action which would alter the status of Jerusalem." That protest barely registered in Israel, as tensions between the archaeologists and Jewish religious leaders reached a boiling point.

Ben-Dov later said that he conceived of a bait-and-switch plan to distract the turf-conscious rabbis. The only building close to the southern wall of the Temple Mount was a girls' school built under Jordanian rule just south of the platform's southwest corner. The one-story structure had since been vacated and was slated to be torn down. In the meantime, the municipality had granted Nissim use of the building for the Great Rabbinical Court.

Ben-Dov paid a visit to Kollek, who was staunchly opposed to the growing power of the religious leaders. The mayor handed the young archaeologist a handwritten note giving the dig team permission to use empty portions of the school as their excavation office. "My new strategy was to try to shift their attention away from the struggle against the archaeological dig to another issue, namely, use of the building," Ben-Dov later wrote.

On the leap day of 1968, fifteen of Mazar's workers gathered at sunrise outside the deserted school. The archaeologists gave instructions for the men to mark out squares to prepare for digging. When the building's charwoman arrived, Mazar brandished Kollek's note, and she dutifully handed over the door key. The first rabbinical court employee arrived at 8:00 a.m. to find the archaeologists settled into their new offices. He telephoned Nissim with the disturbing news.

The rabbi arrived minutes later and demanded the excavators leave the building immediately. "Before long the civil altercation between us had burgeoned into a full-blown dispute," recalled Ben-Dov. The argument ended with the rabbi storming off in fury. Minister of Religions Wahrhaftig then arrived, "followed by a stream of other officials" who begged and cajoled the archaeologists to vacate the premises. "No one breathed a word about the dig," which was already well underway just outside the windows, said the archaeologist. Mazar and Ben-Dov refused to budge, in the hope that within a few days the digs would be too advanced to halt.

By the following day, news of the excavation drew workers assigned by the Ministry of Labor as well as a score of volunteers. Negotiations over the use of the building by the archaeologists dragged on as the excavation quickly became a fact on the ground. Once they were confident their work could not be stopped, Mazar and Ben-Dov conceded to the rabbinical court two of the four schoolrooms they had commandeered.

The rabbis and the minister then tried to halt the excavations, and Nissim even took his campaign on the road, traveling to the United States to drum up opposition, but his efforts proved futile. His fear that the archaeologists could undermine Jewish claims to Jerusalem was prophetic. Ben-Dov soon made a discovery so politically explosive that it was nearly wiped out before it could come to public light.

◆ ◆ ◆

"REMAIN IN JERUSALEM, money will be paid to your account this week." This was the telegram from London that Charles Warren had received in November 1867. The eccentric British officer celebrated by standing on his head on the broad slope beneath the southern wall of the Noble Sanctuary, "where the ground was built up for the cultivation of the most splendid cauliflowers I have ever seen."

One of the most densely occupied parts of ancient Jerusalem remained, a century later, largely unoccupied. When the government of Jordan decided to build the girls' school near the southwestern corner of the platform in the early 1960s, they asked Kenyon and the French friar Roland de Vaux, a protegé of Vincent at the École Biblique, to excavate first to determine what antiquities lay below.

After digging a few narrow trenches, Kenyon and de Vaux encountered the foundations of two substantial buildings they concluded were Byzantine hospices built in the time of Justinian the Great in the sixth century CE, when the area was a busy residential neighborhood. The structures, they added, had been renovated by early Muslim rulers and remained in use until the eleventh century.

Ben-Dov had read their report, and he was contemptuous of their methods of drawing big conclusions from small digs. "The only way to achieve reliable results was to dig up the whole area," he wrote. This was the traditional technique to expose water and drainage systems as well as cellars, providing a far more expansive view of ancient structures, but without the precision and detail that Kenyon's approach required.

Opening a larger area, however, also requires more time, labor, and money. And at a site with millennia of occupation, recording each horizontal layer can be a formidable effort that takes years of concentrated effort; much data can be lost. As a result, larger digs encourage archaeologists to focus on a single time period. In the coming decade, Ben-Dov's approach would win out over Kenyon's.

Busy with his university duties and often ill, the aging Mazar left much of the day-to-day work at the site to Ben-Dov. The young round-faced archaeologist had grown up in a town of Jews and Arabs in northern Israel, where he learned Arabic as well as Hebrew. His soft-spoken manner belied an ambitious and maverick personality. Israeli archaeologists are a notoriously combative tribe, but over the course of a long career, Ben-Dov earned an unusual amount of contempt from many of his colleagues, which he attributed to the envy of those less gifted.

"Ben-Dov is the hero of his own story, which is of the triumph of scientific inquiry over superstition and ignorance," concluded one British historian, who compared his self-confidence and prickly personality to that of Warren.

Before joining Mazar in Jerusalem, Ben-Dov had used heavy machinery to clear thick layers of deposits at a rural site in northern Israel to gain faster access to deeper archaeological layers. This tactic was highly controversial. "A bulldozer is the last thing an archaeologist would normally expect to find at a dig," he later acknowledged. But "if its operator is graced with a sensitive soul, and if an archaeologist is stationed permanently beside its scoop, it can be a very helpful instrument."

In March 1968, with Mazar absent, he secured a bulldozer and scraped away the dense layers left by a full millennium of Ottoman, Arab, and Crusader residents, remains that were sent largely unexamined to a municipal dump. Ben-Dov then parked the machine and had his team expose "an almost perfectly square two-acre building that was flanked on the north by a broad paved street." In the center was a stone-paved courtyard interspersed with what appeared to have been beds for flowers and trees.

The scale and designs stunned the archaeologist. Byzantine builders typically preferred long rectangular basilicas or domed buildings. This huge structure seemed to have more in common with the luxurious palaces built by early Islamic rulers across the Middle East. Yet there was no known mention in letters or other texts of any such grand villas in Jerusalem in this era. The only known monuments constructed in the city by early Muslims were the Dome of the Rock and al-Aqsa Mosque on the Noble Sanctuary, which loomed above the site. This had led many historians to conclude that—unlike for Jews—the city held religious but not political significance for members of the new faith.

There was no doubt of Jerusalem's religious import to Muslims; it played a starring role in the mind of Muhammad, who was deeply influenced by both Jewish and Christian traditions. He had decreed to his first followers that they should pray toward the Holy City, and he honored the Jewish prophets as well as Jesus and Mary. Only later, while he and his followers were in Medina, did the prophet change the direction of prayer to his hometown of Mecca. Five years after his death in 632 CE, a Muslim army arrived at the gates of the city.

By then, the demoralized Byzantine army had fled. Unlike the Babylonians, Romans, and Persians, however, the new conquerors apparently refrained from pillage and destruction. Contemporary sources say that the Christian patriarch Sophronius, the city's effective leader, requested that the surrender be made directly to Caliph Umar, who had been a companion to the prophet. One version has Umar arriving in a simple robe and on a donkey, in startling contrast to the richly bedecked Christian cleric with his glittering retinue.

According to other stories, Umar asked to be taken to the site of Solomon's temple, and he was shown to the top of the platform that lay in ruins as a testament to Christianity's triumph over Judaism. The rocky outcrop near the center, possibly the rock that underlay the Jewish temple's Holy of Holies, was covered in sewage and trash. Appalled by this sacrilege, Umar began to clean it himself and decreed the area sacred to Islam. He didn't linger, but before he departed, the caliph negotiated an agreement with the patriarch allowing some Jews, long banned, to return to the city.

Among those said to have accompanied him was Muawiya I, the son of a Meccan merchant and brother-in-law of the prophet Muhammad. He returned to Jerusalem around 660 CE to receive oaths of allegiance and assume leadership of the empire at a ceremony on the platform that became known as the Noble Sanctuary. But Muawiya designated the more populous, wealthy, and strategic city of Damascus as capital of the new Umayyad dynasty. Aside from ordering construction of the Dome of the Rock and what became al-Aqsa Mosque, the new caliph and his successors appeared to leave Jerusalem on the political periphery.

Ben-Dov's bulldozer, however, revealed a startlingly different picture. When his team cleared a clogged drain in the mysterious building, the archaeologist found clumps of mud and ancient sewage containing coins dated to the early eighth century CE—the early Islamic period. There were also broken bits of vessels identical to those found in Muslim palaces of the era.

To Ben-Dov, the implication was plain: a construction of this scale, dating from that era, could suggest only that Jerusalem had served as a political center of early Islam as well as a religious one. Jews had long argued for stewardship over Jerusalem on the basis that, in essence, Islam's roots in the city didn't run as deep as theirs. The archaeologist's discovery contradicted a view that was, in the wake of the war, political dynamite.

"Mazar was home sick, and he knew nothing about this period," said Ben-Dov, with characteristic acerbity. "So I phoned my former teacher Yigael Yadin. He knew Islamic archaeology and Arabic." Yadin was the nation's most famous excavator, eclipsing even Mazar. He had served as the chief of staff of the Israeli Defense Forces until 1952, when he took up archaeology and wrote popular books like *The Art of Warfare in Biblical Lands*.

Yadin agreed to come immediately to the site. "He arrived at about 4:00 p.m. in the afternoon. He looked around and said, 'You are right, these can't be Byzantine or Roman buildings.'

"Then he told me, 'Look, no one knows about this yet. And no one knows Islamic history. You have a bulldozer. Use it.'"

Ben-Dov was stunned that a prominent archaeologist would order him to destroy a significant and monumental ancient building, yet he understood Yadin's reasoning. Israel was already on tenuous footing, domestically and internationally, after its seizure of the Old City the year before. A major Islamic site posed a political threat.

Ben-Dov may have sanctioned questionable practices as an archaeologist, but he bridled at the thought of following an instruction that placed ideology over science.

"I had friends in radio, and after Yadin left, I called them up," he said.

"By 6:30 p.m., I was at the station." In a live interview, he revealed his discovery. That evening, he paid a visit to Mazar at his home. "I told him what I had found, but he didn't believe me," Ben-Dov said. "He didn't for a long time."

The dig quickly drew the curious, including representatives of the waqf that owned the land. A few days later, while working at the site, Ben-Dov noticed a cluster of ten Islamic clerics and men in dark suits standing at a gate along the perimeter of the excavation. The archaeologist approached them with a greeting in Arabic. "I said come over and spend ten minutes and have coffee," he said. "So they came and I gave them a tour. They couldn't believe it."

Also in the group was the deputy head of Jordan's Department of Antiquities, Rafiq Dajani, who was related to a notable Jerusalem family. "If we could leave politics to the politicians, I would heartily congratulate you on your work," Dajani said. "The finds from the early Muslim period are thrilling, and frankly I am surprised that Israeli scholars have made them public." A nearby reporter overheard the remark, and, with Dajani's permission, quoted him in an Israeli newspaper. Two weeks later, the respected archaeologist—one of the few Jordanians with an archaeology degree—was fired for his public support of the enemy.

Ben-Dov felt little sympathy. "Dajani's attempt to separate politics from science was a naive and futile gesture," he said. Archaeologists could not hope to escape Jerusalem's brutal political realities.

The monumental building proved only part of what was an immense complex of a half-dozen large and impressive square structures, carefully designed, with each opening onto a large central courtyard. They ringed the southern wall of the platform and the southern end of the Western Wall and clearly were built as a single development. Inside the buildings, the team found what Ben-Dov called "vessels of extraordinary splendor, fragments of frescoes, and ornamented architectural stone fragments carved in the finest Umayyad tradition."

The foundation of the main structure, the first one unearthed, was planted more than two dozen feet into the earth, and the aboveground structure reached as high as the platform's southern wall, as did the roofs of some of the other buildings. Mazar, once convinced, wrote later that they were part of "a large and well-planned cluster of great buildings, provided with all amenities, as well as an extensive sewage system" from the Umayyad era. "There is no doubt that this vast building complex . . .

represented an ambitious socio-political and religious plan intended to heighten the prestige" of the dynasty.

One morning, while taking a break, Ben-Dov gazed at a chirping bird. It had perched on a stone protruding from near the top of the Noble Sanctuary's southern wall. He realized that it was the remnant of a bridge built between the roof of the massive building and the platform, which would provide a dignitary—such as, for example, a caliph—with a private entrance to al-Aqsa Mosque. In an era of frequent assassination, such a feature would have proved a useful security measure. He concluded the structure could be nothing less than a palace for a ruler of an empire that would soon stretch from the Atlantic coast to the Bay of Bengal.

The historic find forced a reckoning with conventional Israeli views of the Muslim past; archaeology demonstrated that Jerusalem was not, as had been believed, on the periphery of early Islam. While this disturbed many Israeli Jews like Yadin, who saw this as a threat to their own claim on Jerusalem, it also provided unexpected benefits for the nation. Simply publicizing the discovery demonstrated to international audiences the integrity of Israeli archaeology. Ben-Dov had shown the world that he and his colleagues were not held hostage to narrow ideological interests. But he also had proven that archaeology could upset religious and political assumptions.

A few days after the initial radio broadcast announcing the discovery, Ben-Dov ran into his former teacher Yadin on a Jerusalem street. "Meir, it is good we did not destroy the buildings," the elder archaeologist told his young colleague.

More than five decades later, Ben-Dov shook his head at the memory. "That's what he said—we!"

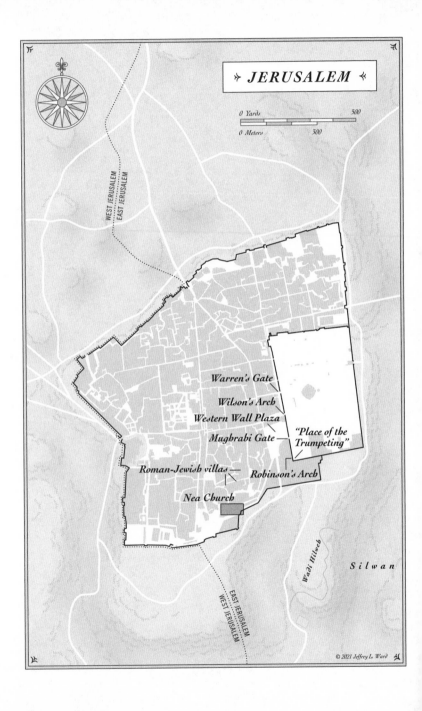

10

The Magnificence of the Metropolis

Israeli archaeologists, professional and amateurs, are not merely digging for knowledge and objects, but for the reassurance of roots.

—AMOS ELON

On June 20, 1969, three bombs went off in an alley near the Western Wall, killing one Arab man and injuring several others. Israel blamed saboteurs from Jordan. An angry Prime Minister Golda Meir quickly approved the rabbinical request to demolish the fifteenth-century buildings clustered around the Mughrabi Gate, where members of the Abu Saud family still lived.

A century after Warren had sparred with the family, the Arab residents were evicted, and Israeli bulldozers leveled the compound without archaeological supervision. Its most famous resident had lived there as a child in the 1930s; his mother was an Abu Saud. Five months before the demolition, he had been chosen to chair the Palestine Liberation Organization (PLO), which had as its goal the liberation of the region from Israeli control. His name was Yasser Arafat.

"On the few occasions he has spoken of his childhood, he mentioned the destruction of the Abu Saud house," noted one biographer. Arafat was already involved in demolition of his own, in the form of bombing attacks against both Israel and Jordan.

Israeli archaeologists, however, were more concerned with the Chief Rabbinate Council than the nascent PLO. They feared the compound's destruction marked the start of a campaign by the rabbis to extend its control south of the plaza. Soon after the bulldozer dust had settled, the clerics forbade archaeological work within thirty feet of the entire southern length of the Western Wall.

Mazar and Ben-Dov boldly ignored the decree. They expanded their excavations from the south slope of the southern wall to the south portion of the Western Wall. Alarmed Orthodox believers backed by the Ministry of Religions quickly created a prayer space south of the gate as a kind of spiritual barricade to block the profane researchers. The conflict threatened to turn violent until the ministry backed down, and the worshippers withdrew.

From then on, the Mughrabi Gate and its sloping ramp formed a second fraught frontier. While the first border separated Muslims on the platform to the east from Jews on the plaza to the west, the second separated religious Jews from their secular counterparts. Israeli archaeologists reigned supreme south of the gate, and rabbinical authorities held sway to the north.

Nowhere were the two starkly competing visions of Israel—one secular and scientific minded, the other traditional and religious oriented— more apparent. South of the border, tanned young men and a few women dug through ancient debris in shorts and tank tops. To the north, men had to wear head coverings and women were kept strictly segregated; all were expected to dress modestly.

Both secular and religious Israeli Jews soon united in surprise and delight by what Mazar's team found. Workers hit a stone inscribed with the Hebrew words for "the place of the trumpeting." That phrase echoed a mention by the Roman Jewish historian Josephus of a spot on the Temple Mount "where it was custom for one of the priests to stand and to give notice, by sound of trumpet, in the afternoon of the approach, and on the following evening of the close, of every seventh day."

The stone presumably had been cemented at the top of the platform wall built at the order of Herod the Great, and it was compelling evidence that this was, indeed, the site of the temple complex during the time of Jesus. When it fell—likely during the Roman destruction of 70 CE—it landed on a broad and well-paved street paralleling the Western Wall.

Subsequently, in a nearby trench, the team came across the fragment of a biblical verse written in Hebrew during the Byzantine or early Islamic period. "And you will see and your heart will rejoice," it said. This suggested a Jewish presence close to the Western Wall long after the temple was ruined, when either Christianity or Islam was dominant.

The discoveries created a sensation in Israel. One newspaper declared the dig "the most spiritual excavations ever in Israel," while another referred to the effort as "a holy work." Leading Israeli politicians, including Prime Minister Meir and the retired Ben-Gurion, visited the site, as did scores of Israeli and international reporters. The media attention also attracted thousands of volunteers from around the world, Christian as well as Jewish, eager to participate in unearthing biblical artifacts.

The finds gave Mazar and Ben-Dov an edge in their battle with the rabbis, since it undercut their claims that archaeology could disturb the area's "sublime sanctity." Work continued in all seasons, employing an army of engineers, surveyors, architects, artists, and photographers as well as laborers, both paid and volunteer. Many of the day laborers were local Arab men. In the first five years, the team moved more than one million cubic feet of earth, or enough to fill a dozen Olympic swimming pools.

The focus of the work was squarely on what Mazar called "the magnificence of the metropolis in the first century A.D.," when Jewish Jerusalem was at the height of its glory. As a result, structures from later periods—from late Roman to Ottoman times—were recorded but removed. "One of the ironies of searching for and preserving the remains of the past is that the archaeological endeavor entails destruction," Ben-Dov explained. "The brutal fact is that if you want to know what lies under a certain stratum, you have no choice but to destroy it."

He added later that "the idea is to remove all the remnants of later periods and leave only those from Second Temple times." This period of Jewish dominance before the Roman destruction of 70 CE was considered the most important, since its ruins were "so impressive and numerous." Yet this decision, as is often the case at sites with multiple layers, came at a cost.

The team, for example, dismantled an elegant room in a medieval Islamic building that in turn revealed a late Roman chamber beneath littered with erotic oil lamps, elaborate rings once owned by Roman soldiers, and a small bronze Celtic cavalryman identical to one that turned up in the River Thames in London. When this area was taken apart, the excavators reached the paved street laid down next to the Western Wall during the time of Jesus. This monumental street remained for future tourists to walk; Israeli researchers judged this era to be of greater interest to visitors than what came after.

Later archaeologists cringed at the speed with which massive amounts of ancient material were swept away with little or no documentation. "It was one of the largest excavations," said one, "and one of the worst." Little of the tons of earth was closely sifted for small artifacts, which are often the most revealing.

Mazar's team was able to solve a number of research questions, including the purpose of Robinson's Arch, the bit of stone springing from the Western Wall near Mughrabi Gate. Warren and others believed it to be part of a massive bridge connecting the Temple Mount with the main part of the city that lay on the slope to the west. Instead, the team determined it was an enormous pedestrian interchange that was a wonder of the ancient world. Such discoveries, Mazar said, confirmed the boast found in the Babylonian Talmud, a foundation of rabbinical teaching compiled centuries after the city's destruction: "Whoever has not seen Jerusalem in its splendor has never seen a fine city."

Orthodox believers had long repeated the phrase, but it was secular Israeli archaeologists who made that splendor tangible.

◆ ◆ ◆

FOILED IN THEIR ATTEMPT to expand the Western Wall Plaza to the south, the chief rabbis wasted no time in taking a page from nineteenth-century archaeologists like Warren. The Ministry of Religions turned its gaze north, to what the British explorer's colleague Charles Wilson had called "one of the most perfect and magnificent remains in Jerusalem."

Unlike Mazar's well-publicized digs, this effort was clandestinely planned and executed. Eventually it would become one of Jerusalem's most popular tourist attractions and extensive prayer spaces. It would also spark frequent protests, two international crises, and leave more than one hundred dead and nearly a thousand injured. Ultimately it would become a major stumbling block in resolving the Israeli-Palestinian crisis.

The fully intact ancient arch named for Wilson had once acted as the final support for a broad stone aqueduct carrying water through the western side of the city to the Temple Mount, though the date of its construction was disputed. By the time the British Royal Engineer examined it with Schick in 1866, the monumental stonework was covered with later structures and the area beneath had been converted into a cistern.

Two years later, Warren had cut through the concrete floor of the reservoir, struggled past boulders and broken masonry, and dug through mud reeking of sewage. His team's efforts paid off when they opened up a labyrinth of ancient chambers, including what he called the Masonic Hall. Massive foundations of medieval Islamic schools to the north halted their progress, and complaints that the work endangered buildings above prompted the Ottoman governor to seal the entrance. No one had entered the space since then. As late as 1965, one American archaeologist noted that "presumably the pasha's wall is still there, waiting to be removed by a yet greater diplomat than Charles Warren."

Neither could have guessed that the work halted in 1868 would be resumed not by diplomats or scientists, but by Jewish clerics. Precisely a century later, Minister of Religions Wahrhaftig approved a plan to dig an underground passage north of the plaza to expose the foundation of the Western Wall. The entire wall is longer than the Empire State Building is tall, with most of its length and height buried under later construction. Accessing it required digging directly beneath the heart of the Muslim Quarter, which was thick with homes and businesses and included some of the city's oldest and most important Islamic structures.

Wahrhaftig's idea had the enthusiastic support of Rabbi Shlomo Goren, the former chief rabbi of the Israeli Defense Forces and a fervent Ashkenazi nationalist. Goren was bitter that the Temple Mount had been left in the hands of Muslims at the end of the 1967 war. This had been done at the direction of General Moshe Dayan, who saw it as a "historical site of commemoration of the past" rather than a place for Jewish prayer; he also hoped to avoid igniting a wider holy war.

In protest, Goren had organized a Jewish prayer on the Temple Mount in August 1967 that resulted in a riot, the first recorded clash between Jews and Muslims on the sacred platform. Exposing the foundations of the Western Wall would seemingly offer a less fraught alternative for Jewish worshippers. A second key supporter of the tunnel was Yehuda Getz, a Sephardic cleric who had just been appointed to the new post of rabbi of the Western Wall.

As a first step, the underground wall built by order of the pasha was dismantled in the summer of 1968. Since Wahrhaftig considered his ministry exempt from the nation's antiquities laws, no dig permit was requested, though an archaeological supervisor was appointed: Ben-Dov served as the project's nominal scientific supervisor for the next eighteen years. Busy with his other excavations, he visited the site only sporadically and published no scientific papers on the effort.

Keeping the project under wraps in its initial stages was vital. "Fear of disapproval within Israel and abroad was so great that all of the work was conducted in the utmost secrecy," wrote the archaeologist Dan Bahat, who took over for Ben-Dov in the mid-1980s.

Rabbi Getz oversaw the work. Born in Tunisia, he came from a long line of Jewish scholars trained in the mystical tradition of Kabbalah that had so fascinated the Finnish scholar Juvelius. This path, which developed in medieval Muslim Spain, influenced and was influenced by Muslim Sufi thought and practices. Kabbalah was rich in stories and imagery of the future Jewish return to Jerusalem, the appearance of the Messiah, and the end of history. By the sixteenth and seventeenth centuries, Kabbalah's dramatic millennial theology had even seeped into Protestant apocalyptic thinking, and echoed distantly in the beliefs of nineteenth-century Christian evangelicals such as the Seventh Earl of Shaftesbury.

After studying law in Tunis and being ordained as a rabbi, Getz left for the new Jewish state in 1949 and settled in the Galilee, north of Jerusalem. There he cultivated an orchard and ran an elementary school. Yet he was anything but a meek rural scholar. Getz immediately joined the military, and rose to the rank of lieutenant colonel in the artillery. When he wasn't in uniform, "he wore a black robe and carried a prayer book and a Bible in his pockets, as well as a pistol at his hip," according to the Israeli journalist Nadav Shragai, who described him as an odd combination of rabbi, officer, and mystic.

Getz was not an archaeologist. In fact, he was hostile to the discipline. "He didn't like what archaeologists were trying to do in the Jewish Quarter and around the Temple Mount," said Isaac Hershkowitz, a religious scholar at Bar-Ilan University who has studied Getz's career and writings. "Their work was too academic and not spiritual enough. He was afraid they wouldn't have the necessary respect."

After one of his sons was killed in the 1967 fight for the Old City, the shaken father resigned his commission and moved to Jerusalem. Soon after, he was appointed as the overseer of prayer at the Western Wall, a position he held for nearly thirty years. A man of contradictions, the rotund rabbi quietly gave to the needy and was known for his gentle compassion. He was also observed punching journalists and treating Christian and Muslim clerics with undisguised contempt.

As director of the Old City's Beit-El Synagogue's yeshiva, which specialized in the study of Kabbalah, the rabbi quickly emerged as a central figure in the mystical tradition. Destroyed in the 1948 war and rebuilt in 1967, the school drew Sephardic Jews from across what had been called the Maghreb, today's Morocco, Algeria, Libya, and Tunisia. But it was the underground spaces that became his true second home.

"Every night at midnight the rabbi used to go to the tunnel," recalled one of his grandsons, Yiftach Getz. "He would wash his hands first, and then put a rug on the floor, and pray with tears the mystical prayer of Tikkun Chatzot, a prayer for the healing of the destruction of Jerusalem and the Temple. He used to cry with deep sorrow while praying. His dream was to hasten the coming of the redeemer." Getz imbued the project with his esoteric beliefs. "The laborers and their supervisors believed they were fulfilling a holy mission," Ben-Dov recalled.

The mission, however, required a strong stomach. When workers broke through the pasha's wall, they could not locate the maze of rooms described by Warren. The enormous underground spaces had since filled up with sewage from the homes and businesses above. Ben-Dov said that "whenever any one of the residents living on the streets used a toilet, the workers below got a revolting shower of fresh sewage poured down on them" in what he called "one of the most malodorous episodes in archaeological history."

Over time, the municipality was able to install a more modern sewage system to limit—but not completely halt—the leakage. The rooms were slowly cleared. As it had in Warren's day, however, the tunneling threatened to unsettle the buildings above. The government of Jordan complained in 1970 that the digging disturbed the foundations of the medieval Ribat al-Kurd mosque and the al-Jawhariyah school. Residents and shopkeepers began to notice cracks in their shops and residences, which the municipality blamed on the sewer work.

Despite official government silence on the project, muddy workers and dump trucks hauling away dirt and rubble were impossible to conceal. "This secrecy created uncertainty and suspicions regarding what was taking place at the sites," noted Bahat. Rumors swirled in Arab Muslim circles about the true nature of the project. They suspected the rabbis sought to dig into the Noble Sanctuary, or even undermine it, much as the residents a century before had feared Warren's true intentions.

In the late twentieth century, the stakes were higher than in Warren's day. "The Jordanians, Israelis, and Americans all had an agreement that we would not go even one millimeter past the Western Wall and under the Temple Mount," said Ben-Dov. As his workers exposed new sections of the tunnel, Getz would place a Torah mark to certify it was a place of prayer rather than a secular archaeological site.

By 1976, after nearly a decade of dirty and difficult effort cutting through the mud, sewage, and thick stone foundations that had halted Warren's work, the team had extended the passage 150 feet north of Wilson's Arch. This is where they encountered the first break in the smooth line of stones running along the Western Wall's lower courses. The site was directly below Ablution Gate that leads into the Noble Sanctuary. Scholars believe the gate, built by Saladin's brother in 1193, houses the world's oldest public latrines still in use.

The break in the subterranean stones was one of four openings in the Herod-era wall mentioned by Josephus. Robinson's Arch and Wilson's Arch were grand affairs set high up that provided direct access to the Temple Mount. Between these two stood what was known as Barclay's Gate, set low near today's Mughrabi Gate.

The fourth entry, a simple door, had been completely concealed from view by later construction. Warren, of course, had beat the rabbis there, and later excavators named it after him. How the British captain accessed the deeply buried site remains a mystery. He may have resorted to crawling through a cistern beneath a nearby Muslim religious school; in any case, he declined to advertise his route. While working on the sacred platform a couple of years before, Wilson had explored a cistern on the other side of the Western Wall, below the Noble Sanctuary and directly opposite Warren's Gate.

This entry may have remained open until just before the Crusader era, providing direct access to the central portion of the platform. When a German pilgrim visited the Noble Sanctuary in the 1170s, he described a set of stairs leading from near the Dome of the Rock into the cistern explored by Wilson. In the recent past, he noted, the passage had led to the city beyond.

The door's modest design belied its prominence. "The gate is the most important of all gates because it is the nearest gate to the Holy of Holies," said Bahat, Ben-Dov's successor in the tunnel.

Many scholars suspect that the Dome of the Rock, which hovers above a rough slab of bedrock, was the site of the cube-shaped chamber within the Jewish temples known as the Holy of Holies. This was Judaism's most sacred space; during the era of the first sanctuary, according to the Bible, it housed the Ark of the Covenant. In the temple's second incarnation, it was said to have remained empty. The Jewish high priest was the only one allowed to enter, and then only during Yom Kippur.

No place on earth is freighted with so much legend. This rough stone is where God created Adam, and where the biblical patriarch Abraham bound his son Isaac—Ishmael in the Arab version—as a human sacrifice to God. It is the rock on which tradition relates that Abraham's grandson Jacob laid his head to dream of a celestial ladder. And it is the Jebusite threshing floor that King David chose as the altar to worship the Israelite god. Here, the birth of John the Baptist was foretold, and Muhammad set off on his momentous visit to heaven. It is the foundation stone of the earth, the navel of the world. And it lay a mere 250 feet to the east of Warren's Gate.

For the next five years, after overseeing the tunnel construction by day, Getz returned at night to the sealed doorway to pray toward the sacred rock.

◆ ◆ ◆

THE DIGS UNDER the Old City absorbed the attention of Israeli archaeologists for more than a decade. As Mazar and Ben-Dov worked close to the Temple Mount, their colleague Nahman Avigad conducted excavations in the partially ruined Jewish Quarter on the slope to the west. As was common practice, his team largely bulldozed away more than a thousand years of Ottoman, Arab, and Crusader layers, including a thirteenth-century defensive fortification, to get at earlier Jewish periods.

Among his stunning revelations was a thick wall and a stout tower dating to the sixth century BCE. Kenyon had long argued the city at that time did not extend so far to the west and north. The finds demonstrated that Jerusalem was a large and formidable settlement in that era, though the rampart ultimately failed to stem a Babylonian attack.

Avigad also uncovered elegant Roman-style villas adopted by the Jewish elite in the century before the civil war and then the Roman attack in 70 CE laid waste to Jerusalem. The city's wealthy class, including temple priests, adopted Roman tableware and styles to a surprising degree; one dining room might have been in Pompeii, save for the lack of human and animal figures in deference to the Jewish taboo on images. Even their meals were cooked in pans identical to those used in Rome. Many of these finds were preserved in innovative outdoor and basement museums highlighting the Jewish past.

Some Byzantine constructions were too monumental to ignore. Along with uncovering long segments of an arcaded Byzantine street, the team identified the massive intact vaults that once supported the long-lost Nea Church, consecrated in 543 CE and rivaled in splendor only by the Holy Sepulchre. Yet a church in the midst of the Jewish Quarter was anathema to many Orthodox Jews, and its vaults and apses were later locked behind gates and doors inaccessible to the public.

Meanwhile, the narrow ridge extending south of the Noble Sanctuary that had for a full century drawn archaeologists from Warren to Kenyon lay forgotten. "I believe that the archaeological evidence for anything more does not survive," concluded Kenyon after completing her dig there in 1967, adding "David's successors have destroyed most of his town" in building later structures. If anyone were foolish enough to attempt another dig, she warned, "I wish the excavators luck."

The complete lack of evidence for a time that the Bible labeled as a golden era was troubling for Israeli archaeologists—as well as for politicians insisting on Israel's claim to East Jerusalem. Mazar had found the magnificent metropolis of Herod the Great. Where was Solomon's?

A dozen years after Kenyon abandoned the ridge, a forty-one-year-old former Israeli paratrooper named Yigal Shiloh took up her challenge. "It is an exciting—even awe-inspiring—story," wrote Hershel Shanks, the editor of *Biblical Archaeology Review*. "Shiloh found things no one had found before."

He launched a large-scale dig on the northeastern slope of the ridge just weeks before the British archaeologist died. Like Ben-Dov, Shiloh scoffed at her excavation method. "Kenyon thought once she took an area and, like a checkerboard, put down four small squares, perforating the area, that she had finished her work," he said. His larger-scale digs exposed stone houses on the eastern slope of the ridge dating to 3000 BCE, in the early Bronze Age. This was the same era in which the world's first cities began to flourish in neighboring Egypt and Mesopotamia. This pushed back Jerusalem's origins by more than a thousand years, to the dawn of civilization.

He also expanded on Kenyon's finds of Middle Bronze Age walls and fortifications dating to about 1800 BCE, and an impressive set of stone terraces from five or so centuries after that. The city at that time had not been large, but it had boasted impressive infrastructure for its day, from towers above to water tunnels below. Shiloh's most provocative result, however, was what he *didn't* find. When it came to the early City of David, the team came up empty-handed.

◆ ◆ ◆

AFTER THREE YEARS of digging, Shiloh's excavations of the past suddenly became embroiled in the politics of the present. On June 30, 1981, Israeli voters went to the polls. Prime Minister Menachem Begin's conservative Likud-led bloc narrowly retained power, but it held only a razor-thin three-vote majority. To maintain the support of small religious parties, he approved a formal agreement requiring that "the law forbidding excavation at grave sites will be strictly enforced."

According to Jewish tradition, disinterring a corpse or disturbing a grave is forbidden except under specific circumstances. Since archaeologists frequently encounter or even seek burials in the course of their work, this law provided rabbis with a legal tool for limiting or halting excavations they deemed sacrilegious. Until 1981, it had been largely ignored. But Begin's frantic attempts to pull together a coalition provided religious parties with the leverage they needed to ensure that excavators adhered to the rule.

After battling for control of the area around the Temple Mount in the late 1960s, archaeologists and rabbis had secured a fragile peace. The new controversy reignited that bitter conflict. During the summer, word spread among strictly Orthodox believers—also called Haredi—that Shiloh's dig had uncovered a late medieval Jewish cemetery. Five weeks after the election, on August 6, more than one hundred protestors gathered to demand a halt to the excavations. They instigated a riot in the Mea Shearim neighborhood in Jerusalem, a Haredi bastion, blocking roads, hurling rocks, tossing Molotov cocktails, and overturning trash cans. Police moved in with tear gas. Slogans like "Death to Archaeology" and "Drivers be careful: pathologists and archaeologists are hungry" appeared on walls.

The demonstrators also vandalized the grave of Theodor Herzl, spraypainting the taunt "Why don't you dig here?" on the stone of the founder of modern Zionism, while marking the tomb of the militant Zionist leader Ze'ev Jabotinsky with a swastika. For these religious protestors, secular figures like Herzl and Jabotinsky were heretics, and archaeologists were their despised descendants. The sudden spread of discontent "was very effectively carried out by dramatic rabbinical sermons" at yeshivas as well as wall posters in conservative Jewish neighborhoods urging protests, according to the political scientist Ehud Sprinkzak.

A perplexed Shiloh insisted that his team had found no human remains. "What we have are really nice things coming out of the Bronze Age—wonderful, wonderful things," he told a reporter. "Unfortunately we are fighting a kind of political fight here. I keep trying to explain we don't mix archeology and politics, but these people are pressuring the government. I'm fighting not just as an archeologist, but as an Israeli who believes in law." He added, defiantly: "We are not moving out from the area."

Demonstrators converged each day at the site that for Arabs was the Silwan suburb of Wadi Hilweh, which Jews increasingly referred to as the City of David. Sprinkzak noted that young religious students would "pray, cry, scream, and tear their dresses in grief" and often throw rocks at the workers in an attempt to halt the excavation. Their efforts did not end there. Shiloh and his wife and two children were subject to "a barrage of personal threats, vilifications, insults, hate letters, and intimidating phone calls," another academic said.

Shiloh was assigned round-the-clock police protection. Once he was attacked by a Haredi protestor and landed in the hospital for stitches above his eye. Another time, two demonstrators spit on his daughter and called her a whore. To Shiloh's satisfaction, she spit back.

At first, mainstream Jewish leaders dismissed the demonstrators as fringe right-wing activists. Shlomo Goren, who had backed the rabbinical tunnel dig, was now the Ashkenazi chief rabbi, and he shocked the government by siding with the protestors. He also obtained the support of the Sephardic chief rabbi. "They don't care about the bones," Goren said in an August 9 radio interview. "They care only about archaeology, and if they can learn something about ancient times. But they do not care about Jewish law."

He ordered the dig shut down, charging that Shiloh had failed to keep his promise to guarantee a rabbinical supervisor was constantly on-site to ensure no bones were found. "Religious law has to be enforced," Goren insisted.

"An archaeological dig or site is not like a kosher hotel or restaurant,"

Shiloh retorted. "Do you think we are really grave robbers? Do you think we are just excavating grounds like these just to find bones and throw them to the dogs?" he asked in a media interview. "If we find human bones, we deal with them according to law, but just because you might find bones, not to excavate at all?"

There was already personal animosity between Goren and Shiloh. The rabbi was said to begrudge the fact that the archaeologist had convinced Israeli leaders to rebury the remains of Jewish rebels found on top of the Dead Sea mesa of Masada, considered a sacred redoubt of resistance to ancient Rome. This move prevented religious authorities from declaring the entire mesa top a religious site, which would have precluded future excavations. "The archaeologists have to learn once and for all that it is forbidden to violate cemeteries," Goren told a reporter. As for the City of David, he promised, "That dig won't be renewed."

Deputy Prime Minister Yigael Yadin, the former archaeologist who had recommended that Ben-Dov destroy the Umayyad palace, waded into the controversy to back his colleague, noting that the excavations "help strengthen the people's roots in this land." In a widely watched televised confrontation with Yadin, Goren claimed to have seen bones littering Shiloh's site. The deputy prime minister dismissed the accusation, noting that previous excavators already had dug in the area without encountering human remains.

"Until now the biggest enemies of our archaeological enterprises have been the Arabs and UNESCO, because they didn't want us to uncover our roots," he said, adding that "it is unthinkable that the government will allow itself to be driven by a group of extremists and anti-Zionists."

The protests gathered steam, attracting international media attention and creating unlikely activists. The Israel Exploration Society, a purely academic organization, threatened to organize demonstrations on behalf of Shiloh. Meanwhile, dressed in sackcloth, Haredi protestors shut down a busy downtown square to perform a mourning ritual. A growing number of Israelis sympathized with the strictly Orthodox. As two Israeli historians later noted, citizens began to question whether it was worth desecrating the bones of their ancestors for the sake of science.

A beleaguered Prime Minister Begin stalled for time. His attorney general set up a special committee to investigate, but the tenuous governing coalition showed signs of strain. The Ministry of Education and Culture, which was led by Zevulun Hammer, a member of the National

Religious Party, had issued Shiloh's dig license. Goren, the nation's Ash-kenazi chief rabbi, threatened to excommunicate the minister if he didn't halt the excavations.

On September 1, Hammer called for a two-week suspension of the excavations. Later that month, Israel's high court overruled the decision. "In our state, which is not a theocratic state," the judges decreed, "the rul-ings of the chief rabbinate do not in any way obligate state officials in their official capacities." The Chief Rabbinate Council responded by issuing a communiqué declaring that religious law superseded secular law.

The unsubstantiated claims by a small fundamentalist sect had morphed into a full-scale national crisis.

Shiloh feared that the future of Israeli archaeology was at stake. "What would happen if every excavation in Israel were stopped because of this coalition agreement?" he asked. But the archaeologist saw a much greater threat in the dispute. He accused "fanatic Jews" of trying to dictate "what it means to be an Israeli and what kind of country Israel is to be. Is it to be a theocratic state or a state of law?"

On August 31, his elderly colleague, Benjamin Mazar, warned that what he called Goren's "fabrication" was indeed "threatening to under-mine a national enterprise."

Goren was unsympathetic to the plight of the archaeologists. "This is their problem," he said. "A place where there is a chance of finding Jewish graves will not be touched without our orders, without our regula-tions . . . even if this means stopping digging in Israel altogether."

◆ ◆ ◆

TENSIONS SUBSIDED AS the summer excavation season ended, but both sides girded for the next round of battle. Goren and the council champi-oned a bill in Israel's parliament, the Knesset, that would declare cemeter-ies to be holy sites, and therefore off-limits to archaeological investigation. This would have precluded digs in large sections of Jerusalem and Israel, since most ancient sites included cemeteries. The measure failed to win support, but Shiloh was forced to compromise with religious authorities by agreeing to limit the scope of his excavations.

The concession wasn't enough to appease religious leaders, who excom-municated him. They urged that devout Jews pray that God punish him.

Shiloh continued the dig, but only with armed guards present. In the summer of 1983, demonstrators burned the site's archaeology office and desecrated the graves of distinguished archaeologists. One protest that season drew several thousand demonstrators. Religious parties kept up pressure to pass a bill allowing Israel's chief rabbis to halt any dig site thought to harbor tombs. This failed, but they managed to impose stricter controls over digs.

Shiloh finished his excavations at summer's end in 1985, at which point he began writing up his results. That December, he was diagnosed with stomach cancer, and two years later he died. Soon after, posters went up in Mea Shearim calling Shiloh an "evil, wicked, abominable apostate" who was now "a dead corpse after suffering great and deserved pain while he was alive. Hell and perdition will now complete his punishment."

Shortly before he passed away, the archaeologist was given the Jerusalem Prize by Mayor Kollek. In one of his last interviews, Shiloh warned that his opponents saw putting a stop to archaeology as a first step toward creating a theocratic state. But he recalled the 1981 legal win that allowed him to keep digging with satisfaction. "It was a sweet victory, I must say," he recalled. "When we got the decision of the Supreme Court [High Court], we almost cried, all of us."

What Shiloh did not know in the charged summer of 1981 was that the rabbis were secretly conducting their own dig less than half a mile away. If his excavation roiled a nation, then this one would spark a crisis that rippled far beyond the borders of Israel.

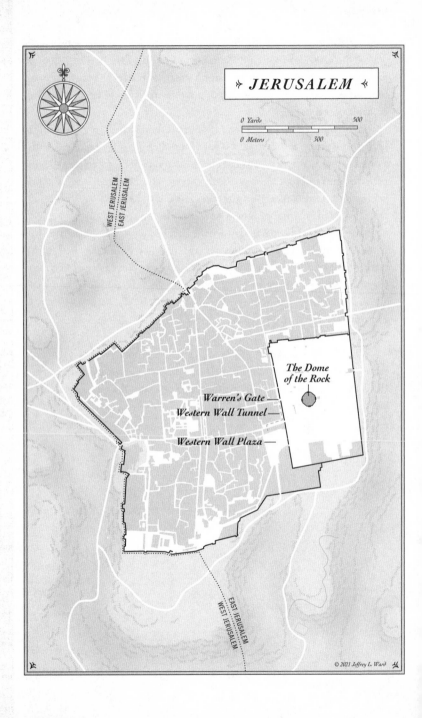

11

The Rabbi's McGuffin

"You and I are very much alike. Archaeology is our religion, yet we have both fallen from the pure faith. Our methods have not differed as much as you pretend. I am but a shadowy reflection of you. It would take only a nudge to make you like me. To push you out of the light."

—*Raiders of the Lost Ark*

Two weeks before Israeli voters went to the polls, *Raiders of the Lost Ark* opened to rave reviews and packed theaters in the United States. The hero, a handsome American archaeologist named Indiana Jones, finds himself trying to outwit burly Nazis who locate the Ark of the Covenant in a vault beneath an Egyptian temple. "The Bible tells of it leveling mountains and wasting entire regions," he explains, which is precisely why the Nazis are so eager to find it.

Before presenting their prize artifact to Adolf Hitler, the team opens the sacred box only to find it filled with sand—and furious spirits, which burn them to death. Jones and his heroine survive, and the container ends up lost again, this time in a mammoth U.S. government warehouse.

In movie parlance, the Ark was the "McGuffin"—the spur for the plot—thought up by one of the film's co-writers, Philip Kaufman. The idea, he later said, came from "an old dentist I went to in Chicago who was obsessed with the lost Ark's legendary powers." His dentist was not the only one fixated on this mysterious artifact; Hitler purportedly had sought the Ark during World War II.

After the movie's June 1981 premiere (it didn't open in Israel until the end of that year), a real-life version of Jones's adventure unfolded beneath the Muslim Quarter of Jerusalem. In this case, the searchers claimed to have found the Ark, though they did not attempt to open it. Nevertheless, their effort released a different kind of furious spirit.

At 1:00 p.m. on July 22, 1981, Getz's construction manager called the rabbi. "He told me about an amazing discovery of a big hall behind the Western Wall with an opening in the ancient gate," the rabbi wrote in his diary. Excited, Getz rushed from his office by the Western Wall Plaza to the tunnel entrance nearby. He unlocked the metal door and walked briskly through the halls originally excavated by Warren. Then he entered the well-lit but perpetually damp passage leading north.

The tunnel was, on average, five feet wide and seven feet high, bored through the stone of medieval foundations and floored with wooden boards that covered yawning cisterns. The lower courses of the Western Wall were on his right, including one of the largest building stones in the ancient world, a forty-six-foot-wide and ten-foot-high behemoth weighing more than four hundred tons. Beyond it lay the honeycombed interior of the Noble Sanctuary.

Near the tunnel's end, he reached Warren's Gate to find what he said was a two-foot-wide hole puncturing the long-sealed entrance leading into the sacred platform's interior. Under the prevailing status quo, no one was permitted to broach this border. Getz's diary does not explain who made the opening or why. He later suggested it was the result of an accident while workers were cutting out a space to accommodate Torah scrolls for a prayer space in the tunnel.

If it was an accident, then it came at a serendipitous moment. The election results had made religious parties coalition kingmakers. Their newfound influence included the potential not just to halt excavations, like those of Shiloh, but to start their own, free of secular interference.

"A long hour I sat there, helpless, with boiling-hot tears running down from my eyes," wrote Getz. "Eventually, I gathered courage and with awe and compassion I entered." The rabbi seated himself on the stairs leading into the chamber and said the Tikkun Chatzot, the midnight prayer expressing mourning for the destruction of the temple.

Then he stood. A set of stone stairs led down from the inside of the gate into a vaulted hall. Twenty-six feet wide, thirty-three feet high, and nearly one hundred feet long, it was partially submerged in the familiar underground Jerusalem cocktail of water, mud, and sewage.

Getz suspected the passageway was used by priests to access the Jewish temple before it had been blocked on both the eastern and western ends to create the cistern. He consulted with his excavation engineer. The two agreed that the first step was to remove the water and muck. Then he ordered the hole to be temporarily sealed "for security reasons" and called Israel's chief rabbis: Goren, the leader of the faith's Ashkenazim, and Ovadia Yosef, now the leader of the Sephardim. Getz also called the minister of religions, Aharon Abuhatzira, nephew to a famous Kabbalah sage from Morocco.

By 6:00 p.m., the four men were examining the interior of the cistern. Goren chanted a few Psalms—somewhat theatrically, according to Getz—and assured him that no one would stop his excavation team. He walked Getz to his Jewish Quarter home, saying mysteriously, "Now we will know the whole truth. I'm blessed that I got that privilege."

The next morning, Getz ordered the project electrician to install lights in a corner of the cistern. The water pump, however, proved ineffective at draining the cistern. The following day, he called the director of Jerusalem's fire department, who agreed to provide a more efficient electric pump and suggested sending a crew of Arab workers to help. "We refused, of course," the rabbi wrote. When that larger pump repeatedly choked on the mud at the cistern's floor, Getz ordered a more powerful model.

On the afternoon of July 30, Rabbi Yosef and several rabbinical judges arrived to discuss turning the drained cistern into a synagogue. Entering the Noble Sanctuary was a Jewish religious taboo. Since the location of the Holy of Holies was not known, it might be tread upon by accident; this was why rabbis a century before had questioned Warren so closely before agreeing to a tour of the underground spaces he had found. These twentieth-century rabbis, however, believed that a spiritual loophole allowed them to enter beneath the Temple Mount. That evening Goren told Getz, "It was clear as the sun that it is allowed to dig."

The next day, Getz lined up a donor to fund the renovations, but he held off on any major construction. Though he had a religious green light to proceed, the former military officer wanted government permission as well.

"Nobody on the outside knew what we were doing inside," Goren later told the American Christian archaeologist Randall Price. "No news of our dig was revealed to any journalist." He added that "we had a budget and only a few people—about ten—engaged in the work, but they took a vow not to tell anything about their work." Some were drawn from the yeshiva run by Ateret Cohanim, a right-wing group recently organized to buy and rent Muslim Quarter properties for Jewish use.

A rare photograph of the work shows several young men wearing mustaches and muddy slacks at the top of the flight of steps leading into the cistern; beyond, two men pick their way carefully across a line of wooden boards leading across the muck to the other side of the reservoir. "Everything was full of water and mud," Goren told Price. On August 11, Getz reported that "the archaeologist gave [him] the administrative go-ahead" to continue the work.

The archaeologist in question was Ben-Dov, but he remembered the scene differently. "Rabbi Getz came to me and said, 'I want to show you something,'" he recalled. "So I went to Warren's Gate, and there were ten people inside. The gate had been blocked with stone, and they had opened a sixty-centimeter hole"—nearly two feet across. "I told him, 'You are crazy!' He said, 'No, it wasn't me, it was an order. We got orders. I didn't tell anyone—not even my wife.' I told him that you can't keep this a secret—people will hear you working!"

Getz's more immediate problem wasn't stealth; it remained how to remove the thick layer of mud laid down over the course of a millennium. For the next two weeks he struggled to obtain the right equipment and electrical connections, and he finally decided to hire workers to scoop it out with shovels and carry it out in buckets. On the morning of August 17, cracks appeared in the ceiling of the cistern, and Getz ordered scaffolding built to conduct repairs. He also ordered "undercover guards" to stand watch in the tunnel to ensure secrecy.

Goren had banned reporters as well as other archaeologists from visiting the site, but word of the discovery spread among senior government officials. In the meantime, Abuhatzira had been charged with bribery—he was later convicted—and was replaced by Yosef Burg as the head of the renamed Ministry of Religious Affairs.

Burg arrived at the site on August 26 looking unhappy. Though a deeply religious Zionist, the German-born politician was wary of the dangers posed by entering the cistern. He was accompanied by reporters from Israel National Radio. They told Getz that Mayor Kollek intended to send in police the following day to shut down what was seen as an illegal attempt to dig under the Temple Mount. Despite Getz's protestations, they refused to embargo the news of the incursion beyond the following morning.

At 8:00 a.m. on August 27, the hourly bulletin opened with a report on the tunnel. The rabbi was heard explaining that he had discovered the cistern a month earlier while investigating water seeping from the ancient wall. It was one of several conflicting accounts he would make to explain the incursion. He added that the gate was one of the entrances used by priests in the days of the Jewish temple. Getz complained later that the broadcast was done "in a very dramatic way that could incite the Arabs and create turmoil."

Senior Israeli officials quickly distanced themselves from the penetration into the Temple Mount. Burg told reporters he was surprised and annoyed that the work had been done in secret, without informing the government. Zevulun Hammer, the education and culture minister, expressed "amazement and anger" that he had not been informed of the effort.

Getz, meanwhile, worried that the news would prompt action by the Muslims above. "I fear 'invasion' from the Arabs so I ordered the workers to close the entrance to prevent their penetration," he wrote August 29. The next day—Sunday, August 30—Israel's deputy prime minister Yigael Yadin publicly criticized the Ministry of Religious Affairs for allowing the secret dig, an ironic stance given that this was the man who had once advised Ben-Dov to quietly raze the Umayyad palace before Arabs made political hay of them. His blistering criticism was echoed by a growing number of government officials.

The following morning, Kollek arrived with a group of people, "one of whom I suspect is waqf," Getz wrote, referring to a member of the Islamic charitable trust charged with managing the Noble Sanctuary. The mayor ordered the rabbi to seal the gate securely and permanently. "I told him that I get my orders only from the chief rabbi or the minister." The crisis exposed the tension between Israel's secular and religious leaders, forcing officials to take sides in an escalating crisis that was taking place simultaneously with the violent conflict over Shiloh's excavations.

◆   ◆   ◆

EARLY THAT SAME AFTERNOON, Arab workers sent by waqf administrators entered the cistern from two manholes in the ceiling and began carrying building materials into the space to seal up the wall. Alerted to the news, Getz rushed from his home in the nearby Jewish Quarter. His alarmed wife followed and was shaken to find him standing in the cistern, now filled with Arabs holding tools. She ran out of the tunnel to the plaza and called on worshippers to protect the rabbi from what she thought was certain death.

"I stood alone in front of them," he said later. "I was not about to go down quietly." He shone a bright construction light on the workers to intimidate them, and then called Goren on a nearby phone to beg for help. When Goren arrived at the Western Wall, he saw what he described as "hundreds" of police, including the chief of police, and hurried to Warren's Gate, where he claimed there were also "hundreds of Arabs" in the cistern "coming in from all sides—and crying and shouting."

In the meantime, Getz said, "the police, including the supreme command, literally had run away," a charge that Goren made as well. The latter told Price that he called Defense Minister Ariel Sharon, who was busy entertaining foreign visitors and refused to act. "Finally, I called to the boys from the yeshiva and a few hundred came with weapons."

Isam Awwad, the waqf's chief architect, told a less dramatic tale. He and his colleagues had been closely monitoring the Israeli incursion and decided it was time to stop the invaders. "We sent ten of our Arab workers into the cistern with bricks and mortar to seal up the wall," he said in an interview. "I was there inside with them."

Getz went back to the cistern to face the Muslims by himself. "I found that the Arabs had entered the synagogue intending to block the entry and allow their men to build a wall," he wrote in his diary. "Backed alone in the corner, I could not stop them." One report had him pulling a gun on the Arabs. Then he heard shouts. Jewish worshippers broke into the space and began to fight with the Arab workers, one of whom was injured by a broken bottle.

Awwad said ten Jewish religious students rushed in and attacked his ten workers, numbers that seem more in line with the narrow space than Goren's claim that there were hundreds. Then the director general of the Ministry of Religious Affairs, Gedalta Schreiber, arrived with a squad of policemen in riot gear who struggled to separate the two groups.

"A border policeman had to be restrained from opening fire with an M-16 automatic rifle, and the two sides were persuaded to withdraw," according to the *Guardian*. Two people were slightly injured in the brief scuffle, and the police arrested several Jews and at least one Arab. A bloodbath was narrowly prevented.

Awwad said he filed a complaint with the police about the attack, "but they didn't want to do anything." He continued work on the wall, adding a layer of reinforced concrete to make it more difficult for another such attempt at penetrating the platform.

That night, before going to sleep, Getz wrote bitterly, "I have never felt the humiliation of Jews like today—and in our own sovereign state!"

On Thursday, police questioned Getz. They said that witnesses claimed he "gave orders to kill Arabs," which he dismissed as a lie. He said he would speak "only in court." In his diary, he railed against "the humiliating weakness and retreat of the government." In interviews with reporters, the rabbi who was opposed to archaeology insisted that it was a crime to prevent "the discovery of the remnants of our past."

At midnight, as was his custom, he prayed outside the now closed Warren's Gate. "I heard the sound of the Arabs inside the tunnel sealing with concrete the brick wall," he said. "Every one of their cries is like a dagger in my wounded heart, and from my mouth came the cry: 'God, the heathen are come into thine inheritance; thy holy Temple have they defiled.' I have to keep strong and not break."

That evening, Awwad's workers refilled the ancient cistern. The next day, September 4, the Supreme Muslim Council ordered all businesses and schools in East Jerusalem to close in order to protest against excavation under the Noble Sanctuary. The Jordanian foreign minister, Marwan Kasim, accused the Israeli government of tunneling fifty feet below the platform as "part of the Zionist effort to seize the holy sanctuary" and endangering Islam's third-holiest site with "total collapse."

He warned that this would "constitute a crime against humanity" that would "almost certainly bring in its wake a serious threat to world peace and security." According to his September 8 letter to the United Nations secretary-general, "the collapse of this holy sanctuary would be nothing less than a cultural, political and spiritual genocide."

The Muslim response largely was confined to the brief strike and harsh words. The quick action by the waqf, combined with the Israeli government's repudiation of the incursion, prevented the sort of riots and demonstrations that rocked Jerusalem after Parker's dig in 1911. Getz never had his day in court; no charges were ever brought. The incident was largely forgotten by the Israeli public, which was led to believe it had been a rogue operation by overly enthusiastic rabbis.

Palestinian Muslims suspected Getz had the quiet backing of the Israeli government, much as the Ottoman regime was implicated in the 1911 desecration. To this day, waqf guards monitor the water levels in the platform's myriad reservoirs. They are always on the alert for a sudden drop that might be a sign of another Israeli attempt to enter the Noble Sanctuary's subterranean depths.

◆ ◆ ◆

GETZ'S PENETRATION OF the platform startled Samuel Lewis, the U.S. ambassador to Israel. Lewis, a career diplomat, was trying to salvage the peace effort begun while Jimmy Carter was president. A Southern Baptist, Carter called the establishment of Israel "the fulfillment of biblical prophecy" and dreamed of brokering a Middle East peace with its Arab neighbors.

Egyptian president Anwar Sadat had given Carter an opening when Sadat made a dramatic visit to Jerusalem in 1977 to negotiate a truce with Prime Minister Begin. The following year, after a summit at the presidential compound in rural Maryland, the two leaders signed the Camp David Accords, which laid out a road map for negotiations between the old enemies and held the promise of eventually putting an end to the regional conflict.

Carter had lost his reelection bid to Ronald Reagan in November 1980, and the new president was on the fence about continued American support for the accords. Reagan's victory was due in no small part to his backing by fundamentalist Christians who were enthusiastic about Israel and opposed to a Palestinian state. Begin had astutely cultivated those Christian Zionists, the spiritual heirs to the Seventh Earl of Shaftesbury and other mid-nineteenth-century evangelicals. The prime minister presented Moral Majority leader Jerry Falwell with a Learjet; the American religious leader was chosen that year to receive the Jabotinsky Award, named for Begin's mentor, the famous Zionist leader Ze'ev Jabotinsky. "To stand against Israel is to stand against God," Falwell often said.

The Temple Mount incursion was just the latest in a series of Israeli actions in the summer of 1981 that infuriated Ambassador Lewis. Five days before the American release of *Raiders of the Lost Ark,* Israeli bombers destroyed an Iraqi reactor, drawing a rare rebuke from Washington. Ten days later, Israeli planes and ships attacked Palestinian forces in southern Lebanon and the nation's capital of Beirut, a campaign that by July had killed hundreds of civilians. Palestinian forces in turn launched a barrage of rockets and field artillery into northern Israel. Three days after Getz had stealthily entered the hole in the Western Wall, both sides had agreed to a shaky truce.

On the day the news of the tunnel was at last made public, Begin was in Egypt negotiating with Sadat the terms of an Israeli withdrawal from the Sinai Peninsula, which had been captured in the 1967 war. The next step would be to discuss the creation of a Palestinian state in the Israeli-occupied areas of the West Bank and Gaza.

On September 1, the day after the scuffle in the cistern, Lewis met for three hours with Ariel Sharon, Begin's newly appointed defense minister, "who was as usual very testy, exuberant and full of himself," Lewis later wrote. The ambassador was skeptical of Israeli government assurances that the dig by Getz and Goren was the work of rogue rabbis. He insisted on a formal investigation into the incident. Wary of alienating his nation's biggest backer, the hawkish Sharon agreed.

The following day, Burg, the minister of religious affairs, acted on the American demand by ordering creation of "an internal committee to examine the digs next to the Western Wall" to determine whether the incursion was accidental or premeditated. He nominated three panel members, including Ben-Dov.

Meanwhile, the waqf architect Awwad was working on his own report about the incident for the Jordanian government, which oversaw Muslim rights on the platform. That study rejected the official Israeli claim that Getz had only been attempting to fix a water leak and concluded that the penetration of the Western Wall was intentional.

The Israeli committee conducted a series of meetings in September, including one in which an engineering advisor to the Ministry of Religious Affairs testified that the hole in the Western Wall had taken two days to create and been cut deliberately by hand. The initial opening, he added, was five feet in width, not the two feet claimed by both Getz and Ben-Dov.

The Israeli engineer's conclusion, like that of Awwad, was that it was no mishap.

"We prepared a thirty-three-page report," said Ben-Dov. In the last sentence on the last page, he said the committee concluded that Goren and Getz had not acted on their own. They had been given a green light to proceed with the excavation by Defense Minister Sharon himself, who had failed to inform the prime minister. Burg was unhappy with that ending. "Change the last sentence to say instead that water was leaking out of the cistern," he said, according to Ben-Dov. "How could we otherwise show our faces again to the Americans?" The members agreed to edit the explosive statement, and the altered report was presented to Ambassador Lewis.

Ben-Dov explained that Sharon's intention, with the encouragement of Getz, was to create a synagogue beneath the platform. This idea of splitting the platform into two different pieces—a Jewish area below and a Muslim area above—would resurface.

◆ ◆ ◆

IN HIS DIARIES, Rabbi Getz comes across as a deeply pious man, one who simply wanted to create a prayer space as close to the Holy of Holies as possible. Yet his writings don't tell the full story. What exactly was the mysterious "inheritance" that he longed for on the night of September 4, as he stood beside the now-sealed gate? And what was "the whole truth" that Goren had alluded to?

In subsequent years, the true goal of Getz, Goren, and senior Israeli government officials came to light. Like Parker and Weill, as well as the fictional archaeologist who concurrently captured the world's imagination, they had been seeking the Ark of the Covenant.

The rabbis were guided in part by Maimonides, the twelfth-century Jewish philosopher—known by some as the Ark of God—who wrote that King Solomon anticipated the temple's destruction and "built a structure in which to hide the Ark, down below in deep and twisting concealed places." That belief persisted. "The legend of the 'Lost Ark' is a non-Jewish invention," said Rabbi Chaim Richman, co-director of Jerusalem's Temple Institute. "We basically know where the Ark is located. The problem lies in reaching it."

Getz passed away in 1995, but his daughter, Lily Horowitz, confirmed the quest. "Dad was striving to find the Ark of the Covenant buried beneath the Temple Mount by King Josiah of Judah," she said. "He wanted to find the Ark of the Covenant to bring salvation closer. Because of its sacredness, my father was willing to risk his life. This was part of the redemption that comes with resurrection."

One of the rabbi's grandsons, Adiel Getz, added that his grandfather had long been convinced that the cistern "could lead to the chamber where the Ark is concealed, and above it, on ground level, to the place of the altar." Another grandson, Yiftach Getz, said that "the dig for him had a messianic meaning. With the discovery of the place of the altar, he hoped, the righteous Messiah could reveal himself. He wanted to find the Ark of the Covenant. He hoped it would be found in the tunnels."

The three confirmed that when Warren's Gate was unearthed in 1976, the rabbi wrote to Menachem Mendel Schneerson, also known as the Lubavitcher Rebbe, who was believed by many of his followers to be the Messiah. Getz asked for a blessing so that he might enter through the gate to find the Ark. Schneerson refused the request because he believed that no modern Jew was pure enough to enter the Temple Mount, whether from above or below.

For five years, Getz had submitted to this ruling as he prayed nightly beside the gate. In his official version, it was only the "chance" hole that led him to enter beyond the Western Wall and beneath the platform, with the goal of creating a synagogue. This was a cover story. Hershkowitz, the Bar-Ilan professor who studied Getz's writings, said that the rabbi took his service as a military officer seriously, and that he was highly unlikely to act without clear government approval. "In a struggle between messianic dreams versus the state, there is no question he would let the state win."

Decades later, a more detailed version of Getz's incursion implicated one of Israel's most notorious intelligence agents in the operation's planning and execution. That man was Rafi Eitan, best known for leading the team that captured Adolf Eichmann, the Nazi official who helped devise the Holocaust. In 1960, Eitan brought him from Argentina for trial in Jerusalem, where Eichmann was hanged. Eitan was also famed for recruiting an American naval intelligence officer named Jonathan Pollard as an Israeli spy. One Israeli sociologist declared Eitan "well known for his limited intellectual horizons, his derogatory attitude toward Arabs, and his joy of battle."

In the early summer of 1981, Eitan and Begin helped plan the Iraqi nuclear reactor attack as well as the bombing of Lebanon. According to a 2003 book by Hila Volberstein, Eitan's busy schedule both before and during that summer didn't prevent him from spending a good deal of time in the Western Wall Tunnel with Getz.

"As the excavation of the tunnels progressed, I met with Rabbi Getz almost daily," he told Volberstein. "Together with him, I studied the structure of the Holy Temple and its dimensions. We drew conclusions as to the location of the Holy Temple and the Holy of Holies." He was eager to explore beyond Warren's Gate, which they both believed had been used by the temple priests to access the sanctuary. "We assumed that if we made an opening in the wall to the east, we could move forward and eventually reach the Holy of Holies. But we waited for the right time to make the opening."

They planned to avoid using noisy and heavy-duty tools. "We thought that in that way, we could advance quietly and secretly to discover the hiding place where the priests had concealed the Temple artifacts and arrive at the spot just under the Holy of Holies, the place where the Ark of the Covenant was hidden."

Those missing treasures stolen by the Romans in 70 CE—some of which are depicted as loot on the Arch of Titus in Rome—include the golden menorah, the laver basin, the table of the showbread, the golden altar, the copper altar, and the curtain that hung across the entrance to the Holy of Holies.

They were not only sacred but extremely valuable on the art market. And just as their treasure-hunting predecessor, Parker, had done seven decades before, Getz and Eitan tapped a person considered to have supernatural powers to pinpoint the precise location of these sacred and valuable artifacts. Hanan Avraham was an Israeli mystic and parapsychologist who dabbled in pendulum dowsing, hypnotism, and telepathy, and who claimed to have taken part in police and military investigations. Fifteen years later, in 1997, he won notoriety for conducting a seance for prominent Israelis in which he claimed to channel assassinated prime minister Yitzhak Rabin.

In his diary of the time, Getz doesn't mention Avraham, though journalists later learned of his participation in the effort. Nor does Getz refer to Sharon or Eitan directly. He does, however, allude to speaking with a person he identifies only as a government anti-terror advisor—presumably Eitan—who promised to bring Sharon to visit the cistern. He doesn't reveal whether that visit took place.

Getz's daughter, Lily Horowitz, confirmed that Rafi Eitan was her father's confidant. "They were good friends," she said. "I remember the phone calls between them." Though Eitan was not particularly religious, she said the two bonded when they both worked for the Mossad, the security arm of the Israeli state responsible for intelligence and counter-terrorism operations. She added that Avraham, while meeting with Getz, pointed to a map that showed where the temple treasures were hidden.

According to Getz's grandson Adiel, the rabbi privately alerted three senior Israeli government officials—Sharon, Eitan, and Deputy Prime Minister Yadin—to the activities within the cistern before the effort was made public. "They all told him to continue the excavation, but not to tell Prime Minister Menachem Begin," he said. "In retrospect, my grandfather said that if he had told Begin, he would have consented along with the others, but that after the story became public, Begin had to stop it to prevent a war."

Price, the Christian archaeologist, reported that Goren felt confident they were on the right track to find the Ark and the temple treasures when he spotted a bug in the cistern mud. "This insect verified that this place was opposite the Holy of Holies," he stated. The rabbi cited a passage from the Mishnah—the first part of the Talmud—saying that "if the priest was found unclean, and therefore unable to get out of the Holy of Holies, [he] should release an insect that would go under the veil" separating that chamber from the outer area. "I have discovered that insect."

Goren said that he and Getz closely examined the eastern end of the cistern and saw several possible openings leading deeper beneath the Temple Mount. They opened one door that revealed a wall beyond. Goren estimated it stood only a short distance from the bedrock beneath the Dome of the Rock.

"We believe that the Holy Ark made by Moses, and the table from the Temple, and the candelabra made by Moses, along with other very important items, are hidden very deep underneath the Holy of the Holies," he told Price. "We started digging and came close to the place; we were not more than thirty or forty yards away."

Price also spoke with Gershon Salomon, who said he was part of the excavation team. Salomon claimed that they had just begun breaking down a wall separating them from the Holy of Holies when the Arabs intervened. "They were afraid that if the Jews found these objects that it would be the surest sign of all of a Jewish presence on the Temple Mount," the Temple Institute's Richman explained to Price. "They were afraid that if these things were uncovered, that we would rebuild the Temple."

The archaeologist Dan Bahat, who knows the rabbinical tunnel as well as anyone, derided the attempt to uncover the legendary artifacts. "I knew very well they would not reach the treasures of the temple," he said. "It had nothing to do with reality. But they thought they were clever." Bahat did benefit from some of the data collected during their effort. "Behind the eastern wall of the cistern is a stairway that goes to the surface" of the Temple Mount, he added. "The only possible date for it is Second Temple period or maybe Roman"—a reference to the late centuries BCE and early centuries CE. "If they had had time, they would have pierced that wall to reach the stairwell."

The religious scholar Sarina Chen, of Ben-Gurion University of the Negev, speculated that Getz was motivated by a mix of Kabbalism, nationalism, and "competition with the archaeologists," all the while trying to give meaning to his son's death.

When he spoke publicly in later years, Getz was coy about his quest. Rumors swirled that he had penetrated the eastern wall of the cistern and continued to explore beneath the Dome of the Rock. Horowitz insisted that "Dad was able to identify the Ark's location." She said a photographer was present, but the images have never been published. One story has him using a mirror to reflect the Ark, which rested around a tight corner. He was also said to have confirmed on Australian television that he saw the sacred object.

"I can confirm to you that we know the exact location of the Ark of the Covenant," he wrote in a typewritten response to a query from a curious Australian viewer dated June 13, 1993, two years before his death. "As you can understand it, this subject is very delicate, and we are not interested at all to diffuse everywhere such information. With my best regards, Rabbi M.Y. Getz."

JERUSALEM

0 Yards 500

0 Meters 300

WEST JERUSALEM
EAST JERUSALEM

Gordon's
Garden Tomb

Western Wall Tunnel —

Madrasa al-Manjakiyya —

Western Wall Plaza —

The Dome
of the Rock

EAST JERUSALEM
WEST JERUSALEM

© 2021 Jeffrey L. Ward

12

Someone of Great Imagination

Then God's temple in heaven was opened, and within his temple was seen the ark of his covenant. And there came flashes of lightning, rumblings, peals of thunder, an earthquake and a severe hailstorm.

—REVELATION 11:19

Ark fever in the 1980s was not confined to theatergoers and rabbis. Just four months after the aborted attempt in the Western Wall Tunnel, a fundamentalist Christian from Tennessee named Ron Wyatt began his own excavation to expose the sacred artifact and the major ritual objects used in Solomon's temple. His saga shows how the search for these fabled objects could shade into a strange obsession peculiar to Jerusalem.

Wyatt was a middle-aged nurse anesthetist and self-trained explorer on a mission to resolve biblical mysteries. He wore a broad-brimmed fedora like that of Indiana Jones, and claimed to have once found, among many other biblical artifacts, the wheels of Pharaoh's chariots that followed the Israelites out of Egypt. The Ark was, so to speak, his ultimate Holy Grail.

He was also a member of the Seventh-day Adventist Church, a Christian sect seeded by the evangelical fervor that swept Britain and North America in the 1830s and ignited the Protestant fascination with Judaism and Jerusalem. One of the church's founders, a New Englander named Ellen White, believed that "righteous men" secreted the Ark with the tablets of the Ten Commandments in a cave shortly before the Babylonians destroyed Jerusalem.

"It was to be hid from the people of Israel, because of their sins, and was to be no more restored to them," she wrote. "That sacred ark is yet hid. It has never been disturbed since it was secreted." Its reappearance would signal Jesus's return and the End Times, and Wyatt believed that time was near.

He also believed that the Ark was hidden beneath the Garden Tomb, the place proclaimed by General Charles Gordon as the true site of Jesus's crucifixion, burial, and resurrection. The same London-based charitable trust that had bought the land just north of Damascus Gate in 1894 still operated the site, which remained a popular attraction for Protestant pilgrims.

Although he had no archaeological training, the charismatic Wyatt succeeded in securing the trust's approval to explore the underground spaces that riddled the site. "He was given permission to access the caves via our property," acknowledged Peter Wells, the trust director. Both men maintained that the dig also had the approval of the Israeli government, a claim that its authorities would later hotly dispute.

According to Wyatt's account, written by his wife, Mary Nell Wyatt, more than a decade later, he dug a shaft on the grounds of the Garden Tomb that led to a dank and dusty passage. On January 1, 1982, he crawled through the space, which was so narrow "that Ron had to exhale in order to squeeze through." At the end was an opening guarded by a stalactite that he broke off. Beyond lay a small chamber. His Arab assistant crawled through first, but "he frantically came back, eyes filled with what Wyatt called 'utter terror.' He was shaking and shouting, 'What's in there?! What's in there?! I'm not going back in there!'" He crawled past Ron and fled, never to return.

Wyatt was undaunted. "Now alone in this vast cave system, he took his hammer and chisel and enlarged the hole, crawling through. With only about eighteen inches clearance, he had to lie on his stomach with nothing but his flashlight in his hand for light." Then he spotted something shiny. Pushing back the rocks, he said he found rotted wooden timbers and ancient animal skins concealing a "gold-veneered table" with a bell-and-pomegranate pattern around the side. This, he realized, was the table of showbread, one of the premier ritual artifacts from Solomon's temple.

"Adrenaline flowing through his veins," Wyatt shone his flashlight around the cave and noticed a crack in the low ceiling in the back of the small chamber that was lined with a black substance. Directly below the crack was a large and flat stone split in two. The black material appeared to have dribbled into the opening between the split stone, but the space was too narrow for Wyatt to peer into. Suddenly, the explorer experienced a flash of insight so powerful that he said he lost consciousness for nearly an hour. "He knew the Ark was in the stone case."

But this wasn't what made him pass out. Instead, he had "the most overwhelming realization" that the black substance was nothing less than the blood of Christ.

The Tennessean had noted a rock hole penetrating the garden's surface that was one foot square. He theorized that this cavity, which lay directly above the cave, had supported the cross of Jesus. As the Galilean suffered the Roman torture, blood would have dribbled down the wooden post and into the hole. At the moment of Jesus's death, according to the Gospel of Matthew, an earthquake shook Jerusalem. Wyatt believed this tremor created a fissure from the base of the cross into the cave below, channeling the blood onto the stone enclosure around the Ark of the Covenant, hidden there since the Babylonian destruction of the city in 586 BCE.

"Ron did not report his experience to anyone at that time," Mary Nell Wyatt noted. He continued to probe the cave on his own, drawing on his medical knowledge to secure a trinkle drill used by orthopedic surgeons and a colonoscope used by gastroenterologists. The drill failed to penetrate the stone, forcing Wyatt to resort to a hammer and a stone-tipped chisel to make a tiny hole. Through that he said he inserted the colonoscope to shine a powerful light into the chamber beneath the split rock. He saw flashes of gold and crown molding—"enough to know for sure it was the Ark."

The catalog of other treasures that Wyatt claimed to have seen in the small cave included a golden incense altar, a golden censer, a golden menorah, an intricate garment worn by ancient Jewish priests, the head covering of the Jewish high priest, oil lamps, an ivory pomegranate, and a large sword. He said that he was also able to identify scrolls within the Ark written on animal skins and "in perfect condition," and he also spotted stone tablets that he said were the Ten Commandments given to Moses by God.

Extracting these objects proved impossible, given the narrowness of the chamber, so Wyatt instead snapped some fuzzy pictures with his Polaroid camera and took samples of the black substance. Wyatt reported that he then sealed up the passage leading to the treasure-laden chamber.

Later, the excavator approached the archaeologist Dan Bahat, who at the time was in charge of the city's directorate within the Israel Department of Antiquities and Museums. "He came to me and said he had found the Ark of the Covenant," Bahat recalled. "So I went with him to the Garden Tomb." The caretakers of the land, the archaeologist said, didn't want to let Wyatt enter—he apparently had become a nuisance—but Bahat used his authority to convince them to let the two men into the walled garden.

Wyatt then led him to a pit. "He pointed at a hole in the ground and said, do you see it? Do you see the metal box?" said Bahat. "I told him I didn't see anything. I just saw garbage. This was where the gardeners dumped their rubbish. Then I left. That was it." The archaeologist added that he had assured the association managers there was no harm in letting Wyatt clean a rubbish-filled cistern.

Wyatt, however, told others that Bahat had been pressured to keep the explosive find under wraps. His wife later elaborated that "the officials that Ron dealt with were serious government servants, concerned with the welfare of the people, and they realized that such an announcement would most likely set off a bloody clash between those who would want to immediately destroy the mosque on the Temple Mount to rebuild the Temple, and the Arabs."

As word spread among Christian evangelical circles of Wyatt's alleged discoveries, volunteers and donations helped expand the excavations beyond the simple cleaning of a cistern. In 1986, the American biblical scholar William Shea met with Bahat to discuss Wyatt's burrowing beneath the garden, an activity strictly forbidden under Israeli law. He reported back to Wyatt in a July 20 letter that "Bahat himself does not want you to do any more tunneling as he says this is not sound archaeological technique."

Wyatt, however, felt buoyed by a vision he had one day while eating lunch in the garden. "Ron heard a voice behind him say 'God bless you in what you are doing here,'" his wife related. "And he looked up. Standing on the much higher ground many feet above him was a tall, slender man with dark hair wearing a long robe and head covering similar to that worn in Biblical times—except that it was all pure white." The figure said that he was on his way from South Africa to the New Jerusalem, then departed. Wyatt took the visitor to be an angel or even Jesus himself.

As his fame grew among fundamentalists in North America, Australia, and New Zealand—some called him the Adventist Indiana Jones—Wyatt became a sought-after speaker and garnered a television deal, though that never came to fruition. In 1994, he opened the Museum of God's Treasures in the tourist town of Gatlinburg, Tennessee, within the Gatlinburg Passion Play Complex. It featured "the discoveries of Noah's Ark, Sodom and Gomorrah, Red Sea crossing, Mt. Sinai, etc.," as well as a mockup of the fissure that led from the surface of the Garden Tomb to the cave below.

At the ceremony inaugurating the museum, Wyatt said that the samples of the black substance taken more than a decade earlier had proven to be dried human blood. He declined to reveal more, asserting that the Israeli government had forbidden him from discussing the results. Later he claimed that scientific analysis by an unidentified lab showed the blood contained twenty-four chromosomes, rather than the twenty-three each human inherits from their mother and father. He concluded that the extra chromosome was that of Jesus's father, God.

In Wyatt's telling, the blood of Jesus that fell on the Ark was physical proof of the new covenant superseding the old one made by Yahweh with the Israelites at Mount Sinai.

As his claims continued to circulate, Israeli officials grew increasingly irritated with the American's insistence that the excavation work was done with their permission and, at the same time, his criticism that they were forcing him to keep silent on the details of his earth-shattering finds. "Mr. Ron Wyatt is neither an archaeologist nor has he ever carried out a legally licensed excavation in Israel or Jerusalem," wrote an exasperated Joseph Zias, an official with the department's successor, the Israel Antiquities Authority (IAA), in 1996. He added that if Wyatt could produce "the lab report on the so-called blood of Jesus along with a sample for independent testing which shows 24 chromosomes, I will then be led along the road to Damascus," a sly reference to the apostle Paul's conversion from Judaism to Christianity.

By then, the Gatlinburg museum had lost its lease, and the excavator had established the Wyatt Archaeological Museum in his rural Tennessee hometown of Cornersville. Zias sent an American biblical archaeologist to investigate, and he reported back that the museum curator dismissed the Israeli authority as "a bunch of unbelievers" eager to withhold the truth from the public. Two years later, after receiving a new round of inquiries from Christians, the IAA was forced to reiterate that "Ron Wyatt has never received a dig license" and that if he excavated in Israel, "he committed an illegal act."

The board of the Garden Tomb trust later acknowledged that Wyatt had continued digging for nearly a full decade, until 1990, before it lost patience and banned his activities. "Members of our staff observed his progress and entered his excavated shaft," according to a board statement. "As far as we are aware nothing was ever discovered to support either his claims nor have we ever been shown any evidence of biblical artifacts or 'temple treasures.'" The board members "totally refute the claim of Ron Wyatt to have discovered the original Ark of the Covenant or other significant biblical artifacts within the boundaries of the garden."

The biblical archaeologist Shea, a devout Christian who had collaborated with Wyatt on some of his other expeditions, concluded that Wyatt "has never brought anything out of the ground to indicate that the Ark is there." He added that Wyatt's theory was based on Gordon's faulty assumption that this was the site of Jesus's tomb. "Ron has the wrong location for his starting place."

The repeated refutations did little to shake the belief of many of Wyatt's followers, even after his death from cancer in 1999. There were subsequent assertions that he was guilty of fiscal improprieties and deceit, but a core group remained devoted to the cause of bringing the sacred artifact to light. "Yes, it is very controversial," said his longtime follower Jim Pinkoski. "No, all the details cannot be verified at this time, but there is a very good chance that the late Ron Wyatt found the Ark of the Covenant."

Like General Gordon, Wyatt possessed a tenacious faith, natural charisma, and an ability to rise above inconvenient matters of fact. "He vilified me, but he wasn't himself a villain," said Bahat. "He was actually a very nice man. I considered him someone of great imagination," he added, with something close to admiration.

◆ ◆ ◆

WHILE WYATT WAS EXCAVATING at the Garden Tomb in late 1981, another Christian from the American South passed by his excavation. He shared Wyatt's devotion to Jesus and his fascination with Jerusalem. Bill Clinton was an Arkansas lawyer, as was his wife, Hillary. During that Christmas season, the couple made their first trek to the Holy City on a tour led by Pastor Worley Oscar Vaught of the Immanuel Baptist Church in Little Rock.

The thirty-six-year-old Clinton was then wandering in the political wilderness. A year before, he had lost his bid for a second term as governor. It was a crushing defeat, and he was searching for a way back into the hearts of Arkansas voters.

Jerusalem provided a welcome distraction and, ultimately, new inspiration. "We visited the holy sites. I relived the history of the Bible, of your scriptures and mine, and I formed a bond with my pastor," he later told the Knesset. "He said that it is God's will that Israel, the biblical home of the people of Israel, continue for ever and ever."

The atmosphere then was tense; the Getz incursion had put Muslims on edge, while two bomb attacks in late November by the increasingly influential PLO had left Jewish residents shaken. "It was the beginning of an obsession to see all the children of Abraham reconciled on the holy ground in which our three faiths came to life," Clinton wrote of his visit. "That trip left a lasting mark on me."

On his return to Arkansas, he announced he would run once again for governor. Clinton acknowledged his political sins in a series of folksy television spots filmed in a New York studio. That risky media strategy asking for voter forgiveness set him on a course to reclaim the governor's mansion the following year.

When Vaught was on his deathbed seven years after the sojourn to Jerusalem, he urged his ambitious church member to run for the American presidency. But he warned the young politician "that if I ever let Israel down, God would never forgive me," Clinton recalled, and he promised, "I will never let Israel down."

◆　◆　◆

SOON AFTER THE CLINTONS returned to Little Rock, Stanley Goldfoot of the Jerusalem Temple Foundation ran across a brochure from the renowned Stanford Research Institute in Menlo Park, California, touting new advances that allowed scientists to peer through solid rock. "Remote sensing now offers an opportunity—for the first time—to explore and unearth some of man's great 'lost' historic sites," the brochure promised. "Egypt and Israel offer particularly important opportunities."

Goldfoot brought to the foundation a zeal for the creation of a new

Jewish temple on the Noble Sanctuary, but he also came with a contro-versial and violent past. South African born, he joined Zionist militants and played a part in their 1946 bombing of the King David Hotel in Jerusalem that killed ninety-one people, mostly British officials. An Israeli court later convicted him of organizing the successful plot to assassinate a senior United Nations official; he spent a few months in jail before the new Israeli government had him released.

By the 1980s he was raising money from the growing numbers of American Christian fundamentalists with a stake in Israel's future. Their predecessors in the nineteenth century wanted to see Jews return to the Holy Land. This accomplished, the next task was to build a new Jewish sanctuary on the Temple Mount in order to fulfill New Testament proph-ecy. The goal dovetailed neatly with the desire by Jewish fundamentalists like Goldfoot, who did not believe in the New Testament but did seek to reinvigorate Judaism's temple ritual.

This meant rebuilding a new sanctuary on the footprint of the old. Given that two millennia had elapsed and no comprehensive digs had taken place on the Temple Mount, no one knew precisely where that foot-print lay, though many believed the Dome of the Rock stood above the former Holy of Holies. If it were possible to locate the Ark and temple treasures as well, then all the better.

In Lambert Dolphin, a senior research physicist at the Stanford insti-tute, Goldfoot found the perfect candidate to help him explore the sub-terranean world of the Temple Mount. Dolphin had used seismographic and geomagnetic devices in the late 1970s to probe inside the limestone mass of the Sphinx and the Chephren Pyramid at Giza with a grant from the U.S. National Science Foundation. He was also a born-again Chris-tian who considered himself a staunch ally of Israel.

When Goldfoot contacted him, the physicist was primed to bring this new technology to bear on what lay beyond the ancient Western Wall. "It was already obvious to me that the Temple Mount was one of the most important unexplored archaeological sites anywhere in the world," Dol-phin wrote later. "It seemed to me . . . that modern science might be able to solve the mystery of where the [Jewish] temples once stood."

In 1982, Dolphin arrived in Israel to meet with Goldfoot, who was accompanied by Getz. In the wake of the previous year's debacle, the rabbi had been intrigued by the idea of exchanging Bronze Age chisels in favor of American high tech. Dolphin also could draw on his connections with wealthy Christian fundamentalists and Silicon Valley entrepreneurs to raise money for the venture. After discussing logistics with the men, Dolphin returned home to ready an expedition. Then a Western Union Mailgram arrived at his California office on April 8, 1983, that postponed the mission; the necessary authorities, he was told, opposed the project.

Dolphin had no intention of giving up the search of a lifetime, so he and a half-dozen members of his technical team flew to Israel anyway. They spent six weeks testing their equipment at various archaeological sites around Israel before they turned to Jerusalem. Getz and Goldfoot planned a night mission. At 10:00 p.m. on May 22, 1983, a van packed with eight people and several boxes of equipment rolled up to the Western Wall Plaza.

"We hoped to locate any large open spaces inside the wall which could indicate water cisterns, a tunnel, or perhaps a secret room where the Ark of the Covenant or ancient temple records had been hidden centuries earlier," Dolphin wrote. Working at night was vital to ensure a minimum amount of noise and vibration for optimal operation of the seismic sounder. "Second, we thought it best to keep our mission quiet because the more people who knew what we were attempting the more complicated things would become."

A guard at the plaza entrance was about to wave the vehicle through when plainclothes detectives suddenly materialized out of the dark. "We identified ourselves and said we had been invited by Yehuda Getz, the rabbi in charge of the tunnel, to do some scientific work for him," Dolphin recalled. But the detectives said they lacked the proper permits, and ordered them back to their hotel.

Dolphin was told to report the next morning to Jerusalem's chief of police intelligence. Goldfoot was there at the police station when his Californian collaborator arrived. They were told by the officer that the waqf that oversaw the Noble Sanctuary had relayed a message: "Scientists from America are going to send electronic signals beneath our Mosque. Please stop them."

Dolphin knew of Parker's ill-fated dig in 1911, and he agreed to postpone his research "to avoid a possible riot and international incident." But he chafed at the refusal. "The Moslems seemingly have veto power over what goes on in the tunnel as well as the Temple Mount," he complained. "It is impossible to keep anything secret very long in Jerusalem." It was a lesson that both he and Parker had learned too late.

News of the scrubbed effort to probe inside the Temple Mount indeed quickly leaked. In an article titled "Slouching Toward Armageddon," the *Jerusalem Post* noted that "there are significant and to some minds worrisome links between a handful of American evangelical leaders and right-wing Israelis like Goldfoot." This led an outraged Dolphin to write a response decrying "the cheap attacks on my good friend" and accusing the newspaper of being "part of a conspiracy" to thwart an important scientific endeavor. He added that as a devout believer in "the Messiah Jesus . . . I would like to see the Temple rebuilt."

According to Dolphin, Goldfoot later organized an Israeli team to conduct ground-penetrating radar studies and infrared measurements of the Temple Mount's interior from belowground as well as from helicopters, though the effort did not produce any published scientific papers. "No one yet knows for certain which of the possible candidate sites on the Temple Mount was the place where the First and Second Temple stood," Dolphin concluded, referring to the periods of Solomon's sanctuary and its successor. "If our team had been permitted to use the sophisticated equipment in the rabbinical tunnel, we have reason to believe we may have been able in time to help solve the problem."

As Robinson and Warren had in the nineteenth century, Dolphin was eager to use the latest scientific methods not just to obtain data but to support his religious faith.

This nagging question of the temples' location, hotly debated among biblical scholars since Robinson's day, soon would take on urgent political significance.

◆ ◆ ◆

THE FLAGRANT ATTEMPTS by Getz and Goldfoot in the early 1980s to probe the sacred platform's interior were part of a new movement to exert Jewish religious control over the Muslim site. While they used shovels and science, others resorted to guns and explosives. On Easter morning in 1982, an Israeli soldier charged into the Dome of the Rock and opened fire, killing two Muslim worshippers. Subsequent riots left a dozen Arabs dead and hundreds wounded.

The following spring, shortly before Dolphin's team arrived in Jerusalem, Israeli police had arrested four yeshiva students attempting to access a tunnel beneath the southern wall of the platform in order to launch an

German explorer Conrad Schick (*right*) stands under the portico of the Tomb of the Kings with his son-in-law (*left*) and Arab workers (*below*). *(Palestine Exploration Fund)*

French senator Louis-Félicien de Saulcy, a former artillery officer, launched the first legal excavation in Jerusalem in 1863.

Charles Wilson, shown here while surveying the boundary between Canada and the United States, led the first British expedition to Jerusalem in 1865. *(Library of Congress)*

This 1886 painting by German artist Gustav Bauernfeind features a gate leading into the Noble Sanctuary, with the Dome of the Rock looming in the background. This image typifies the romantic aura that enveloped Jerusalem for many Europeans in the late nineteenth century.

Charles Warren explored Jerusalem's underground realm in the late 1860s for the Palestine Exploration Society, including the Bahr el Khabeer, or the Great Sea, that lies beneath the Noble Sanctuary/Temple Mount. Scottish artist William Simpson captured the immensity of this enormous cistern in a painting from the same period. *(Palestine Exploration Fund)*

By the turn of the twentieth century, Jerusalem was a popular tourist destination, drawing Jewish as well as Christian visitors. Note that this German postcard bought by a French tourist includes an imagined reconstruction of Solomon's temple (*left*).

In August 1867, Charles Warren (*left*) poses with Jerusalem's Anglican bishop, Joseph Barclay (*center*); photographer Henry Phillips (*seated right*); guide and interpreter Jerius Salame (*standing*); and expedition member Frederick Eaton (*reclining*).
(*Palestine Exploration Fund*)

Deep beneath the ridge extending south from the Old City, Finnish poet and explorer Valter Juvelius (*left*) takes a break with an unidentified member of the Parker expedition in his search for the temple treasures.

British general Edmund Allenby enters the Old City through Jaffa Gate in December 1917 on foot, in studied contrast to German Kaiser Wilhelm's triumphal arrival two decades before.
(Underwood & Underwood)

The Wailing Wall, called al-Buraq by Arabs, is just below the Dome of the Rock in this photograph from the early twentieth century. Extending beyond it is the Mughrabi Quarter, including the Abu Saud family compound, located to the right of the wall.

In the aftermath of the Six-Day War in 1967, Israeli bulldozers demolished the Mughrabi Quarter to make way for today's Western Wall Plaza.

Deep beneath the Noble Sanctuary/ Temple Mount, Israeli soldiers stand between Rabbi Yehuda Getz (*lower center*) and Arab employees of the Islamic waqf during a violent 1981 confrontation.

Muslim authorities opened a new entrance into the Marwani prayer space—formerly Solomon's Stables— on the Noble Sanctuary/ Temple Mount with Israeli government permission in 1999. Israeli archaeologists and religious Jewish groups decried the effort as needlessly destructive.

In 2005, Eilat Mazar announced that she had found the palace of King David within the City of David National Park in the Arab neighborhood of Silwan, a claim still hotly disputed by many archaeologists. *(Courtesy Rina Castelnuovo)*

The Arab homes of Silwan rise up around the Givati parking lot, where a team led by Israeli archaeologist Yuval Gadot (*pictured*) has uncovered remnants dating from the Iron Age to the twelfth century CE.
(Courtesy Simon Norfolk)

A synagogue built into the foundations of a medieval Islamic school in the Western Wall Tunnel, inaugurated in 2017, was swiftly closed due to water and sewage leaks from the Muslim Quarter above.
(Courtesy Simon Norfolk)

This stepped street, which once led to the Temple Mount, was likely built under the patronage of Roman governor Pontius Pilate around the time of Jesus. Arabs living above the tunnel that exposed the ancient path complain that the construction work damaged their homes and businesses. *(Courtesy Simon Norfolk)*

Miriam Siebenberg and her husband turned the basement of their Jewish Quarter home in the Old City into a multilevel museum that showcases ancient Jewish buildings and artifacts. *(Courtesy Simon Norfolk)*

Zedekiah's Cave, also called Solomon's Quarries, extends deep beneath the Muslim Quarter. The site of Masonic rituals since the 1860s, it also is used today for underground concerts. *(Courtesy Simon Norfolk)*

Archaeologist Shlomit Weksler-Bdolah, who excavates within the Western Wall Tunnel, stands in the "Masonic Hall" discovered by Warren and illustrated by William Simpson in the late 1860s. *(Courtesy Simon Norfolk)*

attack. In another instance, police uncovered a plot to crash a plane loaded with explosives into the fourteen-hundred-year-old Muslim shrine.

On a cold January night in 1984, a Muslim guard surprised four armed Israeli men entering the Noble Sanctuary. They fled, but not before dropping a backpack containing fifteen grenades and twenty-eight pounds of explosives belonging to the Israeli Defense Forces. When captured, they said they intended to blow up the Dome of the Rock to clear the way for the new Jewish temple. One man was given jail time; the others were committed to psychiatric care.

While Rabbi Getz insisted he did not condone such violence, he told one interviewer not to worry about the Muslim shrines on the Temple Mount: "The Almighty will destroy them. We will lend him a helping hand."

His tunnel along the Western Wall proved its own unintended weapon of sorts. Two months after the near-bombing incident, the earth next to a fourteenth-century former religious school called al-Madrasa al-Manjakiyya gave way. This was the headquarters of the waqf responsible for the adjacent Noble Sanctuary. At the time, the king of Jordan appointed and paid members of its administration, which was run by a general director. The grand mufti of Jerusalem handled the site's Islamic affairs. Both men had their offices in the medieval school—located directly above the rabbinical tunnel.

Three of the stone steps leading into the building vanished into a gaping hole nearly ten feet long and six feet wide. The hole cracked the foundations and exposed the tunnel thirty feet below. The collapse took place at two thirty in the morning, so no one was killed or injured. By dawn the next morning, furious waqf officials were meeting with Ministry of Religious Affairs and municipal officials to demand that they shore up the endangered building.

Adnan al-Husseini, the general manager in charge of construction and maintenance of waqf properties in Jerusalem, inspected the area and concluded that "earth has been removed during these excavations and this has weakened the foundations which can no longer support the buildings above them," he wrote. "Cracks will gradually appear, threatening the buildings with total collapse," he added in a report to the Jordanian government presented to the United Nations.

Jordan's UN representative, Abdullah Salah, accused Israel of deliberately planning "the destruction of the Islamic and Christian Holy Places and the ancient historic landmarks in the city of Jerusalem" through tunneling "underneath the western wall." The excavation's purpose, he insisted, was to "shake the subterranean foundations of the Islamic religious buildings" until they collapsed.

Israeli officials dismissed this claim as spurious. Bahat later blamed poor construction of the steps for the collapse. But the ignominious episode prompted Prime Minister Yitzhak Shamir in April to suspend work in the tunnel.

That summer, the UN secretary-general dispatched Raymond Lemaire, a leading architectural historian from Belgium's University of Louvain, to examine the area. Lemaire had reported on damage to buildings above the tunnel since 1971, and had warned the Israelis the previous November about the instability of the area above the tunnel. After his visit, he concluded that cutting through unstable rubble and beneath cistern walls unsettled the foundations of the structures above. The resulting cracks threatened the buildings above, "some of which form part of the fundamental Islamic heritage of Jerusalem."

Engineers had since reinforced the tunnel with concrete. The "structure of the tunnel is now solid and there is no danger of the building above it collapsing," he reported. But Lemaire added that it was "very probable that slight movements will continue to cause cracks in the edifice for some time to come, probably for several years." He recommended that al-Husseini be allowed to inspect the tunnel, a suggestion rejected by the Israelis.

The UN representative also wrote that "it is regrettable that the tunneling, which constitutes an excavation in the deep subsoil of Jerusalem, has not been monitored by an experienced archaeologist." That gap, he added, "can only be condemned" since there was no scientific recording of data. "Whole pages of the ancient history of Jerusalem may be lost for all time," he concluded.

Some Israeli archaeologists blamed the troubles on new sewage lines, but Mayor Kollek and the Ministry of Religious Affairs accepted Lemaire's conclusions. They also insisted that a new archaeologist be appointed to oversee the scientific work. The tunnel would no longer be a private fiefdom of the rabbis. Getz's incursion and the collapse of the very steps of the waqf's headquarters shone an embarrassing international spotlight on what seemed, at best, a poorly engineered and scientifically suspect effort.

In fact, the work beneath the heart of Jerusalem's Old City was little short of a scientific catastrophe. Tons of soil and debris were hauled away without being systematically examined for artifacts. Stratigraphic deposits went unrecorded. Doors were cut through ancient walls, and concrete used freely to cover original surfaces that were not first mapped. This was the conclusion not of the United Nations but of Israeli experts. "For almost twenty years the work of the tunnel was characterized by uncontrolled digging that contravened all ethical principles of archaeological investigation," wrote Gideon Avni and Jon Seligman, two respected archaeologists with what would become the IAA.

Prime Minister Shamir's government convened a committee to review the tunnel effort. The panel recommended lifting the mantle of secrecy and injecting more science into the effort. In 1985, the southern end of the passage, with its many chambers first explored by Warren, was opened to the public. Work on the tunnel's northern end resumed. Ben-Dov, who had been largely absent from the scene, was now replaced by Bahat.

Appalled by the lack of records and data, Bahat scrambled to piece together the dizzyingly complex subterranean world. It proved a daunting task. "There was no archeological supervision of the site," he complained. "The whole dig was run for political purposes, under the Ministry of Religious Affairs." Massive use of cement to stabilize the tunnel made it impossible to examine parts of the site. Ancient stairs leading up to Warren's Gate had been damaged by the rabbi's workers.

A garrulous man with a bald head and a walrus mustache, Bahat called himself a "radical secularist." He sparred frequently with Rabbi Goren, despite the fact that he had grown up on the same block in Tel Aviv where the cleric lived. He was on more cordial terms with Getz, saying, "He was a good person and knowledgeable about Orthodox matters." But Getz had no use for science. One day he insisted that King Solomon built the Western Wall, a notion long dismissed by researchers. Getz "became so angry that he later wrote me an apology—while insisting I was wrong."

Bahat wanted to know what the tunnel could tell researchers about the evolution of the platform and its surroundings. As they prepared the Western Wall two millennia ago, workers cut through older features such as water and sewage conduits and moats. These alterations provided clues to the size and shape of the platform in its early stages of development before the 586 BCE Babylonian destruction. Bahat was able to determine that Herod and his successors had doubled its size during and after the first century BCE. He also discovered that the street and wall near the Western Wall's northern corner came to an abrupt end. "At this point," he wrote, "the Temple Mount was never completed."

Not long after he took over, Bahat received a phone call from the project engineer. The team had broken into an enormous roughly hewn passage covered high above with thick stone slabs. When he reached the site, he realized this immense channel was where Warren had made his strange journey on a boat of doors across a sea of sewage. Now dry, it wound north for 250 feet. Soaring as high as thirty-five feet, but in places as narrow as three feet, the natural rock of many hues gave it the feel of a dramatic subterranean canyon rather than a prosaic sewer.

Beyond, the excavators encountered an underground dam six feet high that led to a large rectangular pool brimming with dark water. The medieval street that ran above was the Via Dolorosa, the route Christian pilgrims believed was taken by Jesus on his way to Golgotha. At this point, sixteen hundred feet after it began, the Western Wall ended, deep in the Muslim Quarter. The northern wall continued to the east, buried beneath later structures.

By 1987, the tunnel—extending nearly a thousand feet—was nearly complete. "Fresh air is pumped into the shaft, electric cables and bare bulbs have been installed and it is possible to walk the entire length unhindered," a *New York Times* reporter noted. "For visitors, the single-file walk along the underground section of the wall takes about fifteen minutes. At the end of the excavated part of the aqueduct is an ancient underground cistern. There is a stairway at the cistern, leading above ground."

This ancient set of steps had been sealed off years before when the Israelis had repaved the street. Its reopening would set in motion a chain of events that would shake Jerusalem, and the Middle East, for years to come.

◆ ◆ ◆

THAT DECEMBER, a collision between an Israeli army truck and a Palestinian car set off the first intifada, or Palestinian uprising. The protests began peacefully but grew increasingly violent. Israel responded with an "iron fist" policy, flooding the streets with soldiers to contain the growing rebellion. Six months later, at 8:00 a.m. on July 3, 1988, Bahat's workers quietly opened the old stairway that led to the Via Dolorosa in order to cart away mud from the tunnel's north end.

Within two hours, the narrow street was filled with angry Palestinian demonstrators. The protest quickly turned ugly, with Arabs throwing bottles and rocks at the Jewish workers. Police arrived and fired rubber bullets and tear gas to disperse the mob; several demonstrators were injured.

"I decided to extinguish the fire as soon as it started," said Bahat. "I went with the commander of the Old City police—we waded right through the middle of the riot—to speak to the waqf sheikh, and said we would close the exit. By two in the afternoon, all was quiet again." Bahat added that he was slated to brief Pope John Paul II on Jerusalem archaeology the next day, "and it wasn't suitable to go there with rioting in the background."

Muslims claimed that the tunnel was designed to penetrate the platform, a charge Bahat dismissed. "I can tell you, they have nothing to worry about," he assured the *New York Times*. Lemaire was not so sanguine. He warned that any attempt to reopen the northern exit would create a crisis. "Clashes between believers of the two religious communities might . . . well occur here, and it would be undesirable to create potential arenas of confrontation."

Meanwhile, Lemaire learned that some of the foundations beneath Mamluk-era buildings above the tunnel's southern end "had alarming bulges in them, and that one of the vaults was extremely unstable." Their collapse would destroy part of a fourteenth-century religious school; this was the same area that Jerusalem's city council had determined was under threat from Charles Warren's excavations in the late 1860s. The instability also threatened the yeshiva run by Rabbi Getz. Emergency repairs were hastily made to shore up the walls.

In October 1988, Israeli authorities created the Western Wall Heritage Foundation to oversee the tunnel work and maintenance around the wall itself. The director, Mordechai (Suli) Eliav—a son-in-law of the former education and culture minister Zevulun Hammer, who had battled with Rabbi Goren—set out to complete the passage. A few weeks later, the Palestine National Council, the PLO's legislative body, adopted a declaration of independence for a state of Palestine with its capital in Jerusalem. That would make it the only city in the world that was capital of two distinct nations.

In 1990, after twenty-two years of work, the tunnel was finally opened to the public. But without an exit at the north end, visitors were forced to double back to the Western Wall Plaza. "There were nonstop collisions," recalled Bahat. Eliav and the Ministry of Religious Affairs repeatedly asked for government approval to open a northern exit, but a succession of prime ministers refused. Even as the intifada waned, Israeli leaders remained reluctant to take the risk of igniting violence for the sake of tourists' convenience.

By the start of 1993, keeping a lid on violence assumed even greater importance. On the evening of January 20, two Israeli professors and three PLO officials met at the Oslo home of the Norwegian minister of defense. At virtually the same time, standing before the U.S. Capitol on a bright cold midday in Washington, Bill Clinton took the presidential oath. The start of the secret talks in Oslo gave the new chief executive an unexpected opportunity. Clinton, as he later explained, now had a chance to indulge his passion to "see all the children of Abraham reconciled on the holy ground in which our three faiths came to life."

For the next few months, American diplomats played a minor role in the Norwegian-orchestrated effort. The negotiators hammered out what became known as the Oslo I Accord, which called for Israeli forces to withdraw from parts of the West Bank and Gaza strip occupied by Israel in 1967, and for talks to commence on Palestinian autonomy. Israel accepted the PLO as the sole representative of Palestinians, while the PLO renounced terrorism and recognized Israel's right to exist. The agreement effectively ended the intifada and opened the way for a Palestinian state.

When the time came for Israeli prime minister Rabin and PLO chairman Arafat to shake hands on the deal that September, it was a crisp morning on the White House lawn. The six-foot-two-inch Clinton towered over the two men, who each barely cleared five feet, his long arms spread in an Abrahamic-style blessing. "The descendants of Isaac and Ishmael have embarked together on a bold journey," he said.

The president had spent part of the sleepless night before reading the Bible's book of Joshua, in which the Israelites conquer Jericho from the Canaanites after blowing their horns that shook the city's walls to the ground. This inspired him to choose a blue tie with gold horns for the occasion. "Now the horns would herald the coming of a peace that would return Jericho to the Palestinians," he later wrote.

But would peace return Jerusalem to them as well?

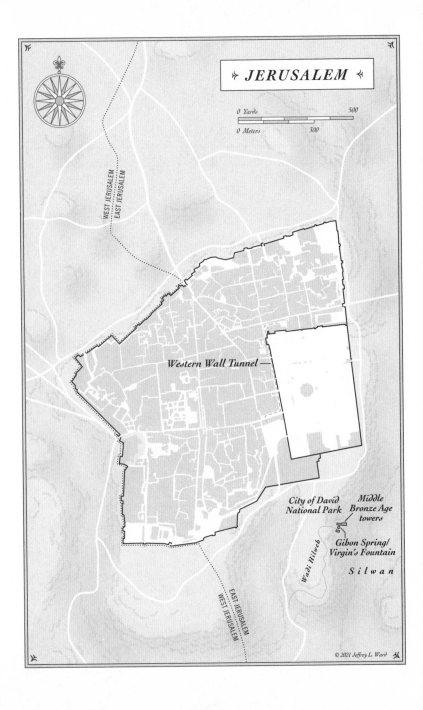

JERUSALEM

0 Yards   500

0 Meters   300

WEST JERUSALEM
EAST JERUSALEM

Western Wall Tunnel —

City of David
National Park

Middle
Bronze Age
towers

Wadi Hilweh

Gihon Spring/
Virgin's Fountain

Silwan

EAST JERUSALEM
WEST JERUSALEM

© 2021 Jeffrey L. Ward

13

A Free People in Our Land

Be strong and courageous, because you will lead these people
to inherit the land I swore to their ancestors to give them.
—JOSHUA 1:6

David is the rare figure esteemed by all three monotheisms; his very name comes from the Hebrew word for "beloved." He is, however, venerated for different traits. For Christians, David serves as the anchor for the royal line that ended with Jesus. The Qur'an hails him as a gifted poet and righteous ruler who authored the Psalms. For Jews, he is a flawed but accomplished leader who founded their first state, to which they are heirs.

That fame extends far beyond scripture. Michelangelo made him the subject of the world's most famous sculpture, depicting the shepherd boy and his lethal slingshot just before his battle with Goliath. Caravaggio and Rubens painted the legendary fight in dramatic detail. The biblical ruler was the king of spades on traditional French playing cards and even the subject of a 1997 musical theater production. David is the second-most-popular masculine name in the United States, with nearly one hundred thousand Davids born each year. In Jerusalem, he figures prominently in art galleries, and his name graces everything from postage stamps to grand hotels.

Yet despite extensive excavations across the Middle East, no one had found any contemporary mention of David or his son Solomon. Outside of the Bible, which scholars agreed had been written centuries later, they were strangely absent from the historical record. This did not prevent

Jerusalem's mayor, Teddy Kollek, from announcing plans in 1993 to celebrate the three thousandth anniversary of King David's triumph over the
Jebusites.

Kollek decreed that the celebration would begin in the fall of 1995,
"since most researchers, experts and archaeologists estimate that the conquest took place in year 1004 BC," according to a document published by
the municipality. This was, at best, wishful thinking. The calculation was
based on the Bible's account of how long various royals reigned; the only
date that could be independently verified was that of an Egyptian military
campaign. The municipality acknowledged, parenthetically, that "some
uncertainty still remains."

A month after Kollek's announcement, as Israeli and Palestinian negotiators in Oslo were still meeting in secret, a spectacular clue to David's
existence outside the biblical text emerged from an ancient mound called
Tel Dan near the Syrian border. Israeli archaeologists dug up pieces of
a stone slab with thirteen lines of broken text. Its date was estimated as
anywhere from 850 BCE to 750 BCE.

The inscription referred to Israel as well as the "House of David." The
latter wording was a common Middle Eastern phrase designating the first
in a lineage of leaders; it is used more than two dozen times in the Hebrew
scripture. "There has never before been found a reference to the House
of David other than in the Bible," said the excavator, Avraham Biran of
Hebrew Union College and a former deputy military governor of Jerusalem. Eric Meyers, a Duke University archaeologist, called it "a stunning
discovery" that would shed light "on a kind of dark age in biblical history."

For many scholars, it confirmed the reliability of scripture. "At a single
blow, the finding of this inscription brought an end to the debate and settled the question of whether David was an actual historical person," wrote
George Washington University archaeologist Eric Cline. Not everyone at
the time was convinced; there is still a linguistic debate over whether the
word translated as "David" refers to the Israelite leader, to a god, or to
Jerusalem itself. The inscription also is not contemporary to David, as it
was written at least a century after he presumably lived.

But the discovery triggered yet another surprise. After hearing news of
the Tel Dan find, the French scholar André Lemaire—no relation to the
Belgian architect Raymond Lemaire—examined a well-known artifact
that had been on display in the Louvre for more than a century. Called
the Mesha Stele, it was set up as a royal monument around 850 BCE,

and is the sole other ancient inscription mentioning Israel aside from the Merneptah Stele found by Petrie in Egypt.

The story of how it was found and then shattered, and how its pieces finally made their way into the Louvre, is a classic tale of the nineteenth-century European scramble to obtain biblical artifacts at any cost.

In August 1868, as Warren was tunneling in Jerusalem, Bedouin living in the desert fifty miles west of the city led an Anglican missionary to an inscribed stone. Both the Prussian consul and the French diplomat and archaeologist Charles Clermont-Ganneau, who later assisted in Weill's search for the tomb of David, heard rumors of the find.

Fearful the Prussian would buy it before he could arrange purchase, Clermont-Ganneau dispatched an Arab assistant to travel to the site and make a "squeeze," an impression made by putting wet paper on the inscription, allowing it to dry thoroughly, and then carefully peeling it off. As the man was making the copy, a fight broke out among tribe members. Amid a shower of gunfire, he was forced to rip the still-damp paper from the rock face and flee.

When the Ottoman government sought to obtain the artifact at the request of several Europeans, the Bedouin smashed the stone to pieces. Warren, the Prussian, and Clermont-Ganneau raced to collect the fragments. Clermont-Ganneau managed to get the most; the Palestine Exploration Fund later donated Warren's portion to the French. Eventually, those retrieved by the Prussian also found their way to the Louvre. The damage, however, made a full reconstruction of the text impossible

Using the remains and the blurry squeeze, Clermont-Ganneau translated the inscription, which celebrated the victory of King Mesha, leader of the Moabites, over Omri, king of Israel, and his sons. But the stone contained another secret, one that took 126 years to spot. Lemaire surprised his colleagues, and the world, when he deciphered one incomplete passage to read "the House of David." Though there remain a few skeptics, Lemaire's interpretation has since gained wide acceptance.

This second piece of evidence strengthened the case for a historical David, and it also revived the search for the elusive remains of his famous era in Jerusalem.

◆ ◆ ◆

BENJAMIN MAZAR, who had dug with Ben-Dov along the walls of the Temple Mount, was heartened by the Tel Dan and Mesha Stele revelations.

He was, however, too elderly and frail to undertake new excavations. As he lay dying in 1995, he discussed the project with his granddaughter Eilat Mazar, a promising excavator who had worked beside him since age ten. He encouraged her to start by closely examining the biblical text. "Pore over it again and again, for it contains within it descriptions of genuine historical reality," she recalled him advising.

The Mazars, while secular Jews, strongly believed that the Bible contained invaluable clues to archaeological truth. "I work with the Bible in one hand and the tools of excavation in the other," Eilat Mazar once said, echoing a view that could be traced back to Edward Robinson's expedition in the 1830s.

One passage that drew her again and again described David descending from his palace to Jerusalem's fortress. "There is no reason to doubt the accuracy of the biblical description," she said later. "The Bible is quite careful in its use of going up and going down." She reasoned that David would have built a new and imposing royal residence just north of the heavily fortified Jebusite city that he had conquered.

That settlement would have clustered close to the spring that poured out about halfway down the eastern flank of the ridge. The region from the spring to the southern edge of the ridge, based on digs by Kenyon and Shiloh, had likely been densely occupied when the Israelites arrived. "Choosing a site for his palace adjacent to the northern side of the Jebusite fortress would have been a very logical step for someone who was already planning a northern expansion of the city," Mazar said.

That expansion to the north led to the ridge above, later known as the Temple Mount, where the Bible says David built an altar. The most plausible location for the palace, then, was between the city and that altar, adjacent to the city's northern Jebusite wall. Studying the geography of the ridge, she decided that a narrow neck of land that was only 165 feet wide was the logical place for that wall, since it would require a relatively short fortification that was easy to build and defend.

Next, Mazar examined an apron of stone that lay on the edge of the eastern cliff near that narrow neck. It was connected to a set of impressive terraced walls, rising sixty feet, that held up the steep hillside. The dates for these—called the Large Stone Structure and the Stepped-Stone Structure—were hard to ascertain.

When Mazar examined the 1960s dig reports by Kenyon, she noted that the British excavator cited a massive wall and a pilaster capital close to the structures described as typical of Israelite building. Kenyon had concluded that "during the period of monarchic Jerusalem, a building of some considerable pretensions stood on top of the scarp." If true, she could limit her search for David's palace to a relatively small area, on land that Rothschild had bought for Weill's dig a century before; now, conveniently, it was owned by the National Parks Authority.

Mazar's desire to search for the lost palace only intensified when a Tel Aviv University archaeologist named Israel Finkelstein published a controversial paper questioning more than a century of academic and biblical assumptions. After studying pottery from sites across the region, he concluded that the archaeological "clock" used to date materials was off by a century or so. This meant that buildings dated to 950 BCE actually were built around 850 BCE. This difference of a century or so might seem an academic detail, but the implications were dramatic.

"This, of course, would change the entire understanding of the history of Israel," wrote Finkelstein, who has been described as the enfant terrible of Israeli archaeology. Though little from this era was known to exist in Jerusalem, a host of monumental gates and buildings at ancient sites around Israel had been attributed to the "Solomonic" era of the tenth century BCE. In Finkelstein's revision, they were the work of later rulers. David and Solomon may indeed have existed, but they had not been the powerful and wealthy monarchs described in the Bible. They were more akin to tribal chieftains who had taken over an established city but had built little of consequence.

Scripture, then, harked back to a golden age that never took place; this explained the lack of archaeological evidence for this era in the City of David.

Finkelstein's theory infuriated Mazar, a blond woman with a round face and a ready smile that belied a tough and stubborn personality. As a Mazar, she held a status in Israel akin to that of being a Leakey in Kenya. Yet as a woman in an overwhelmingly male-dominated field, she faced serious challenges. Not yet forty, she was still working on her PhD and lacked the institutional support needed to launch her own excavation and disprove this new assertion.

Frustrated, she published a public call for action, laying out her theory and throwing down the gauntlet. "Excavate King David's Palace!" was the blunt headline given to her 1997 article in *Biblical Archaeology Review*. "Let us put it to the test in the way archaeologists always try to test their theories—by excavation." Mazar noted the lands were "owned by the state and are barely built up at all. Who will heed the call to find King David's palace?"

Her plea was ignored. By the time she made the call to arms, other archaeologists were at work near the site, but not to test her theory. Then personal tragedy struck when her husband unexpectedly died, leaving her to raise four children largely on her own. She would have to wait a full decade before she could answer her own call.

◆ ◆ ◆

ON A HOT AFTERNOON on September 4, 1995, Israeli prime minister Yitzhak Rabin stood beneath a tent adjacent to an archaeological excavation to launch the celebration that was Kollek's brainchild. The site was at the base of the ridge that Jews now called the City of David. For Palestinians, this was the Silwan suburb of Wadi Hilweh, or "beautiful valley." The gentle fields of cauliflower and grazing land of Warren's and Bliss's day had given way to concrete houses and dusty streets. Security was tight as Israeli forces patrolled the roofs of nearby Arab homes.

"Three thousand years of history look down upon us today in the city from whose stones the ancient Jewish nation sprang," Rabin said that day. He also praised the 1967 capture of the Temple Mount, which loomed just to the north, "liberated from the yoke of strangers." That comment, ignoring more than thirteen centuries of Muslim control of the platform, was bound to infuriate Palestinians who saw the Jews as the interlopers. Later that evening, a fireworks display and laser show lit up the sky.

The event, which took place amid tense peace negotiations, was seen as more politics than history by Palestinians and foreign ambassadors, including U.S. ambassador Martin Indyk, who steered clear of the celebration. "They glorify occupation," said Faisal Husseini, the senior Palestinian Authority official in the city. "Jerusalem was not built three thousand, but five thousand years ago. The recent occupation is trying to celebrate the old one."

Kenyon's and Shiloh's Bronze Age discoveries, made close to where Rabin spoke, had provided Palestinians with their own origin story, one predating that of the Jews. Husseini declared himself descended from the Jebusites—"the ones who came before King David." They were, he added, "the original landlords" of Jerusalem. "Our forefathers, the Canaanites and Jebusites, built the cities and planted the land," said Arafat.

Five days after Rabin's speech, Benjamin Mazar died; his old nemesis, Rabbi Yehuda Getz, had passed away just three weeks before. The two men represented the bitter divide between Israeli religious and secular nationalists. The rapidly shifting political reality would soon bring these two feuding parties into closer alignment.

On September 28, Rabin and Arafat agreed to a plan to elect Palestinian Authority leaders and set up the authority's autonomous areas in the West Bank, including Jericho. The Israeli prime minister predicted an era of peace was at hand. That era proved as elusive as that of David. A month later, a twenty-five-year-old religious Zionist who feared Rabin would give away Israel's "biblical heritage" shot and killed the seventy-three-year-old former general. At his funeral in Jerusalem, attended by both King Hussein of Jordan and President Hosni Mubarak of Egypt, a grieving Clinton called him a "martyr for peace." The assassination marked an abrupt turning point for Clinton, Israel, Palestine, the peace talks, and Jerusalem.

Following Rabin's death, Palestinians overwhelmingly chose Yasser Arafat as the first president of the newly created Palestinian Authority. Radical Muslims quickly moved to derail the peace talks by launching a wave of missile and suicide attacks. The Israeli government, now led by the Labor Party's Shimon Peres, responded by sealing the border with the West Bank and Gaza, preventing tens of thousands of Arab workers from reaching their Israeli jobs. Israel also invaded southern Lebanon, dropping shells on a UN compound that killed more than one hundred civilian refugees, causing an international outcry.

The turmoil gave Israeli hawks, who were also intent on halting the peace talks, an unexpected opportunity. The young new leader of the Likud Party, a former military officer who grew up in Jerusalem and Pennsylvania, campaigned vigorously against the Oslo Accords. His party scored a narrow victory in the Israeli general elections in late May. The forty-six-year-old Benjamin Netanyahu was now prime minister.

◆ ◆ ◆

AMONG THE THREE HUNDRED GUESTS at Rabin's September 1995 appearance at the City of David had been Ronny Reich, the archaeologist in charge of the excavations next to the tent. He knew the honeycombed interior of the ridge better than any researcher of his day. While in the Israeli army, he had given tours of the area for fellow soldiers, and he grew fascinated with the caves and passages that riddled the area. In the wake of the 1967 war, he earned an archaeology degree and worked in the Jewish Quarter excavations.

In 1970, after a long summer day of digging, he and a colleague had walked through the Old City's Dung Gate and hiked down to the ridge carrying a sledgehammer. Six decades before, Parker's expedition had blocked access to one of the underground channels with a wall of field stones on the eastern slope of the ridge. The two young men knocked a hole in the wall big enough to squeeze through, and spent a couple of hours exploring the underground chambers. It was a bracing adventure, but it left Reich doubtful that there was anything left to find. (Shiloh's digs, as well as his own, later proved him wrong.)

Decades later, Reich and his colleague Eli Shukron were given the job of conducting a couple of small excavations around the base of the ridge as part of the IAA's contribution to the 1995 celebration. They began work in April and wrapped up the digs by August. "We did not find a great deal," Reich reported later, though the archaeological trenches served as a useful backdrop for Rabin's speech.

The following year, Reich was summoned to a meeting with the IAA's director, Amir Drori, to discuss a new opportunity in the area.

The right-wing political victory in May 1996 was good news for a private organization named the City of David Foundation, widely known by its Hebrew acronym Elad. The group had proposed building a visitor center on National Parks Authority land that covered a portion of the northeastern slope of the ridge, a plan that had the enthusiastic support of Kollek's successor, Ehud Olmert, and senior members of the new conservative government.

Under Israeli law, developers were required to pay for archaeological excavations before construction on a site could begin. At the meeting to discuss the work, Elad founder and director David Be'eri expressed unhappiness at having to shoulder the costs of the dig, though eventually he relented. The IAA director turned to Reich and told him to manage the excavation.

Now it was Reich's turn to bridle; he adamantly refused. "They had a religious view that Jews should settle and get rid of the Arabs," he said of Elad. For the left-wing Reich, cooperating with Be'eri and his organization was anathema.

The two men shared similar backgrounds. The forty-nine-year-old Reich was only six years older and both had grown up in Tel Aviv suburbs with parents who survived the Holocaust and grandparents who did not. Both were avowed nationalists; during the September ceremony with Rabin, Reich found himself deeply moved to hear the Israeli national anthem, which speaks of "a free people in our land, the land of Zion and Jerusalem," sung for what he imagined was the first time in the City of David.

Yet Reich and Be'eri also epitomized the old rift between secular and religious Zionists. Reich's father was killed in combat with Arab forces in 1948, and as the only son of a widow, he served in non-combat positions in the Israeli Defense Forces. When he was discharged from the army he took up an academic career and cultivated his European-language skills, eventually translating English and German poetry in his spare time. Clean-shaven and wearing glasses, Reich dressed with a little more flair than typical for Israeli archaeologists, and his European habits extended to his religious skepticism. "I am a Jew but an agnostic one," he explained. "I don't believe there is what others call God. I grew up without religion and politics."

Be'eri, by contrast, remained with the military until 1979. He then taught at the school run by Ateret Cohanim. Associates said he was sympathetic to those right-wing groups in the early 1980s that sought to destroy the Muslim shrines on the Noble Sanctuary in order to encourage construction of a new Jewish temple. Be'eri wore a bushy mustache and a distinctive uniform of open shirt and sandals, whatever the weather.

In 1986, Be'eri visited Wadi Hilweh and found it in "a state of disrepair and neglect," with former excavations buried under "garbage and waste," according to the Elad website. "Inspired by the incredible archaeological significance of the site, and the longing of the Jewish people to return to Jerusalem after 2,000 years," he founded Elad with Rabbi Yehuda Mali. Both men were eager to find remnants of the time of David and Solomon. The primary goal at first, however, was to acquire land, as Ateret Cohanim was doing in the Old City, not to dig beneath it.

Soon after founding Elad, Be'eri was called back to active duty as deputy commander of the newly formed Israeli Defense Forces Unit 217, also known as Duvdevan—for "cherry" in Hebrew, as in the cherry on top of the cream of the IDF. Brigade members often impersonated Arabs in order to gather intelligence and foil attacks against Jewish Israelis. Elad's activities stalled in Be'eri's absence.

Then, in 1990, Ariel Sharon was named minister of housing and construction. Sharon gave Be'eri his strong support in a petition, noting "the City of David is a place of immense importance to the Jewish people" and adding that "it could fit in well with the areas of Jewish settlements around it." He welcomed the new organization's "activities to purchase the rights in the houses in the City of David and to populate them."

The houses, of course, were already populated—with Arabs. According to his wife, Michal, Be'eri used deception to ingratiate himself with the residents. In one case, he befriended an Arab homeowner by posing as a tour guide in order to obtain one home. "Of course, it was all staged," she later said. When the Arab family refused to move, Elad officials broke into the house, destroyed the furniture, and waved the Israeli flag from the roof.

An Israeli law approving seizure of property owned by Jews prior to the Six-Day War offered Elad a prime tool in expanding Jewish holdings in East Jerusalem. An Israeli court later ruled that the foundation falsified a deposition claiming the property in question fit that category. Such practices prompted the Israeli government to set up a commission in 1992 led by the director general of the Ministry of Justice. The panel uncovered high-level government involvement in the ostensibly private schemes of groups like Elad and Ateret Cohanim, labeling these "a serious conflict of interest."

Prime Minister Rabin ordered a further investigation that was later dropped—according to a government source, to avoid embarrassing the government. But now, with left-wing Labor out and conservative Likud in, Elad could depend on friendlier faces in power.

Reich's refusal to cooperate with Be'eri's group reflected a history of hostility between archaeologists and the organization. IAA managers had long been at odds with what they viewed as Elad's cavalier attitude toward cultural heritage on the ridge. The legal counsel wrote that the organization "has been directly responsible for offenses of damaging antiquities and of illegal construction, forcing the IAA to summon the police."

Drori, the IAA director and a former deputy chief of staff for the Israeli Defense Forces, was determined to heal this rift. At the meeting with Be'eri, he grew furious with Reich's defiance. "You do what I say you do!" he snapped. "Even in the army, I was a general and you were a corporal!"

"No, I was a sergeant," Reich responded, eliciting laughs and breaking the tension.

Reluctantly, the archaeologist obeyed the order. "I said to myself, there is nothing to find in the City of David. A couple of weeks and I can move on." Those couple of weeks became more than a decade and a half. His time on the ridge would produce not just reams of data but a new and bitter divide among the nation's archaeologists as well as the further alienation of Palestinian residents.

◆　◆　◆

IN AUGUST 1996, Reich and Shukron began their excavation for Elad. The site was close to the spring that was Jerusalem's original reason for being; at Reich's insistence, the excavators hired Palestinian workers from Silwan, still the backbone of Jerusalem archaeology.

Their first year of grueling work involved clearing two dozen feet of gravel and soil. The potsherds that surfaced all seemed to date no earlier than the first century CE, and only at much greater depths did they find pottery from the Iron Age, that is, from the centuries before the Babylonian destruction of 586 BCE. Beneath those, the team uncovered large stones. Reich's first thought was that they were part of the wall mentioned in the Bible as built by King Manasseh in the seventh century BCE.

The prospect of finding biblical-era remains excited Be'eri. The man once wary of archaeologists quickly became enamored of excavations that could bring to life the Judean past. Reich endured the constant presence of the Elad founder, usually known by the diminutive Davidele for his short stature. "He and his men came every second minute to ask if we had found King David's palace or his tomb," the archaeologist recalled. "At first, he didn't know what he was talking about, but over time he learned. Then he realized that archaeology going on all the time can promote a site."

At the time, there was little to pull tourists to an area considered by many Israeli Jews to be a dangerous and drug-ridden neighborhood. Be'eri—as Warren had learned long before—grasped that excavations themselves could be their own draw, generating both publicity and funding.

Reich and Shukron soon realized, however, that they had not found Manasseh's wall, but something much older. As they dug in 1997, those large stones turned out to be the top of a tower with twelve-foot-thick walls. It measured forty-five feet by fifty-five feet, nearly as large as the base of the Washington Monument. The structure was built with gargantuan blocks of rough stone, some as big as a garden shed. "We immediately recognized that we might well have discovered the remains of a tower built around the spring to protect it," the two men later wrote. "And what a tower!"

A second adjacent structure was just as impressive. The discoveries proved to be part of a complex system of fortifications, underground channels, and pools built around the vital spring. In the crevices of the massive stones, the excavators found tiny bits of pottery dating to about 1700 BCE. This matched the date of sections of massive city walls that Parker, Kenyon, and Shiloh had found in the vicinity. Such big stonework was a classic characteristic of construction in the Middle Bronze Age, a time of wealthy independent city-states that periodically fended off Egyptian invasions.

When the Israelites arrived seven or so centuries later, the remarkable system was still in working order. After a millennium of use, it went out of service around the eighth century BCE, about the same time Judeans dug a tunnel to funnel water to the base of the ridge; this was the channel that Robinson and Warren had crawled through and which had harbored the inscription Schick had publicized.

The team also cleaned two blocked underground channels dating to the Bronze Age, including one that Schick had emptied more than a century before. They stumbled on more recent artifacts: rusted iron buckets used by Parker's expedition between 1909 and 1911, as well as a wooden pipe enjoyed by one of its members. Reich and Shukron also exploded the myth that David's soldiers had used a steep passage within the ridge to conquer the Jebusite fortress, an idea first suggested by Warren. The Israeli excavators determined that this nearly vertical corridor had not been accessible during that ancient era.

While the archaeologists dug below, Elad officials were pressing above for the Israeli government to grant their organization operational control of the City of David National Park. This proposal drew immediate criticism. Elad's role in settling Jewish families in an otherwise Arab neighborhood was controversial enough, but turning what was one of the top heritage sites in the nation over to a private group was highly unusual.

Archaeologists from Hebrew University took the lead in opposing the move, filing a 1998 suit in which Israel's High Court of Justice ordered the government to consider a disinterested party, rather than Elad, to take over management of the site. The official position of the IAA was that "it is essential to preserve the City of David and not allow any construction there." Elad, in other words, was a fox that should not be allowed in the chicken coop.

The Netanyahu government, with Sharon as minister of infrastructure, ultimately overrode those concerns. Elad was granted "guardianship and maintenance" under the National Parks Authority. Practically speaking, however, the change granted the organization effective control of the site. The foundation then set to work making their dig a tourist-friendly locale. To accommodate the bewildering array of steep, uneven, and often narrow passages beneath the ridge, the foundation had the archaeology team insert wooden and, later, metal beams, offering safer and wider paths for visitors. Shukron's brother, an accomplished welder, advised the team on how to place the trusses into the precariously loose soil.

Use of this technique marked a revival of the old method favored by European excavators like Warren, Bliss, and Parker. Tunneling defined early Jerusalem archaeology but fell out of favor by the early 1900s, when British control made it unnecessary to hide digs from prying Ottomans. By then, archaeologists also had realized that boring a tunnel was like driving a car without peripheral vision; you can see only what's ahead but not to the left or right. The universally accepted practice became to shovel straight down from the surface. This allowed a clear view of the layers built up over time, the approach championed by Petrie. It was also safer for workers. There were rare exceptions to the rule, such as work done on Nero's palace in Rome, which was otherwise difficult to access because of later structures.

The archaeologists dug their way through the underground network of passages and caves. In the muck within a rock-cut pool dating to the Middle Bronze Age, the team found hundreds of clay seals used for packages, as well as more than ten thousand fish bones dating from the eighth century BCE to the sixth century BCE. Analysis showed that most of those bones were from sea bream caught in a lagoon along the coast of the Sinai Peninsula. There were also perch from the Nile, a sign of urban prosperity and long-distance trade among Judea and its neighbors.

Reich and Shukron's excavation of the ancient tunnels and completion of a well-lit path deep beneath the ridge turned a visitor center with little to show into one of Jerusalem's most exciting destinations. Tourists could enjoy a breathtaking experience below the surface of the modern town that outclassed the Western Wall Tunnel and even the tours given by Warren more than a century before.

Descending a series of stairs and ramps, visitors found themselves passing through dramatically lit passages and caves. They could lean over the subterranean pool fed by the spring, marvel at the size of the enormous towers, and choose to wade through the eighth-century BCE tunnel that sent its waters into a Byzantine-era pool, or take a dry tunnel that exited just to the east. The old entrance to the spring, long used by local Palestinians, was sealed.

The Elad director bragged that the complex involved so much iron bracing that it was "holding up the mountain" and had increased the price of metal in Israel. Yet the fabled metropolis of the early Judean kings remained stubbornly absent. It was an embarrassing void at a visitor center named for King David's city.

Meanwhile, Jerusalem had entered one of its bloodiest cycles in modern times. As Reich and Shukron began their City of David excavation in the summer of 1996, Netanyahu was confronting his first major test as leader. It did not involve suicide bombings or foreign invasions. Instead, it began with a Saturday morning underground brawl between Christian monks and Palestinian factory workers.

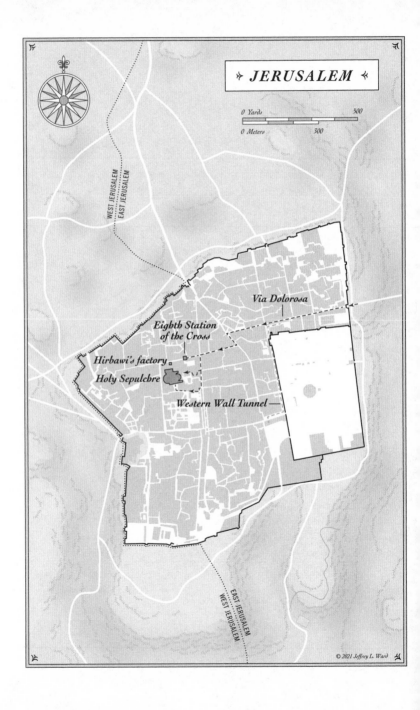

❦

14

The Cellar Crusade

No matter how low you go, there's always an unexplored basement.

—F. SCOTT FITZGERALD

At dawn on July 13, 1996, as the rising sun reflected off the dull gray dome of the Church of the Holy Sepulchre, a fifty-year-old Muslim businessman named Abdel Salam Hirbawi made his way up a narrow alley in the Christian Quarter, which still lay in shadow. The stone-lined lane was part of the Via Dolorosa, the path that the famous Galilean was said to have taken on his way to execution.

Within hours it would be clogged with knots of praying pilgrims. Now, however, it was deserted except for Hirbawi and bakers pushing wheeled carts with warm *ka'ak bi simsin,* the oblong sesame-covered bagels peculiar to the Old City. He halted in front of a hulking three-story medieval building and pulled out a set of heavy keys to open the door to his factory, where he employed 150 men and boys in making fashionable jackets from fine Turkish leather. After he entered, sleepy workers began to drift in for their Saturday shift, the Monday morning of the Muslim world.

The calm was broken by muffled noises emanating from below. Puzzled, Hirbawi lifted a square metal hatch in the floor, the only access into the dirt-floored basement. To his surprise, the faces of a dozen drunken, black-bearded Egyptian Coptic priests in robes glared back at him. They clearly had been on an all-night bender. A second shock was the basement itself. He remembered it as a dank crawl space. Now it was a forest of stone columns and arches extending into the shadowy distance.

The Muslim factory owner didn't appreciate trespassers, particularly Christian clerics, partying in his cellar. A Coptic official later claimed Hirbawi and fifty of his workers jumped down the hatch and attacked the monks; one of the Copts was slashed in the head with a knife while two others sustained minor injuries. Hirbawi denied he was involved in the violence, but the fracas was serious enough to draw Israeli police. They separated the two groups and sealed the factory door.

The Copts explained to the police that the space was part of a chapel and monastery that belonged to them but had fallen out of use. In the intervening centuries, it had filled with trash and debris. The monks had used a subterranean door leading from the north side of the neighboring Holy Sepulchre to clear the area.

What they didn't say was that the Israel Antiquities Authority, the new government agency tasked with protecting Jerusalem's heritage, had learned of the illegal dig and shut it down. Eager to make use of a rare opportunity to examine Christendom's most important site, Israeli archaeologists later allowed the work to resume under their supervision, but in strict secrecy. The unusual joint team of Egyptian monks and Jewish archaeologists gradually carted away the compacted garbage, which reached heights of twelve feet, exposing remains of the thousand-year-old ancient chapel and monastery.

Then they came across an uncharted space. As they dug through the debris, they picked out glass bottles that once contained sacred oil for nineteenth-century Russian pilgrims as well as the desiccated remains of dead dogs and donkeys. What slowly emerged was a cavernous hall covering the area of two basketball courts and soaring twenty feet above the stone floor. A Gothic *A* carved onto a column revealed it to be the work of European Crusaders some eight centuries earlier.

About a third of the structure lay directly below Hirbawi's leather operation, so the team was careful to excavate only when the factory was in operation, since the noise of the machinery above drowned out their digging. The project was nearly complete when the monks held their impromptu underground celebration, only to be discovered by Hirbawi while deep in their cups. What the Muslim businessman had thought was a shallow basement had actually been the top of an enormous old trash heap. Unknown to him, his factory had always rested on the stately Crusader vaults.

Immediately after the police broke up the brawl, Hirbawi, who was an Israeli citizen, asked the local Israeli court for a temporary injunction to halt the underground work. The judge quickly complied, a move that infuriated Anba Abraham, the city's senior Coptic cleric. For the Egyptian monks, who lived on a rooftop aerie of the Holy Sepulchre, an easy stone's throw from Hirbawi's factory, the legal decision was unacceptable meddling in Christian affairs by Israeli authorities.

Abraham carried the formidable title of Metropolitan of the Holy and Great City of Our Lord, Jerusalem, Holy Zion, Archbishop of the Holy Archdiocese of Jerusalem, All Palestine, Philadelphia of Jordan and All the Near East. He called on the world's most famous Copt for help. UN secretary-general Boutros Boutros-Ghali, married to a Jewish-born woman who had converted to Catholicism, was well versed in Jerusalem politics. In 1977, he had written the speech that Egyptian president Anwar Sadat gave in his surprise appearance before the Israeli Knesset, a landmark visit that led to a truce between the two enemy nations—and, ultimately, to Sadat's assassination four years later.

The secretary-general requested the intercession of Sadat's successor, President Hosni Mubarak. Mubarak asked Palestinian Authority leader Yasser Arafat to intercede in the matter. For Arafat, it was a chance to show the new Israeli leader that he was determined to exert control over the Old City of Jerusalem.

Six days after the underground scuffle, in the middle of the night, a half-dozen armed men burst into the Hirbawi family home on the northern outskirts of Jerusalem. They declared that they were there at the behest of the Palestinian Authority, but the businessman refused to go with his abductors. One of the men changed Hirbawi's mind by firing two bullets into the floor at his feet. They took him to Ramallah, the provisional headquarters of the Palestinian Authority in the West Bank, where the businessman refused $2 million in exchange for rights to the cellar.

When Netanyahu received word of the kidnapping of an Israeli citizen on soil that Israel considered its own, he had just returned from Washington and his first meeting with Clinton. The president had been infuriated by the prime minister's refusal to meet with Arafat to restart the stalled peace talks. "Who is the fucking superpower here?" the outraged American leader asked his aides later. All that Netanyahu had agreed to was an easing of travel restrictions imposed on Palestinians entering the country following a spate of spring terrorist attacks; thousands of Palestinians could return to work the following week.

The Israeli leader demanded Hirbawi immediately be freed, threatening to keep the border restrictions in place unless the Palestinians complied. He then ordered Israeli tanks and soldiers to besiege Ramallah. No one was allowed to enter or leave the city. Alarmed, Clinton and Jordan's King Hussein scrambled to prevent a slide into war.

Hirbawi was soon released, and diplomats around the world breathed a sigh of relief as both sides edged away from open conflict. But the battle of the basement was far from over. The Muslim businessman and the Christian Copts assembled legal teams that scoured archives for medieval maps, nineteenth-century sewer blueprints, and fragile documents dating back as far as 1189 to prove their respective claims to the Crusader hall.

The litigation would plague Netanyahu, his successors, a revolving door of government ministers, a courtroom full of lawyers, and several benches' worth of judges for the next twenty years. At stake was far more than who owned a musty cellar; the deeper question was who should reign over Jerusalem's vast underground realm.

◆ ◆ ◆

"MANY SITUATIONS OVER TIME have changed the map," said Father Antonious, a tall and regal Coptic cleric dressed in a long black robe that contrasted sharply with a cumulus cloud of silvery beard. "There is a lot of politics." He was referring to Holy Sepulchre real estate. The Copts, the largest Christian sect in the Middle East, once lived and worshipped in a monastery just north of Jesus's tomb. Now they are relegated to the compound's roof, which they share uneasily with monks from the Ethiopian Orthodox Tewahedo Church.

In the mid-1980s, the Copts decided to restore their small abandoned chapel, which by then lay abandoned underground. Under Israeli law, excavating without a license was illegal. But the Copts, like other Christian sects, bridled at the idea of asking the Israeli government for permission; they considered the Holy Sepulchre to be on illegally occupied land. Instead, they began to excavate slowly and surreptitiously. In 1992, they were spotted hauling bags of dirt to a nearby dump.

"We knocked on their door and asked what was going on," said Gideon Avni, the IAA archaeologist then in charge of the Jerusalem directorate. "They said this was their property, but we stopped them." Avni had spent decades studying the evolution of the Holy Sepulchre. He was appalled by the illicit digging, but also excited at the rare chance he was presented to excavate within its precincts. The IAA proposed to allow the excavation to continue under the supervision of Avni and his colleague Jon Seligman. The Egyptians agreed, and both sides kept the unusual arrangement secret.

This unlikely dig team made up of Coptic monks and Jewish archaeologists soon uncovered a courtyard surrounded by small rooms next to a large chapel, an ancient monastic cloister. The prayer space included a nave and two aisles separated by massive square pillars, with an apse on the east side. Dating the church proved challenging. Based on the pottery and glass fragments, Avni and Seligman eventually concluded it was built after the arrival of Islam in the seventh century CE and was used as late as the tenth and eleventh centuries.

Its use may have ended in 1009, when an Egyptian caliph, widely believed to have been mentally unbalanced, ordered the Holy Sepulchre demolished. How much of the church actually was damaged is not clear, but the chapel may have been a victim of the destruction. Yet the Christian complex had grown in the centuries after the arrival of Muslims and prior to the mad caliph. Historians had long assumed that members of the new faith made life difficult for Christians. "The construction of a new Christian church in Jerusalem under Islamic rule might seem surprising," the collaborators noted in an academic paper. "But when evaluating the recent evidence from excavations elsewhere in the city, it proved to be the rule rather than the exception."

Finds such as that of the Coptic chapel explained a puzzling comment made by the Muslim historian al-Muqaddasi. He complained in 985 CE that most of Jerusalem's population remained Christian. This was more than three centuries after Muslims took control of the city. Not only were Christians allowed to continue their rites, they were permitted to expand their prime religious complex. This was in stark contrast to the Crusader policy a century later, when Jews and Muslims not massacred were evicted, as were some Christian sects deemed too cozy with the previous Islamic rulers.

When the Copts and Israeli archaeologists dug below the foundations of the medieval structure, they found large stone blocks similar to those used in the original basilica of Constantine, along with pottery dating to the fourth and fifth centuries CE. They also uncovered a square foundation of what Avni speculated might be the original basilica's long-lost baptistry.

Under these remains, the team encountered a quarry similar to others uncovered beneath the complex. Since quarries were located outside town, it was an additional piece of evidence that the Holy Sepulchre, the traditional site of Jesus's crucifixion, had indeed been outside of the city gates at the time.

By 1995, the excavators had reached an area north and west of the chapel and monastery. To their delight, they encountered a buried but magnificent and intact hall built on bedrock with high stone arches. The style of the stonework and the mason's marks confirmed it was the work of Crusaders. Avni suspected that it was part of a complex called the Convent of the Canons of the Holy Sepulchre mentioned in contemporary texts.

The hall was almost completely filled with debris, however, and removing the dirt was time-consuming and back-breaking labor. It was as they dug farther north that the excavators found themselves directly beneath Hirbawi's noisy leather workshop. "We knew we were working under him, so we stopped digging at 4:00 p.m., when it closed down for the night," said Avni. This allowed the excavators to work without fear of discovery.

The Copts' ill-advised and raucous party, which lasted until the early morning hours of July 13, ended the dig before it could be completed. "Everything exploded," Avni said. "We backed off, because we didn't want archaeology in the spotlight. And that was the end of our excavation." No news reports at the time mentioned the involvement of Israeli Jewish excavators, a fact that Egyptian as well as Israeli officials preferred to keep from the public.

Avni and Seligman waited seven years to publish their finds, in order to avoid getting sucked into the controversy. Even then, Hirbawi's suit was still winding through the courts, on its way to becoming one of Israel's longest-lasting and most fascinating legal cases.

◆ ◆ ◆

REUVEN YEHOSHUA WAS Hirbawi's lawyer. His hair, black when the case began, now was white, while his infant daughter then was today an Israeli Defense Forces officer. "It was crazy," he said, lighting a cigarette and leaning back in his chair in his West Jerusalem office soon after the litigation was finally closed. Then he got up to retrieve a thick hardbound book from a crowded shelf.

"There were two legal ways to deal with the problem," he explained. "There is civil law, and there is law pertaining to the holy places."

Laws pertaining to the holy places have their own peculiar history that extends back to the eighteenth century. Faced with bickering among Christian sects that could flare into violence, Ottoman sultans froze all changes in claims and use of the Holy Sepulchre and other Christian sites in Jerusalem, as well as Bethlehem's Church of the Nativity. Only a personal decree by the sultan could alter this status quo. France's attempt to force the sultan to do so in the 1850s had helped spark the Crimean War with Russia.

Mindful of such danger, the major European powers backed the Ottoman policy in the 1878 Treaty of Berlin. After World War I the British expanded the concept to include Jewish and Muslim sites as well, and the British monarch replaced the sultan as final arbiter in any disputes. After the British withdrew from Palestine in 1947 and Jordan occupied East Jerusalem, the Jordanian king became the overseer of the status quo.

Since there were no major Muslim or Christian holy places in Jewish West Jerusalem, the 1967 victors arrived in the Old City with little direct knowledge of the status quo's baroque intricacies. The agreement was not a formal document. It was instead a motley collection of largely oral tradition as to which group could use an altar and make a procession and whether a religious painting could be repaired and by whom. These were deadly serious matters; if one sect cleaned a stair claimed by another, it was viewed as an attempt to grab territory, and violence could result.

At first, Israeli government officials declared they were not bound by an arrangement that seemed so antiquated; they had little interest in arbitrating disputes among quarreling Christians. Nor did many of the Christian clergy welcome Jews adjudicating their issues; many harbored anti-Semitic beliefs and had openly backed Jordan's claim to Jerusalem. While many Protestants viewed the advent of Jewish rule in 1967 as a blessing, for most of the city's other Christians it was a curse. Until 1965, Roman Catholic dogma blamed Jews for the death of Jesus—Greek Orthodox dogma still does—while the Vatican did not recognize Israel's status as a nation until 1993.

But as all those who rule Jerusalem eventually discover, arbitrating bitter disputes among competing religious groups is an exasperating yet inevitable part of governing the city.

Less than a year passed in the wake of Israel's takeover of the Old City before conflict arose between Armenians and Copts over minor repairs in the Holy Sepulchre. The matter was referred to an Israeli court, but the Jewish judge, wisely avoiding the complicated and fraught issue, cited an old British law that denied his court jurisdiction. Only the head of the government, he concluded, could rule on disagreements involving holy places. This punted responsibility to the ruling party, which also had no interest in involving themselves in the complex Christian matter. The case languished for years.

The Hirbawi dispute proved even more nightmarish for Israeli politicians and judges. First, it pitted Muslims against Christians, and it was complicated by Egyptian and Palestinian support for the Copts. Second, Hirbawi was an Arab Muslim but an Israeli citizen with close ties to Jewish business leaders. To make the situation even more awkward, the dispute came at a perilous time, when a new government was under pressure from the right to kill the peace process and from Clinton to complete it.

The key question was whether the Crusader hall excavated by the Jewish archaeologists and the Copts should be considered a holy place or not. If it were, then the prime minister had the final say. That would give the Copts a better chance of influencing the outcome, given their support from Egypt. If it was not, then the decision was a simple property dispute left to the courts. That result might give Hirbawi the upper hand.

At first, the Israeli government reflexively sided with the Copts. A week after Hirbawi's release, the Ministry of Religious Affairs declared the entire Crusader hall, including the portion beneath Hirbawi's factory, to be part of the Holy Sepulchre complex. "This means that it is a holy place, subject to the status quo, and it is the government which must decide, no other body," said Uri Mor, head of the ministry's Christian Communities Division.

Hirbawi's lawyer, however, insisted that the hall was never a holy place, and that the portion beneath the factory was the property of the Muslim religious trust that owned the building and had granted Hirbawi's family a long-term lease. "By Israeli law, what is below and above until the heavens is yours," Yehoshua said. "This was true in ancient Islamic and Ottoman law as well. So we argued the dispute should be resolved by the courts rather than politicians."

Years passed before the Israeli government ruled on whether politicians or judges would tackle the case. Ministers came and went. A decade passed. "The attorney general would ask for more information," said

Yehoshua. Both Hirbawi's lawyer and the Israeli firm hired by the Egyptians assembled mountains of travel guides, medieval maps, blueprints of old sewer lines, and documents dating back as far as 1189 to bolster their respective claims.

Archaeological data ultimately tipped the balance in favor of the factory owner. Ironically, it was the very excavations undertaken by the Copts with the Jewish archaeologists that undermined their position. "We were asked to give expert opinion a number of times by Hirbawi's side," recalled Avni. "We knew it was a church from the ninth to twelfth centuries—and from then on it was deserted."

After the Crusader era, the hall became a garbage dump. "People in ancient times lived within walls for a reason," Yehoshua explained. "If you left them, you could be robbed or killed. And there were no toilets or municipal services. So you threw your waste wherever you could. Even in your own cellar. Even dead dogs and donkeys. The whole underground area was used like a giant trash compactor until it was filled to the brim."

Chemical analysis of the remains revealed a thousand years' worth of decaying trash and dead animals. "I told the Minister of Religious Affairs, 'Just how holy could a garbage dump be?'"

In 2011—fifteen years after the basement brawl—the ministry, with the prime minister's approval, declared that the hall was not a holy site. The matter therefore was a property dispute for the courts. The furious Copts appealed that decision to the Israeli High Court. After months of deliberation, the court declined to overturn the government's decision and sent the case to a lower court.

But the judges there were no more eager than the politicians to make a ruling. Years of hearings and appeals followed. "This should have been a clear-cut case," Yehoshua said. "But the judges handling the file were afraid to deal with it because it was so politically sensitive." Two lower courts determined that neither Hirbawi nor the Copts had proved ownership over the space and refused to make a ruling.

The Copts then appealed again to the High Court of Justice, an extremely rare instance of a case going twice to the nation's highest court. Rather than handle the hot-potato issue directly, the justices appointed retired High Court justice Ayala Procaccia to arbitrate and agreed to back her decision.

Then a peculiar case became even stranger.

"Bizarrely, I received a phone call from a person I don't know, who introduced himself as someone who works—I think he said—at the National Security Council and asked to meet with me about this case," the retired justice told the lawyers during one meeting. "I was very surprised and said we were conducting a formal mediation and arbitration proceeding, and asked whether he was connected to the case. He said he wasn't but was representing the state's interests."

When she suggested that the government submit a formal position, none ever materialized. The incident spawned suspicions that Israel's government had attempted to intimidate the court, with the goal of handing the space over to the Copts in order to extract concessions from the Egyptians and Palestinians.

The retired justice eventually ruled that the portion of the cellar beneath Hirbawi's shop belonged to its legal owner, a Muslim waqf. She concluded that Saladin had given the area to the trust to prevent the expansion of the Holy Sepulchre following the defeat of the Crusaders in 1187.

The Copts appealed that decision, sending the case back to a lower court. The lower court judge eventually rejected the Egyptian appeal. The Copts were undeterred; they filed a new appeal in district court, this time against the Israeli government. Finally, in January 2016, the judges upheld Muslim control over that part of the hall beneath Hirbawi's factory. The court ordered the two sides to build a wall to separate the two portions to avoid future trouble.

By then, both Hirbawi and Abraham, the Coptic metropolitan, had passed away. Hirbawi's son Saleh and the new Coptic leader continued the battle where their elders had left off. Saleh said his legal bills topped $300,000.

A few weeks after the final judgment was handed down, Saleh lifted the same hatch that his father had opened to find the drunken monks beneath. The leather factory had since been converted into a grocery store, and the hatch was now located in the middle of the potato-chip aisle. Hirbawi climbed down a rusty ladder planted on a mound of earth, not yet excavated, that sloped down into the opened portion of the hall.

A Coptic delegation came through a small door to the south, in the wall of the Holy Sepulchre, the only other entry to the space. Along with their attorneys, the monks and Hirbawi plotted a line for the new wall. While discussing its location, according to the Israeli newspaper *Haaretz,* they quickly began to quarrel over what amounted to six inches. The Coptic attorney threatened to call for a new survey.

"I am afraid my father is looking down at me from above and will be angry that I gave up ten centimeters," said Hirbawi. In the end, the Muslim businessman agreed to accept the Coptic line. Hirbawi shook hands with the lead monk and embraced him. Two decades after the July 1996 underground scuffle, the battle of the basement had ended in a draw.

But Hirbawi's kidnapping and the subsequent siege of Ramallah during that fraught summer proved to be a dress rehearsal for a far deadlier crisis that metastasized in September. This calamity would prove an underground dispute that no court could resolve.

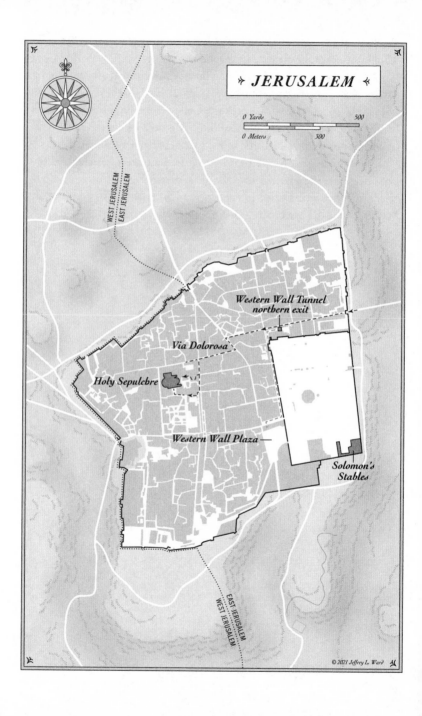

15

The Bedrock of Our Existence

In Jerusalem, the mythology is so great that something doesn't
have to be true to set off an electric shock.
—DENNIS ROSS

I n early January 1996, Dan Bahat's phone rang. On the other end of
the line was Adnan al-Husseini. Bahat was the self-proclaimed "radical
secularist" who had overseen the Western Wall Tunnel excavation for
the religious foundation that controlled the site. The caller managed the
Noble Sanctuary on behalf of its eight-hundred-year-old waqf. The two
men were cordial if wary colleagues.

The kingdom of Jordan funded and appointed members of the waqf,
which conducted its business from the medieval building that had lost some
of its steps to the collapse of the tunnel. Since 1967, Israel had claimed
the platform as part of its territory and controlled its security, and any
significant change required Israeli approval. Jordanian officials and Muslim
clerics, however, refused on principle to acknowledge Israeli sovereignty.

Like any busy religious and tourist site, particularly an ancient one,
the platform requires constant maintenance and conservation. The Muslims and Jews found ways to work beneath the political radar to ensure
smooth functioning of the site. For nearly two decades, over mint tea or
Turkish coffee at the waqf's headquarters, al-Husseini and his colleagues
kept Israelis like Bahat apprised of their work and occasionally made use
of Israeli experts.

Al-Husseini explained to Bahat that the holy month of Ramadan, the
peak time of Muslim pilgrimage, would begin by January 22. Forecasters

were calling for unusually heavy winter rains just as vast crowds would arrive to pray. Waqf officials wanted to turn the empty underground area of Solomon's Stables into a temporary prayer space to provide shelter for worshippers. The proposal wasn't wholly new; they had made it in late 1993 but nothing had come of it.

Solomon's Stables was the popular name for the vast underground space in the southeastern corner of the platform. The vaults took their present form under the rule of the Umayyad caliphs in the seventh century CE. The dynasty's first leader, Caliph Umar, who was said to have accepted Jerusalem's surrender, built a rudimentary prayer space that a contemporary Christian pilgrim reported stood on ruins and could hold three thousand men.

This temporary structure was replaced with al-Aqsa Mosque in time for the investiture of Umar's successor Muawiya I in 660 CE. The American art historian Beatrice St. Laurent, who worked extensively at the site, concluded that Solomon's Stables is that original prayer space. If she is correct, then it was built a half century *before* the Dome of the Rock, which would make it the world's oldest existing Islamic structure.

In Muawiya's day, the space had two impressive entrances through the southern wall of the platform: the Single Gate and the Triple Gate. On the north side, nine high and broad arches provided access to the platform's surface. With the construction of al-Aqsa and the dazzling Dome of the Rock, the large but unadorned space fell out of fashion and then out of religious use. The two exterior gates were sealed and the plaza facing north became a convenient dumping ground for trash and construction debris. As with so much else in Jerusalem, the old prayer space eventually sank from view.

By the time the Crusaders thundered into Jerusalem in 1099, the entire structure was buried. King Baldwin II granted the conquered Noble Sanctuary to the Knights Templar, also known as the Order of the Temple of Solomon. The martial monks of this order turned the Dome of the Rock—which at the time was imagined to be the Jewish monarch's famous sanctuary—into a church. Al-Aqsa Mosque became their headquarters, and the underground space to the east became their storeroom and treasure house as well as home to their horses, as iron rings drilled into the pillars and stone feeding troughs, still visible, testify.

After the Crusaders were driven out of Jerusalem, the space was again largely abandoned. When Wilson arrived in 1864, he described "a sloping heap of rubbish" at the southeastern corner. Three years later, Mark Twain descended into the space to marvel at its "wilderness of pillars." For three-quarters of a millennium, the stables had remained the world's largest forgotten basement, hiding what archaeologist Meir Ben-Dov called "a stunning underground world." That long vacancy soon came to an abrupt end.

◆ ◆ ◆

"I TOLD HIM that I thought this was not a bad idea," Bahat recalled of his conversation with al-Husseini. "But we have to have some give-and-take." In exchange for turning a blind eye to the conversion of the underground space into a prayer place, Bahat had his own request. He wanted to open a northern exit to the Western Wall Tunnel so that tourists could enter at the Western Wall Plaza and exit to the Via Dolorosa.

"I waited for his response," the archaeologist said. "There wasn't a yes or a no. But he said he questioned what the street [the Arab public] would say." He knew that Bahat's decision to open this same exit to the Western Wall Tunnel in 1988 had resulted in violence. There was no reason to think this time would be different, unless waqf officials were motivated to prevent or at least tamp down any protests.

After he hung up the phone, Bahat relayed the gist of the conversation to the Jerusalem district police commander, Major General Arye Amit. The commander then passed the news to the office of Israeli prime minister Shimon Peres, who faced an electoral challenge from the young Netanyahu of the conservative Likud Party. Likud members suspected that Peres would trade away the Muslim Quarter of the Old City as part of a deal with the Palestinians.

Al-Husseini's phone call proved a godsend for the embattled Israeli leader. Opening the tunnel exit in the quarter's heart, as part of a quid pro quo with Muslim clerics, would demonstrate to skeptics his resolve to hold on to the heart of the Old City. Peres's internal security minister, Moshe Shahal, quickly arranged for members of the Israeli government to meet with waqf officials to discuss the conversion of Solomon's Stables into a prayer area.

During the gathering, the Israelis agreed not to oppose the move. Then they mentioned their plan to open the northern exit of the Western Wall Tunnel. The Muslim officials remained silent, voicing neither assent nor protest. An informal agreement seemed to have been struck. "Both sides emphasized the need to keep the plan a secret," wrote journalist Nadav Shragai.

But the Jerusalem police commander, Amit, broke with the under-the-radar tradition and put the deal in writing. "I said don't do it!" Bahat recalled, citing the previous good faith of waqf officials. "They have never broken an agreement!" No waqf official could acknowledge such a deal without endangering their job or even their life, Bahat added.

Ramadan had already begun when the January 24, 1996, letter was sent to two leading waqf officials. "In the course of the meeting you put forward a request to open Solomon's Stables because of the forecast of heavy rain and concern for the worshipers on the Fridays during the blessed month of Ramadan this year," it stated. "In reply to your request, I agreed to the opening of the place to worshipers during the blessed month of Ramadan."

The missive went on: "In the meeting, I said that the atmosphere of peace which prevails in the region paves the way for the opening of the Western Wall tunnels in order to achieve economic goals and to increase the flow of tourists, a development which will serve the general interest, and I shall implement this soon." The same day, Peres's security cabinet approved the deal.

The appalled Muslim leaders responded just as Bahat had predicted. "Naturally the director of the waqf had to answer that we don't agree," he remembered. On February 6, Sheikh Abdul Azim Salhab, the chairman of the waqf's board, wrote that "the position of the Muslim Council and the Waqf concerning the opening of the tunnel is clear. It will generate an atmosphere of tension and dissatisfaction and will be harmful to the city's economy and to its image in the eyes of visitors from every corner of the world, and therefore we demand that this tunnel not be opened."

He added that conversion of Solomon's Stables into a prayer space on the platform was purely a waqf matter, and not subject to Israeli approval. Neither the Jordanians nor the Palestinians could be exposed conducting a horse trade with Israel. They were done no favors when Israeli politicians dismissed the waqf response as a necessary public denial of a private deal.

The ancient stairs at the Western Wall Tunnel's northern end that had been briefly opened in 1988 were inadequate for large numbers of visitors. Mordechai (Suli) Eliav at the Western Wall Heritage Foundation had secretly ordered Bahat to create a larger exit. This work, conducted between 1990 and 1994, meant cutting away forty-five feet of rock, ending just shy of the street.

"It was very simple," Bahat said. "We were left only with the last few centimeters," a shallow membrane separating the Western Wall Tunnel from the Via Dolorosa. That winter, heavy winter rains lashed Ramadan pilgrims and flooded the tunnel. Solomon's Stables remained empty, the northern exit closed.

◆ ◆ ◆

THE VAST SPACES BENEATH the sturdy vaults of the stables had attracted the attention of more than just Muslim clerics who wanted to keep their flocks dry. As early as 1983, Prime Minister Yitzhak Shamir, in a letter to the nation's two chief rabbis, had suggested converting it into a synagogue. The subterranean hall had particular appeal since it could be used—under some interpretations of Jewish religious law—without breaking the taboo against treading on the Holy of Holies, which had been located somewhere on the platform's surface above.

Eliav was already busy turning other underground spaces into Jewish prayer sites. Wilson's Arch had long provided shelter for Western Wall worshippers, while in the adjacent tunnel, workers planned a large synagogue in the medieval foundations of what had been an Islamic religious school. After Rabbi Getz's passing in 1995, a small synagogue was dedicated to him opposite Warren's Gate.

At about the time that Bahat received the phone call from al-Husseini, Jewish religious activists approached Avraham Shapiro, Israel's chief Ashkenazi rabbi, to discuss turning the area below Solomon's Stables into a Jewish prayer space. The latter discussions were duly reported in the Israeli media, setting off alarm bells in the waqf.

Meanwhile, the turmoil unleashed by the peace process had led some Muslims to challenge the waqf's jurisdiction over the platform. The Palestinian Authority was demanding a role in administration at the expense of Jordan, while the Northern Branch of the Islamic Movement in Israel began to exert its growing power.

Led by an Arab Israeli named Sheikh Raed Salah Abu Shakra, this increasingly influential charitable association was the Muslim answer to Israel's Haredi organizations. By providing local communities with medical help, schooling, and sports activities for youth, it had gained adherents among Arabs in Israel as well as in the Palestinian territories. Protecting Muslim holy places, and the Noble Sanctuary in particular, became its popular rallying cry.

Salah's work drew the attention of the Israeli government. Eager to find out more about his goals and motives, Gideon Avni, Bahat's successor as the head of Jerusalem's archaeology directorate, was given the task of sounding him out. The archaeologist led him on a tour of the Western Wall Tunnel that spring and was surprised to find him well briefed. "He had an interest in and knowledge about archaeology," Avni recalled. "He had done his homework." It was the first of several unusual meetings between the charismatic Muslim leader and the low-key Jewish scientist.

Salah told Avni that "because this was an exclusively Muslim sacred area, archaeological data are of no relevance to the Islamic identity of the site," Avni later wrote. "In his view scientific research at such a site contradicts the religious character of the sacred enclosure, and any such research at the site should be avoided." Salah maintained that any digging should be done solely for the benefit of improving the site for worship. "Muslim believers need no further proof to reinforce" their ties to the platform, he added.

Soon after, the Israeli historian Gershom Gorenberg paid a visit to the Islamic Movement's offices in the northern Israeli town of Umm al-Fahm. The directions, Gorenberg recalled, were as forbidding as they were amusing. "Drive south past Armageddon and turn right." (Armageddon, also known as Megiddo, is an ancient city at a strategic crossroads.)

He asked one of the movement's lieutenants, Ahmad Agbariya, about Solomon's Stables. "Information reached us that Jews want to take it for a synagogue," Agbariya said. He was also concerned about the increasing talk of rebuilding a Jewish temple by ultra-religious Jewish groups. When Gorenberg inquired about when that might take place, the Islamic Movement official was very specific. "In three years," he said. "And three years will be up in August 1999."

Both Gorenberg's and Avni's contacts with the Islamic Movement came to an abrupt end in the wake of Netanyahu's electoral victory in May. By July, as Netanyahu was grappling with the problem of Hirbawi's basement, Muslim workers quietly had begun to turn Solomon's Stables from storeroom to prayer space. Drawing on more than a half-million dollars in private donations and the help of volunteers, the Islamic Movement coordinated the renovation.

Avni contended that the group now dominated decisions on the Noble

Sanctuary. Waqf officials insisted they worked with rather than for Salah. What was indisputable was that the quarter century of coffee-drinking chats between Israeli and Palestinian professionals was over. A new era had begun, one in which religious fundamentalists on both sides held greater sway.

♦ ♦ ♦

THE PROSPECT THAT Solomon's Stables would become a mosque out-raged many strictly Orthodox Jews. On September 4, the same day that Netanyahu met Arafat for the first time in person, Jerusalem mayor Olmert secured a court injunction ordering the work in Solomon's Stables halted until the city issued a building permit.

The grand mufti of Jerusalem, Sheikh Ekrima Sabri, then argued that the underground space was outside Israeli jurisdiction, and he kept city inspectors at a distance. The national government's only recourse to enforce the court's order was to send in police, which would only risk sparking a bloodbath.

Six days later, the Temple Mount Faithful—a right-wing group that had sparked a deadly riot in 1990 when members tried to lay a cornerstone for a new temple—increased the pressure on the Israeli government to intervene by asking the High Court to "prevent the site from being turned into a mosque." The group had long accused the IAA of abetting waqf efforts at "eradicating Jewish identification with the Temple Mount." The suit argued that the illegal renovation was destroying ancient Jewish heritage.

The Netanyahu government countered that the Solomon's Stables alterations were "an internal change" that "did not cause practical harm to antiquities." The Israeli archaeologist Jon Seligman noted that "a stone floor was laid by hundreds of volunteers of the Islamic Movement, and electrical cables and light fixtures were attached to the columns." Carpets donated by the Moroccan king were laid. Some of the work violated con-servation principles—such as drilling holes into stone walls—but it did not inflict significant damage, he added. On September 16, the judges rejected the Temple Mount Faithful's complaint, and concluded that no building permit was required.

The crisis averted, Netanyahu secretly gave the green light that same day for Bahat to prepare to open the Western Wall Tunnel's northern exit.

Israeli intelligence officials, however, were alarmed. Friday sermons and Palestinian Authority rumblings suggested this move would elicit violence. "I was against the opening," said Yisrael Hasson, the Jerusalem chief of the country's security agency, Shin Bet, and who later would direct the IAA. He begged officials in the prime minister's office to wait. "Just give me three months," he recalled saying, "and I will find a way to open it peacefully." They refused.

Netanyahu's motives are disputed. One Israeli historian concluded that the new prime minister was misled into thinking that a quid pro quo with the waqf was in place. His government had ensured the stables' renovations could proceed without interference, and now it was time for the waqf to hold up its end of the bargain. Saeb Erekat, a senior Palestinian Authority diplomat, saw a more nefarious goal: "It was part of his strategy to get rid of any prospects of a just and lasting peace."

Dennis Ross, who worked as a Middle East peace negotiator for Clinton, said the decision resulted from pressure exerted by Olmert, the mayor and Likud rival angling to outflank his prime minister on the right. "I had a call from our ambassador in Israel saying that Olmert was pushing Bibi [Netanyahu's nickname] to open the exit, even though all the intelligence agencies were against it," he said. "This was Olmert's doing. Bibi just acquiesced."

American diplomats urged the Israeli prime minister to tread cautiously. Anywhere else in the world, making a new exit in an underground tourist attraction would hardly be newsworthy, much less draw an explicit warning from the world's sole superpower.

◆ ◆ ◆

THE JEWISH FAST of Yom Kippur, the holiest day on the Jewish calendar, ended at sunset on Monday, September 23, 1996. After midnight, Bahat's workers, protected by darkness and Israeli soldiers, hammered away at the last foot of rock separating the new tunnel's new stairway from the Via Dolorosa. They then closed the hole with a temporary wall.

The new exit lay directly across the street from the Franciscan monastery commemorating the first two stations of the cross, where Jesus by tradition was condemned and forced to take up the instrument of his execution. Around the corner was one of the primary gates for Muslim worshippers to enter the Noble Sanctuary.

The next morning, Jerusalem's senior Jewish religious and political figures gathered on the narrow street outside the new exit, which Mayor Olmert predicted would benefit the city. He also made it clear to the media covering the event that Israel was sending a pointed message to Palestinians.

"The government says, 'Hey guys, we are not playing games here.' We will not agree that everything that happens in Jerusalem will be subject to negotiations." Then he himself wielded a sledgehammer to open the stairway, and the group chanted Psalms in Hebrew in praise of Jerusalem.

A prominent spectator was Grand Mufti Sabri. "He was standing there, watching the television cameras and the officials," recalled Hasson, the Israeli intelligence official. "He pulled out his phone and called Arafat. I heard him—he was as close to me as you are now. I heard it with my own ears. He told Arafat that the Jews were digging under the Temple Mount."

When he hung up, Hasson told him, "'Look, Sheikh Sabri, this is not under the Temple Mount.' He said, 'I don't care! This goes under the Temple Mount!'" Hasson quickly dialed Arafat, whom he knew well. "I said the tunnel does not go under the Temple Mount. But there was no talking to him."

The dispute echoed the conflict instigated by Warren more than a century before, when he excavated beneath the city's Islamic court near the Wailing Wall. A delegation from Jerusalem's city council had visited the digs and declared that the British officer was working beneath the Noble Sanctuary. To avoid such allegations, Bahat had given waqf officials tours of the Western Wall Tunnel.

As European Christians did in the 1860s, Israeli officials dismissed Muslim complaints that the platform was under threat as inaccurate and alarmist. Yet many of the city's oldest and most important Islamic buildings were constructed next to the Western Wall. Muslims considered them part and parcel of a sacred zone that extended beyond the wall itself.

"We opposed the tunnel from the beginning," Ziad Abu-Ziad, a member of the Palestinian ministerial council, told the Israeli newspaper *Haaretz*. "There are Islamic structures above the tunnel that are ancient, and culturally, historically and religiously valuable. There are active offices of public institutions and religious organizations, and Arab families also live there. The tunnel works endanger the buildings. But it's not just a safety issue. It's hard to get rid of the impression that the Israeli goal is aggressive."

In less than an hour, hundreds of Arab residents were marching through the streets of the Old City. Police fired rubber bullets to prevent them from reaching the site. After the noon Muslim prayers, the crowds thickened. "They started to shout from the minarets that Jews were penetrating the Temple Mount," said Bahat. "That was enough."

A truck and a car were set ablaze outside the Old City, sending a column of smoke into the early autumn sky. When dozens of young Muslim demonstrators began to throw rocks from the platform onto Jewish worshippers at the Western Wall Plaza, police briefly closed both the plaza and the platform. "Why did they put it in their minds to open it now?" a distraught al-Husseini said to a *Los Angeles Times* reporter. "It means the peace is over."

Arafat warned that "the Palestinian people will not stand with their hands tied." He demanded that the UN Security Council intervene. His cabinet subsequently called for a general strike. Other Arab leaders also denounced Netanyahu's move. Morocco's King Hassan II warned the same day that the tunnel opening put the peace process "in a state of crisis." Jordan's King Hussein said the new exit was an insult to Muslims. The Arab League in Cairo warned that Israel "has provoked outrage among Muslims in the world," and demonstrations spread from Jordan to Morocco.

In what proved remarkably bad timing, Netanyahu had just arrived in Europe on a diplomatic visit designed to charm skeptical leaders into believing his sincere desire for peace. At first, he was unrepentant. "It should have been done before, and I'm proud that we did it today," he told reporters. "There is no truth to the wild claims made that we were digging under the Temple Mount. Every leader in the Arab world knows that there is no truth to these things. All we did was allow visitors, Muslims, Jews or Christians, instead of making a U-turn, to go directly out of the tunnel."

This goal of ensuring a smooth flow of people had been Bahat's aim for years, but that argument held little weight with Muslims. For them, the convenience of tourists was an excuse used by the Israeli government to extend its influence beneath their feet. Netanyahu had acknowledged that the tunnel was far more than a tourist site when he paid a visit the previous year and praised it as a vital expression of Jewish identity. While underground, he said he felt he had touched "our rock of existence."

The protests and riots quickly took an ominous turn in the West Bank and Gaza when some Palestinian police attacked Israeli forces. For the first time, Palestinian Authority personnel were locked in battle against the Israeli Defense Forces. By nightfall on Wednesday, 4 Palestinians lay dead and 240 were injured. "Nothing like this had happened since the beginning of the Oslo process," the American diplomat Dennis Ross wrote. "The violence seemed to have a life of its own."

Meeting with French president Jacques Chirac in Paris, Netanyahu confronted a growing storm of international criticism. The tunnel opening created "a new and regrettable factor of tension," the French Ministry of Foreign Affairs said in a statement. The U.S. State Department also implicitly criticized Israel, urging both sides to avoid "obstacles" that could make the situation worse—a clear reference to the exit.

In a rare united rebuke to an Israel leader, the leaders of France, Germany, and the United Kingdom released a joint letter to Netanyahu expressing "our grave concern at the tragic events." They also "welcomed the announcement of the decision to close the tunnel under the Holy City," a sign that the prime minister intended to reverse the controversial move.

Thursday brought a new round of violence. At the traditional site of Joseph's Tomb in the city of Nablus, hundreds of Palestinian demonstrators and police attacked the holy place, killing a half-dozen Israeli soldiers and trapping 42 in an adjacent Jewish religious school. A rescue operation by the Israeli Defense Forces proved costly. By day's end, a total of 39 Palestinians and 11 Israeli soldiers were dead, with 762 Palestinians and 44 Israelis injured.

"I deeply regret the injuries and loss of life we've seen in the West Bank and Gaza in the last few days," a somber Clinton told reporters at the White House. "I ask both sides to end the violence." But the situation continued to escalate.

Netanyahu returned to Israel that night. He met with his cabinet for seven hours, until the early hours of Friday, September 27. Defense Minister Yitzhak Mordechai told him that "the Palestinian Authority has no full control over what is going on in the streets" and counseled compromise. Others rejected that course. Faced with the loss of so many Israeli soldiers and under pressure from the right not to retreat, the prime minister hardened his position.

At a press conference in Jerusalem on Friday morning, Netanyahu reiterated that the new exit posed no threat. He accused Palestinians of turning the tunnel into "a religious issue of fanaticism" and insisted the riots "were not spontaneous at first, but organized by the Palestinian Authority." He reiterated that the tunnel was "the bedrock of our existence." Meanwhile, Arab newspapers warned that a new and more violent intifada was underway.

What had begun as a secret effort by rabbis to expose Herod's ancient wall to increase their prayer space was now on the world's front pages and at the epicenter of the Israeli-Arab conflict.

Faisal Husseini, Jerusalem's Palestinian Authority leader, was injured later that day when he joined protestors attempting to reach the exit. "I told them this tunnel would lead to this," he said to a *New York Times* reporter from his hospital bed. In the Palestinian city of Jenin alone, more than ten thousand protestors marched through the streets carrying signs opposing the tunnel opening.

In Washington, Clinton grappled with how to prevent not just the collapse of the peace process but the outbreak of a full-scale war between Palestinians and Israelis that could morph into a wider regional conflict. Secretary of State Warren Christopher "burned up the phone lines" with Netanyahu and Arafat to stop the bloodshed, the president recalled in his autobiography.

He added that "the Israelis had opened a tunnel that ran under the Temple Mount in Jerusalem's Old City." This statement revealed how difficult it was for politicians to grasp the subtleties of the ancient city's complicated subterranean world. When Clinton first visited Jerusalem in 1981, the Western Wall Tunnel was still closed to visitors. On his 1995 return as president, his advisors made sure he steered clear of the controversial project. "Olmert wanted to bring Clinton on a tour of the tunnels, and we decided we didn't want to do that," Ross later said. "It would have caused a huge issue, and symbolism here is so important."

Alarmed by the continued chaos, Ross suggested to Clinton that he call for an unprecedented meeting at the White House of Israeli, Jordanian, Egyptian, and Palestinian leaders. "Only a dramatic step would suffice," the diplomat said. But it was an unpopular idea among the president's advisors. His bid for reelection was less than five weeks away, and Clinton's Republican rival, Bob Dole, had criticized the Democratic incumbent for pressuring Israel to make concessions in the peace talks.

"Can we get Netanyahu to close the tunnel?" asked Clinton, according to Ross's account. "Probably not," the diplomat responded. "But we could use the summit to launch a new round of negotiations." Clinton agreed. "I invited Netanyahu and Arafat to the White House to talk things over," he wrote. But Arafat first insisted that the Israeli leader close the tunnel exit, while Netanyahu demanded an immediate end to the violence.

By Friday afternoon, riots erupted again on the Noble Sanctuary, where hundreds of Israeli police using rubber bullets and tear gas clashed with stone-throwing Arabs. Eyewitnesses reported use of live ammunition. "The blood is all over the ground, especially in front of al-Aqsa Mosque," a Muslim shopkeeper from East Jerusalem named Abu Khalil told the *New York Times.* He claimed Israeli forces had opened fire on unarmed protestors. A later Israeli investigation found no evidence of this, but it did conclude there was "unjustified firing of rubber bullets at a forbidden range."

From his Gaza headquarters, Arafat said, "It is necessary to calm the situation down. But the attempt to attack worshipers inside the mosque is something that cannot be tolerated." In retaliation, Israeli helicopter gunships fired on the West Bank city of Ramallah, while tanks surrounded Nablus. Dozens were killed and injured in sporadic violence across the region. At one Jewish holy site outside Jerusalem, Rachel's Tomb, Palestinian police held back Arab demonstrators to avoid further bloodshed. "I have not seen such hysteria and such determination on the part of Palestinians," one shocked Israeli border guard told a reporter.

Israel's Labor Party, meanwhile, lambasted Netanyahu for needlessly triggering the violence, while the country's Arab community launched a general strike to show their solidarity with Palestinians. A former tourism minister called the government's move to open the exit "a monstrous decision that can only confirm the concerns of the Arab world from Israel."

At the United Nations, the Saudi Arabian ambassador delivered a complaint to the Security Council decrying the Israeli move to open "an entrance to the tunnel extending under the al-Aqsa Mosque in occupied East Jerusalem." The council debated a watered-down resolution calling for "the immediate cessation and reversal of all acts which have resulted in the aggravation of the situation, and which have negative implications for the Middle East peace process."

Angry at what Clinton saw as an unnecessary Israeli provocation, and at Netanyahu's intransigence, the U.S. delegation abstained from the 14–0 vote on September 28, allowing the resolution to pass. Even in abstention, it was an unusual public rebuke of Israeli actions by its leading ally.

By Sunday, the violence began to subside, but not the protests. Thousands of left-wing supporters of the Israeli organization Peace Now marched from the grave of assassinated prime minister Rabin to Netanyahu's home in a show of support for the peace talks. The prime minister was defiant. "I do not regret that we opened the Western Wall Tunnel, which has no effect on the Temple Mount, and expresses our sovereignty over Jerusalem," he said in a press conference.

The same day, Netanyahu and King Hussein agreed to attend an emergency meeting at the White House hosted by Clinton. Arafat hesitated.

He told an Israeli newspaper that "the closing of the tunnel would show prudent judgment," adding, "We expect the situation at the tunnel to go back to the way it was. Then the storm will fade." Once it became clear Netanyahu would not back down, he accepted the American president's invitation.

On October 1, while Arafat was at the White House, the Palestinian Authority called on Israel to close the Western Wall Tunnel permanently. At a lunch the same day, Ross joined Netanyahu and Arafat for two hours of private talks. "Arafat had felt that Bibi was taking him for granted—this was a chance to show him that he had to deal with him," Ross recalled. He said that Netanyahu told Arafat, "We can surprise the world." Arafat's response was a simple "Okay."

In the end, those discussions led to a January 1997 agreement over how Israeli and Palestinian forces would jointly police the holy city of Hebron, a possible template for an agreement to handle Jerusalem. It came at a dreadful cost. Four days of violence left seventy-four Palestinians and sixteen Israeli soldiers dead, and more than a thousand Palestinians and fifty-eight Israelis wounded.

Netanyahu refused all face-saving suggestions on the tunnel, said Ross. King Hussein had suggested suspending its opening until archaeologists could show it posed no threat to the platform, a proposal the Israeli leader rejected. He also said he would not allow the waqf to renovate Solomon's Stables—a renovation that was, however, already underway. According to Ross, Clinton berated Netanyahu privately for his inflexibility.

Some supporters of Israel charged Arafat with orchestrating the violence to suppress archaeological truth. Writing in the *Washington Post* on Sunday, September 29, the president of the Zionist Organization of America, Morton Klein, said that Palestinians feared "a much larger number of people will be able to view the ancient archaeological sites beneath Jerusalem's ground—sites that provide vivid testimony to the 3,000-plus years of Jewish history in Jerusalem."

He added that "every visitor to the tunnel views a wide array of evidence testifying to the long Jewish presence, including an ancient Jewish water system used in the time of King Solomon (nearly 3,000 years ago) and an aqueduct built by the Maccabees, in the second century BCE— evidence of Jerusalem's deep Jewish roots. This shatters the Arab propaganda claim that historically, Jerusalem has been an Arab city."

In fact, outside the Bible, there was no evidence that King Solomon had existed, much less that he had constructed a water system. There was ample historical and archaeological evidence that Jews had deep roots in Jerusalem, yet no credible historian denied that Arabs had controlled the city for nearly half of the past three millennia, far longer and much more recently than Jews.

The threat of a regional war or a renewed intifada gradually receded, though occasional demonstrations and sporadic violence continued through the fall. In October, police dragged dozens of Jewish as well as Muslim protestors away from the tunnel exit. "We have shed enough of our blood and are not willing to pay more for a tunnel," said Sergio Yani, an Israeli Jew who was among them.

In the meantime, the Knesset learned that neither Israel's intelligence nor defense leaders had been given time to prepare for the violence that flared in September. The defense minister revealed that he only learned about the tunnel opening five minutes before it took place. "A thousand tunnels are not worth a Jewish or Palestinian son killed in a riot," one Arab Knesset member said.

Amid the carnage and recriminations aboveground, workers on the Noble Sanctuary continued their subterranean work in Solomon's Stables. On December 19, five thousand Muslim worshippers filed into what was officially dubbed the Marwani prayer space. The name was carefully chosen. Marwan I was the caliph who founded the line of leaders who turned early Islamic Jerusalem into a political as well as religious center, precisely what Palestinians hoped to accomplish with their new state.

By then, tourists could make their way through the entrance of the Western Wall Tunnel at the Western Wall Plaza, take in the underground sights, and then exit at the Via Dolorosa. From there, they were escorted by Israeli soldiers out of the Muslim Quarter. Soon, the number of visitors quintupled. Bahat had been right; it soon became Jerusalem's third-most-popular tourist attraction after the Holy Sepulchre and the Western Wall itself.

The impact of the tunnel on the peace process was just beginning. In the wake of the riots, the underground passage was about to play a central role in undermining Clinton's last desperate effort to reconcile Abraham's quarreling children.

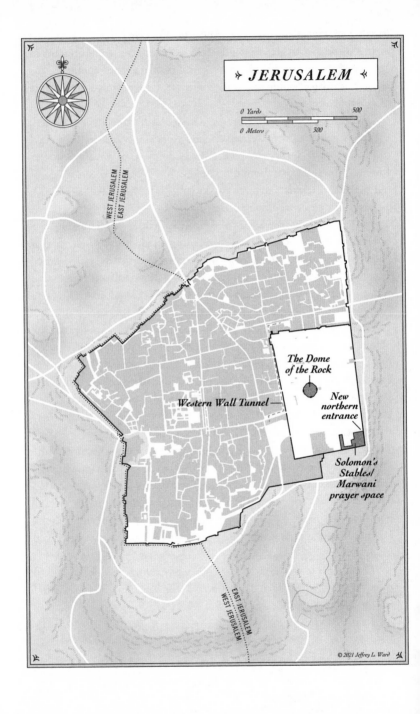

JERUSALEM 2021

0 Yards   500
0 Meters   300

WEST JERUSALEM
EAST JERUSALEM

The Dome
of the Rock

New
northern
entrance

Western Wall Tunnel —

Solomon's
Stables/
Marwani
prayer space

EAST JERUSALEM
WEST JERUSALEM

© 2021 Jeffrey L. Ward

16

Millennial Madness

If you aren't writing your story, others will write it for you.
—WAJAHAT ALI

On Monday August 9, 1999, a six-foot-wide hole materialized in the southern wall of the Noble Sanctuary. Waqf managers explained to Israeli officials that they had removed a few stones in order to provide better ventilation for the large but windowless new Marwani prayer space. Skeptical Israeli security agents suspected it was the first step in creating a new entrance into the sacred platform.

If it were true, it would mean thousands of Muslim worshippers trooping through the archaeological ruins on the slope below to enter the platform. For the Israeli government, this would be the Palestinian equivalent of opening the northern exit of the Western Wall Tunnel, a provocative threat to the status quo.

Israel's newly installed prime minister assembled his cabinet for an emergency meeting. Tired of twenty-two years of war in Lebanon and perpetually stalled peace talks, Israeli voters in May had ousted Netanyahu in favor of Ehud Barak, the leader of the left-wing Labor Party.

With Israeli riot police on alert, Palestinian workers quickly installed an iron grate over the opening to calm the prime minister's concerns. This failed to satisfy Barak. "We will not accept violations of the law," he said. "We will not accept a unilateral act." He warned that he was prepared to order the police to block the offending window. Muslim leaders got the message. By dawn on Tuesday, it had been sealed.

Swift negotiations between Israeli and Palestinian leaders had averted a potentially bloody calamity. What newspapers did not report was that the two sides had cut a secret deal. In exchange for Muslim agreement to seal the window, the Israelis approved creation of a second Marwani entrance.

This practical compromise took place in the shadow of the millennium's turn, as much of the world wondered whether computers would freeze up at the stroke of midnight. In Jerusalem, the concerns were of a different sort. The pope had declared 2000 a jubilee year for the Catholic Church, and record numbers of pilgrims and tourists were expected to descend on the Holy City. There were fears that extremists might take the opportunity to launch terrorist acts to gain public attention.

There were also concerns that the celebration could spark an outbreak of Jerusalem syndrome, a mental affliction in which patients lose a sense of their selves and the present, and can take on the personalities of prophets or Jesus, often with the help of a hotel bedsheet. An uptick of cases in the fall of 1999 prompted authorities to put a medical team from a Jerusalem hospital on alert, and an emergency room with twelve beds was set aside for those afflicted with the typically temporary psychosis.

The primary concern of Israel's Ministry of Religious Affairs was more prosaic. Massive crowds might overwhelm popular sites like the Holy Sepulchre, which had only one exit. "What will happen if there is a fire?" asked ministry official Uri Mor in a newspaper interview in June 1999. "During Greek Easter, there are about 17,000 people gathering in the church. It takes them three to three and a half hours to evacuate through this door peacefully."

Both Israelis and Palestinians shared similar fears about the Marwani. The enormous space could hold up to fifteen thousand worshippers, yet it had only one access point. This was a single narrow doorway from the small room known as the Cradle of Jesus, the same entry that Mark Twain had used in 1867. Individuals had to line up to enter and exit. Ten years before, more than fourteen hundred Muslim pilgrims had died in a tunnel in Mecca during a stampede. Were a similar disaster to befall Jerusalem, the Israeli government would surely be considered culpable.

"We needed to prepare for 2000," Sheikh Azzam al-Khatib, who later became director of the Jerusalem Islamic waqf, explained. "People were coming from all over." The IAA's Seligman agreed the lone entry "was clearly inadequate for some 15,000 believers who would now fill the new prayer hall. The necessity for an emergency exit to the new mosque is clear."

Ramadan was slated to begin December 9, 1999, followed three weeks later by the start of the new millennium. Waqf authorities quickly came up with a plan approved by Barak's office. Nine large sealed arches lined the north side of the buried building. Opening one of those would allow Muslims to enter and exit directly from the platform, according to Yusuf Natsheh, director of the Haram al-Sharif's tourism and archaeology department. The olive grove just north of the Marwani was cleared in preparation.

On Thursday, November 28, the eve of a Jerusalem weekend, workers began to excavate by hand from the platform's ground level to reach the arch that had long ago been covered in debris. The initial digging showed that the "accumulation of earth was larger than anyone expected," Natsheh said. Exposing a single arch meant leaving a precarious wall of earth on either side, so the decision was made on the spot to open more than one.

"Both the waqf engineers and the Islamic Movement knew that these arches were access gates on the surface in the past," added the Palestinian archaeologist Ehab Jallad. "What was outside had since been filled with soil and garbage, so they decided to uncover two of the gates."

What happened next is a matter of dispute. "The waqf was in charge; it did the design and the entire project was conducted under the supervision of Israeli police," insisted Sheik Azzam. But several eyewitnesses said that the waqf excavation team halted its work when it hit the top of the arches in order to allow Palestinian conservators to inspect the area before they continued; this was standard practice with an ancient site. The dig team and waqf officials then stopped work for the weekend; Natsheh himself said he was on vacation at the time.

After they departed, heavy equipment roared through Lions' Gate on the northeast corner of the Old City, the same entry used by Israeli soldiers to conquer the walled town in 1967. Three bulldozers and a fleet of dump trucks then took a left turn that brought them to the Noble Sanctuary's northeastern entrance and onto the platform itself. This was no rogue operation; Israeli guards carefully monitored all comings and goings from the Muslim site at all hours. The guards waved the bulldozers through, a clear sign that the effort had the stamp of approval of Israeli authorities.

"Things were tense then," said Jallad. "The Israelis didn't seem to care about the planned exit construction, and if they were, they could always have closed the gates." The vehicles rumbled south across the platform's east side. In the open area in front of the long-buried Marwani, the bulldozers began to gouge a broad ramp out of the soil in order to expose the buried arches.

Eyewitnesses said officials from the Islamic Movement, not the waqf, oversaw the operations. According to the Israeli media, the group's leader, Sheikh Salah, had even sent a letter to the grand mufti boasting that he intended to open seven arches for "what the engineers refer to as 'emergency exits.'"

The noise and dust drew at least two alarmed Palestinian archaeologists who lived nearby. "Nobody is allowed to take bulldozers there," said Nazmi Jubeh, a Birzeit University historian and archaeologist. "No bulldozer should be used at any archaeological site. Not even on the upper layer!" He sought out the project supervisor, who assured him the work had the approval of the Israeli prime minister.

"I was there in a private capacity to see what was going on," Jubeh recalled. "I have nothing to do with the waqf; I was just watching. Everybody knew that if they didn't move quickly, the Israelis would stop it. There was a war on! You cannot blame them for using bulldozers when every day there was a threat to the mosque." But he was relieved to see that the area under excavation appeared to be "absolutely a dump" that showed no trace of architecture.

Jubeh said he nevertheless carefully monitored the operation. "I remember exactly when they reached the virgin strata. I stood there and said 'Khalas!' No more!" When the bulldozer powered down, he said, "no architectural remain had been removed—not a single stone. The only pieces were columns that supported a part of the city wall, but they were not removed, and they are still in place." Natsheh, though not an eyewitness, agreed with this assessment. "There was no archaeology," he said of the Marwani dig. "No one found even a capital or a column."

One young Palestinian archaeologist, who was present but preferred anonymity, saw the situation differently. "I knew what was going on," he said. "It was destruction. Nothing was recorded. We lost data." Torn between his scientific training and his identity as a Palestinian, he found himself unsure of what to do. "So I did nothing," he added. Two decades later, there was still anguish in his voice.

This disagreement over whether the Marwani dig was an act of wanton destruction marked a generational as much as a political or religious divide. Israeli archaeologists, such as Mazar, Ben-Dov, and Avigad, had used bulldozers in the 1960s and '70s to remove layers without detailed analysis. For an older generation, dumps from later periods were obstacles to finding ancient residences, palaces, and shrines.

Younger archaeologists, by contrast, tended to view dumps as treasure heaps. Thanks to scientific advances, seeds, ceramics, bones, and even human fecal matter could provide a wealth of data on past health, diet, and trading patterns. Such practices, however, were slow to catch on among Israeli archaeologists in Jerusalem, and were absorbed at an even slower pace by the small and poorly funded coterie of Palestinian excavators— who, in any case, were forbidden from digging within Jerusalem.

From the perspective of Arabs who were not archaeologists, the bulldozers could even be seen as preserving rather than destroying cultural heritage. Opening the new exit increased the numbers and safety of worshippers in one of Islam's oldest prayer spaces; in that sense, it strengthened Muslim tradition.

◆ ◆ ◆

MORE THAN THIRTY dump truck loads, carrying enough material to fill three and a half Olympic swimming pools, passed through Lions' Gate to municipal waste sites. The prime minister's office, which knew of the excavation plans, had left the IAA out of the loop. "We didn't get wind of it until Saturday," said IAA archaeologist Jon Seligman.

Barak and Arafat were locked in tense negotiations, and the prime minister apparently preferred to keep the matter quiet. Not until the start of the country's work week on Sunday morning did the IAA convince the Israeli government to order the work halted. By then, the excavation had been underway for a total of thirty-six hours. "Barak didn't realize why this was so important and what damage it would cause," added Seligman's colleague, Gideon Avni.

When Seligman arrived at the platform on Sunday, he found a 140-foot-wide dirt ramp sloping for more than 100 feet to the north side of the Marwani. Two of the arches had been unblocked, and a third was partially opened. Three additional arches were fully exposed and portions of three more were visible. "The extraction of the ancient layers without supervision, recording and systematic archaeological excavation, resulted in the loss of archaeological data of supreme value," he later wrote. In addition, he spotted damage to a nearby medieval covered passageway and an ancient wall, as well as a cistern and water channel.

Seligman blamed "the recent radicalization of the waqf, catalyzed by the Islamic Movement" for what he characterized as an archaeological disaster. He believed that the Islamic Movement took advantage of the moment, with the cooperation of the waqf. "They knew exactly what they were doing," he added. He railed against a "disastrous" excavation that "should be not tolerated and must not be allowed to recur."

Avni took a more nuanced view of the event. He saw it as a result of a long-standing power struggle between the comparatively moderate waqf and radical fundamentalists. "The Islamic Movement didn't ask anyone" for permission to use heavy machinery, he said. Desperate officials from the waqf had phoned Israeli archaeologists during the weekend. "They said, 'Help us, they are destroying everything!' They said they couldn't do anything." Neither could Avni or Seligman until it was too late.

Strictly Orthodox Jewish groups had long shown more contempt than sympathy for excavations. Now they decried the Marwani dig as an act of desecration—even cultural genocide. The Muslims were guilty of the "systematic destruction of Jewish remains," thundered an editorial in *Hatzofeh,* a newspaper run by the National Religious Party. The writer ominously warned that "there are more and more Jews" willing to take up arms to defend the Temple Mount, and predicted a "very high certainty of an insane Jewish outburst of violence" over what had taken place.

Other Israelis pointed out that Christians had conducted dozens of excavations within the Holy Sepulchre, many without proper professional supervision. "The church is an extraordinarily important archaeological site, but at no time did we hear the workers there being accused by [Israel] Antiquities Authority chairman Amir Drori of committing an 'archaeological crime,' as he said the waqf is now doing," noted one commentator. "The reason is that the site of the tomb of Jesus is of no interest to the Jews, whereas on the Temple Mount a protracted struggle is underway by Jewish groups who want to wrest the compound from Muslim hands."

Waqf officials dismissed Jewish criticism of the Marwani dig as hypocritical. "The Israelis used bulldozers to destroy archaeological sites in the Mughrabi Quarter, and no one complained about that," Sheikh Azzam acidly noted.

The growing outcry among Israelis forced Barak to convene a meeting of senior government officials, including Drori, to address the crisis. The prime minister acknowledged that the Muslim authorities acted with government authorization, but added that the work "went beyond the bounds of reasonableness" by exposing two additional arches.

Shlomo Ben-Ami, the minister of public security, warned Barak that any forceful Israeli response could led to a repeat of the 1996 bloodbath that followed the opening of the Western Wall Tunnel. Attorney General Elyakim Rubinstein agreed. At the end of the meeting, the prime minister decided to insist that the waqf close off all but two arches.

Ben-Ami assured waiting reporters that "no Jewish archaeological damage has been done. The main damage was to medieval findings of the Muslims themselves." Drori agreed in his December 14 testimony to a Knesset committee. "I can say that there was antiquities violation, but I can say that what was damaged was mainly Muslim from the Middle Ages."

A petition filed by the litigious Temple Mount Faithful demanded the government stop the activity and restore the platform to its previous state. In an affidavit submitted to the High Court, Drori acknowledged the excavation as "an archaeological crime" but explained that the Muslim authorities already had lined the bottom of the trench with concrete to make the entrance gate. The damage was done. An IAA document submitted to the High Court added that, "to the best of the authorities' knowledge," no Jewish antiquities were harmed.

Data submitted by the IAA contradicted this claim. The results of a brief survey of the dirt taken to a municipal dump estimated that one-third of the material dated to the era before the 70 CE Roman destruction of Jewish Jerusalem. Nevertheless, the attorney general warned the High Court that approving the petition "is almost certain to bring about the shedding of blood and the inflaming of passions that could easily spread from the Temple Mount and Jerusalem to the territories and all of Israel."

His public position was directly at odds with his private beliefs. "The vestiges of the Jewish people's history are being trampled," he declared in a private meeting reported in *Haaretz*. "We must tell the waqf and the Muslims: We, too, have a history. Do not run roughshod over our history!"

Barak's attempt to stem the furor failed. Mayor Olmert denounced Barak's secret agreement with Islamic clerics as a "capitulation" to "Muslim extremists."

◆ ◆ ◆

A FEW DAYS BEFORE the new millennium began, more than three thousand demonstrators gathered on Mount Scopus, overlooking the distant Temple Mount, to protest the archaeological destruction. On that brisk day, the Dome of the Rock gleamed in the distance with its new coating of gold; the Jordanian king had recently sold a London home to pay for the upgrade to demonstrate his personal commitment to the platform.

"It was the largest demonstration Temple activists had ever pulled together, a sign of growing support on the radical wing of 'redemptive Zionism,'" noted the Israeli historian Gershom Gorenberg. "The bulldozers unnecessarily exposed an old divide," he added. "What is a living holy place for Muslims is a historic symbol for Jews."

The protest was unusual not just for its large numbers, but for including individuals from both sides of the old secular and religious rift in Israeli Jewish society. As the new millennium was about to begin, these old adversaries found themselves allied in their demand that Jewish heritage be protected and respected by Palestinians.

A thin, dark-haired sophomore at Tel Aviv's Bar-Ilan University named Zach Dvira watched coverage of the rally on television. He grew up in a household that wasn't very religious and he had worked in software. But, like many in his generation, he had embraced his Jewish religious identity, and even changed his name from the German-Yiddish Zweig to a Hebrew word meaning "Holy of Holies." He gave up programming to study the Bible, which led him to archaeology.

That semester he was taking a course on the era around 1000 BCE, when the Israelites were thought to have conquered Jerusalem and made it their capital. Images of bulldozers scooping up tons of earth on the Temple Mount had both appalled and excited him.

"I knew the material would be out of context, but I thought of doing what you do during an archaeological survey," he said. "You pick up artifacts that are 'floating' on the ground. This can give you a lot of data before you actually excavate. And since there had been no archaeological digs on the Temple Mount, this seemed a unique opportunity."

He read a report in *Haaretz* that was vague about exactly where the trucks had dumped the material, so Dvira called the article writer, Nadav Shragai. He pointed him in turn to Yehuda Etzion, who had tracked the trucks when they left the Noble Sanctuary.

Etzion was a controversial figure, having hatched an early 1980s plot to blow up the Dome of the Rock in order to trigger the construction of a new Jewish temple. An Israeli court convicted him and he was imprisoned, though he remained unrepentant. "The one thing I am sure of is that the Dome of the Rock is a temporary building," he told a reporter in August 1999. "It must come to an end. Exactly when and exactly how I cannot say." That November, he had filed a private petition with the High Court to block the changes to Solomon's Stables, which the judges dismissed.

Etzion told Dvira that he had seen the trucks take bulldozed material to the Kidron Valley, about a quarter mile south of the Old City, and to a municipal dump two miles to the east. On Sunday, December 12, the college sophomore made a brief visit to the Kidron site, which had been a refuse area for Jerusalem since ancient times. Three days later he convinced his brother and a few friends, along with Etzion, to come with him to do a preliminary survey of the material.

The sun was setting by the time they parked the white Fiat in the unpaved lot. It was easy to spot the huge mound of freshly dumped dirt. But with darkness descending, the group only had time to collect about thirty pieces of pottery and bits of stone. The others eventually left, leaving Dvira and his brother behind. They soon discovered they were not alone.

"To our surprise, about ten young Muslim guys came up with an older guy," Dvira recalled. That older man "said that he was from the waqf, and we had to leave the site immediately. He threatened to call the police. It was absurd! Here was a representative of the very group responsible for this violation."

The waqf official explained that the dirt had been dumped there with the permission of the Israeli prime minister and Mayor Olmert. He warned them to be careful at night there, since they might be attacked. He also told them not to "plant" any Jewish coins so that they could claim there was a Jewish temple on the platform. The man, whose name he did not get, added that there were only Muslim and Christian remains to be found there.

"I didn't want to get into a fight," said Dvira. "It felt like a dangerous situation, so we left." He called IAA chief Drori to alert him to the presence of antiquities in the dump. When he didn't hear back by the next morning, he phoned Gideon Avni. "He tried to calm me down and say it wasn't that bad, that the material was just fill from medieval times." Avni assured him there was nothing of archaeological value to be found by pawing through the piles of displaced dirt; random artifacts ripped from their original context could provide little data.

Later that morning, at the university, Dvira showed some of the objects he had taken from the dump to Bahat, who identified a tool from the early centuries BCE. Two days later, on Wednesday, December 15, the student rounded up fifteen volunteers, plus Etzion and some of his supporters. The team first visited the East Jerusalem dump and spent two hours gathering pottery and using a metal detector, a device illegal in Israel outside of licensed excavations. Then they headed to the Kidron site. Along the way, to Dvira's surprise, they encountered an ABC *Nightline* crew as well as Shragai from *Haaretz*. The media-savvy Etzion had invited them to join the expedition.

When they arrived at the Kidron site, however, their work was cut short. "Within five minutes, the IAA's anti-theft unit showed up and told us to leave," he said. "The inspectors told us not to touch a thing." According to the unit's leader, Amir Ganor, who testified in court, Etzion and the others turned hostile. "Everybody gathered around me and began shouting 'Israeli Nazis! Go catch the Arabs on the Temple Mount who are destroying antiquities!" Etzion then continued to dig, but Ganor decided to avoid confrontation. Meanwhile, Dvira recalled, Arab youth on the slope above began throwing firecrackers at the group, and the Israelis eventually left.

Later that night, Dvira's volunteers came to his apartment with the materials they had dug out of the dump, and he began to catalog the finds. The next day he took the artifacts in several dirty bags to each of his archaeology professors. Some refused to examine what they said were looted items, since they were acquired without a dig permit. Others seemed unsure as to the date of the material. His last stop was at the office of Gabriel Barkay, who was teaching the course on the tenth century BCE.

A bearded and bearish figure with a thick Hungarian accent, Barkay had spent thirty-five years probing Jerusalem's ancient past. He had found two silver amulets with inscriptions considered the world's oldest biblical-related texts, dating to the seventh century BCE, and earned a Jerusalem Prize for his decades of work. Barkay was excited by the unique chance to examine artifacts fresh from the Temple Mount.

The two agreed that the student should present the finds at the annual conference on Jerusalem archaeology to be held at Bar-Ilan University on December 23. This big affair draws hundreds of academics and government officials to hear about the latest excavations in and around the city. Seligman, who had just succeeded Avni as head of the Jerusalem directorate, ordered Dvira not to give a public presentation.

The student's advisor, archaeologist Hanan Eshel, encouraged him to go ahead with the talk but to avoid mentioning Etzion, a notorious right-wing activist. In his presentation, the student showed cornices, figurines, and other evidence of architecture dating to ancient Jewish times. "There was a lot of commotion in the hall," Dvira recalled.

Avni, now the IAA chief of excavations, stood to declare that the finds were from an illegal dig, and criticized the university and meeting organizers for allowing looted artifacts to be presented. But archaeologist Ronny Reich, who even then was excavating in the City of David, defended Dvira and called for archaeologists to unite behind him. The uproar made the front page of Israel's leading newspapers, the *Jerusalem Post* and *Haaretz*.

◆ ◆ ◆

DVIRA PROFESSED TO BE apolitical until the events surrounding the Marwani excavation. At the prompting of the journalist Shragai, he decided to organize a demonstration to protest the IAA's decision to downplay the waqf's destructive activities.

Barkay warned him that "archaeologists are not the kind of people used to public controversy," but he nevertheless proceeded with his plan. On January 6, 2000, more than two dozen archaeologists gathered at the Kidron Valley dump to show their solidarity. Among them was Eilat Mazar, the granddaughter of Benjamin Mazar, who was then excavating just south of the Noble Sanctuary. The rally's slogan was "Archaeology Trashed." Barkay gave a rousing talk to the assembled international media. "We have been given a corpse after its murder," he said, pointing to the piles of dirt. "This is a terrible disaster for archaeology."

"The scholars weren't going to riot," wrote the historian Gorenberg. "But their response mattered, because for many Israelis"—religious or not—"archaeology is the science of cultivating Jews' tie to their land." While their constituents were perhaps not as passionate as the Haredim, they were potentially far more numerous and certain to get sympathetic attention from mainstream media.

Five minutes before the rally was to begin, Dvira said that Ganor of the IAA's anti-theft unit had called and asked him to come by their office at the Rockefeller Museum, on the other side of the Old City. After the protest, the student drove into the well-guarded compound across the street from Lions' Gate. He walked up the steps to Ganor's office and handed over all the material from the Kidron that he had in his car. "He asked me if I had political intentions, and I said that's not really my nature," Dvira later said.

Ganor then raised a topic completely unrelated to the Marwani dig or the municipal dumps. He said that his unit suspected that Dvira was involved in looting a cave on a sheep farm in the suburbs of Jerusalem. Dvira acknowledged that he knew of the cave but that he had alerted his professors when he heard it was being illegally excavated. "They said I was doing something illegal, but I was framed," he said. Dvira refused to divulge the location of the site. "That's when they threatened me. They said they would raid my house."

For his part, Ganor recalled telling Dvira, "You have a chance here to be an archaeologist and not an antiquities thief." He gave Dvira a week to come clean.

Meanwhile, Israel's High Court was meeting to determine whether the Marwani dig had been done without the necessary permits. On January 11, the judges ruled that it had. But given the "unique" nature of the Temple Mount, they deferred to the politicians and rejected the Temple Mount Faithful petition. Public safety trumped archaeological legalities. The court also noted that the government promised "to renew cooperation with the Muslim waqf and to use this way also in order to prevent further damages on the Temple Mount."

On January 17, after Dvira refused to cooperate, the IAA made good on its threat. Early that morning, Ganor and three other officials from the anti-theft unit arrived at Dvira's apartment in a Tel Aviv suburb with a search warrant. The team conducted a thorough inspection. "They took all the artifacts, which I had told them I had wanted to return," Dvira said. "They were disappointed when they didn't find any coins, since those are valuable and would have linked me to antiquities theft."

Ganor later told a court hearing that they found a metal detector, a flashlight, and gloves—tools of both archaeologists and looters—in Dvira's bedroom wardrobe. They also seized a bag of potsherds that the student acknowledged came from the cave on the sheep farm. When they sat him down at his kitchen table, however, he refused to talk. "So we called a patrol car," Ganor added. He was then taken to a nearby police station for interrogation.

"By now the story was all over the media, and they were pissed," the student recalled, referring to the IAA officials. "They tried to get me to cooperate, but I refused. This is when I lost my faith in the authorities." He asked to speak to an attorney, but they told him that was "only in American movies." Under Israeli law, he had a right to stay silent but not to legal representation. He insisted on speaking only to the police. After seven hours, the station commander ordered Dvira released.

His experience with the IAA turned a mild-mannered college student into a radical organizer. He joined with Barkay and Mazar to form the Committee for the Prevention of the Destruction of Antiquities on the Temple Mount.

The new organization sent Barak a letter—published as an advertisement in *Haaretz* in June—denouncing "serious acts of vandalism" and "massive destruction" on the part of the waqf. The committee accused the Islamic organization of "making every effort to obliterate all remnants" of the Jewish and Christian past. The Temple Mount was, the petition stated, "a site of supreme historical importance in the annals of all human culture, in particular of the Jewish people."

Signed by former mayor Kollek, present-day mayor Olmert, and dozens of Knesset members, artists, writers, and other prominent Israelis, including many leftists, the petition urged the government to make the Noble Sanctuary more accessible to all visitors. Its conclusion was unambiguous: "No nation on earth would stand by while its most important historical relics are destroyed." The petition marked a turning point in relations between secular and religious nationalists, and between Israel's right and left. The actions on the platform united these warring groups in their condemnation of Muslim authorities.

The IAA sent its own unambiguous message. Six weeks later, on July 17, 2000, it filed suit against Dvira for antiquities theft.

◆ ◆ ◆

THAT SAME DAY, at his wooded retreat in the Maryland mountains, Clinton was tantalizingly close to clinching the Middle East peace that he had dreamed about since his 1981 Jerusalem visit. With his second term winding down and the truculent Netanyahu out of office, he had seen one last chance to secure a sweeping agreement between the two bitter enemies. The gathering at Camp David, which *Time* characterized as "the world's highest-stakes poker game," was his gamble to break the impasse.

Arafat, Barak, Clinton, and their negotiating teams had begun that game six days earlier. At the core of the discussion would be what the *New York Times* termed "the single most explosive piece of real estate on the planet"—the sacred platform.

The recent Marwani excavations had only intensified passions over the site. Barak told his delegation that the Temple Mount was "the Archimedean point of our existence, the anchor point of the Zionist struggle." Arafat, meanwhile, warned his delegation, "Do not budge on this one thing: the Haram [the Noble Sanctuary] is more precious to me than everything else."

Both men faced restive religious constituencies. Israel's chief rabbis had warned the government against transferring sovereignty or ownership of the Temple Mount. "Even the very discussion of such a possibility is considered blasphemy," concluded the Chief Rabbinate Council. Jerusalem's grand mufti, Sheikh Sabri, likewise rejected any notion of handing over any part of the Noble Sanctuary, including the Western Wall, which Muslims considered an essential part of the sacred enclosure. He mocked the American president's naivete. "Is it a cake, that Clinton can divide?"

During the first week of the Camp David talks, neither side would budge on the issue of Jerusalem and the platform. On July 17, *Time* magazine's West Bank correspondent, Jamil Hamad, explained to readers the disconnect among the negotiating parties. "The Israelis and Americans cannot understand why Arafat cannot give up Jerusalem," he wrote. "The Americans think of it simply as property, or land. They haven't grasped what Jerusalem means in the minds and hearts of Palestinians—as Arabs and Muslims it represents something extremely powerful. In the same way, the Palestinians have failed to understand the emotional significance of the city for Jews, and why Barak can't move an inch on Jerusalem. And this is the basic problem. There's very little mutual understanding among the parties at the talks—they talk past one another."

That afternoon, under pressure from Clinton, Barak broke the deadlock. He said that the Israelis would consider Palestinian rule in the city's Arab neighborhoods. The Old City would be split between Israeli control of the Jewish and Armenian quarters and Palestinian control in the Muslim and Christian quarters. Israel would maintain sovereignty over the platform, and Jews would be allowed to pray there, but the Palestinians would have "custodianship." No excavations would be allowed, except under an international regime.

The president was delighted. "You are the bravest man I have ever met," an enthusiastic Clinton told him, according to Barak's chief of staff.

The next day, Clinton and Arafat met to discuss the Israeli proposal. The Palestinian leader said he was willing to accept a commitment to ban all excavations on the platform, and would consider Israeli sovereignty over the Western Wall and Jewish Quarter, according to Shlomo Ben-Ami, now Israel's foreign minister. But he balked at the idea of continued Israeli sovereignty over the Noble Sanctuary and a plan to allow Jewish worship on the platform. That could suggest the building of a synagogue—or even constructing the Jewish temple that radicals like Etzion demanded.

American negotiators scrambled to come up with creative compromises. A coalition of Islamic countries, the UN Security Council, and even God were proposed as alternative sovereign powers to rule the sacred enclosure. Neither side, however, was prepared to give up either their territorial or spiritual claims. Time was running out. Clinton planned to leave July 19 for a G8 summit in Japan.

Hours before he left, Arafat and Clinton quarreled over the Palestinian's rejection of the Jewish assertion that their temples once stood on the platform. This statement infuriated Clinton, a devout Southern Baptist who often mixed politics and religion. During a 1994 speech to the Knesset, Clinton had said, "It was God's will that Israel, the biblical home of the people of Israel, continue for ever and ever." He opened each cabinet meeting with a prayer, and long ago, he had promised his preacher never to let Israel down.

"In our Bible, the place is called the Temple Mount because the Jewish temples stood there," Clinton told Arafat angrily. The president, according to one report, "almost shouted" at the Palestinian leader. "It is impossible," he told the Palestinian leader, "to ignore the rights of Jews on the Temple Mount!"

Arafat, however, refused to back down. He insisted there was no archaeological evidence for Jewish temples on the platform, and suggested they had been located in the West Bank city of Nablus. (Later he placed it variously in Yemen and Saudi Arabia.) It was an almost comical scene: an American president citing scripture while the devout Muslim demanded scientific proof. The mood, however, was anything but amusing. Clinton issued a stark warning to Arafat, accompanied by a fist banged on the table: "You are leading your people and the entire region to disaster!"

In a meeting with French president Jacques Chirac that fall, Arafat remained emphatic that the platform had never been a center of Jewish worship. "But the ruins of the temple don't exist!" he told the French leader. Archaeology, he insisted, had never found evidence to support the Israeli claim. Arafat cited the "absence of any trace of the temple under the plaza of the mosques. For thirty-four years the Israelis have been digging without success."

In that instant, the future of peace in the Middle East revolved around an arcane question that scholars had been arguing about since the nineteenth century. Where had the famous Jewish temples stood?

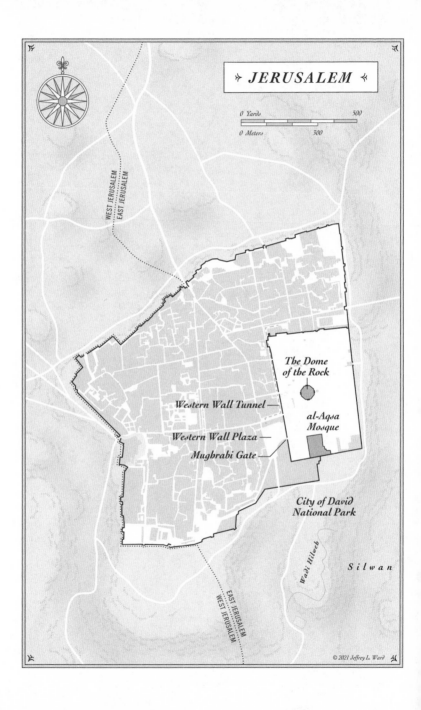

JERUSALEM

0 Yards 500
0 Meters 300

WEST JERUSALEM
EAST JERUSALEM

The Dome
of the Rock

Western Wall Tunnel —

al-Aqsa
Mosque

Western Wall Plaza —
Mughrabi Gate —

City of David
National Park

Wadi Hilweh

Silwan

EAST JERUSALEM
WEST JERUSALEM

© 2021 Jeffrey L. Ward

17

Ruins in the Mind

They saw in Jerusalem, in the Aqsa Mosque, and especially the
Holy Rock, the causeway connecting them to heaven.
—SHAMSUDDIN AL-KILANI

S trictly speaking, Arafat was correct. There was no reliable physical
evidence confirming the existence of Solomon's temple or its successor, renovated at the order of Herod the Great and destroyed soon
after by the Roman army. On this, Israeli and Palestinian scholars agreed.

"Of the Temple proper, there are no remains," concluded Israeli
archaeologist Joseph Patrich of Hebrew University. "No remnants of
the Temple have survived," concurred Palestinian historian Kamil Jamil
al-'Asali. After two centuries of fierce debate, intensive study, and even
some limited archaeological work, academics had come up with dozens of
hotly contested theories, hundreds of artists' conceptions, and thousands
of books and research papers—but very little hard evidence.

"The mystery of this sacred place has been heightened, providing fertile ground for flights of fancy concerning the two temples that formerly
occupied the site," wrote archaeologists Shimon Gibson and David Jacobson. "Even serious scholars have had to make do with hypotheses concerning the position and layout of these ancient complexes."

No building has attracted so much devotion, spawned so many legends, and engendered so much controversy as Solomon's temple. Its
precise measurements are laid out in the Bible. The objects within are
cataloged, and even the robes worn by the priests are specified in rich
detail. There are, however, no known contemporary descriptions. This

text, which scholars say was written after the building's destruction, is the only undisputed source for its existence.

"We seem to be a long way yet from fixing the position with any degree of certainty," said Charles Warren about even the location of the inner temple enclosure. Little has changed since 1869.

According to scripture, King David built an altar on Mount Moriah, on land he purchased from a farmer who used the breezy hill for threshing grain. This lay above and to the north of the Jebusite city he had conquered. His son Solomon then constructed an elaborate shrine on the spot to house the Ark of the Covenant. Most scholars estimate this would have taken place sometime around the tenth or ninth century BCE.

In the sixth century BCE, a Babylonian general conquered the city, which resisted rule by what was then the Middle Eastern superpower. "He set fire to the temple of the Lord, the royal palace and all the houses of Jerusalem. Every important building he burned down," the biblical text reports. There is extensive archaeological evidence for this destruction in layers of ash and Babylonian spear points from this time, and little doubt that a main temple would have been a prime target for the invaders.

A few intriguing clues related to Solomon's sanctuary have surfaced over the years, though the desire to profit from the temple's fame has also produced clever forgeries that can fool even experts.

In 1979, an antiquities dealer bought a thumb-sized piece of hippopotamus bone carved like a pomegranate. Carved with the Hebrew words "Holy to the Priest of the House of Yahweh," it was thought by excited archaeologists to have adorned the scepter of the Judean high priest inside Solomon's temple. In 1988, the Israel Museum paid $550,000 for the item and gave it its own room for display. It was later declared a forgery, though some still maintain its authenticity.

Shortly after the Camp David meeting, a small inscribed stone tablet appeared on the art market that was said to have come from the Muslim cemetery just east of the Noble Sanctuary. The inscription described renovations to the "storied structure" of the temple by King Jehoash, who may have lived around 800 BCE. The artifact created an international sensation and was offered to the Israel Museum for $4 million. Later it was also debunked as a fake.

Two more convincing pieces of evidence emerged in 1997. Archaeologists working at Tel Arad, south of Jerusalem, found a scrap of sixth-century BCE pottery mentioning "the House of Yahweh," which could be a reference to the Jerusalem temple. The same year, Israeli researchers published the results of their analysis of wooden beams removed from the eighth-century CE al-Aqsa Mosque after a 1927 earthquake. Radiocarbon analysis showed they might be nearly three thousand years old and could conceivably have been used in the first sanctuary; more recent study of the wood suggests it dates to Roman times.

Jewish scripture holds that the second iteration of the temple, of a far more modest scale than its predecessor, was built after members of the Judean elite returned from a half century of captivity in Babylon. Little is known about this structure until the first century BCE, when contemporary writers say that Herod the Great ordered a massive renovation of the temple as well as a major expansion of the platform.

There is a large body of textual evidence for this final renovated sanctuary, including dozens of reports, letters, eyewitness accounts, and religious texts from Greek scribes, Italian tourists, Jewish priests, and Roman military officers, not to mention Jesus and his apostles. "Jerusalem is the capital of the Jews. In it was a temple possessing enormous riches," noted the Roman historian Tacitus a few decades after the city was destroyed in 70 CE. The Roman Jewish historian Josephus, a temple priest whose accounts have often proved to be highly accurate, provides extraordinary detail about its operations and personnel.

Yet there is no contemporary map and no single stone that archaeologists can say with certainty was part of Herod's rebuilt temple, or even an object that can be said was housed within its walls. Nor is there anything approaching consensus on the precise location or design of either the first or second sanctuary. Arafat was therefore strictly accurate when he insisted to Clinton and Chirac on "the absence of any trace of the temple."

But his claim was also a disingenuous technicality. There is extensive physical evidence for Herod's temple *compound,* if not the temple itself.

Like today's Dome of the Rock, the Jewish sanctuary was only one building among many on the sacred platform. As early as 1871, an inscription was found warning Gentiles, on pain of death, against entering the inner court of the temple; a second similar one was discovered in the 1930s. Nearly a half century later, Mazar unearthed his "trumpeting stone," presumed to have fallen from the wall of the Temple Mount as reconstructed during or just after Herod's reign. These carved signs were mentioned by Josephus as part of the temple complex. The elaborately decorated domes and passageways that still survive intact beneath al-Aqsa also are widely recognized by art historians as dating to the period just before the Roman destruction.

The most prominent remains of the Jewish temple complex are, of course, its walls. Early Western explorers like de Saulcy and Warren argued that they were built at the order of Solomon. Though some sections could well be that old, most archaeologists now accept that the majority of the stones were laid during and just after Herod the Great's reign. Israeli archaeologists like Dan Bahat and Eilat Mazar showed that Herod nearly doubled the size of the platform.

Such academic nuances were lost in the increasingly heated political debate over the future of the sacred platform. In the aftermath of Arafat's comments questioning the existence of the Jewish sanctuaries and pointing out the lack of archaeological evidence, what came to be called "temple denial" swept the Arab Muslim world.

In fact, Solomon's temple had a well-established place in Muslim scripture and tradition. The Qur'an says that demons and spirits made for Solomon "whatever he wished of sanctuaries and statues, and bowls like pools, and heavy cauldrons." This description closely echoed the picture painted of Solomon's temple in the Hebrew Bible—the sacred building, the cherubim, and the enormous bronze basins for purifying the priests.

In the collection of the prophet's sayings called the hadith, Muhammad led the Jewish prophets, including Jesus, in prayer at al-Aqsa—"the farthest"—before taking his celestial journey. This was associated from the early days of Islam with the Jerusalem temple. The city itself was called Beit al-Maqdis, a term derived from the Hebrew Beit HaMikdash, meaning "the sanctified house" or sanctuary. Solomon's temple is "in a central position in Muslim sacred geography," wrote historians William J. Hamblin and David Rolph Seely.

Yet as negotiators began to consider the future of Jerusalem, the deep Jewish roots of Islam proved problematic for Palestinians demanding a nation apart from the Jewish state. "You have a whole culture around us seeking to prove the existence of the Jewish capital and temple," said Sari Nusseibeh, a philosopher, Palestinian activist, and former president of al-Quds University. Temple denial, he said, "is a result of twentieth-century politics."

From the Muslim perspective, the central thrust of Israeli archaeology in Jerusalem since 1967 had been to buttress Jewish claims to the city and the Temple Mount. Pointing out the obvious lack of physical evidence for the actual temples was a way for Palestinians to neutralize that claim. Many Jews, meanwhile, denied the religious centrality of the platform within Islamic tradition, dismissing the prophet's journey to heaven as a fairy tale. "To us, the Temple Mount is the gate to heaven," Rabbi Goren had said in 1989. "Why else have we come here other than to return to the Temple Mount?"

It was all part of a new mythological arms race. Israeli Jews and Palestinian Muslims were competing to convince themselves and the outside world that they held the clearest title to the city and its acropolis, and they cherry-picked the evidence to back up their respective claims. It was like the fight between Hirbawi and the Copts writ large. In this case, however, there was little archaeology and no court to settle the matter, only the forces of politics and arms.

◆ ◆ ◆

A FEW HOURS AFTER Clinton and Arafat argued over the temple, the president left Camp David for Japan. A furious Barak shut himself up in his cabin; he later withdrew his proposal to share Jerusalem. The stalled Camp David effort fell apart soon after Clinton returned on July 23. The next day, the president called Arafat to his lodge and threatened to end the talks and "let hell break loose."

Arafat took the threat in stride. He insisted on full Palestinian sovereignty over the platform as well as all the Jerusalem territory conquered by Israel in 1967. When Clinton pressed him again, the chairman exploded. "I can't betray my people!" he exclaimed. "Do you want to attend my funeral? I will not wait for them to shoot me; I will shoot myself if I agree to relinquish Jerusalem and its holy places."

Barak characterized Arafat as "a great actor," and some American diplomats, including Dennis Ross, viewed this tirade as pure theatrics. The secretary-general of the Arab League, however, said, "No Arab leader is allowed to relinquish Jerusalem." And others believed Arafat could not win approval for any peace plan that allowed the Israelis to claim control over the Noble Sanctuary. "If there were any compromises at all, he would be charged with having sold Islam out the window, and there would have been a fatwa [an Islamic legal judgment] on his head the next day," said Edward Walker, the U.S. ambassador to Egypt and then Israel during the late 1990s. "It has nothing to do with personal weaknesses. It was an absolute fact—he would have been assassinated!"

In the early morning hours of July 25, Arafat sent a letter to the president thanking him for his peace efforts, but asserting that "we cannot accept any Israeli sovereignty in the Muslim and Christian holy places." The Jerusalem summit ended in failure. A grim Clinton told reporters the next day that resolving the issue of Jerusalem was akin to "going to the dentist without having your gums deadened." For his part, Ross said he left the presidential camp with a feeling that, despite the disastrous end of the talks, "something profound had happened."

Before departing Camp David, Arafat mentioned to Barak press reports that Ariel Sharon, the conservative Likud opposition leader who had approved Getz's incursion into the Temple Mount almost two decades earlier, intended to visit the sacred platform in the coming days. Sharon was angling for Barak's job, and such a high-publicity event would boost his approval among right-wing Israelis. The Palestinian warned the prime minister that such a move could spark violence, but the Israeli leader ignored what was either a plea or a warning—or both.

Within two weeks, Arafat assured Clinton that he was willing to resume talks on Jerusalem. In an effort to bring Arab pressure to bear on the Palestinians, Ross met with Egypt's foreign minister, Amre Moussa, at a beach resort near Alexandria. He spread out a map of Jerusalem on a seaside table beneath a blue canopy protecting them from the fierce August sun. The Palestinians, the American said, would have oversight of the platform, while the Israelis would control the Wailing Wall—that is, the Western Wall Plaza—and the Western Wall Tunnel. An international regime would govern excavations on and below the platform.

When Ross met with Barak the next day, the prime minister insisted that Israel would not surrender its sovereignty over the Temple Mount. But Clinton's negotiator was heartened that he did not rule out some sort of shared sovereignty. Two days later, on August 21, the American diplomat met with Arafat. "Of course, the temple did not exist in Jerusalem, but in Nablus," the Palestinian leader reminded him.

"Mr. Chairman, regardless of what you think, the President of the United States knows that the temple existed in Jerusalem," Ross replied. "If he hears you denying its existence there, he will never again take you seriously. My advice to you is never raise this view again in his presence." Arafat took that advice, though he continued to maintain his position in media interviews.

A convert to Judaism who was widely seen as sympathetic to the

Israeli cause, Ross was personally affronted by Arafat's claim. "He was challenging not just the Israelis but the core of the Jewish faith, which is really unacceptable," he said later. This spurred him, however, to consider another way of seeing an otherwise intractable problem.

He recalled his visits to the Western Wall Tunnel and Solomon's Stables. "I thought, let's create an above ground and a below ground." For Israelis, he said, "what is most significant is a dead reality—where the Second Temple was. But in terms of symbolism and faith, it is fundamental." By contrast, Muslims honored what lay on the surface of the platform, particularly the Dome of the Rock and al-Aqsa Mosque.

If Jews were allowed access to the realm under the platform—the spaces that Wilson had found "perfectly honeycombed with passages and cisterns"—then they could pray without interfering with Muslim devotions above. Just as Jewish worshippers flocked to the Western Wall Tunnel prayer places without disturbing Muslims living and working above, so could they do so beneath the surface of the Temple Mount. "I even checked with my rabbi at the synagogue to see if this would create a problem from a religious standpoint," Ross said, "and he said no."

Clinton was immediately drawn to the idea. "He was attracted to it because he saw this as a creative way to meet what both sides need," Ross recalled.

Both men recognized the danger posed by excavations; the 1996 tunnel riots were still fresh in their minds. Palestinians would oppose any Israeli dig as an attempt to prove their historical claims. Israelis, meanwhile, would suspect that any Palestinian excavations were concerted efforts to hide or destroy evidence of the Jewish past.

"We explicitly said there will be an international committee with representatives from both sides that would have to approve any excavations," Ross said. "We saw how it created a political problem every time something was done. Given what it took to stop the violence in 1996, we were highly sensitive to this."

President Chirac was intrigued by Ross's idea and pressed Arafat about the subject in a September 20 meeting in Paris. "What do you think of the formula according to which you would have sovereignty over the plaza of the mosques and a certain below-ground depth?" he asked the chairman.

"We reject the horizontal division of sovereignty," Arafat replied brusquely, reiterating that there was no archaeological evidence for the temple.

Chirac retorted that archaeological truth was beside the point: "Whether these ruins do or don't exist should not be taken into account. It's the idea of the ruins in the mind of the Israeli people that has to be reckoned with, not so much the ruins themselves." What mattered, he added, was that Palestinian sovereignty "would be active" while that of the Israelis would be passive, "since it would pertain to an inert underground area."

Arafat remained emphatic. "But the ruins of the temple don't exist!" he told the French leader. "Our studies show that these are actually Greek and Roman ruins." Chirac, running out of patience, said that "this isn't a debate on the reality of the temple but on the way the Israeli people hold it in their minds. Right now we've got all the elements of a historic peace agreement on the table. If it isn't concluded, the situation will become unstable again, and there'll be a return of terrorism and Israeli aggression against the Palestinians."

The clock was ticking down as Clinton's final term neared its January 20 end. "You have three or four weeks in which to reach an accord and sign a historic peace treaty, or else find yourselves back in the worst kind of trouble," Chirac warned.

Eight days later, the worst kind of trouble erupted.

◆ ◆ ◆

ON SEPTEMBER 28, 2000, Israeli and Palestinian negotiators were holed up in the Ritz-Carlton hotel next to Washington National Airport. Their American mediators were optimistic that the two sides could reach a deal. That morning, the *Jerusalem Post* quoted Barak as confirming that Jerusalem would be capital of the new Palestinian state. Peace suddenly had never seemed more possible.

Ben-Ami, who served as both foreign minister as well as internal security minister, knew that Israeli opposition leader Ariel Sharon intended to visit the Temple Mount that day to underscore Jewish claims to the area. While in Washington, he ordered Sharon and his entourage not to enter any prayer areas, but he was not overly concerned. He calculated that publicly banning Sharon would cause more trouble than allowing him to score a political point.

Sharon came through Mughrabi Gate in a suit and a striped tie, wearing sunglasses against the rising autumn sun. The politician was accompanied by a half-dozen other Likud lawmakers and a thousand Israeli police, many in riot gear and carrying clubs, as a police helicopter hovered above. "I bring a message of peace," he told reporters. An Israeli archaeologist gave the opposition leader a tour of the platform.

Despite the instructions of the government, Sharon attempted to visit the Marwani prayer space, a move that would please those supporters still furious over the bulldozing on the platform not quite a year earlier. But when he and his entourage tried to walk down the stairs leading to the underground hall, the way was blocked by some two hundred Muslims, including Israeli Arab members of the Knesset. He and his party withdrew.

When Sharon left the platform, protestors began to throw rocks and chairs. The police responded with tear gas and rubber bullets. Among the two dozen injured were three Israeli Arab lawmakers and the top Jerusalem official for the Palestinian Authority, Faisal Husseini. Later that day, Sharon insisted that the platform was "the holiest site in Judaism and it is the right of every Jew to visit the Temple Mount." He added, echoing the cry of 1967, "The Temple Mount is in our hands."

Husseini saw it differently. "They have military might, they have the power of occupation, but not sovereignty," he told the media. "Sharon Touches a Nerve, and Jerusalem Explodes," read the *New York Times* headline.

The next day was Friday, the Muslim sabbath, and it brought thousands of angry Palestinians into the mosques and then out into the streets. Israel deployed some two thousand soldiers and sharpshooters on and around the platform. When worshippers left al-Aqsa, they threw stones that injured several dozen Israelis, prompting the soldiers to storm the mosque in a blaze of live ammunition as well as rubber bullets.

By the time the sun set, marking the start of Rosh Hashanah, the Jewish new year, four Palestinians were dead and more than two hundred lay injured. Some Israelis mark the ambush of a Jewish soldier two days earlier as the true start of the uprising; but whatever the date of its inception, what became known as the al-Aqsa intifada had begun in earnest. During the first week, Israeli soldiers killed fifty Palestinians, while the Israelis counted five civilians dead. Muslim protestors threw rocks from the top of the platform onto the Western Wall Plaza, and Israeli soldiers responded with live ammunition. Riots erupted after funerals and were harshly put down by Israeli forces.

Emergency talks between Arafat and Barak failed to control the violence. On October 10, a Palestinian mob ransacked the Jewish holy site of Joseph's Tomb, and two days later another Arab mob in Ramallah lynched two Israeli reservists suspected of posing as Palestinian protestors. Soon after, helicopter gunships dropped bombs on Arafat's Ramallah compound while the chairman was there, as well as on Palestinian police stations in Gaza and the West Bank. Arafat and his forces found themselves outnumbered, outgunned, and besieged.

A summit convened on October 16 and 17 by UN Secretary-General Kofi Annan at the Sinai beach resort of Sharm el-Sheikh brought together Clinton along with the Egyptian president and the Jordanian king. Arafat was permitted to leave his compound, which remained surrounded by Israeli forces. The Palestinians and Israelis agreed to issue public statements calling for an end to the violence and a resumption of peace talks.

The worst of the violence ebbed, helped by unusually early winter rains and winds. By November 9, Arafat was sitting in the Oval Office. Three days later, Barak arrived for his own private talks with the exiting U.S. president. Ross had just announced he planned to leave government service at the end of the year.

By the time Barak departed Washington, at least 228 Arabs were dead, along with a dozen Israeli soldiers and another dozen Israeli civilians. Some seven thousand Palestinians were injured, nearly a third by gunshot wounds. The fragile Palestinian economy was in free fall due to a strict Israeli blockade and widespread destruction of buildings and damage to agricultural lands.

On December 11, Ross and Arafat met in Morocco in a last-ditch effort to come up with a deal. Ross told the Palestinian leader that Barak wanted sovereignty over "the Jewish cemetery on the Mount of Olives, and the City of David in a part of the Silwan neighborhood," while the Arab portions of the Old City would be under Palestinian rule but guided by a special regime. As for the Noble Sanctuary, the Israeli prime minister would agree to "live with your control over the surface as long as he has control over the subsurface."

When Ross asked if this was acceptable, he said Arafat replied with a single word: "Yes."

On December 19, Israeli and Palestinian negotiators landed at Bolling Air Force Base on the southeastern outskirts of Washington. Unlike the warm and rural setting of Camp David, the accommodations were stark, and snow was forecast.

Foreign Minister Ben-Ami quickly shocked his own delegation by making a proposal that went far beyond the directions of his government. He asked Yisrael Hasson, the Shin Bet official who had witnessed the start of the 1996 tunnel riots and was part of the Israeli team, to translate his new plan into Arabic; Hasson angrily refused. "I threw the paper on the table and said you can kill me; I will never ever, ever say these words," he said later. "It was the second day of Hanukah. I told him, 'My father was a rabbi and I can't say it!'"

The paper proposed giving Palestinians full sovereignty over the Noble Sanctuary, so long as they agreed to "recognize the sanctity of the place to the Jewish people, and the centrality of the site in the history, tradition, and identity of the Jewish people." The Palestinians would agree not to excavate beneath the platform without international approval. Finally, it granted Jews the right to pray on the Temple Mount "in an area that will be agreed upon." Ben-Ami later admitted that he put forward the proposal without consulting his own prime minister.

The breakthrough spurred the White House to action. On December 23, Israeli and Palestinian negotiators met in the Cabinet Room. Clinton stalked in wearing jeans and a serious expression. He said he had in his hands a set of "parameters" that represented a basic agreement—and each side had five days to respond with a yes or a no. Then he slowly read the 1,376-word paper.

The president said that the way out of the impasse over the sacred platform was for each side to "accord respect to the religious beliefs of both sides." He proposed Palestinian sovereignty over the Noble Sanctuary and Israeli sovereignty over the Western Wall "and the space sacred to Judaism of which it is a part" or "the Western Wall and the Holy of Holies of which it is a part." This agreement also would include "a firm commitment by both not to excavate" either beneath the platform or behind the Western Wall, unless there was mutual consent.

After he finished, Clinton looked up. "This is the best I can do," he said. Then he left the room.

"Why so late?" said an exasperated Hasson to the American delegation after the president departed. "Everything would have been different if you'd submitted this proposal in September or at Camp David!"

The Israeli cabinet accepted the parameters, though with reservations. Arafat asked for, and received, a brief extension. He said that his negotiators were jarred by the introduction of the mention of the Holy of Holies, a spot that many Jews believed was located under the Dome of the Rock.

"I came up with the 'Holy of Holies' or 'holy space' language as a way of addressing the existence of the temple without mentioning it," Ross later explained. "According to Jewish tradition, the Ark of the Covenant, the place in the temple where the Ten Commandments were kept, was in the Holy of Holies."

But the mention of the Western Wall and the Holy of Holies in one breath spooked Palestinian negotiators. The reference to the wall could mean just the section in the prayer plaza, or it could also mean the Western Wall Tunnel that extended deep under the Muslim Quarter. The exact site of the Holy of Holies was uncertain, though most theories placed it near or just beneath the Dome of the Rock. The language, while creative, left it unclear exactly who would control what.

Ross's last day on the job was New Year's Eve of 2000. By then, 328 Palestinians had been killed since the violence began on September 28, along with 45 Israeli Jews and 13 Israeli Arabs. On January 1, 2001, Clinton called Arafat. The Palestinian agreed to come to Washington to explain his reservations with the plan. At the meeting the next day, Arafat told the president that he could not countenance giving Israel sovereignty over the entire Western Wall—that is, both the Wailing Wall and the subterranean portion revealed by the Western Wall Tunnel.

"From our side, we were clear that al-Aqsa Mosque compound should be under Palestinian sovereignty, with the Islamic waqf continuing as today," said Saeb Erekat, the top Palestinian negotiator, shortly before his death in 2020. "We could certainly not support the normalization of an Israeli violation, such as having the tunnels under al-Aqsa Mosque compound under Israeli sovereignty." The Noble Sanctuary, he added, "is one undividable unit."

Barak, meanwhile, had said he would never hand over full sovereignty of the Temple Mount to a Palestinian state. The two sides remained at loggerheads.

George W. Bush was sworn in as Clinton's successor on January 20, 2001. Four days later there was a final effort to iron out the differences, though without American participation. An agreement again was tantalizingly within reach. At the Egyptian coastal town of Taba, both sides tentatively agreed to Israeli sovereignty over the Western Wall, though they still disagreed over whether that meant the traditional area of the Wailing Wall or the entire wall and the tunnel running alongside it.

As for the platform itself, "both sides were close to accepting Clinton's idea" of an upstairs-downstairs approach, according to the notes made by the European Union mediator. The talks soon broke up, however, because of the impending Israeli elections. Those would put conservative Ariel Sharon in the prime minister's office in February.

"This was the end of the road," Ross said. He and Clinton had tried to broker the ultimate Solomonic deal. In the Bible story, the would-be mother gave up her claim to a child when King Solomon proposed cutting the baby in two. In this instance, splitting the sacred platform had seemed the magic solution that would harm no one, but Palestinians were unwilling to cleave it in two.

Arafat was widely criticized for missing this opportunity to secure peace. "There were three words in the Clinton parameters that were hard for Arafat—end of conflict," said Ross. "He was defined by conflict. He wasn't prepared to make any compromises of his own." Yet Arafat's team compromised on a number of issues, from refugees to West Bank territory. On the Noble Sanctuary, he had remained remarkably consistent since at least 1990, when he said, "I am absolutely unwilling to concede even the tiniest part."

Ross and Clinton had failed to grasp not just the power that Islam's third-holiest site exerted over Palestinians, but the long history of threats to the platform posed by Christians like Warren and Parker and, later, by Jews like Getz and Goren—not to mention the attempts by Jewish fundamentalists to blow up the Dome of the Rock. Arab newspapers speculated that Sharon planned a synagogue on the Temple Mount "in anticipation of the establishment of 'Solomon's Temple.'"

Little wonder, then, that the Palestinian rallying cry of "al-Aqsa is in danger" could bring thousands into the streets. Just as the Wailing Wall took on political meaning for secular Zionists at the turn of the twentieth century, so the Noble Sanctuary had formed the kernel of Palestinian nationalism. It had become a last Islamic redoubt in the rising sea of Israeli Jews, a kind of Palestinian Masada for which Arab Muslims were ready to die rather than compromise. It is therefore not surprising that when it came time to consider sharing Jerusalem's ancient acropolis, the Palestinian leader balked.

"The brutal fact is that for decades to come neither Arab nor Jew could relinquish Jerusalem without committing psychological suicide," the writer Colin Thubron predicted after a 1970s visit. "Everything else is negotiable, but not this city. It stands like a rock in the path of peace." In the middle of that rock stood the sacred platform that, in turn, surrounded the rough stone that lay under the great golden dome.

The collapse of the peace process in 2001 coincided with the creation of a novel and powerful alliance between two old foes. In the new millennium, Israeli archaeologists and Jewish religious nationalists would work, sometimes uneasily, together. Their combined efforts—shaped also by real estate and tourist interests—would transform Jerusalem's long-hidden realm of mud- and sewage-filled vaults into an underground attraction unlike any in the world. In so doing, they would come to dominate the mythological arms race, altering the way millions of foreign visitors perceived the city's ancient past—and, therefore, its conflicted present.

PART III

Jerusalem
is each lie treated like truth,
and each truth treated like a lie.
Jerusalem
is a divine crime scene,
a crime committed with the hands of the holy.
Jerusalem
is a beheading of the hydra,
a lynching of those who speak just.

—MOHAMMED AL-KURD

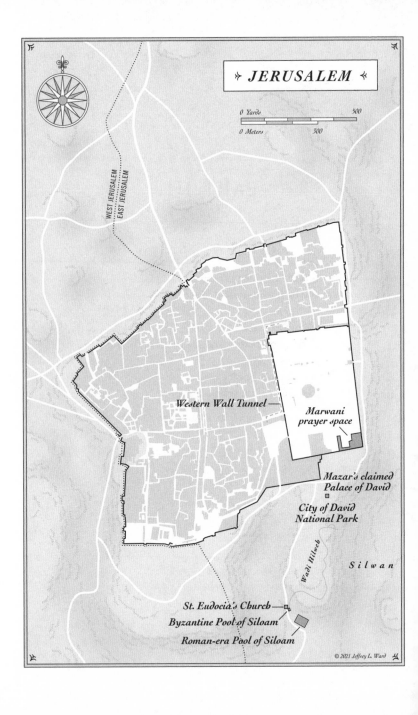

18

Reality Is Always Stronger
Than Belief

Readers are touchingly loyal to the first history they learn—
and if you challenge it, it's as if you are taking away their child-
hoods. For a person who seeks safety and authority, history
is the wrong place to look. Any worthwhile history is in a
constant state of self-questioning.

—HILARY MANTEL

At his October 2001 court hearing, the Bar-Ilan student Zach
Dvira faced charges of looting material taken from the Marwani
dig and deposited in the Kidron Valley, as well as for illegally
excavating a cave on a sheep farm outside Jerusalem. His defense argued
that he had only gathered a few potsherds that were worthless on the art
market. "The defendant, a sophomore archaeology student, took no coins
nor King Solomon's treasures," his lawyer reassured the court.

His archaeology professor Hanan Eshel testified at a later hearing that
Dvira made "a beginner's mistake," and that while what he did was wrong,
he was not an antiquities thief. "What we have here," he explained, "is an
excess of motivation." The prosecution, however, insisted that Dvira had
clearly broken the law forbidding excavations without a permit. The case
became a cause célèbre for right-wing Jews, who argued that the waqf, not
an Israeli Jewish archaeology student, was guilty of antiquities destruction.

In January 2003, the IAA quietly dropped its suit against Dvira, who in
turn withdrew his accusations of unfair treatment by the IAA. The judge,

however, did not let him go unpunished. She told Dvira that because he had technically broken the law, his punishment would be to give ten archaeology lessons to high school classes—and suggested that she would be happy if it were at her own children's school.

Meanwhile, Dvira and his elder mentor, the archaeologist Gabriel Barkay, were struggling to obtain both an IAA license and enough private money to launch what became known as the Temple Mount Sifting Project. After three years of effort they succeeded, and in 2004 they moved the first of what would be more than three hundred truckloads of soil from the Kidron site to Tzurim Valley National Park, just below Mount Scopus.

Then they began to sort through the material. Picking through the dirt initially produced only a few larger potsherds. One day, after a hard rain, the archaeologists noticed the artifacts were suddenly more visible.

The team began to separate larger bits of material from plain dirt by passing it through a screen. This was then soaked in buckets to dissolve the remaining soil. The bucket was then again dumped into a screen and sprayed with water, exposing the smallest pieces of bone, metal, coins, and other artifacts. This procedure, called dry and wet sifting, had never been used in Jerusalem for all excavated soil, only select samples.

The first of six thousand coins plucked out of the mesh screens bore the Hebrew phrase "For the Freedom of Zion"; they had been minted during the first Jewish revolt around 70 CE. For the following dozen years, some two hundred thousand volunteers—most of them tourists eager for a chance to recover a bit of ancient Jerusalem—retrieved jewelry, terra-cotta figurines, Egyptian scarabs, Roman playing dice, Byzantine floor tiles, burnt sheep bone, Bronze Age arrowheads, and beads made from lapis lazuli imported from Afghanistan. Out of the dirt emerged a gold coin bearing the image of de Saulcy's patron, the French emperor Napoleon III.

There was pottery from the Bronze Age, signet rings worn by Muslim clerics in the Ottoman era, and 1920s British military badges. A ten-year-old Russian boy spotted a seal of brown limestone carved with two animals that likely dated to the tenth century BCE.

A seventh-century BCE seal turned up in another screen inscribed with a Hebrew phrase that referenced the son of a man mentioned in the Bible as "chief officer of the house of God." Such artifacts had clear political as well as archaeological significance. At a June 2019 meeting with

Prime Minister Netanyahu, the minister of Jerusalem affairs and heritage showed off the seal, noting that "finds of this nature illustrate our connection to the Temple Mount."

Even powered by volunteer labor, however, the effort proved expensive to operate. In 2005, the project found a willing partner in Elad, the right-wing foundation run by David Be'eri. "We worked hand in hand with them," said Barkay. "Yes, they have a political agenda for which they are well known. I couldn't care less. My purpose is to do archaeological study, and if I got help from Satan, that would be acceptable."

After a dozen years of work, the volunteers had collected a half-million artifacts from all periods of Jerusalem's history, which then were sorted by a team of twenty part-time professionals. Barkay claimed to have found extensive pottery and other artifacts from the era of David and Solomon, as well as floor tiles from Herod's temple plazas. Christian mosaics and marble suggested the Temple Mount had not been empty in Byzantine times, as historians long believed. The project, he concluded, shed welcome light on Jerusalem's great "black hole of history."

Other archaeologists were skeptical. The IAA archaeologist Yuval Baruch, who received a permit to study the material while it was in the municipal dumps, concluded that much of the material might have been brought onto the platform from nearby locations during repair and renovation work. The artifacts might or might not be related to the Temple Mount.

Barkay contended that there was no evidence that massive amounts of soil came from outside the platform, and dismissed such criticism as having more to do with politics than science. "Our very existence reminds the IAA of its inability to guard the antiquities of the Temple Mount. They don't like others in their business. So they don't like us," he said. "But reality is always stronger than belief."

Dvira and Barkay suffered a major blow in 2017 when, after a dozen years of financing, Elad abruptly withdrew its support. "They were not interested in research," said Barkay, who characterized the split as a divorce. A foundation spokesperson explained that their organization was disappointed by the project's lack of progress, saying, "Before we start pumping more and more money into this, we need to all be on the same page." Sifting operations ground to a halt for two years while Barkay and Dvira regrouped and opened another sifting site.

Elad's decision demonstrated the growing power of right-wing Jewish groups in setting the agenda for resource-short archaeologists working in the heart of Jerusalem. By the early 2000s, the City of David visitor center run by the organization had become a major hit with tourists, thanks to the tunnels and passages made accessible by Reich and Shukron. Sharon, the new prime minister, remained a staunch supporter of the organization and its most valuable ally.

Be'eri, meanwhile, embarked on frequent trips to the United States to woo potential donors. With his sandals and halting English, he proved a humble but highly effective salesman for the dual efforts to install Jewish families aboveground and to uncover Jewish antiquities belowground. In 2007 alone, Elad's New York–based Friends of Ir David took in $2.5 million. This growing political and financial muscle helped Be'eri launch what would become the most ambitious, costly, and controversial excavation on earth.

◆ ◆ ◆

IN THE WINTER OF 2003, a flash flood swept through the Kidron Valley. This narrow defile separates Wadi Hilweh on the rocky ridge extending south of the Noble Sanctuary from the core of Silwan, which lies just across the valley to the east. Raging water ripped away chunks of asphalt on a road at the base of the ridge, exposing a concrete sewage main. On the morning of May 30, 2004, a municipal maintenance crew arrived to replace the pipe. A bulldozer roared to life.

Eli Shukron, Reich's excavation partner, was taking a break from their work at the underground spring located just up the hill. Shukron had heard about the planned repair work and was curious. Donning sunglasses against the glare of the late morning sun, he wandered down the steep hill just as the bulldozer raised a cloud of dust. "It was very noisy," he recalled. "But then I heard the sound of steel scratching stone." Shukron waited for the loud bang of rocks being dropped into the waiting dump truck. Instead, he heard only the soft thump of earth landing in the truck bed. "The second or third time this happened, I knew there was something large below."

The burly archaeologist yelled for the bulldozer operator to halt the digging. Then he asked one of the workers to get into the hole to see what was creating the scratching sound. "There's nothing here," the man shouted, climbing out of the trench. "There has to be!" replied Shukron impatiently. He jumped into the newly made pit dug into the gravelly silt.

"Give me a shovel," he called out. Within moments, he had uncovered three broad stone stairs. "Look, guys, there *is* something here!" he told the crew.

This serendipitous find could easily never have happened. An IAA inspector was designated to watch the crew's work, but he had gone missing at that critical moment. Excited, Shukron called his boss. "If Eli had not stopped that giant bulldozer, those steps would have been torn out without anyone noticing," said Reich, who rushed to the scene when he heard the news.

The construction crew was sent away, leaving the archaeologists to puzzle over the purpose of the carefully dressed rectangular limestone slabs. The steps led up the slope, which quickly turned into the rock cliff towering above. It seemed a staircase to nowhere.

Then Reich had a brainstorm. The steps weren't going up the slope. They were going down, in the direction of the orchard that stretched to the south. "These must be steps going down to the Pool of Siloam during the Second Temple Period," he told Shukron.

The pool had been filled with the waters from the eighth-century BCE tunnel explored by Robinson and Warren that had yielded the inscription published by Schick. The underground spring on the eastern flank of the hill where Reich and Shukron were then excavating sent water coursing into the tunnel that emptied into an open-air reservoir at the southern base of the ridge.

The name Siloam is a Greek version of the ancient Hebrew Shiloach—"to send forth"—and is the origin of the Arabic word Silwan. The prophet Isaiah mentioned the "gently flowing waters of Shiloah" and the Judean exiles returning from Babylon in the sixth century BCE were said to have rebuilt "the wall of the Pool of Siloam by the King's Garden," in the small but fertile valley below the City of David. Over time, the pool would silt up and require either reconstruction or an entirely new basin. There were, therefore, several successive pools of Siloam.

By the second century BCE, a sophisticated network of tunnels and aqueducts brought fresh water from the distant hills near Bethlehem, rendering the pool less essential to the city's well-being. But at least until the time of Jesus, it remained a well-known gathering spot. It plays a starring role in the Christian New Testament. One day, according to the Gospel of John, Jesus encountered a man blind since birth. The Galilean carpenter spit on the ground, made a mud paste, and put it on the afflicted man's eyes. "Go," he told him, "wash in the Pool of Siloam." He was summarily healed.

Sometime after the fourth century CE, Byzantine Christians hewed a smaller rectangular pool out of limestone just uphill, on the southwestern side of the ridge, just below the tunnel outlet. In the late fifth century, the Byzantine empress Eudocia built the Church of Siloam next to the reservoir to commemorate the miracle. One Italian pilgrim in the 570s reported "two basins constructed of marble, which are separated from each other by a partition. Men wash in one and women in the other, to gain a blessing. In these waters many cures take place."

The church eventually fell into disuse and was buried under later debris, but the water from the tunnel continued to flow into the adjacent pool.

In the 1890s, Bliss and Dickie encountered remains of Eudocia's church while tunneling beneath the ridge. Soon after, "the Siloam people took advantage of our excavations to erect a small mosque" on the northwest side of the pool, Bliss noted. The pool was thought to have healing properties, particularly for eye afflictions, among local Arabs. But some archaeologists suspected the pool from the days of Jesus lay at the base of the hill, under a garden tended by Greek monks.

Standing beside the newly exposed steps, Reich recalled that Bliss and Dickie had dug a tunnel nearby and reported finding a stone staircase. He immediately jumped into his car and drove around the Old City to the Rockefeller Museum. Under the whitewashed vaults of its library, he found a century-old report by the excavators mentioning stairs found at the same site. These steps, however, were at a ninety-degree angle to the ones Reich and Shukron had uncovered an hour before. Reich grasped that the two came together in a corner, a compelling clue that this was one corner of the lost pool.

Reich, a man with a strong competitive streak, then rushed to his Jerusalem apartment to email pictures of the find to Jon Seligman, the head of the city's archaeology directorate. "I had to make sure that this discovery, despite the bureaucracy of the IAA, would fall to us."

The sliver of land where they had made their discovery was municipally owned, sandwiched between Greek Orthodox owners on the slope below and a waqf that oversaw the mosque property above. Reich and Shukron quickly secured a permit and uncovered three segments of stairs separated by landings that ended in what appeared to be a broad plaza.

One set of steps extended more than two hundred feet from east to west. They didn't simply end, however, but continued south into the orchard before vanishing under land owned by the Greeks.

Though they couldn't excavate the entire complex, the archaeologists gathered enough data to say with certainty that the stairs created a trapezoidal space half as large as a football field. Fragments of columns and other carved stones that they unearthed provided evidence that the complex was surrounded by an elegant classical colonnade. Coins embedded in the cement of the complex dated to between 103 and 76 BCE, shortly before the Roman general Pompey the Great conquered the city. This meant the steps were built in the era just before the time of Jesus.

Two days before Christmas 2004—just when American and European editors were hungry for Holy Land stories—media reports of the "miracle pool" discovery flashed around the world.

Reich was eager to excavate the entire area to gain a fuller understanding of the site, much of which lay beneath a verdant orchard of pomegranates and figs owned by the Greek Orthodox Church. But at that moment, there was more than one Greek patriarch, and the two clerics were locked in a bitter feud with international repercussions. One had been ousted after being accused of selling church land to Jewish settlers, but the new leader required the joint approval of Israel, Jordan, and the Palestinian Authority. The stalemate put the pool out of reach.

So Reich turned his gaze up the hill, to the north. He had realized in his research that the bathing complex was just part of a much larger construction project. "We know today that the Siloam Pool is connected to the Temple Mount," he had told the Associated Press. "There is a road that connects the two elements. The entire system is clearer today."

At the time, no one, not even Reich, grasped the full implications of this offhand comment. "That was the starting point of a catastrophic event for Jerusalem archaeology, the reopening of horizontal tunneling," said one rueful Israeli archaeologist.

· · ·

EILAT MAZAR, the granddaughter of Benjamin, had to wait a decade to heed her own call to find King David's palace. When Reich and Shukron had begun their excavations at the City of David's visitor center in 1996, they focused on the spring and the web of underground spaces radiating out from the all-important water source. They had ignored the area at the ridgetop that Mazar believed was the key to finding the palace of the most famous Judean king.

Soon after, her husband—also an archaeologist—died of a heart attack, leaving her with four children to raise. By the millennium's turn, she had secured her PhD and more excavation experience, though not a professorship at a university that could provide the funding necessary for a dig. She needed a private patron.

The Bronx-born investment banker Roger Hertog stepped in to help. The New York philanthropist chaired the Shalem Center, an Israeli neo-conservative institute that sought to bolster right-wing positions through scholarly work. It was founded in 1994 to confront what its founders saw as a flagging commitment to Zionism. Mazar became a fellow. Hertog described his contributions to her dig—funding that would top half a million dollars—as "venture philanthropy." His unabashed goal was to show that "the Bible reflects Jewish history."

Elad's Be'eri welcomed the excavation. Mazar wanted to dig for his beloved namesake's home in the middle of the visitor center. It was just the sort of project that would excite the Israeli and American donors as well as visitors.

On a chilly February day in 2005, just a half-dozen weeks after Reich and Shukron announced their Pool of Siloam discovery, Mazar and her team began to excavate beneath the arcade of the visitor center. The site was a few dozen yards from the steep drop off the eastern side of the ridge.

"Almost from the start, ancient remains, preserved beyond all expectations, were unearthed," she recalled.

Five feet below the surface, the team encountered remnants of the impressive Byzantine-era House of Eusebius. Two British archaeologists had given it that name in the 1920s when they found it stamped on a tile at the site. Below that was an arched roof covering a plastered pool with steps, a ritual bath from before the Roman destruction of 70 CE. Embedded in that room were large stones from an earlier era. The British excavators had assumed the large stones were from a Jebusite wall that David destroyed when he conquered the city, and didn't search further.

When Mazar dug down, she discovered walls made of the same large stones that extended to the eastern edge of the ridge—the Large Stone Structure—that was nestled against a twelve-story-high terrace—the Stepped-Stone Structure—supporting the cliff face. Though difficult to date, that terrace was thought to be the remnant of an old fortification built before 1000 BCE, possibly the one that David and his men had overwhelmed as described in the Bible.

The walls uncovered by Mazar seemed to be part of that terrace. This impressive complex, she said, was "not just any public building, but a structure that was clearly the product of inspiration, imagination, and considerable economic investment." It was also outside the original Jebusite city, since there were no earlier ruins associated with it. "It's very clear this is one huge construction," she added. It was, in fact, larger than a hockey rink. There was no doubt it was an important find.

But who had built it, and when, remained uncertain. There was no floor to seal older remains below, which made dating the walls problematic. "One cannot just *assume* that they belong to one and the same building, this has to be *proven*," wrote one skeptical archaeologist. Everything depended on interpreting potsherds littering the site. By midsummer, the team was able to discern a second phase of construction and possibly a third. By carefully comparing the subtle differences in potsherds from these phases, Mazar dated the first phase of the building to the middle of the tenth century BCE, "when the Bible says King David ruled the United Kingdom of Israel."

Radiocarbon dates from organic samples seemed to back up her dating, although this technique generally can't pinpoint a date within a century or so without taking large numbers of samples and using advanced statistical methods. The structure, she added, was in use until as late as the Babylonian destruction of 586 BCE. But its purpose was difficult to ascertain. In the ancient Near East, monumental buildings typically were either temples or palaces. According to the biblical texts, the temple was constructed in Solomon's day to the north, on the hill above the ridge.

That appeared to leave only one logical possibility; she had found David's palace.

Mazar's claim to have uncovered the first physical evidence of the reign of one of the most famous figures in the Bible—and history—went public in August. Major newspapers and networks around the world gave it prominent play. Religious publications also spread the news widely. "Dr. Mazar's discovery of King David's palace ought to fill you with wonder and hope!" wrote one Christian newspaper. Mazar had succeeded in her funder's dream that the dig would show "the Bible reflects Jewish history."

Her conclusion, however, quickly came under fire from both Israeli and Palestinian academics. Four professors from Tel Aviv University, after examining Mazar's site, concluded that the dating evidence was shaky and that most of the architectural elements—such as column capitals—were from the second century BCE. That was nearly eight centuries later than Mazar claimed. Her academic nemesis, Israel Finkelstein of Tel Aviv University, concluded the building could have been constructed as late as the sixth century BCE, just prior to the Babylonian destruction.

After analyzing her materials in greater detail, Mazar strengthened her case by showing that at least some of the walls she uncovered indeed were connected to the terrace and dated to the early Iron Age, that is, from about 1200 BCE to between 1000 and 950 BCE. Based on the pottery finds, she suggested a date at the end of that period, precisely when she believed David had lived.

Others, however, came to different conclusions using the same data, arguing that the terrace and part of the walls Mazar found were from a time closer to 1200 BCE—when the Jebusites, presumably a tribe of Canaanites, still dominated the city. They argued that while King David might have reused the stronghold as a palace, there was no evidence he constructed the impressive terrace and its associated walls.

Reich, among others, attacked Mazar's interpretation as wishful thinking. Her reading of the Bible suggested King David's palace might be buried on the ridge. Given that reasoning, he said, "she certainly would find the building." But Hershel Shanks, the editor of *Biblical Archaeology Review,* countered that "Eilat had a hypothesis, and she wanted to test it by digging."

Mazar's attempt to link David to a complex she viewed as a "product of inspiration, imagination, and considerable economic investment" unsettled many scholars, even those who agreed with her interpretation. The implication was that Canaanites were less likely to be inspired or imaginative than Israelites. This was a rather dubious proposition given that the massive Bronze Age towers, walls, and tunnels they built in previous centuries dwarfed anything known to survive from Israelite rule.

Her attempts to match the archaeological finds to the biblical account also seemed better suited to the early days of the Palestine Exploration Fund than to the twenty-first century. Mazar was skeptical of more recent scientific techniques, even carbon dating, in part because they were more expensive than the old method of ascertaining dates by reading pottery. She wasn't alone in that skepticism. "Carbon-14 is like a prostitute,"

Barkay had said. "Given the margin of error, radiocarbon allows everyone to argue the position they already hold."

Tel Aviv's Finkelstein, by contrast, was a fierce advocate of employing advanced research methods, and he dismissed Mazar's claim to have found King David's palace as technically flawed. Yet even if Mazar were right and Finkelstein wrong, the discovery of a single building could not alter the growing consensus among archaeologists that the Bible had wildly exaggerated the glory of Jerusalem in the days of David and Solomon.

"We all agree Jerusalem was not a major city; it was a small town," said Mazar's cousin, the archaeologist Amihai Mazar. Shanks, a fan of Mazar and her Bible-as-guide approach, also acknowledged that Jerusalem was "a capital of a few small villages." Even her most ardent supporters envisioned the city as covering, at most, a dozen acres and housing a thousand or so people.

That may have qualified as a major center in the desolate Judean hills, but it was hardly impressive when matched against contemporaries such as Egypt's Thebes, Mesopotamia's Babylon, and China's Xi'an, each of which boasted more than a hundred thousand residents living amid monumental walls and buildings. The myth of Jerusalem's splendid past remained a staple of yeshivas and Sunday schools, but archaeologists had shown that—even with a palace of David—it contradicted the facts on the ground.

Archaeology had confirmed the likely existence of a historical David, but also demonstrated that the scribes who composed the scripture, most writing a half a millennium or more later, burnished the distant past into a suitably golden age. This was common to all Middle Eastern societies, in which kings boasted of victories what were in fact defeats, and exaggerated wealth to impress both subjects and outsiders.

Such debates would be of interest only to scholars and armchair explorers if they dealt with, say, Luxor or Babylon. But Mazar's find was thrust quickly into the political arena. The *New York Times* predicted that her claim would be ammunition "in the broad political battle over Jerusalem— whether the Jews have their origins here and thus have some special hold on the place, or whether, as many Palestinians have said, including the late Yasser Arafat [who had died six months before] the idea of a Jewish origin in Jerusalem is a myth used to justify conquest and occupation."

Palestinian scholars decried what they saw as an obvious case of science twisted in the service of Zionism. Hani Nur el-Din, an archaeologist at al-Quds University, said that some Israeli archaeologists searching for remains from the days of David and Solomon "try to link whatever they find to the biblical narration. They have a button, and they want to make a suit out of it."

As the controversy over Mazar's discovery raged aboveground, another excavation had quietly begun just a short stroll down the ridge. If the magnificence of the metropolis under its early Judean rulers remained out of reach, then the city's heyday under its last Jewish kings was waiting to be revealed.

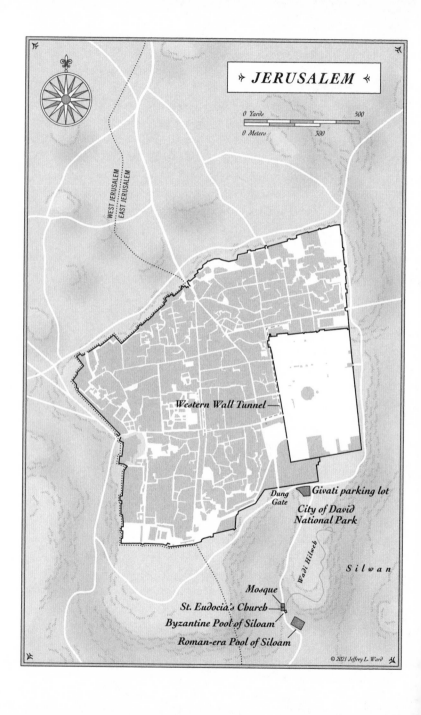

JERUSALEM

0 Yards 500
0 Meters 500

WEST JERUSALEM
EAST JERUSALEM

Western Wall Tunnel —

Dung Gate — Givati parking lot

City of David
National Park

Wadi Hilweh

Silwan

Mosque
St. Eudocia's Church —
Byzantine Pool of Siloam
Roman-era Pool of Siloam

© 2021 Jeffrey L. Ward

19

The Rebel Dig

I want to dig a subterranean passage. Some progress must be
made. . . . We are digging the pit of Babel.
—FRANZ KAFKA

As Mazar was at work near the top of the ridge, Reich and Shukron tried without success to follow up their finds at the Pool of Siloam, which lay at its base. Not only did the Greek Orthodox Church and the Islamic waqf refuse their requests to dig, but the IAA itself blocked further excavations. Their immediate boss, Jon Seligman, would not approve excavations even along the narrow strip of municipal land. Funding and manpower were in short supply. Then David Be'eri intervened on their behalf.

The discovery of the pool had proved a boon for Elad; tourists now could exit the water tunnel at the base of the ridge and see a famous archaeological site. Any additional remains would only add to the appeal. According to Reich, the Elad chief convinced Shuka Dorfman, the new head of the IAA, to overrule Seligman.

With Seligman's grudging green light, the archaeologists made a trench stretching from the eastern edge of the pool to the western end. To their delight, the stone-paved esplanade continued, though it was covered with thick heaps of rubble, presumably left by the destruction of 70 CE, as well as some twenty feet of mud that had accumulated in the subsequent two millennia.

The steps marched up the slope of the ridge, in the direction of the Temple Mount. But they led directly beneath land owned by the waqf, and its managers soon complained that the work threatened to undermine a nearby kindergarten as well as the century-old mosque. Reich suspected that heavy rains rather than the excavation were to blame, but the team was forced to suspend its work.

Before doing so, they cleared out a nearby underground rock-cut channel for about 150 feet, and the soil revealed coins and pottery just predating 70 CE. Reich realized that this channel was roofed with the treads of a stepped street that still lay buried above, tantalizingly close.

Though no known text directly mentioned it, Reich was sure that this was a monumental path connecting the pool with the Temple Mount. There had been hints of its existence for more than a century. Warren had first encountered remains of a wide paved road next to the Western Wall, while Bliss and Dickie's team had uncovered similar pavement near the pool; they surmised it was part of a single great staircase and road system dating to the period of Herod the Great's temple renovation that began in the first century CE. Later, Kenyon had hit the same pavement halfway up the ridge.

Reich believed that pilgrims entering Jerusalem from its southern gate would have performed ritual ablutions at the pool and then made their way up the stepped street to worship in the temple. But there was no chance to pursue his theory. "We were faced with a real dilemma," the archaeologist recalled. "We could not dig the area because it exceeded the limitations of our permit, which was only to clear the channel. Neither could we dig from above ground because of property-ownership issues."

Once again, Be'eri came to their rescue. A street might not be as compelling as, say, the Ark of the Covenant or David's palace. But if it could be exposed, visitors would have a chance to walk in the literal footsteps of pilgrims—including Jesus and his disciples—who had made the trek up to Judaism's sacred sanctuary.

One day Be'eri took his managers to examine the flagstones that Reich and Shukron had already uncovered. "He pointed up at the Old City walls and said, 'This road is going to connect the City of David to the Old City,'" recalled Doron Spielman, Elad's international development director. "It was such a far-off dream, but he was so resolute. I remember thinking this was the voice of a true visionary. He had only uncovered a handful of stones, but he could see the road."

This would require tunneling beneath Muslim property. The Elad chief informed Dorfman, the IAA director, that Israeli law allowed excavation beneath private property, recalled Reich. This was not true, and Reich added that he was not fooled. "I did not believe this claim," he later admitted, "and I was hoping that if anyone countered it, the matter would be dealt with by lawyers rather than archaeologists." The excavators began to tunnel into the hillside, though Reich acknowledged that he was breaking the law and that tunneling "is not proper archaeological procedure."

When Gideon Avni, who headed the IAA's excavations section, learned what they were doing, he shut down the dig. Dorfman reversed that decision, and Reich and Shukron bored a horizontal passage, about six feet high and six feet wide, more than fifty feet into the soil, which Reich said contained only later debris, and therefore justified this unconventional approach. The chance of exposing what the excavators believed was a monumental street from the glory days of Herod the Great and his successors was too tempting to ignore.

The team made a passage above the drainage channel to expose the steps as they climbed the grade. The workers, most of them Arabs from Silwan, quickly exposed the foundations of ancient shops along the carefully laid stone slabs. Based on coins and pottery, it was clear that everything had been buried in the destruction debris from 70 CE. Reich was delighted by what he called "the 'rebel' dig." Soon after, however, the team's progress was blocked by Eudocia's church, which Bliss and Dickie had encountered in the 1890s. Destroying such an important and monumental structure was out of the question—at least for the time being—so they stopped their work.

Not easily deterred, Be'eri offered to pay for a dig beneath one of Elad's properties halfway up the ridge. The site was auspicious. This was close to where Kenyon had made a small trench in the vicinity in the 1960s and noted a section of stepped street. Reich and Shukron happily began a traditional top-down excavation. But when they reached the level that seemed to correspond with the first centuries BCE and CE, there were no steps to be found. (Only later would they learn that they had missed the monumental stairs by less than three feet.)

The team did stumble on a small passage that seemed promising. One of the slimmer Silwan boys slipped into the opening and crept his way to a wider underground channel that led nearly three hundred feet to the south before it proved impassable from debris. Coins dating to near

70 CE showed that it was in use just before the destruction, while unusual finds of fully intact pottery suggested it was used as a hiding place from Jewish rebels in the Roman siege.

The drain obviously had been built to channel water that landed on the stepped street that had been above. Either the stairs had not been completed or the stones had later been removed for a construction project—yet another example of Jerusalem recycling itself.

Removing the mud and silt in that channel meant extending the work beyond Elad's property and beneath Arab homes and businesses. When Dorfman came to inspect their work, Reich and Shukron argued that since the tunnel already existed, the work would not really constitute excavation, nor could it harm the modern structures above; they were simply cleaning an existing channel.

Once the old sewer was cleaned, it could serve as an underground path. Tourists could enter at the visitor center on the northeastern slope of the ridge, descend to the underground spring, and then follow the old water tunnels down to the Pool of Siloam at the base of the hill. Then they could enter this drainage channel, which spanned the western side of the ridge, and work their way back up to the visitor center underground. It was narrow and barely six feet high but could be made accessible to the public. This would allow tourists to make a complete circuit while avoiding the streets of Wadi Hilweh altogether.

Dorfman again allowed them to proceed. The Silwan workers began to shovel tons of silt and rock in the tight, hot, and humid space, hauling it to the surface for sifting at another site. Some areas had collapsed, which required insertion of steel beams. The excavation, however, was controversial among some IAA archaeologists. "They are saying they're 'only' clearing debris, but debris is important, too, and should be removed from top to bottom, not chipped away from the side," complained Yoram Tsafrir, a Hebrew University archaeologist and the chair of the IAA advisory committee.

He also worried that archaeologists were inadvertently poisoning long-term relations with the local Arab community, which already was at odds with Elad for its dogged attempts to purchase real estate to increase the Jewish presence in Wadi Hilweh. The digs below were easily seen as extensions to those settlement efforts above. "Someday there may be peace here, and the Palestinian residents will agree to a proper excavation," Tsafrir warned. "It is unacceptable that the political needs of Elad dictate the pace." But there was little doubt that Be'eri had become the area's prime mover. *Haaretz* dubbed him the ruler of "the Republic of Elad."

◆ ◆ ◆

THE UNDERGROUND WORK CAUGHT the attention of Rafi Greenberg, a professor at Tel Aviv University. He had fond memories of Wadi Hilweh, where he began his career during Shiloh's excavations and had met his wife. But when he returned two decades later, he was shocked to find the sleepy neighborhood transformed.

"The place I knew as an Arab village with archaeology turned into a place with armed guards, with guns ready to be pulled out at any moment, a place with amplified symbols of Israeli presence—huge flags, watchtowers, cameras filming twenty-four hours a day."

Greenberg watched with mounting concern as Elad increased its hold over the neighborhood—both above- and belowground. With government funding of archaeology in decline, he wrote, "the IAA has been lured ever deeper into the City of David ventures." He worried about the "feverish pace by IAA archaeologists bankrolled by the settler NGO Elad." The excavation work, he contended, is "connected by its umbilical cord to politics."

By 2006, Greenberg and a few of his colleagues were offering visitors an alternative tour of the City of David that highlighted the impact of the digs on the Arab neighbors. The following year they organized Emek Shaveh, a nonprofit dedicated to shining a light on the role of archaeology in Israeli-Palestinian relations, particularly in Silwan and its suburb of Wadi Hilweh. The name of the organization meant, roughly, "middle ground" in Hebrew. Like the defense of Shiloh and the protests against the Marwani dig, it was a rare instance of Israeli archaeologists taking an overtly political stance.

Middle ground proved hard to find. Dorfman refused to halt Reich and Shukron's tunnel work. In the ensuing controversy, the Silwan workers quit their jobs. The loss was a bitter blow to Reich. "Over all those years, I made only one demand of Elad, that we employ laborers from Silwan," he wrote. "I believe that people fortunate enough to live near an important antiquities site should be able to make a living rather than bringing in outside labor." He blamed Greenberg and Tsafrir for "stirring the cauldron for political reasons."

This marked the end of nearly a century and a half of collaboration between Arab laborers and archaeologists stretching back to Warren's day. They had moved hundreds of tons of soil by hand, often in cramped, dirty, and dangerous circumstances. Despite regime changes, wars, riots, and intifadas, the village's workers had maintained their excavation expertise under British, French, German, and Israeli archaeologists. Their knowledge and experience working in the peculiar Jerusalem underground had been passed down through generations. At the same time, their relationship to archaeologists had remained a wholly subordinate one. They had been accepted as skilled labor but had never risen to senior management.

While Reich blamed his Israeli colleagues, Elad put the onus on Palestinian "evildoers" who intimidated the workers into leaving Israeli Jewish employment. "Most of the Arab workers left in fear for their lives, and because one of them was beaten and his car set on fire," the foundation said in a statement. Another Israeli archaeologist who worked at the site told a different story that hinted at tensions between the Jewish overseers and Arab employees. "One night the Silwan workers broke into the compound and stole all the equipment," he said, "and Elad said enough is enough."

In January 2008, a section of the road on the main street of Wadi Hilweh collapsed. Residents blamed the excavations that Reich and Shukron were conducting directly beneath. Seven Palestinians filed charges in Israeli court contending that the work—which still had not been officially made public—was damaging their homes and businesses. They added that they should have been consulted about any digging beneath their property. The next day, five were arrested for allegedly damaging the City of David visitor center, though the charges were dropped.

"The claims are bogus," said Elad's Spielman, when asked about the lawsuit, in an echo of Warren's dismissal of the Abu Saud complaints. "We are simply cleaning out tunnels that were already dug by King Herod."

As in Warren's day, the soil beneath Jerusalem was notoriously fickle, capable of suddenly turning from solid to liquid. Tunneling or a heavy rain, or some combination of the two, could unsettle what lay below for weeks or months before the ground gave way. Proving the cause of cracks and cave-ins was as difficult in the current day as it had been when Abu Saud complained about damage to his home by the British archaeologist. And also as in Warren's day, distrust and lack of communication between the two sides exacerbated tensions.

The growing controversy drew Israeli Jewish as well as Palestinian

Arab activists into the streets of Wadi Hilweh. One banner hoisted over the main road read, "To dig a tunnel means to kill a village," while protestors handed out leaflets to tourists that said, "Yes to archeology, no to re-writing history" and "Enter a tourist, exit as a settler." When three demonstrators—one Israeli and two Palestinian—attempted to file a complaint about the digs at a police station, they reported that they were arrested on suspicion of disturbing the peace and held in custody for thirty-six hours.

Israel's High Court ruled in 2009 that "the importance of investigating the past does not negate the interests of the present." Justice Edna Arbel warned the government that "it cannot tread upon the right of residents of the excavation area to live in tranquility." Yet she concluded that the excavation was legal as well as archaeologically important, and rejected the claim that the work was damaging buildings above. Work on the channel continued, and it was soon cleared and incorporated into Elad's growing underground network of passages.

In a repeat of Warren's tunneling days, suspicions grew among Arabs about what was really taking place beneath their feet. "Tunnels allow you to get on with business away from prying eyes," said Greenberg. "One may well wonder what science it is that conducts its business underground."

Be'eri dismissed the idea that there was tension between the Jewish and Arab residents. "There is a lot of trust between us," he told a reporter, extolling the "really excellent neighborly relations." In striking contrast, Greenberg pointed out that the Israeli government paid a security agency to protect the area's Jewish settlers, and Jewish children regularly were ushered to and from school by armed guards.

The controversy took a toll on relations between the two longtime collaborators, Reich and Shukron. "I have a somewhat laid-back personality, while Eli took things very emotionally," Reich said. "And he has a fundamentalist bent which I didn't know at the beginning." Shukron's fascination with finding remains to verify biblical accounts made him a favorite of Be'eri but irritated Reich. It also led to deep disagreements over how to interpret their wealth of finds.

Eventually, they ceased speaking to each other, and publication of their work ground to a halt. The search for the stepped street came to a standstill. Be'eri's dream of pilgrims and tourists marching up from the Pool of Siloam to the Temple Mount on treads hewn in Jerusalem's Jewish heyday would have to wait.

* * *

IN 2007 ALONE, more than 360,000 visitors filed through the open courtyards of the City of David and the tunnel system below exposed by Reich and Shukron. A nighttime light show was added that splashed color on the ruins and told the story of Jews returning from Babylon to rebuild Jerusalem. "Here it began and here it continues," thundered the narrator as recorded music swelled. "The return to Zion!"

Though the focus was on an event more than twenty-five centuries before, the link to the 1967 Israeli occupation of the area was hard to miss. "Archaeological evidence is not what is at stake," wrote the Dutch archaeologist Margreet Steiner. "Imagination, religion, nationalism and emotion set the tone here."

The 2008 tunnel dispute put a spotlight not just on Elad's support for underground excavations, but on the way it presented the archaeological finds seen by Israeli schoolchildren, foreign tourists, and Israeli Defense Forces soldiers. The soldiers were among the largest group of visitors, led by guides trained by the military's education unit, who in turn were briefed by Elad officials. One unit officer noted that "training focused solely on Judaism," while another reported "they talked only about the Jewish narrative."

Elad officials were unapologetic about this approach. "Sixty percent of the Bible was written on this little hill," said Spielman, in a film aired in 2008. "I can tell you with certainty that David, Solomon, Bathsheba, Jeremiah, Isaiah—all the prophets and all the kings of the ancient world, perhaps the queen of Sheba—they all stood here," he added. "I feel King David's hand as I put my hand on this stone."

Greenberg argued that Elad "selectively exploited" the data gleaned by archaeologists to push its "crude amalgam of history, nationalism, and quasi-religious pilgrimage." He argued that archaeologists had an ethical responsibility that went beyond simply operating in a proper scientific manner. "There are things archaeologists have to consider when they dig in a community," he said, calling for what he termed "inclusive archaeology" benefiting residents as well as researchers and their patrons.

Archaeological digs were not just producing data, they were reshaping the city's underground political geography. The spaces, Greenberg noted, benefited "ideological-religious organizations located in the heart of the Old City," including not just Elad but the Western Wall Heritage Foundation, which oversaw the Western Wall Tunnel, and right-wing yeshivas. The subterranean spaces "serve as a virtual lifeline, attracting thousands of tourists and providing an unrivaled opportunity for hours of indoctrination."

Academic colleagues and students at more liberal universities, such as Tel Aviv, tended to agree with that assessment, while others dismissed the criticism as putting unrealistic demands on researchers. Reich was among those archaeologists who insisted that what was done with their sites after they dug was simply not their business. His job was to gather information, not to police guides and signage. "What I create for them is a by-product of my science," he said later. "I don't have a say. I use their money. They were looking for a place to sell Coca-Cola." He concluded that "their agenda is not archaeology, but business."

For Reich, who remained staunchly left-wing in his political views, the price of working with a right-wing group was well worth it. "It created for me a name, a scientific reputation. I knew this would be my opportunity. And I know some people might not like it." As for Mazar, she insisted "my obligation is to show the facts. What they do with them, how they present them, I can't control. They are like children. You educate them, but you cannot be responsible for everything they do when they grow up."

Yet even Reich and Mazar had their limits. When Elad interpreted a Byzantine cistern at the City of David visitor center as the pit into which the prophet Jeremiah was thrown by a wicked Judean king, they both objected. "This was nonsense," said Reich, who had excavated the cistern in 1998. "It was like saying, here, we found the place where King David committed adultery, let me show you."

Mazar made a written complaint in 2011, dismissing Jeremiah's Pit as a "gimmick" that the IAA shamefully refused to condemn. She also criticized Reich, complaining that under Elad's direction, he intended to destroy one side of the cistern for tourist purposes. That would endanger her King David palace excavation only a few yards away. She had completed the dig in 2008 but hoped to resume excavations in the area.

The IAA responded icily that "Dr. Mazar is trying to appropriate the site to herself and we regret that." An Elad attorney dismissed Mazar's criticism as "nothing but an attempt to stop legitimate and vital work being carried out by our client, for reasons of ego and credit only, camouflaged as pseudo-professional complaints." The attorney also noted that Mazar had signed a contract with Elad agreeing not to have "any claim or complaint against Elad regarding future excavations."

The foundation threatened to sue Mazar if she continued her attacks. She never excavated at the City of David again. The threat was a stark warning that opposing Elad could hurt one's career—and even one's health. "Excavating in Jerusalem, you need the skin of an elephant," Mazar said later. "It has taken a toll on me and made me sick. It is so hard."

In May 2021, she passed away after a long illness at age sixty-four. While her interpretations of data rankled many colleagues, they esteemed Mazar for her tenacity and impressive publishing record.

By the time of her complaint, Elad had built an iron catwalk slung beneath the center's plaza that allowed visitors a clear view of the jumbled stones and stubs of rough walls from her trench. It became a centerpiece attraction of the City of David, presented with few caveats.

"The whole use of archaeology as a legitimizer of the state has become a hallmark of Netanyahu," Greenberg told *Haaretz* in 2006, referring to the decade of work at the City of David. "Archaeology has become part of the conflict." Other archaeologists viewed Elad primarily as a private organization driven by real estate and other business concerns—"to sell Coca-Cola," as Reich put it. But it made no bones about its political intentions. When the foundation launched a publicity campaign that year, Be'eri told the same newspaper that its goal was to inform the public that the City of David lay only a couple of hundred yards from the Old City. "Therefore, in any negotiations, it must remain in Israel's hands," he said. "We must not give up."

The tenacious Elad leader not only didn't intend to give up, he was bent on expanding his foundation's footprint on the disputed ridge. Soon he found a chance to expose a chunk of Jerusalem's past as part of a massive real estate development in one of the city's prime locations.

◆　◆　◆

DUNG GATE PIERCES the south side of Jerusalem's Ottoman walls, leading directly to the Western Wall Plaza and the Jewish Quarter. It obtained its odd name as the primary disposal point for the medieval city's waste. A stone's throw to the south was a dusty public parking lot that drew tour buses and Palestinian boys looking for a flat area to play soccer in their hilly neighborhood. It also served visitors to the City of David complex that lay to the east, just across the narrow street bisecting the narrow ridge. The Jerusalem municipality dubbed the site Givati after an Israeli Defense Forces infantry brigade attacked there in 1986 by militant Palestinians.

In 2002, soon after the Sharon government took power, part of the site was acquired by an Elad subsidiary. Other portions came under the organization's control in 2007. The foundation envisioned an underground parking garage below a large building with shops, tourist facilities, and meeting halls. The plan appalled some senior IAA archaeologists such as Jon Seligman, who argued that the site—just outside the Old City and untouched by modern construction—almost certainly covered important ancient structures and artifacts.

Dorfman gave the development a go-ahead, subject to an archaeological survey paid for by Elad. "If distinctive antiquities are found, no construction at all will be permitted," he said in meeting notes, though he then contradicted this by adding that "the archaeological findings will be integrated into the structure." In the summer of 2005, Reich and Shukron started work on what quickly became the single largest excavation in Jerusalem.

Contractors who wanted to build on sensitive sites in Jerusalem paid for archaeological work prior to construction, and those jobs accounted for more than half of the IAA's budget. The clients might be run-of-the-mill commercial builders, religious groups like Ateret Cohanim, or the quasi-governmental Western Wall Heritage Foundation, which oversaw the plaza and tunnel complex. Elad was quickly becoming one of the IAA's largest customers. By the early 2000s, it accounted for nearly one out of every ten shekels the IAA spent on archaeological digs.

To shore up the trenches and prepare for the deep foundation required for a large building, concrete pylons were driven into the edges of the lot, just a few feet from the Arab houses that lined the southern and western boundaries. Soon after work began, Seligman proved correct; the site revealed an unusually rich layer cake of Jerusalem history.

In 2007, the IAA archaeologists Doron Ben-Ami and Yana Tchekhanovets took over the project. They found signs of a busy market and industrial area dating to the early Islamic period of the ninth century CE. Below that was a hoard of gold Byzantine coins and a mansion from that era. Under these lay a luxurious Roman villa from the first century CE. The excavators also found what may be the remains of the Akra, a long-lost second-century BCE Hellenistic citadel, as well as the ruins of an impressive two-story building with an elegant reception room, destroyed in 586 BCE by the Babylonians.

According to internal IAA documents from 2007, Elad pushed to dismantle medieval Muslim and Byzantine layers of the parking lot cake "to expose the layer from Second Temple time." Such a decision was in the end the province of the IAA, but the documents chart Be'eri's growing frustration with the slow pace of excavations that were holding up the development. The digs coupled with the delays were costing Elad millions of shekels annually.

The archaeologists were, in effect, creating the foundation for what Elad hoped would be a seven-floor building with more than 175,000 square feet and 250 parking spaces. "We are talking about a building with the attributes of a shopping mall," complained the IAA archaeologist Yuval Baruch. Even Dorfman was unhappy with the proposed "immense building." But he went on to argue that this was just "a modern architectural layer" on top of subterranean cake.

Early in 2008, as protests gathered force in Wadi Hilweh over Reich and Shukron's tunnel work down the street, Ben-Ami and Tchekhanovets encountered a cemetery from medieval times below the parking lot and removed the remains of a dozen or so individuals who appeared to have been Muslim. Had they been Jewish, such a discovery would have had the potential to delay or even halt a development project. "I asked him to stop digging in places where bones were discovered, and I also asked him to keep things quiet," wrote Baruch, who now led the IAA's Jerusalem directorate.

The find was not reported to the Ministry of Religious Affairs, as required under IAA procedures. It was, the authority admitted later, without apparent irony, "a grave mishap." In 2013, the team came across additional ancient graves that also went unpublicized. Later that year, Arab residents filed a petition in the High Court arguing that the work, like the tunnel, was damaging their properties and lacked proper licensing; they also demanded to be included in the excavation and development planning process.

The dig was temporarily halted, but resumed when the court rejected the suit. "The City of David tells the story of the thousands of years of Jerusalem's history, as can be gleaned from the Bible and elsewhere," wrote

Justice Edna Arbel. "National and international importance attaches to revealing the secrets of the City of David."

In 2012, Tel Aviv University stunned many archaeologists by partnering with the IAA at the Givati dig. The site was located in an area that the international community considered occupied territory, where such excavations were considered illegal under international treaties. Digging to build necessary infrastructure was allowed, and so Israeli officials labeled the excavation a salvage dig. Given that the project was to construct a tourist attraction, however, this was a legal fig leaf.

In addition, Elad's aggressive role in settling Jewish families in an Arab neighborhood was viewed with loathing by many left-wing Israeli Jews. The university, home to Greenberg and other Emek Shaveh supporters, was a well-known bastion of such liberal views.

"We will cooperate with Elad, since they run the site, but we will maintain our standards," insisted the Tel Aviv University professor Oded Lipschitz, adding, "We won't agree to be subjected to political interests." The university also promised, without providing details, that "a great deal of attention will be paid to the needs of those living nearby."

More than eighty academics signed a petition protesting the university's decision to be involved with a group they characterized as "an extreme political organization." Tel Aviv University would be enabling Elad to obtain the "international recognition it desires." Greenberg denounced the deal as "a clear politicization of research." He argued that "when you take money from settlers you are in the heart of politics," and that pretending to be above politics in a place of conflict like Wadi Hilweh was itself a political stance. "No amount of sieving, sherd-counting, text criticism, or ancient DNA analysis can alter that equation."

The university's move was widely seen as another sign of Israel's rightward tilt; such a cooperative effort a decade before would have been unthinkable. But media attention was diverted by the steady stream of archaeological discoveries from what had by then become Jerusalem's biggest and longest-running excavation. Emek Shaveh officials characterized these revelations as distractions that "not only deflected potential opposition, but even aroused public sympathy and support for the excavation among the Israeli public."

The publicity indeed drew hundreds of Israeli Jewish volunteers, as well as Jews and Christians from around the world eager to participate in the discovery of ancient Jerusalem. "The excavation project in the Givati lot is one of the most important archaeological operations carried out in Israel during the past generation," the IAA said in a 2014 statement, while Elad insisted that "all the professional archaeological decisions are being made by the IAA."

A Tel Aviv University archaeologist named Yuval Gadot later assumed control of the Givati excavations in collaboration with his AIA colleague Yiftah Shalev. Tall and gregarious, the academic had been sympathetic to Emek Shaveh and had even signed some of its petitions while he was a student. "I've since learned to appreciate the gray in what seems black and white," he said later. "The archaeology should be done there anyway, and I wanted a project that was my own."

In the competitive discipline, managing a large and well-funded excavation was a plum assignment. "Do people think that if Yuval Gadot stops digging the Israeli-Palestinian conflict will end?" he asked. "This ownership of the past is a kind of game. It is not about who owns the past, but about the legitimacy of your claims. We are living with two different ideologies." Archaeologists, he said, cannot hope to be critical players in a game that is all about political advantage. At best, he said, he hoped to do good science and have input into the way the site was interpreted for tourists, "so this can be a more neutral place." For Greenberg, such talk of neutrality was simple denial.

In June 2015, Israeli authorities rejected a request by Emek Shaveh and other groups to cancel the development project, but they did order its size scaled back. Both sides claimed victory. By then, a far more expensive and more divisive excavation was well underway just down the hill from the Givati site. This time excavators had hit pay dirt.

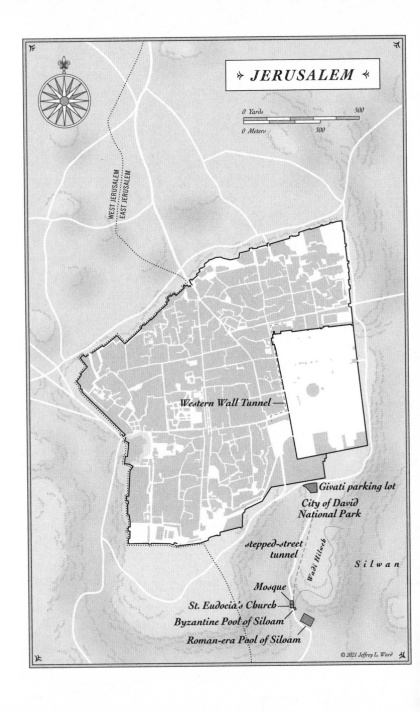

JERUSALEM

0 Yards 500
0 Meters 300

WEST JERUSALEM
EAST JERUSALEM

Western Wall Tunnel —

Givati parking lot
City of David
National Park

stepped-street
tunnel

Wadi Hilweh

Silwan

Mosque
St. Eudocia's Church —
Byzantine Pool of Siloam
Roman-era Pool of Siloam

© 2021 Jeffrey L. Ward

20

Resistance by Existence

Once well underground . . . you know exactly where you are. Nothing can happen to you, and nothing can get at you. You're entirely your own master.
—KENNETH GRAHAME, *The Wind in the Willows*

It wasn't until July 2013 that archaeologists resumed their hunt for the monumental street connecting the Pool of Siloam with the Temple Mount that Be'eri had dreamed of uncovering. "Reich and Shukron began excavations here, going from the top down," said Joe Uziel, the young and energetic excavator who was put in charge of the revitalized project. "They did hit the drainage channel and clear it out, but what they didn't find was the stepped street. That is where we are about to go."

The Israeli archaeologist stood at the bottom of a square pit cut into the middle of the Wadi Hilweh ridge, halfway between the Givati dig to the north and the Pool of Siloam to the south. Concrete Arab houses bristling with electrical wires and satellite dishes crowded above on three sides, while the fourth bordered the neighborhood's main street.

The rising winter sun had yet to pierce the bottom of the deep pit. Uziel then stepped into a broad opening that led from the pit into the earth. Inside, lights blazed within a subway-sized tunnel arched in bright steel. A metal track installed above rattled loudly as plastic buckets heavy with soil jostled by. He grabbed a battered yellow hard hat and began to stride downhill, to the south. "Nothing of this kind can be seen anywhere else," said Uziel, gesturing around the wide passage and raising his Brooklyn accent over the clattering noise.

"Here the stones are missing," he said, pointing down at the packed soil beneath his feet. The Roman-era pavers, carefully carved and fitted, had later been extracted and reused elsewhere. Then he pointed a few yards downhill: "There they are intact." From that point, broad stone slabs, the color of honey and gleaming in the glare of the lights, fell in regular waves before the tunnel took a turn to the southeast.

After walking a few dozen yards, Uziel paused in front of a metal hatch in the stone floor. "This is where we started," he said. Instead of digging down from the surface, they had dug up through the drainage channel. "We worked north until we got to the opening where Reich and Shukron were digging. Then we started working south."

The avenue they exposed proved to be twenty-five feet wide, the usual width of a Roman road and broader than the average American street today. It was paved with rectangular stones more than one and a half feet thick. Each side was flanked by curbstones. In all, some ten thousand tons of fine limestone had been quarried, cut, and carefully laid in what was a massive public works project.

The thoroughfare likely began at the city gate that two thousand years ago lay south of the Pool of Siloam. Then it climbed the western side of the ridge before paralleling the Temple Mount's Western Wall, ending just north of Warren's Gate. "It wasn't as big as the temple renovation project, but it was definitely monumental," Uziel added.

As he strolled down the steps, he gestured at the fine workmanship of the treads. "You can buy a Kia or a Ferrari, and this road is a Ferrari. A lot of effort was put into it, and it was lined with a lot of grandiose buildings. You can imagine traffic jams of people walking up it—the Hebrew word for pilgrimage is 'to go up.' Imagine you had arrived from Rome or London. You might want to change your money to shekels and buy a Coke, so you can imagine there were shops to service those walking up."

The modern-day project was even more ambitious than the one it sought to expose. Be'eri's plan meant digging beneath the entire length of Wadi Hilweh, past the Givati lot, under the Ottoman wall and into the Old City. The subterranean tube then would continue to the southwestern edge of the Temple Mount. At that point, it would measure more than two thousand feet in length, twice as long as the Western Wall Tunnel.

A second stage of construction would extend the passage along the Western Wall to the Mughrabi Gate, and conceivably pass under the plaza beyond, connecting with the rabbinical tunnel. "We support continuing the excavation along the current route," said Mordechai (Suli) Eliav, director of the Western Wall Heritage Foundation. "It is important to us that it will link up with the Western Wall Tunnel."

That would allow visitors an uninterrupted stroll beneath the city for nearly a mile, from the Pool of Siloam to the Via Dolorosa steps, with the bulk passing directly under Muslim homes and businesses. It was an astonishingly bold vision of a revived biblical Jerusalem, far removed from the messy reality aboveground, that even Warren could not have imagined.

◆ ◆ ◆

LIKE THE AMERICAN-BORN Frederick Bliss in the 1890s, Uziel didn't fit the mold of his predecessors. He was not Israeli by birth and had struggled to master Hebrew. His specialty was the more obscure Middle Bronze Age, not biblical or classical times. And while many of his older colleagues fought in the Six-Day War, 1967 marked the year of his birth.

A Cuban American, Uziel was raised in Brooklyn by a secular father and a religious mother. At eighteen, he went to Israel to study in a yeshiva. "I was on a bit of a Zionist kick," he explained. Later, while studying at Bar-Ilan University, he did a brief stint excavating a Byzantine church. "The idea that you could do something academic while getting dirty appealed to me," he said. In time, he "took off his kippah"—the male Jewish head covering—and left his Orthodox faith.

He joined the IAA in 2009 and co-directed a small excavation in southern Israel. When he was offered the stepped-street tunnel project, it was considered something of a poison pill, given its location beneath an Arab neighborhood and the sponsorship of a notorious right-wing organization. But for an ambitious excavator looking for a major project, overseeing such a challenging research effort could launch a career.

"This is not like any other archaeological dig," Uziel said. "We are trying to keep a balance of exposing a major archaeological site while not damaging the existing urban fabric on the hill today." To do that, the team drew on the approach pioneered by Reich and Shukron at the spring on the east side of the ridge. First, engineers inserted metal rods into the soil to support the earth above. Workers could then safely remove the material underneath. The sturdy stone steps became the floor of an ever-expanding tunnel braced by steel arches.

Uziel was determined to try a more scientifically defensible approach than that taken by an older generation. "Without being too critical, archaeologists in Jerusalem have had a tendency to be quite conservative—they weren't using the latest scientific techniques." Instead of simply bagging up and disposing of the material excavated in a tunnel section, for example, the team removed soil from the top of the section and worked its way down. Once they reached the floor, they would begin anew with the next section.

This mimicked a more conventional excavation trench, and theoretically allowed Uziel to record artifacts based on their stratigraphic location. This technique, pioneered by Flinders Petrie at a dig outside Jerusalem in the 1890s, allows researchers to date objects by understanding their relation to one another. In practice, Uziel's approach proved devilishly complex. He and his colleagues struggled to stitch together a coherent picture of each archaeological layer using a variety of computer programs.

As Reich and Shukron had, and as was done in the Temple Mount Sifting Project, the material was then carefully examined. "We take all the dirt and either dry sift or wet sift it, and some we put in a flotation tank to collect seeds and other material," he said over the rattle of the bucket conveyor belt.

At a typical archaeological dig, the excavator had wide latitude in choosing where to dig and the size of the trench. Uziel's work was strictly constrained by engineers. "They determine the width of the dig, based on what is above us," he explained. They forbade him from probing more deeply. "The further down you excavate, the more you weaken the steel arches."

Tunneling technology had improved immeasurably since the days of Bliss. Jerusalem's volatile soil had not. The project was repeatedly halted by collapses caused by the unpredictable mixture of rubble, gravel, and dirt that has long been the bane of archaeologists here. Warren was in a state of constant anxiety. More than once, he wrote, "the shingle would suddenly burst in like water, burying our tools and sometimes partially our workmen."

Uziel shared this fear, coupled with concerns about unmapped buried power lines. Even potholes on the surface could pose unexpected dangers. One afternoon after a heavy winter rain, a small sinkhole opened up in the parking lot of the mosque near the Byzantine-era pool. The municipality dispatched a contractor to fix the hole. When he unleashed a long stream of liquid cement into the gap, he was puzzled that it never seemed to fill up. One of Uziel's deputies raced to the surface. The material was oozing into the tunnel itself, and he begged the worker to stop the flow that was rapidly filling the newly excavated space.

Soon after, a contractor sprayed a special foam in the tunnel designed to prevent such leaks, but the toxic material was distributed too quickly. It caught fire, putting a hold on work in that area for months. The litany of mishaps and near disasters left some project members shaken. "What they are doing is very, very dangerous," said one experienced engineer who worked on the effort. "It is actually irresponsible." There have been no major reported injuries, but Elad has kept a careful lid on public disclosures of the project's technical troubles.

Uziel paused at one side of the street to point out a small hole. At intervals, his team had probed beneath the treads to determine when the street was built—and by whom. The style of the street was consistent with the early Roman era, which began in 63 BCE when the fast-growing city on the Tiber first came to dominate Judea.

The Parthians, Rome's enemies who lived in what is today Iraq and Iran, conquered Jerusalem in 40 BCE. In response, the Roman Senate made a local noble named Herod the region's client king; Roman forces then helped him retake the city and claim the throne three years later. His father and mother were of Arab origins—both came from what is today Jordan—but he was raised Jewish.

Herod befriended Mark Antony, Julius Caesar, and Octavian, the future Augustus, while trying to fend off attempts by Cleopatra, the Egyptian queen, to usurp his territory. His adroit if brutal politics—he is said to have executed a wife accused of adultery and three sons he suspected of conspiring against him—brought him enormous wealth, which he channeled into massive building projects that earned him the moniker "the Great." He ruled not from Jerusalem but from the Mediterranean port of Caesarea Maritima, a cosmopolitan city he filled with statues and temples to Roman deities that were anathema to pious Jews.

But his most ambitious project was to renovate the Temple Mount in order to please his Jewish subjects, a titanic endeavor that included doubling the size of the platform and renovating the sanctuary without disturbing its continuous animal sacrifices. Some eighteen thousand people, including large numbers of slaves, may have been employed in the effort at any given moment. Historians had long credited Herod with oversee-ing the work, though archaeologists suspected it—including, perhaps, the monumental stepped street—went on long after his death in 4 BCE.

Shekels dropped from the pockets of long-dead laborers provided Uziel with the evidence he needed to date the street with precision. The coins trapped beneath the pavement and the hardened mortar that was used to level the space before installing the heavy slabs had lain undis-turbed. The latest were from 31 CE, which meant that this portion of the street was completed shortly before then. Herod had long been dead, and his grandson Herod Agrippa I only assumed power in 41 CE.

The patron of the monumental staircase, then, ruled Jerusalem in the third decade of the first century. He was neither Jewish nor royal; he was also one of the most notorious Romans known to history. His name was Pontius Pilate.

The procurator of the Roman province of Judea, Pilate to this day is vilified by some Christians for his role in executing Jesus and despised by many Jews for his alleged callousness and cruelty.

Pilate served under Emperor Tiberius, and began his decade-long reign around 27 CE. Contemporary writers mention incidents in which the governor incited Jewish anger by ignoring the taboo on graven images. He was criticized for using temple funds to build a new aqueduct to benefit Jerusalem's population. Scholars have long speculated that his poor gover-nance set the stage for the rebellion that resulted in Jerusalem's destruction in 70 CE by Roman forces. Pilate therefore seemed an unlikely candidate for constructing a grand and expensive street for the convenience of Jew-ish pilgrims and the glory of Judaism.

"Part of it may have been to appease the residents of Jerusalem, part of it may have been about the way Jerusalem would fit in the Roman world, and part of it may have been to aggrandize his name through major build-ing projects," said Nahshon Szanton, a young Tel Aviv University archae-ologist who took the lead in dating the street.

Szanton suspected that the monumental path might have been inspired by the Via Sacra, the main street of ancient Rome that led to the top of the Capitoline Hill, which was crowned by an enormous temple to Jupi-ter, his consort Juno, and the goddess Minerva. (Later Romans were said to have built a shrine to this holy trinity on the ruined Temple Mount.) If correct, then this suggested that Pilate respected the religious nature of Jerusalem enough to model the project on the empire's most famous avenue. That challenged the old view that long-term Roman disdain for Judaism sparked the Jewish revolt. Pilate was, perhaps, not simply a villain after all, but rather one in a long line of Jerusalem's rulers who wanted to be remembered for beautifying it.

"New Archaeological Evidence Shows Pontius Pilate Not as Bad as We Thought," read an American headline when the news broke. The discovery recalled a scene from *Monty Python's Life of Brian,* as Judean rebels struggle to justify their fight: "All right, but apart from the sanitation, the medicine, education, wine, public order, irrigation, roads, a fresh water system, and public health, what have the Romans ever done for us?" (The movie is required viewing for new IAA archaeologists.)

Uziel continued his walk down the street, and halted where it suddenly bent to the southeast. Here his crew had encountered the foundations of a long and sturdy building constructed after 70 CE. The stones sat partially on top of the older path. This was another surprise. Historians had long maintained that in the wake of the destruction, little was built south of the Temple Mount. Here was a substantial structure that might have served as barracks for Roman soldiers.

As intriguing as the find was for Uziel, Roman barracks were not what Elad officials wanted to find. In the organization's artists' conceptions of the finished project, tourists climbed steps unobstructed by the later remains of pagan Romans. Whether to keep or remove the building was ultimately an IAA decision. But as the developer and an influential player in Israel's politics, Elad's desires could not be ignored.

"We have a lot of input," said Uziel, pausing by the entrance to the late Roman building and choosing his words carefully. "It is not an easy decision. Excavation is destruction. But you want to leave some representations from other periods, not just one. We attempt to balance it out so there is a little bit of everything." That meant providing visitors with an experience that embraces many eras, not simply that of Jewish Jerusalem in the first century CE. He patted the stone wall. "And we are not going to take this apart."

As he continued down the steps, the paving stones again vanished completely, leaving behind rough-hewn boulders that were difficult to navigate. This was another reality that Elad had not anticipated. Large sections of the stepped street were missing. Whether to replace them with modern stone treads resembling the old ones or to build a metal staircase instead was yet another decision to be made.

Suddenly, Uziel veered from the main tunnel and disappeared into a dark and narrow passage to the right. "You are going to have to duck down a bit," he warned. A thumping fan above nearly drowned out his voice. He slipped his thin frame easily through the twisting and narrow tunnel studded with protruding rock, using his iPhone to light the way. "This is Bliss and Dickie's tunnel," he said over his shoulder.

After a few dozen yards, he emerged into a space that was the size and height of a comfortable suburban living room. His light picked out an upright stone cylinder in a cavernous space. "It's a Byzantine column," he proclaimed with a hint of pride.

The upright pillar still supported portions of the fifth-century church built by order of the Byzantine empress Eudocia. In her, classical Greece met Christian piety and royal wealth. A poet and philosopher, she grew up in a mansion on Athens's Acropolis and married the Byzantine emperor, only to be banished after losing a power struggle in the treacherous court of Constantinople. The exiled royal made the flourishing pilgrimage center of Jerusalem her home. She set out—like Herod, Pilate, and so many after her—to add her own legacy to the Holy City.

The archaeologist crouched down to pull back the sandbag, revealing a smooth white surface. "This is a portion of the marble floor," he said, "and there's a bit of mosaic in place." Eudocia's small but lavish sanctuary commemorated the traditional spot where the blind man was cured by a paste that was made of Jesus's spit and Jerusalem dirt and then washed in the healing waters of the nearby Pool of Siloam. As a consequence of neglect, earthquakes, or invasions, the building eventually fell out of use and vanished beneath later accumulations of debris.

Bliss and Dickie had rediscovered the ruin in the 1890s but paid it little heed, so intent were they on finding remains from the City of David, though local Muslims had marked the site with a small mosque above. The underground church was the structure that had forced Reich and Shukron to halt their excavation. Now, for the second time in a decade, the building lay in the path of the stepped street.

Elad had even less enthusiasm for retaining a Christian church than for preserving Roman barracks. IAA officials said that some of the organization's managers, including Doron Spielman, lobbied hard to have the structure destroyed. "There was a point where they wanted to dismantle the walls," said one archaeologist. "If it were up to them, the church would no longer be there. It was a big debate."

Uziel declined to discuss the matter, but one excavator said that he had adamantly refused to take apart the church. Yuval Baruch, by then the head of the IAA's Jerusalem directorate and Uziel's immediate boss, was reluctant to override his archaeologist's recommendation. To resolve the dispute, IAA chief Yisrael Hasson—who in 1996 had tried to calm Arafat's fury over the Western Wall Tunnel exit—met with Elad chief Be'eri at the subterranean site. He was joined by Uziel and Baruch.

A compromise was floated that required removing a few stones so that tourists could squeeze through a corner of the church in order to continue along the stepped street. "You can't imagine the pressures," one IAA official said. "Six stones standing in the way of a multimillion-dollar project!" In the end, it came down to four stones. Hasson agreed to remove these, on the condition that they be numbered and stored so that they could be put back in place if necessary in the future.

The decision had a paradoxical effect. Had the tunnel been routed around the structure entirely—an expensive but technically possible alternative—the church would have been invisible to visitors. Now it was an unavoidable feature.

"Anyone walking from the Pool of Siloam up the street is going to get Byzantine up the nose," said Uziel, as the stair treads reappeared beneath his feet. Bright winter sun poured in from the tunnel's southern end. Beyond lay the sharp angles of the steps leading to the bathing platform of the Pool of Siloam, where Shukron had made his chance find a decade and a half before.

◆ ◆ ◆

BE'ERI RARELY TALKS to the media or in public, and in encounters with English-speaking reporters he feigns an inability to speak the language. Spielman, promoted to vice president of Elad, does much of the interfacing with journalists. A trim and clean-shaven native of the Detroit suburbs, he left a job in Israeli high-tech to help the fledgling organization create a business plan. He was fervent in discussing the bright future of the City of David.

"If the next ten years are like the last ten years, this"—the City of David—"will be the number one archaeological spot in the world," he predicted in a 2018 interview. "There are more archaeologists working here than on any other site in the country." He also anticipated a mass increase in visitors, to as many as two million a year by 2030. Indians and

Chinese accounted for a growing percentage. "There is a fascination for a people who have existed for thousands of years," Spielman explained. "This isn't like an Akkadian site. The people who began here"—the Jews—"are still here."

In his telling, the development of the City of David complex had benefited both Jews and Arabs. "People buy their Popsicles and drinks from Arab stores," he said. "And there is a lot of security that benefits both Arabs and Jews." The mixing of the two groups—Jews now make up one out of ten residents—"will be a model of co-existence. People will be living together within an active archaeology site with a lot of opportunity."

That harmonious day seemed far in the future. The growing number of Jewish families moving to the neighborhood generally lived in newly constructed buildings behind high gates patrolled by armed guards and watched over by security cameras. Machine-gun-toting men escorted their children to and from school, and when they returned, they shot hoops on fenced courts reserved for Jewish residents. Palestinians, by contrast, generally resided in older homes. Their village, a short walk from the Old City's Dung Gate, lacked a single public playground.

Nor has the influx of tourists provided obvious trickle-down benefits for Arabs. "Business is terrible!" said Abd Yusuf, who ran a small shop close to the local mosque that sits above the new tunnel. "We used to have so many tourists, but now no one comes. They take all the tourists to *their* shops," he added, referring to the City of David's concessions up the hill.

Then he pointed to cracks in his wall. "I have had to replace my door three times because the earth shifts beneath." He also claimed that Israeli Jews pressured him to sell, but he refused. "We have been ninety years in this place—it is a family business and we live here."

Elad's activities prompted local activists in 2009 to organize the Wadi Hilweh Information Center, housed in a modest storefront just up the hill. "The excavations pose many challenges," said Sahar Abass, a former English teacher and the center's deputy director. "They are looking for heritage and history, but it will never give them the right to consider those more important than the people who live here. But that is what is happening. Our homes are being damaged and destroyed."

She estimated that forty houses have been damaged, half of them severely, while five families have been evicted from dwellings considered unsafe. "This is politics. If they can't control us from above, they start to control us from below." For Abass, simply remaining was a form of protest. "Resistance by existence," she said. "They want to move us from this area, but we will keep existing."

Across the street and down a narrow alley, Arab resident Arafat Hamdan, a retired barber with silver hair and a fast smile that fades quickly, lived with his extended family directly above the Elad tunnel. His home had a lush yard studded with orange trees. "I built this house in 1964 with a thick concrete foundation," he said. "But look what has happened," he added, pointing at wide cracks that creep up to just below the first-floor windows. "That is from the last two years."

On the side of the house, he pointed to piles of rubble. "One evening last August we were sitting on the porch when the house began to shake," he recalled. "We could hear them working below with heavy machinery. If you put your hand to the floor, you could feel the vibrations. We fled the house to neighbors, and then we heard a bang—and we could see the cloud of dust rising from where our outdoor kitchen had been."

In a basement apartment, a family member lived with a bathroom riddled with large cracks. "The house was shaking day and night," she said, her voice slightly tremulous. "And the windows and doors won't open." She added, "Every time I enter the bathroom I have fear."

Across the street, Miriam Bashir, an older woman in a scarf and a coat, was in no mood to talk. "I just want to be left alone," she said angrily. "We are lost. We don't know what to do!" After a few minutes, she relented and showed the damage to her interior walls, which seemed to affect only one side of what otherwise appeared to be a well-built house. "The cracks began three years ago, but became more obvious in the past year and a half," she added. As she said goodbye at her gate, beside pots of petunias, she smiled for the first time. "We are peaceful people who live here, and we will stay here despite the damage."

Spielman dismissed the concerns of Arab residents. "Yes, we are working under people's homes, which is not an issue if it is engineered well, which it is." In a later email, he warned against providing a stage for "the claims of politically motivated, anti-Israel, special interest groups."

In the nineteenth century, the Palestine Exploration Fund denied Abu Saud compensation for the alleged damage to his home by Warren. But his complaint drew the attention of senior British government officials and his cause was even championed by the British Foreign Office. Twenty-first-century Arab residents of Wadi Hilweh, by contrast, said they lacked the funds or the faith in the Israeli judicial system to take legal action.

• • •

ON JUNE 30, 2019, shiny black SUVs crowded the dusty parking lot next to the mosque built above Eudocia's Byzantine church. It was the same lot where the cement mixer had tried in vain to fill a pothole, only to send the liquid gushing into the tunnel below. Armed Israeli soldiers patrolled the perimeter under a relentless late afternoon summer sun.

At the base of the ridge, a vast white tent spanned the northern sliver of the Pool of Siloam and the adjacent steps excavated by Reich and Shukron. Inside, the pool's edge had been covered by a stage and hidden by bleachers. Laser lights played on the white backdrop, which also served to screen out the jumble of Arab houses in the distance.

Clustered at the front were an array of VIPs, including the American ambassador to Israel, David Friedman; Senator Lindsey Graham (R-SC); and Sara Netanyahu, the wife of Israel's prime minister. White House Middle East envoy Jason Greenblatt was also in attendance. Other seats of honor were filled with major donors, including several prominent Americans, who had contributed millions of dollars to the project. A few black hats signaled the presence of more traditionally religious Jews, but the majority of the crowd was composed of young and middle-aged Israelis in elegant clothes, women in heels and men in tailored jackets.

"We lay down and wept for thee, Zion," crooned a slim and clean-shaven young man in black, accompanied by a live band. "We remember thee, Zion."

As the singer continued his chant, the emcee climbed onto the stage. "The Jerusalem of King Herod was enormous," he told the crowd. "He challenges his architects to build a building that will be the jewel of the kingdom, the temple," he said, speaking in the historical present tense. "But he doesn't stop there. He expands the Pool of Siloam and orders the construction of a grand thoroughfare to traverse the city, leading pilgrims from the City of David, the ancient capital."

Once completed, he said, "thousands of excited worshippers dress in their finest. Pilgrims climb the stairs, arriving at last at the temple, the most beautiful structure in all the world." Then his voice sank: "The days of peace and prosperity are short-lived. In the year 66, the citizens of Judea revolted against the oppressive Roman Empire. The Jewish rebels hide in the drainage channels beneath the pilgrimage street, just a few meters away from where we are now. Jewish freedom fighters continue to strike back against the Romans."

They were, he added, brutally slain, and in 70 CE, the future emperor Titus destroyed the city. "Once again the Jewish people are exiled," he cried, "but beneath the rubble, the remains of the pilgrimage road of the Second Temple period of Jerusalem awaits." Behind him, a film showed snippets of David Ben-Gurion and the 1967 capture of Jerusalem. There was a shot of Israel's first prime minister at the Western Wall. "We have returned home," he concluded to applause.

Near the end of the ceremony, Be'eri took to the stage in a rare public appearance. Unlike the other men, he was wearing his usual white open shirt and rumpled khaki pants below his white kippah. He spoke in halting but fluent English about an incident that took place decades earlier. He had crawled with his young son Barkai through a drainage channel emptied by Silwan workers, when Reich and Shukron were overseeing the work.

"He told me, Abba, I can't continue, there is a pit ahead." Be'eri encouraged him to jump across it. They then found themselves in a narrow tunnel with stones black from the Roman destruction and surrounded by intact vessels used for food and drink by the beleaguered Jewish rebels who desperately fought the invaders. The Romans, Be'eri explained to his son, had broken into the tunnel "and killed the last Jews in Jerusalem."

They paused there in the passage: "I said to Barkai, I want to tell you a story. My parents come from the Holocaust. They came to Israel and they never spoke about the past. Not one story. But before he died, my father told me one story that I want to tell you here. He said that when he came to Auschwitz, the Germans asked him if he had a profession. He understood it was better to say yes, so he said, yes I am metalworker. And they took him to work in the factory of the Germans—the V2 rockets. He worked in this factory."

The weapons were built in tunnels in order to protect production from Allied bombs. There, his father befriended the factory commander. As the Russians approached from the east in the final days of the war, the German guards marched the prisoners west.

"If you fell down you were killed," Be'eri said. "Only a small group of Jews survived, and they tried one night to escape. The Germans caught them, put them before a pit and shot them with machine guns. All of them died. Only my father got a bullet in his leg. He fell down into the pit and was covered by the dead people."

Be'eri had asked his father what that felt like. "He said, 'I felt that I was the last Jew in the world,' and he thought, 'This was my end.' Then he looked up and saw someone look down. It was the German commander. He crawled in and saved his life."

There, sitting with his son in a very different tunnel and in a very different time, he said, "I have a mission. You see this tunnel? Here, two thousand years ago, the Romans thought this was the end of Jerusalem, the end of Jewish life. We come back to say, 'No! We are going to continue!'" He held up his left index finger. "It took us two thousand years to come back, and to say to the world, we are going to dig. We are going to . . . show all of them that no one can cut our connection to Jerusalem."

This, the Elad chief told the hushed audience, was what inspired him to propose the stepped-street project. To enthusiastic applause, he brought to the stage his son, now a grown man and a member of the same elite commando unit his father helped lead.

Archaeologists and religious nationalists together had created the new attraction, but their goals were radically different. For Reich, Shukron, and Uziel, the excavation had been about exposing an ancient street in order to shed light on Jerusalem's past. For Be'eri, it was about staking a claim to Jerusalem's present to exorcise the ghosts of the Holocaust.

◆ ◆ ◆

A YEAR BEFORE the event, the United States became the first major nation to move its embassy from Tel Aviv to Jerusalem. American policy had long been to support UN resolutions calling for Jerusalem to be internationally administered and outside the control of either Israel or Jordan. The United States therefore had refused to acknowledge the Israeli government's 1950 move to make Jerusalem its capital. After 1967, it considered East Jerusalem as occupied territory.

The decision by President Donald Trump to reverse this policy prompted celebrations by many Israeli as well as American Jews and Christians. Friedman, his ambassador, told the dignitaries assembled under the tent that "the spiritual underpinnings of our society, the bedrock of our principles in which we honor the dignity of every human life came from Jerusalem." He added that "this place is as much a heritage of the U.S. as it is a heritage of Israel." The words were eerily reminiscent of those of the

Anglican bishop who laid claim to the Holy Land at the founding meeting of the Palestine Exploration Fund.

"We want to tell the truth," Friedman continued. "We want to respect history, we want to respect science." Then he pointed offstage to the right, where a path led to the mouth of the tunnel that Reich and Shukron had begun and Uziel had continued. "This, this is the truth. Whether you believe or not, these are largely secular scientists, archaeologists, with no particular agenda. This is the truth. And truth is the only foundation on which peace will come to this area."

The ambassador said the tunnel "confirms with evidence, with science, with archaeological studies that which many of us already knew, certainly in our heart: the centrality of Jerusalem to the Jewish people."

After the speeches, a man dressed in white blew a shofar, a traditional ram's horn trumpet, and the VIPs trooped down the path and into the tunnel. The rest of the audience watched a large screen as the dignitaries swung hammers to break down a stone wall in the tunnel—not an ancient one, but a faux wall built shortly before the ceremony that could be easily demolished.

"What is truth?" Pilate famously is said to have asked Jesus, though he received no reply. The Roman governor's name went unmentioned during the course of the elaborate ceremony, although he likely oversaw the construction of the street for the glory of both Rome and Jerusalem. The only reference to the governor was a cryptic quote buried in a packet of media information distributed by Elad, in which Uziel and his colleagues noted "the importance of the rule of the Roman procurators in shaping the image of Jerusalem."

Pilate wasn't the only significant person missing from the ceremony. Reich declined to attend, while Uziel and several of his colleagues, who had spent long years unearthing the stepped street, were also conspicuously absent. Only at the very last moment, after an angry phone call from an IAA manager, had Elad officials thought to invite the very people responsible for bringing the ancient street to light.

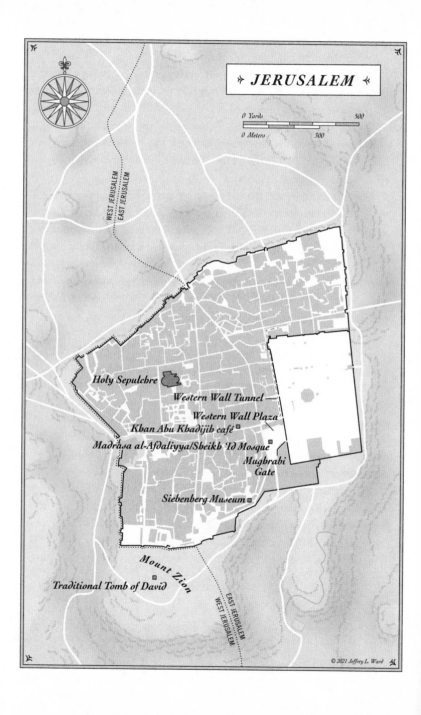

21

Here We Will Stay

> The cherubim are to have their wings spread upward, over-
> shadowing the [Ark] cover with them. The cherubim are to
> face each other.
>
> —EXODUS 25:20

In August 2009, the Israeli archaeologist Benjamin Kedar stepped off a train in the German town of Friedrichshafen. He walked through the twisting medieval streets to a Bauhaus-style building on the shore of Lake Constance, the inland sea nestled beneath the Alps. Though now a scenic tourist destination, Friedrichshafen was once the high-tech center of the world's rigid airship industry. During World War II, its booming factories used slave labor from concentration camps to build V-2 rockets, among other weapons. Some of the workers, including many Jews, were housed in the zeppelin hangars before Allied bombing raids destroyed most of the town.

Like Be'eri, Kedar grew up in Israel with parents who suffered in the Holocaust, and he had served in the Israeli military. They both were close to Ariel Sharon, the prime minister from 2002 until he was felled by a stroke in 2006. Sharon even wrote a foreword to Kedar's book about his experience in the 1967 war.

But Kedar, who chaired the IAA board of directors, broke with Be'eri on the matter of interpreting scientific results. The previous year, he had castigated the IAA for allowing Elad to present the history in what he called "a biased manner" and deplored what he saw as nationalist religious forces playing an increasingly influential role in Israeli archaeology.

That same year, he also had published a groundbreaking book on the sacred platform that included contributions from Palestinian as well as Israeli Jewish scholars. In addition, Kedar pioneered the use of aerial images as aids to Israeli excavators. He believed that bird's-eye views could "help us better confront, comprehend, and come to terms with our recent history, now so befogged by selective, self-righteous and often inflammatory 'narratives.'"

People might lie about the past, but cameras did not. That is what brought him to Friedrichshafen.

Years before, he had come across an image taken during a flyby of the *Graf Zeppelin* above Jerusalem on the morning of Saturday, April 11, 1931; this was before the Nazi regime came to power and emblazoned its fins with swastikas. The world's largest airship had circled the Old City four times. Then the vessel hovered above the Holy Sepulchre, which was only half as long as the zeppelin. Thousands of Christians were crammed into the plaza outside in anticipation of the annual Holy Fire ritual that would soon take place on that Greek Easter Saturday. The sleek craft dropped its nose three times in respect as the stunned crowd gaped in astonishment.

In the zeppelin, a photographer snapped dozens of images of the scene below, rare records of 1930s Jerusalem from above. The Friedrichshafen building housed the zeppelin archives, and a librarian ushered Kedar into the small reading room set aside for researchers. He spent the summer afternoon working his way through three dozen prints of photographs taken during the flight over the city. Before leaving, he requested enlargements of a number of the images, which arrived in a large envelope at his Jerusalem office the following month.

One photo captured the southwest part of the Noble Sanctuary, including one side of al-Aqsa Mosque and the sprawling Mughrabi Quarter just to its west, its narrow alleys crowded with squat houses. The resolution was fine enough to count a dozen or so black-clad Jewish worshippers praying in the small courtyard of the Wailing Wall.

But Kedar, who specialized in the medieval period, was searching for a less well-known sacred place. "I had no idea where exactly it was and how it looked," he said. "So I didn't spot it immediately when I was in the archive. That only came later, after I returned home and enlarged the photo I received."

He suspected that a rectangular building topped with a dome located at the far western edge of the image was the monument he had long sought.

A half-dozen years after the Kurdish general Saladin expelled the Crusaders from Jerusalem in 1187, his son al-Afdal Ibn Salah ad-Din endowed an Islamic law school while he was ruler of Damascus and Jerusalem. That school was the kernel of the Mughrabi Quarter, which became home to centuries of immigrants from North Africa and Spain.

"I had been curious about it for a long time," Kedar later said. "Conventional wisdom put it elsewhere. But with this aerial photo we knew where to look." He then compared the photo with old maps and contacted experts in post-Crusader Jerusalem to see whether his hunch was correct. His colleague Tawfiq Da'adli of Hebrew University, one of Israel's few Arab Muslim archaeologists, checked medieval Arab sources for more information on what was named the Afdaliyya after its founder.

Records were sparse, but they learned that five centuries after it was founded, the school was famed as the resting place of a revered Sufi sage named Sheikh 'Id. By the late nineteenth century, it was known simply as the mosque of Sheikh 'Id.

Buried deep in the IAA's files, Kedar later uncovered a brief 1943 report from what was then the British Palestine Department of Antiquities. An Arab staff member described a building in the Mughrabi Quarter with a domed central chamber and two cross-vaulted halls. Under the western chamber stood a wooden grave marker, presumably that of Sheikh 'Id. The architectural style he described was typical of the Ayyubid period that followed the Crusaders' expulsion, and a particularly common design for religious schools of the day.

The staff member also attached a photograph of what he called "a medieval doorway" from the mosque. It was made up of a pointed arch that featured a strange medley of architectural fragments—possibly from older Crusader buildings. Inside the arch, below a chipped lintel, was a wooden door sunk below the contemporary street level, a sign of its antiquity. A quarter century later, the 775-year-old structure, along with more than one hundred buildings around it, was demolished when Israeli bulldozers leveled the quarter in June 1967.

"If the excavation at Solomon's Stables was an archaeological crime," Kedar said, "then this was one too."

The zeppelin image retrieved from Germany allowed Kedar to confirm the mosque's design and its precise location. He quickly realized that the location matched the very site that his IAA colleague Shlomit Weksler-Bdolah had recently excavated. For nearly four years, she had been digging beneath part of the Western Wall Plaza in preparation for a new building. The dig had wrapped up only months before.

"He came to me and said, 'Look, what did you find?'" Weksler-Bdolah recalled. The two went through her notes. Her team had found medieval structures lining what originally was one of Jerusalem's main thorough-fares dating to late Roman times. Among the remains were the ruins of a domed building with two wings and pieces from what appeared to be a medieval doorway.

At the western end she had found a grave sealed with stone slabs. When the excavators opened the grave, they found the skeleton of a man laid out in traditional Muslim fashion facing south to Mecca. Weksler-Bdolah had recorded the finds, while a physical anthropologist examined the bones, which were determined to be those of a man approximately thirty years old. The structure was then dismantled so that the archaeolo-gist could reach deeper layers, and the bones were reburied in an undis-closed location.

"We researched it, and concluded that this was, for sure, the mosque," said Kedar. "It was most unfortunate," he added, with a note of anguish in his voice. They examined fragments of stone that clearly had belonged to the doorway in the 1930s image. "If I had found the zeppelin photo earlier I could have intervened and told her not to destroy what she had found." Yet while most of the mosque found beneath the Western Wall Plaza was removed, parts of its eastern end remained intact. "Part of it is not yet excavated," said Kedar, "and I hope it will be preserved."

Soon after, another team excavated around the Mughrabi Gate, the entry into the Noble Sanctuary from the vanished quarter. The ramp lead-ing up to the gate was built on top of the foundations of the Abu Saud compound, but it collapsed in February 2004 amid heavy rain, snow, and an earthquake; Arafat, who had lived as a child at the site, died nine months later. A temporary bridge was built, but Noble Sanctuary officials objected to subsequent IAA excavations in preparation for a permanent bridge.

"The Waqf fears that the archaeological excavations will destroy the last remains of the Mughrabi Quarter and remove the archaeological evi-dence" from medieval Arab periods, a UN report found in 2007. Work proceeded despite the objections, and the team uncovered a Byzantine bathhouse and pillars from an Umayyad palace.

They also found a 1955 Jordanian coin. Hair clippers and scissors attested to a barbershop, apparently suddenly abandoned, while several pairs of shoes awaited repair at a cobbler's workshop. "Finally," the dig report stated, "the discovery of porcelain coffee services, among many other objects, illustrate the hasty departure of the inhabitants in 1967."

Kedar's research and the Mughrabi ramp excavations demonstrated that while archaeology could be a tool for national, economic, and religious interests, it could also bear witness to neglected portions of Jerusalem's past.

◆ ◆ ◆

THE VAST MAJORITY of digs in and around the Old City of Jerusalem are not, however, conducted by Israeli Jewish archaeologists, and their finds are far more likely to reach local antiquities shops than scientific journals; Israeli laws are notoriously loose on the trade in ancient artifacts.

When Emdad Abu Khadijih was growing up in Jerusalem, his father ran a tiny convenience store no more than five feet deep along a main street in the heart of the Old City's Muslim Quarter. Today his bushy mustache is gray, but as a youth he surreptitiously began to excavate the back wall of the shop. He scooped earth into bags, concealed from customers by only a curtain.

"I used to lie on my stomach as I was digging," he recalled. "My dad told me, 'You are trying to empty the sea with a teacup!'"

Khadijih, who has no archaeological training, sent the uncounted bags of dirt he amassed to the municipal dump outside Lions' Gate rather than through a sifter. After three decades, that patient work removing five centuries' worth of dirt and trash revealed a large hall of elegant arches resting on stone pillars. The added space allowed him, by then middle-aged, to transform the cramped shop into an atmospheric café popular with foreigners.

The business also brought the attention of the IAA's anti-theft unit, a team of archaeological police responsible for punishing illegal digs.

"I don't read Hebrew," said Khadijih with a shrug as he pulled out a sheaf of papers from a cabinet in his shop. He was arrested in 2015, and the documents ordered him to halt the work unless it was done under IAA supervision. He also was fined the equivalent of $30,000, including back taxes on the additional real estate he had uncovered.

A homeowner in Rome or a businessman in Istanbul could expect to face similar punishment for conducting an illegal excavation. In Jerusalem, however, the preservation of the past is inextricably tied to the political conflict aboveground. Khadijih complained that the fine came as he was under increasing pressure from Jewish developers to sell his shop. "Do you have children?" he thundered. "Would you sell your children? I will not sell my child to anyone!"

The café owner linked his scrap with the IAA to the calls for him to sell. "This is the story of our life," he said, adding that the Israeli government "want us to owe money so they can take our properties." IAA officials dismiss such talk as absurd. "He broke the law," said one Israeli archaeologist. "It is as simple as that." Desperate for financial assistance, Khadijih turned to the Turkish government, which provided monetary help to keep the café afloat and in his name, and even supplied fez-wearing waiters. That assistance prompted fears among Israeli officials of an expanding Turkish influence in the Old City.

When the IAA team members were surveying the café, they were surprised to find that Khadijih had only scratched the surface with three decades of emptying his sea with a teacup. Beneath the hall cleared by the café owner was another hall, this one a vast space half-filled with dirt and refuse. It dated to an even earlier era, in the time of the Crusaders. Its stone floor was gashed by a rough hole that revealed a trash-filled cistern. One excavator who examined the site suspected this tank might provide access to an even deeper level, that of late Roman times, which remains one of the less known eras of ancient Jerusalem.

Despite its obvious importance, however, the site is unlikely to be excavated anytime soon. Few Jewish donors would step forward to support a dig under a Muslim-owned café. And since such an effort would require IAA permission and involvement, Muslim support is also unlikely. It could be viewed as legitimizing the Israeli occupation.

As a result of the distrust between Israeli archaeologists and Palestinian residents and shopkeepers, illegal digs in and around the Old City are alarmingly common. White bags filled with dark earth—unmistakable signs of an emptied cellar or a cleared back room—line the alleys on Saturday, the Jewish sabbath, when there are fewer IAA patrols. Jerusalem's underground realm, built up slowly over millennia, is being hollowed out; each week the city dumps take in a little more of its ancient heritage.

Such illicit digs are not solely an Arab phenomenon. A ten-minute walk to the south of the café, in the rebuilt Jewish Quarter, is the two-story home of a sprightly octogenarian named Miriam Siebenberg. Her roof deck boasts a postcard view of the Western Wall and Temple Mount, but her basement is even more striking.

Siebenberg and her late husband, Theo, built the house in 1969, after the Six-Day War. She was raised in Tel Aviv, but the Belgian-born Theo had escaped the Nazis in an arduous winter flight across the Pyrenees. A history buff, he grew curious about what lay beneath their home. "It took us eighteen years of work," Siebenberg said with pride. "Despite the bureaucracy and our neighbors' concerns, we prevailed."

The couple dug below their own foundations, a treacherous undertaking in a structure perched on a steep slope. They sunk shafts as deep as the house is high, eventually transforming a musty cellar into a multilevel underground museum.

During a tour, Siebenberg affectionately patted a huge stone carved like a trough. "This is my private faucet, part of the old aqueduct," she said. Thick stone walls nearby were, she asserted, part of an ancient Judean palace from the second century BCE that overlooked the Temple Mount. "The one percent lived here," she added with pride.

The Siebenbergs' effort broke any number of antiquities laws, but as twentieth-century one-percenters who counted famous Israeli archaeologists among their friends, they avoided prosecution. The glass cases in her stylish midcentury house were filled with artifacts found below that ranged from delicate bone tools used to apply makeup two thousand years ago to a rusted machine gun from the 1948 war between Jews and Arabs.

Miriam Siebenberg's relationship to what lay beneath her home contrasted sharply with that of Khadijih. Both felt deeply and passionately rooted to their piece of land. For the Arab café owner, what lay underground was valuable for the practical benefits it bestowed. What mattered was additional land, and perhaps a valuable old coin or two, that could help a family prosper. What lay underground was there to harvest so that life could continue above.

Growing up in a world where the very survival of the Jewish people was in question, Siebenberg viewed what lay below her feet quite differently. The underground spaces were more than real estate, and the artifacts were not important because of their monetary value. Instead, they were powerful affirmations of her threatened identity.

"We were here," she explained, as her genial manner suddenly gave way to implacable resolution. "And we came back. Here we are, and here we will stay." Like the cherubim on the Ark cover, the Jews and Arabs of the Old City face each other, perched proudly above their claimed real estate, close yet never touching.

◆ ◆ ◆

MORE THAN A CENTURY after Parker competed with Rothschild to recover the Ark of the Covenant, the dream of unearthing the world's most famous lost artifact still draws adventurers to Jerusalem from around the world.

Ron Wyatt's American followers continued the search after his 1999 death, probing Zedekiah's Cave, which runs under the Muslim Quarter, across the street from the Garden Tomb. Jerusalem's largest underground space, covering the equivalent of two Manhattan city blocks, is the ancient quarry where Warren held the city's first recorded Masonic ritual; it still draws Freemasons to its cavernous halls for secret rites. The Ark, however, was not to be found.

Others believe the sacred box lies beneath Mount Zion just south of the Old City's walls. This is where Bliss began his search for the early Judean city before moving to the ridge a half mile to the south. Home to what is called the Tomb of David, a shrine housed within a late medieval monastic complex, this compact neighborhood is riddled with ancient passages, tombs, and caves.

"There are a lot of mysteries and bizarre stories concerning this mountain," said Amit Re'em, an IAA archaeologist. He had spent years excavating Ottoman barracks beside the city's citadel that revealed a rich layer cake of Jerusalem history. The site was a short stroll to Mount Zion, and Re'em was drawn to a place dense with both sacred sites and legends, but largely unexplored by archaeologists. "It has always drawn bizarre people—I don't want to say lunatics—but certainly strange and extremist people."

In 2013, rabbinical authorities who control the so-called Tomb of David wanted to install a new electrical line, and Re'em conducted an investigation before it was laid. Working at night so as not to disturb the Jewish and occasional Muslim worshippers, he and his small team dug down a foot and a half but found nothing of consequence. "Then we reached the area under the east window, and spotted blocks of stone that seemed to cover a shaft," he recalled. As dawn approached, however, he had to abandon the effort.

Re'em later brought a ground-penetrating radar into the tomb, again under cover of night, to probe without the need for destructive excavation. The data revealed what appeared to be a massive void under the stone floor. This intrigued the Brooklyn-born rabbi Yitzhak Goldstein, who took over from his father operation of the nearby Diaspora Yeshiva, which controls much of the land around the tomb.

"I remember when I was ten, the director of the religious ministry came to visit, and said that he had been in a cave beneath the tomb," he said. "And an old Muslim woman who used to live here"—a member of the Dajani family that for centuries served as the tomb's caretakers, when it was controlled by Muslims—"told the same story."

Goldstein was convinced that Mount Zion was part of the early City of David. "Jerusalem was a great city—it would be a disgrace if it were that small then," said the rabbi, a tall man made taller with his black-brimmed Borsalino hat. "And that means King David is here. But no one has really excavated."

To secure the necessary funds, Goldstein tapped one of the yeshiva's longtime members, Rod Salinger. Salinger was an Australian millionaire and Jewish convert who made a fortune on minerals, wine, and weapons. Like Wyatt, the Australian had grown up a Seventh-day Adventist, the sect that believed the discovery of the Ark would signal the start of the End Times. Salinger later converted to Judaism and became Goldstein's student.

The rabbi and the Australian businessman professed to be on the hunt for David's actual tomb, which they suspected lay in a cave beneath the medieval cloister. But Salinger, who was as tall as Goldstein but sported an Indiana Jones–style fedora, coyly hinted that his ultimate goal was to find the Ark and the temple treasures. He cited lore claiming "all the gold from King Solomon" was hidden away as the Babylonian army approached in the sixth century BCE.

"Everything was packed away," he added. "And it is so clear where it was put. I can't go into details, but this will be a great and exciting story—I'm thinking *National Geographic* or Steven Spielberg."

At first, Re'em was encouraged by Goldstein's willingness to allow excavations beneath yeshiva land and Salinger's apparently deep pockets. He backed out when Salinger insisted on a major role in the actual dig. Not long after, Interpol accused the Australian of illegally exporting a door that once led to the room above the traditional Tomb of David, which many Christians consider the site of Jesus's Last Supper.

"They say it was stolen and that it was ancient," Salinger said later. "But it's not true; it was not an antique." Nevertheless, the IAA forbade any of its employees from working with him until the matter was resolved.

As with many of Jerusalem's other treasure seekers, Salinger claimed that hostile forces were at work to halt the effort. "We are stalled at the moment," he said, his voice dropping to a low growl. "There is a Russian spy trying to destroy everything. She is in a very top position. They stole five hundred thousand dollars earmarked for this project. It was a shock to discover that the honey pot was gone. There's money laundering involved, tiny electronic transfers that whittled away a vast amount of money. And there are others—treacherous bastards—trying to make secret excavations at nighttime to beat us to the punch."

He paused. "Everything I tell you is dinky-di," Australian slang for "on the level."

In the summer of 2019, Salinger abruptly left Israel for Canada. He explained that he had been bitten by a Palestinian viper, called a Land of Israel viper in Hebrew, an extremely poisonous creature, which months before had been declared Israel's official snake. His recovery was slow, and he wasn't sure when he would return. "Indiana Jones didn't like snakes and neither do I," he said.

There is little doubt that neither snakes nor permitting problems will deter future adventurers from seeking the Ark and Solomon's wealth. "Indiana Jones is burned into everyone's head," said Yehiel Zelinger, an IAA archaeologist who has collaborated with and befriended Wyatt's followers. "It is an obsession." He should know; his wife is a psychologist who has worked with Jerusalem Syndrome patients.

But Spielberg shouldn't shoulder the full blame; the Hollywood director only modernized and amplified an old and powerful legend that mixed spiritual longing with earthly rewards. "Nothing changes," said another Israeli archaeologist. "Crazy people with money come from the West to find treasure—and the locals are ready to exploit them."

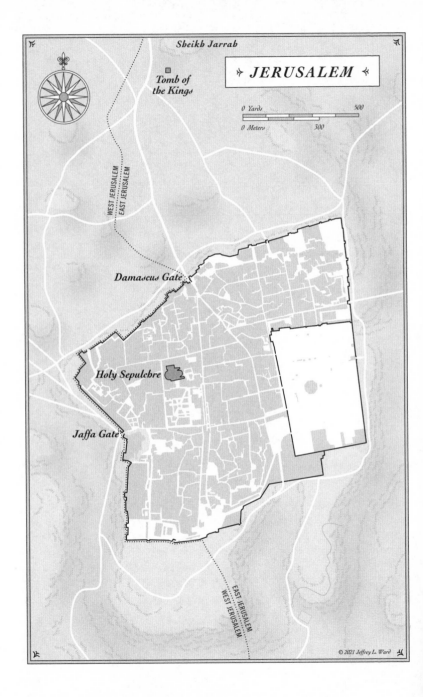

JERUSALEM

Sheikh Jarrah

Tomb of
the Kings

0 Yards 500

0 Meters 300

WEST JERUSALEM
EAST JERUSALEM

Damascus Gate

Holy Sepulchre

Jaffa Gate

EAST JERUSALEM
WEST JERUSALEM

© 2021 Jeffrey L. Ward

22

Return of the Queen

The very ink with which history is written is merely fluid
prejudice.

—MARK TWAIN, *Following the Equator*

In 2010, Rabbi Yitzhak Mamo and his businessman friend Haim
Berkovits left Jerusalem to visit Paris. Berkovits had immigrated to
Israel from France, and he took Mamo on a tour of the city's Grand
Synagogue. Work on the building began in 1867, as Warren was tunneling beneath Jerusalem. The classical structure with neo-Byzantine touches
was funded in large part by the Rothschild family, and it had since served
as the heart of the French Jewish community and seat of the nation's chief
rabbi. This is also where the French officer Alfred Dreyfus was married
before his 1894 arrest on charges of being a German spy.

"I happened to notice a sign on the wall that said 'Tomb of the Kings
of Judah' in English, French, Arabic, and Hebrew," recalled Mamo. "It also
said that the tomb was bought by Madame Péreire and given to France."
Curious, the two strictly Orthodox men asked synagogue employees
about the tomb's location and the identity of the woman. No one knew.
"One guy said they found it in the basement and put it there. Later, I
began to wonder, what is the story?"

Middle-aged and affable, Mamo worked as the director of a West
Bank company that specialized in buying Palestinian lands in the occupied territories for Jewish settlers; his successor had close ties to former
conservative prime minister Ariel Sharon. Berkovits, a heavyset man with
a baby face, was a successful Israeli software entrepreneur. Both men were

involved in the campaign to settle more Jews in East Jerusalem and the West Bank, and to assert Jewish control over the area's tombs and shrines.

Intrigued by the mysterious synagogue sign, they set out to uncover its meaning. The search turned out to be more than a historical lark. "You have to find Dan Brown's telephone number," Mamo said later. "This is an amazing story of archaeology and the politics of the past through so many generations."

Their discovery would reignite the nineteenth-century controversy over the first legal excavation in Jerusalem, the 1863 dig by Félicien de Saulcy. It also would spawn years of demonstrations, legal suits, and a violent scuffle that sharpened tensions between France and Israel.

But first, the two men, with help from a young Israeli historian, scoured archives from France to Turkey. Over time, they unearthed the paper trail detailing what happened to the Tomb of the Kings after de Saulcy left Jerusalem for Paris with his sawed-up sarcophagus and bags of bones.

◆ ◆ ◆

BY THE TIME the governor of Jerusalem bade farewell to de Saulcy at the end of 1863, the Jewish community was in an uproar. The Frenchman's callous treatment of the human remains found within the Tomb of the Kings prompted them to complain to Russian and British envoys about the desecration, and to campaign against the dig in European newspapers.

By then, however, the heavy stone sarcophagus identified as that of an ancient Judean queen and fragments of her skeleton were safely on a steamship bound for France. De Saulcy's patron, Emperor Napoleon III, dismissed foreign criticism and welcomed the artifacts, and the sarcophagus became a magnet for visitors to the Louvre.

One Jewish Parisian named Berthe Lévy Bertrand was so moved—or disturbed—by the display that she set out immediately to purchase the land around the tomb. "I have no other goal than the conservation of this ancient and venerable monument," the prospective buyer later stated in a certified document. "It is in memory of my ancestors that I want to preserve the tomb from all desecration, the tomb of the kings of Israel."

It was a bold move by a nineteenth-century Frenchwoman—particularly one married to one of de Saulcy's closest collaborators.

Born in 1840, she had grown up in Paris but her mother came from a Portuguese Sephardic Jewish family in Bordeaux; her father was a distinguished mathematician and geologist who died a year after her birth.

Finding herself in dire financial straits, the widow placed their daughter in a Catholic convent to ensure a solid education.

In 1860, the twenty-year-old Berthe married the forty-year-old Alexandre Bertrand, one of France's first archaeologists and the person who established the field of European prehistory. Alexandre and de Saulcy were colleagues and friends within the intimate circles of French scholarship. The two men published in the same journals, reviewed each other's writings, and served on the same committees. They even jointly excavated a Gallo-Roman cemetery in eastern France, recovering iron swords and gold rings, shortly before de Saulcy left for Jerusalem. Those discoveries had prompted a visit from a curious Napoleon III.

Three months after de Saulcy's return from the Holy Land, with the emperor's blessing, a committee of leading scholars organized France's first national archaeological museum. Bertrand was named its director. Simultaneously, as British and American newspapers were filled with vitriol against de Saulcy, Bertrand's wife—now Berthe Lévy Bertrand—launched her effort to buy the land around the tomb. What her husband and de Saulcy thought of this initiative, or whether they knew about it at all, isn't known.

Her task was no simple matter; foreigners were forbidden from owning Ottoman land. So she turned to Jacob Pascal, an Armenian who served in Jerusalem's Austro-Hungarian consulate and was known to be sympathetic to Jews. His three-year effort failed, however, and he returned the vast sum of 30,000 francs—roughly half a million dollars today—that she had sent for the purchase. The problem was that the tomb was part of an Islamic trust, and therefore not easily sold.

Berthe Lévy Bertrand was, however, tenacious. A decade later, in 1874, she asked the new French consul, Salvator Patrimonio, to attempt the purchase. As a foreign diplomat, he had the legal right to buy Ottoman property. On April 23, 1874, she paid a visit to the chief rabbi of Paris at the Grand Synagogue, which was nearly completed, to relay the news that the sale had gone through. The rabbi had a certified document drawn up attesting to her desire to ensure the tomb was protected. The document also made clear her pride in her Jewish heritage.

Five days later, the chief rabbi scribbled on the document that "the words spoken and written by Madame Bertrand née Lévy are in all respects reliable. I am certain that the land acquired by her on which is the Tomb of the Kings will remain forever Jewish property preserved from any profanation." He added a note in Hebrew to the attention of Jerusalem's chief rabbi: "The words written here are true and we must base ourselves on these words. I know that the land called Tomb of the Kings will not come out of this family, the family of Israel, and will not be desecrated in any way."

He asked the Jerusalem rabbi "to lend a hand in carrying out the formalities required by Ottoman law, so that we have the joy and the happiness of preserving this venerable and ancient monument in the midst of Israel." But the formalities of registering the land were not concluded until 1878, when Patrimonio reported its acquisition "on behalf of Madame Bertrand." That same year, the ubiquitous Conrad Schick noted that Bertrand had paid to have the area cleaned up and have a protective wall built around the tomb.

Even still, the question of ownership was not settled. Under Ottoman law, a private person could not own a holy place or cemetery. In 1886, the French government asked a man named Henri Péreire to turn the site over to the state. He obliged in a written contract, with the stipulation that "no changes will be made to the actual purpose of this monument."

Péreire was grandson to Isaac Péreire, one of the two famous Péreire brothers, who had founded Crédit Mobilier and helped invent industrial capitalism; a Paris Métro station today bears their name. Key players in making France an industrial powerhouse second only to Britain, they grew up impoverished in Bordeaux, where they had known Berthe's mother and were distantly related to her.

Oddly, Berthe Lévy Bertrand is not mentioned in the document, though she is likely the "Madame Péreire" on the sign at the Grand Synagogue. The Péreire brothers may have fronted Bertrand the money to purchase the tomb in 1864. The grandson's stake in the Imperial Ottoman Bank and close ties to senior French politicians likely explain why he stepped in to help resolve a delicate matter between the two governments.

Although she lived until 1913, Bertrand vanishes utterly from the archives. Any documents or correspondence about the Tomb of the Kings went up in flames a quarter century later, when the family burned their papers as the Nazis approached the French capital.

There was yet another wrinkle, though. The 1886 contract was unsigned, raising doubts as to whether it was officially certified. Nevertheless, the French government took charge of the site, hoisted the French flag, and opened it to visitors. The donation of a Jewish site by a Jewish man to the French government infuriated Theodor Herzl, the founder of Zionism, who visited the site in 1898. "This is how impossible people would consider it that the Jews ever own anything themselves," he fumed.

The Péreire family put up a sign at the site dedicating it to "science and the veneration of the true children of Israel." For more than a century, this potential contradiction—a tomb set aside for both scientific and religious purposes—lay dormant. What the "actual purpose of the monument" was remained unclear; the site became one more Jerusalem tourist destination, if one outside the Old City that was a little off the beaten track.

• • •

IN DE SAULCY'S DAY, the area around the tomb was covered in olive groves and dotted with other graves and shrines. One of these was the resting place of Sheikh Jarrah, Saladin's physician and the namesake of a nearby village. In subsequent decades Sheikh Jarrah became a fashionable neighborhood of villas built by the city's wealthy and influential old Arab families. It also drew a small community of Jews who lived close to the Tomb of Simeon the Just, a Roman grave that medieval tradition attributed to an ancient Jewish sage.

After the 1948 war, the area's Jewish residents fled when it fell under Jordanian control, and Palestinian refugees took over the abandoned homes. In the wake of the 1967 war, Jewish settlers began to file suits to evict them from homes the settlers claimed belonged to the departed Jews. Following the second intifada in the early 2000s, Haredim began to flock to Simeon's tomb in larger numbers, and the pace of evictions—along with communal tensions—increased.

In 2010, the same year that Mamo and Berkovits paid their visit to Paris, President Shimon Peres warned that Jewish settlement in Sheikh Jarrah could spark an Arab backlash.

The intensifying conflict in Sheikh Jarrah also disturbed French officials, who opposed Jewish settlement in what they saw as occupied territory. The same year that Peres sounded the alarm, the French government closed the tomb indefinitely, ostensibly for repair and renovation. The decision drew protests from Israeli archaeologists as well as Haredim.

In a move designed to placate Israeli critics of the French move, the Louvre agreed to loan its sarcophagus excavated by de Saulcy to Jerusalem's Israel Museum. The decision came only after intensive negotiations involving the French ambassador to Israel as well as the directors of both museums. "The French gave me a hard time," curator Hagit Maoz Lin from the Israel Museum told *Haaretz*. "Perhaps there were concerns that once the sarcophagus arrived in Israel, someone would want to keep it here."

After more than a century and a half, the queen's stone casket was returning home, if for only a brief four-month visit, to be part of an exhibit on pioneers of biblical archaeology. Before the heavy stone coffin was shipped, however, France's deputy consul in Jerusalem invited Mamo and Berkovits, as representatives of a Jewish religious foundation that claimed the tomb, to come to Paris to inspect the casket and to show that it contained no human remains.

Accompanied by senior members of France's Jewish community and the French foreign ministry, the two Israelis were taken deep into the Louvre's vast underground storerooms, where the object was kept. "There were no bones," Mamo recalled, "so I said, okay. It belongs in Israel but I will not start a fight between Israel and the Louvre." The exhibition went off without a hitch, and the casket was returned not to a dusty storeroom but to a special hall in the Louvre devoted to de Saulcy's excavation.

The tomb's closure, meanwhile, gave French archaeologists a chance to examine the complex more thoroughly. A French Dominican monk and scholar named Jean-Baptiste Humbert, who had lived next door at the École Biblique for more than half a century, lamented that the important monument "had sunk into oblivion." After reviewing the evidence, he made a startling suggestion.

Scholars had largely not questioned the assumption that the tomb was that of Queen Helena of Adiabene, and the stone coffin was her final resting place.

Humbert, however, asserted not only that it wasn't built for her, but that the sarcophagus found by de Saulcy did not contain her remains. He argued that the tomb's design pointed to a royal Judean sepulcher rather than that of a foreign convert. The French monk believed it was constructed for the grandson of Herod the Great, Herod Agrippa I, who reigned over Judea after Pontius Pilate, from 41 to 44 CE.

Raised in the Roman court, Agrippa was beloved of Roman Emperor Tiberius and a favorite of his successor, Caligula. When that emperor announced that he planned a second career as a sun god in Egypt's Alexandria, assassins stabbed him to death. According to Josephus, Agrippa then encouraged Claudius to stand up to the Senate and accede to the throne. In exchange, Claudius made him ruler of Judea. Humbert believed that Agrippa then set about building a sepulcher fit for his royal family, only to die suddenly. The French scholar noted that parts of the tomb's exterior were unfinished. Helena, as a wealthy aristocrat, would likely have been able to purchase the incomplete complex.

It was, the monk concluded, a tomb designed for a king but bought by a queen. He also cited new research suggesting that the inscription dated to as much as a century after Helena's death, and suggested the casket had been reused. In addition, Humbert noted that Josephus said Helena returned to Adiabene, where she died, and her bones were later returned to Jerusalem. An intact skeleton, such as the one de Saulcy had encountered, would hardly have survived such a long journey. If the monk was right—and his theory is controversial—then the remains sought by Mamo in the bowels of the Louvre may have been those of a queen, but one who lived later, and one who perhaps wasn't even Jewish.

As the renovations dragged on, Haredim began to criticize France. In 2016, an impatient Mamo filed suit against France in rabbinical court to force France to hand over the deed to the tomb. French officials insisted the court had no jurisdiction over a sovereign nation. Under pressure from Israeli officials, Mamo dropped the suit. "So I could be walking in Paris, and someone in the Mossad will kill me," he said, referring to the Israeli intelligence agency. "And that will be the end of the story."

Blocked from taking legal action, Mamo and Berkovits launched regular protests at the iron gate of the tomb. Twice a week, Haredi demonstrators would gather to sing and dance and to demand that the French allow Jews to pray at what they insisted was their holy site. The demonstrations eventually drew the notice of Israeli politicians. While on a state visit to Paris in January 2019, Israeli president Reuven Rivlin complained to French president Emmanuel Macron about the closure, and Macron agreed to open the tomb to visitors. After what the Israeli Foreign Ministry called "long and strenuous negotiations," the site was slated to open in the summer.

Just a few weeks after the French and Israeli leaders met, Mamo and Berkovits, assisted by Bar-Ilan University historian Reut Odom, found what they believed to be proof of French mendacity. An official 1876 Louvre publication titled "Monuments from Palestine kept at the Louvre Museum (Judaic Room)" includes a list mentioning not just the Helena sarcophagus but five boxes with human bones obtained between 1864 and 1870, including "a lower jaw dipped in gelatin."

Though the publication did not specify that the boxes came from the Tomb of the Kings, the collection included "fragments of the scapula to which the meshes of a linen fabric edged with gold thread adhere." This description matched the gold thread of clothes or a shroud that de Saulcy noted was in the sarcophagus after the bones disintegrated upon touch.

The possibility that museum curators had lied about the presence of human remains during their 2010 visit infuriated the Israeli men, who asked Louvre officials to respond to the new information. "Either they are hiding the bones or they have lost them," said Mamo. Two weeks later, in June, museum management pledged to study the matter and respond "as soon as possible." No response was forthcoming. But the French government did announce it would reopen the Jerusalem tomb at the end of June for a limited number of guided tours. All visitors would be required to register online and pay a small fee.

Just after 9:00 a.m. on the morning of June 27, 2019, a dozen Haredi men in black coats and hats crowded around a black iron gate topped with a sign that read "Republic of France, Tomb of the Kings." Beyond, a tricolor flapped in the hot morning breeze. Two dozen registered tourists passed through the gate under the watchful eyes of two security officers from the consulate.

The Jewish men, however, had refused to register. Many avoided use of the Internet altogether, while they found the fee insulting. "I asked the guy in charge, where do people pay to pray?" said Mamo, who led the group. "What church, what mosque, what synagogue?"

When the guards reopened the gate to allow the first batch of visitors to leave, the Jewish believers began to push and shove their way inside. The guards resisted. "They were very violent," Mamo said later of the actions by the gendarmes. "One of them tried to put his hand on me, in a sensitive place."

In the scuffle, one of the gendarmes had his thumb disjointed and was briefly hospitalized, while the other was punched in his side. "Our security officers did not hit anybody," a French official insisted later. "One had his glasses broken. We were not the aggressors." Mamo claimed that the hospitalized guard was faking his injury, adding that the Israeli police had arrested him. The French official denied this: "The Israeli police were on the sidewalk, but they did not intervene."

When he heard the news of the melee, a furious French consul ordered the tomb once again shut and suspended all visits. "We deplore the violent incidents that took place today at the entrance of the site, during which agents of the consulate general of France in Jerusalem were assaulted," said a statement from the consulate. Since making a formal complaint to Israeli authorities might have endangered the diplomatic immunity of the guards, the French government did not pursue the matter.

Relations between the two countries were already strained by a series of anti-Semitic incidents in France. The controversy also put a spotlight on the French refusal to acknowledge the Tomb of the Kings to be on Israeli soil, a stance that had long irritated the Israeli government.

French lawmakers, meanwhile, saw the push to take over the tomb as part of a larger campaign by religious Zionists to secure sacred sites in Sheikh Jarrah in order to expand their presence at the expense of local Arabs. The effort was "part of a global strategy of territorial nibbling on the part of religious nationalists," declared French senator Gilbert Roger in October. "The conflict began when religious people . . . tried to claim possession over the grave because of the location in East Jerusalem."

On October 24, with Israeli security forces deployed nearby to prevent violence, the French reopened the tomb to visitors. The protestors once again tried but failed to enter. The indefatigable Mamo then changed tack. A week later, on behalf of the tomb's Jewish religious foundation, he and Berkovits sued the French Ministry of Europe and Foreign Affairs. They demanded that France give up the Tomb of the Kings to Jewish religious control.

The men also sued the Louvre for repatriation of the bones that de Saulcy had dug out of the underground warren. After all, France had recently returned skulls of indigenous Maori people to New Zealand. "The respect due to the dead requires that the bones of the deceased are not separated from their land of origin," stated the second suit, which also requested the court fine the Louvre a single euro per day "in compensation for its moral prejudice."

An official with the French foreign ministry, meanwhile, insisted that France had no intention of turning over one of the nation's premier Holy Land sites to Israeli religious nationalists. "Settlers have an interest in grabbing this site, which is in such a sensitive area," the official said. "But they can buy a ticket. We won't prevent them from praying."

As the suits were filed in Paris, a new French consul named René Troccaz arrived in Jerusalem to take up his post. On November 6, he led a procession of robed Franciscan monks attended by Muslim guards in gold piping and fezzes through the stone-paved streets of the Old City to the Holy Sepulchre, where the French diplomat was blessed with holy water and given the place of honor in front of the altar at a Catholic Mass. After the ritual, the celebrant bowed to the consul. Troccaz was then led through the small door and into the traditional tomb of Jesus to pray.

It was, perhaps, Jerusalem's strangest ceremony. France is, after all, one of the world's most rigorously secular nations, but it tenaciously clung to its role as protector of the Holy Land's Christian sites, even submitting to the overtly religious rites required to maintain that status.

Much had changed since de Saulcy made his controversial discovery: France was no longer a colonial empire ruled by a Catholic emperor, and the state of Israel, then just a gleam in the eye of a few Christian Zionists, now controlled Jerusalem. Yet the struggle over the Holy City has, if anything, become increasingly volatile. In May 2021, demonstrations against pending Arab evictions in Sheikh Jarrah erupted into regional violence. Bloody clashes spread to Damascus Gate and the contested acropolis. Some four thousand rockets were fired from the Gaza Strip into Israel, while Israeli warplanes pummeled the Palestinian territory. Within two weeks, more than two hundred and fifty Palestinians and a dozen Israelis were dead and thousands more were injured. The conflict was a sobering reminder that Jerusalem remains a powerful symbol of peace as well as the epicenter for one of the world's most intractable conflicts.

"A good friend of mine is a history professor," Mamo recalled with pride soon after the lawsuits against France and the Louvre were filed. "He told me that he liked my work. He said I use history for now." Beneath the Holy City, the real treasure is neither the Ark of the Covenant nor the riches of Solomon, but the ability to mine the past in order to dominate the present and future.

Taken from her sealed subterranean tomb as a biblical trophy, the queen found by the French explorer so long ago is still being pressed into the service of those intent on claiming what is above. Jerusalem may be a gateway to heaven, but its abiding power remains bound up in its underworld.

Epilogue

We are not meant to spend the rest of our lives underground.
We need to go home and tell a strange story that no one will
believe.

—COURTNEY M. PRIVETT, *Cavelost*

In a September 23, 2011, speech before the UN General Assembly, the Israeli prime minister said he kept in his Jerusalem office a 2,700-year-old signet ring found near the Western Wall inscribed with his family's adopted Hebrew surname, Netanyahu. It was, for him, both evidence of his ancient tie to the land and a reproof to Israel's foes. "It has been proved without a doubt that Jerusalem is the main artery of our national consciousness," he added in 2017. "The root of Zionism is in Zion."

Palestinian Authority president Mahmoud Abbas, meanwhile, has criticized Israel's "never-ending digging" as part of a Zionist conspiracy to "vindicate the Israeli narrative" by erasing nearly fourteen hundred years of Muslim presence. As one author noted about William Faulkner's fictional Mississippi county, Jerusalem is "a land where the dead past walks."

Archaeologists in Jerusalem, more than anywhere else on the planet, have always confronted a past that remains stubbornly present, whether the city's rulers were Ottoman, British, Jordanian, or Israeli. They inevitably depend on patrons who invariably come with agendas, and they also must anticipate opponents who, at the recovery of a bone or clearing of a drain, might launch a street riot. And there are more digs taking place in fast-growing Jerusalem—with a population nearing one million—than in any other city in the world.

"It is like working at the ground zero of world archaeology," said Tehillah Lieberman, a twenty-something IAA excavator who, as a woman and a Jewish Orthodox believer, represents a new generation of Israeli archaeologists quite different from the secular men who long dominated the field. "Everything is so tense from political and religious and archaeological angles—everything. That makes it exciting. It also means we have to be as professional and precise as we can."

The tension is not just between Jews and Arabs, but among the many variations of nationalists and believers on both sides of that divide. Lieberman said she doesn't share much about her work with her Orthodox community, lest it create misunderstandings. Even though she excavated a small Roman theater under Wilson's Arch by the Western Wall with the help of Palestinian Arab workers, as a woman she was forbidden from entering the Jewish prayer space directly above.

"Jerusalem is a city of minorities," said Ronnie Ellenblum, a historical geographer at Hebrew University who made a career of studying the city before he passed away in early 2021, just before violence once again engulfed the city. "And every minority has its own sacred places, its own taboos. It is tribal. Each hates the others. They believe they should be the only one. The past is always used to acquire this supremacy. By all of them. The fighting is over the narrative—whose narrative will prevail?"

Archaeologists in Jerusalem—who since 1967 have been nearly all Israeli and Jewish—have replaced the prophets of old as the city's storytellers. Their ability to construct tales of the past using the tools of science has given them a level of clout rare elsewhere. In the last century, many attained the status of national heroes. Their discoveries fill Israeli newspapers and websites, create entirely new attractions, and draw millions of dollars in donations from around the world. They have been instrumental in making Jerusalem one of the planet's fastest-growing tourist destinations.

Unlike their predecessors in the 1960s and '70s, today's excavators are unlikely to bulldoze away layers postdating the Byzantines. Lieberman, who gets "pottery emergency calls" from colleagues to identify ceramics from all periods, maintained that she is just as dedicated to cataloging medieval Arab pots as those used by ancient Jews. She and her colleagues are busy reconstructing a greater totality of the city's past than ever before, from early Bronze Age homes to the barbershop of 1967. They employ tools and methods, backed by private and public funding, that are the envy of many of their colleagues abroad.

Yet Jerusalem's "biblical" millennium still looms large in the minds of both patrons and the public. "Every week or two, there is another news article about a ritual bath, another seal mentioning a biblical figure, another Iron Age wall," said one retired Israeli archaeologist. "You never hear about the Abbasid cesspit." Non-biblical finds tend to vanish into specialized journals read by few. The lack of publicity, in turn, can make it more challenging to obtain funding for digs unrelated to the eras between David and Jesus.

"People come to Jerusalem to hear a story," explained Lieberman. "If you try to be very objective and show everything from every period, it is kind of boring." Most visitors are Jewish and Christian, and, like Mark Twain, they typically arrive expecting to see something related to the familiar Bible tales from their childhood. Jeremiah's pit has more resonance to most than an Umayyad palace. The city's top underground destinations—the City of David, the Western Wall Tunnel, and the museums of the Jewish Quarter—give visitors what they have demanded since the days of Warren: a re-creation of a biblical Jerusalem removed from the inconvenient political and religious reality above.

Such archaeological attractions also demonstrate that "we're not interlopers or migrants, we're not survivors of the Holocaust that Europe dumped here," said Michael Oren, a former Israeli ambassador to the United States, in 2018. He was speaking at the opening of an exhibit of Eilat Mazar's finds near the Temple Mount, digs funded by an unaccredited evangelical Christian college in Oklahoma. The work is, he added, central to "our validity, legitimacy, and security . . . Archaeology is not just about revealing the past. It is about acquiring the present and ensuring our future." Yet the results can reinforce the notion of a biblical Jerusalem in which Arabs are cast as intruders.

Using archaeology for political or religious ends is, of course, not unique to the Holy City; nearby ancient Jericho, for example, is controlled by the Palestinian Authority rather than Israel, and its history as presented to visitors is given a clear pro-Arab slant. What sets Jerusalem apart is the millions of visitors who troop through the Old City each year, the scale of the subterranean sites devoted to the era of Jewish dominance, and, most important, the stakes in what narrative will prevail.

Once a dig is done and the report written up, does an excavator have any further ethical responsibility? "We must be realistic and look at the power of archaeology," said Yuval Baruch, who heads the IAA's Jerusalem directorate. "It is very limited. The most powerful is the economy—tourism." And in this contested city, tourism is intimately linked with businesspeople, politicians, and religious leaders.

Professional excavators are, in any case, often predisposed to shy away from nonacademic controversy. "We became archaeologists because we were attracted to pure science," said Anne Pyburn of Indiana University, who writes about the societal challenges facing her discipline. "We didn't want the interference of politics or to be scrutinized by a thrill-seeking public. Dead people are pretty nonjudgmental. But practicing archaeology today amounts to activism—whether we intend to be activists or not. We are messing with people's heritage."

In Jerusalem, this is true as nowhere else. But just as archaeologists here were slow to adapt new tools and methods, so too are they increasingly reluctant to stray beyond a role restricted to harvesting artifacts and analyzing data. "I have no responsibility for what the public or nonscientists do with archaeology," said Yonatan Adler, an up-and-coming archaeologist at Ariel University in the West Bank. "The most important thing is that we do not allow our own ideological, religious, or personal issues—or outside influence—to affect our work."

It is a view widely shared by Israeli excavators, including many in a younger generation struggling to secure a job in their highly competitive field. In a society that has shifted to the right of the previous generation, they typically prefer to keep their political heads down while trying to uphold academic standards. Many argue this approach works. The discovery of Pontius Pilate's role in constructing the stepped street may have been inconvenient for Elad, but it was sound science that made international headlines. Yet this required ignoring the bitter complaints of Arabs living above the tunnel. And the focus by funders like Be'eri and politicians like Netanyahu on a triumphant Jewish narrative can cloud the facts as revealed by professional excavators.

"If you say you are just doing your job, you are playing the innocent," said Eran Tzidkiyahu, a Jerusalem-born political scientist who has studied the intersection of archaeology and politics. "There are many archaeological sites around the world where communities profit from excavations through tourism and jobs. But the digs at the City of David, for example, are clearly aimed at expropriating from the people that live there not just their land but their history. Elad has built an empire of archaeology."

Excavating is expensive, and archaeologists have always needed wealthy backers. In Jerusalem, those patrons invariably have a political or religious agenda—or both. Ellenblum, part of a fading generation, nevertheless mourned what he saw as a willingness by his younger colleagues to accept financial support in exchange for maintaining silence on their profession's impact on locals and the way their finds are interpreted by others. This is not a new concern; after all, the French scholar Vincent was quick to defend Parker's unethical behavior. But the focus on gathering data while overlooking the wider repercussions may come at a steep price.

"Archaeologists can be slaves to those funding their digs," added Ellenblum. "Some of them are like dear brothers to me, but they don't even know when they sell their souls."

◆ ◆ ◆

JUST BEFORE the Six-Day War, when he was eleven years old, Nazmi Jubeh worked with Kathleen Kenyon at her excavation by the girls' school close to the Noble Sanctuary. This was the site where Ben-Dov's team would later uncover the Umayyad palaces.

Jubeh's father sold spices from a shop in the Old City, but the experience with Kenyon hooked him on excavations. He went on to study archaeology in Germany and at Birzeit University, a Palestinian institution in the West Bank. Shortly before Kenyon's death, the elderly British academic visited Birzeit while Jubeh was a student.

"She remembered me," he recalled. "I asked her how, after her Jericho excavations, she had been able to sleep at night." Kenyon, a devout Anglican, had found no evidence that the Israelites with their Ark and trumpets had made its walls collapse, as the Bible stated. "She said, 'I didn't resolve the conflict. My heart is with the holy book, but my head is with the science, and I stand behind my results.'" Like the devout Schick, she tried to accommodate the data while maintaining her beliefs.

Kenyon then told Jubeh that some balm came from studying the Islamic approach to scripture. "Muslims understand that the stories of the Qur'an and Bible are a source of wisdom, not factual history," she told him. "Therefore we don't have to change the Old Testament, just how we understand it."

Jubeh bemoaned the dogmatism that has enveloped Palestinian views of Jerusalem's past, a Muslim mirror of fundamentalist Jewish and Christian attitudes. He also said that he doesn't doubt there are Israeli archaeologists who put science before ideology. What happens later is another matter. "I went on an Elad tour," Jubeh added. "The guide said David went down this path, down these stairs. The group replied, 'Hallelujah!' They were convinced by David's palace, and that he drank from the Pool of Silwan."

For Jubeh, such pervasive ideas predate the state of Israel and even Zionism. "What we see today of archaeological interpretation is actually the result of more than one hundred fifty years of work begun by Europeans and Americans and continued by Israelis," he said. "It is a totally Christian idea. The meal was already prepared; they just had to eat it."

The responsibility of European and American Christians in sowing the seeds of today's violence has been largely ignored by born-again believers like Carter and Clinton. The American author James Carroll concluded that "Western civilization with its Jew hatred and imperialist racism" is the "unindicted coconspirator" of the conflict, "an invisible hand operating behind the curtain of history."

Palestinians, meanwhile, missed the feast altogether. "For a long time we were not capable, we were not trained," said Jubeh. "We didn't have a state, and even those who managed to study abroad had trouble finding a job here. There was no university; they had to go to the American University in Beirut." Western academics did little to train local Arab excavators, and no Palestinian archaeologists were permitted to dig legally in Jerusalem after 1967—nor would they likely agree to take part in an Israeli excavation, lest they be tarred as traitors.

A decade later, in 1977, the American archaeologist Albert Glock began to teach at Birzeit. He focused his research on the history of Palestinians in the Holy Land during the Ottoman period. His goal was to use excavations to shed light on an era long ignored by Western and Israeli researchers who tended to focus on biblical-era sites. Glock faced an uphill struggle. His Arabic was never fluent, and he confronted long-standing Arab Muslim suspicion of a discipline they associated with European Christians and Jews they perceived as bent on conquest.

His choice of dig sites compounded that challenge. Instead of pursuing remains from the glory days of Islamic power in the region, he launched an excavation at a former Palestinian refugee camp near Jericho. His mission to help shape a Palestinian identity based on scientific finds was cut short in 1992, amid the terror of the first intifada. An unknown assassin shot him to death while he was on his way to campus.

One of Glock's protégés was Jubeh, who now teaches archaeology at Birzeit. Palestinians, he said, must create their own stories based on their own investigations, rather than simply responding reflexively to those told by Israelis. "I know we are living in a conflict and that narratives are part of the conflict," he said. "In the end, however, there is only one narrative—that of science."

◆ ◆ ◆

AS IMPERCEPTIBLY AS water trickling through Jerusalem's porous lime-stone, researchers have refashioned our understanding of the city's past in ways often at odds with the dictates of scripture, the pressure of politics, or the desires of patrons. Science at its best is wild, beholden to no country or faith.

Archaeologists have sometimes found hard evidence that upheld cherished stories, such as the king named David, or the Babylonian destruction of the city. But researchers also have dissolved other favorite myths, such as that of a dazzling capital city ruled by a rich and powerful Solomon.

One of the most pervasive legends of biblical Jerusalem is that it existed in a kind of splendid isolation, preyed upon on occasion by wicked pagans. This idea is reinforced by Israel's modern isolation from its Arab neighbors. Until recently, archaeologists perpetrated this idea with terms like "First Temple Period" and "Second Temple Period" that suggest an inward-looking city set apart from its neighbors amid the fast-shifting currents of Middle Eastern history.

Fish bones from the Nile, furniture made from Anatolian wood, and incense from Arabia now attest to Jerusalem's prosperity when larger and more powerful empires imposed peace on the region. The rise of Babylon, Assyria, the Hellenistic states, and, later, Rome and Constantinople, ushered in the city's greatest periods of economic growth, as reflected in the elegant homes and villas uncovered by excavators. (Israel Finkelstein, the Tel Aviv University archaeologist, noted that little has changed, citing his country's boom under the protective shadow of the American empire.)

This recognition of Judean Jerusalem's place in the wider Middle East is reflected in the terms favored by younger archaeologists, such as "Persian period," "early Roman times," and the "late Roman era," which put the city in its larger regional context. Of course, Jerusalem sometimes gambled on the wrong rising power, found itself politically outmaneuvered, or rebelled at an inopportune moment, reaping the whirlwind. In this, the city was not so different from its neighbors.

Ultimately, of course, it is religion that sets Jerusalem apart. Monotheism, a central temple rite, a sacred day of rest, and a plethora of complicated rules for eating, dressing, working, and socializing are just some of the spiritual innovations attributed to this otherwise unremarkable hill town. Scribes produced many if not most of the books of the Hebrew Bible—the Christian Old Testament—within its walls, a remarkable accomplishment given the city's modest size and relatively low rates of literacy.

Yet new finds demand a rethinking of some of these comfortable assumptions. The Givati dig revealed images of Athena and other signs of Hellenistic influence at Jerusalem's heart in the early centuries BCE, as well as the occasional bones of pigs, catfish, and other foods prohibited by Judean religious laws.

In 2012, at a site called Tel Motza located a mere three miles from the sacred platform, archaeologists uncovered the stone foundations of a large sanctuary matching the measurements of Solomon's temple given in the Bible. An offering table, human and animal figurines, and butchered animal bones suggest rites similar to those presumably performed on the Temple Mount. It was in use at roughly the same period, from the ninth century BCE until the Babylonian invasion—long after the Bible said that competing altars and shrines had been destroyed.

This mysterious sanctuary goes unmentioned in scripture, yet it would have been a major religious and, perhaps, political center, standing virtually in the shadow of the Temple Mount. Such discoveries allow for greater understanding of how Israelite and Judean beliefs and practices influenced and were influenced by local as well as regional neighbors. At the foot of the Temple Mount, for example, excavators found images impressed in clay of Assyrian cherubim that scholars believe refer to the local Judean god, Yahweh, while other finds point to Egyptian religious rites.

It is now clear that Judeans absorbed rituals, traditions, or doctrines from Canaanites, Philistines, Babylonians, Greeks, and Persians. Adler of Ariel University argues that, based on the material record, Judaism did not coalesce into a distinct religion until as late as the first century BCE, a thousand years after the Israelite arrival in the area. That makes Christianity a younger cousin, but only by a century or so. Six centuries later, Islam drew heavily on both Jewish and Christian views rooted in Jerusalem events and texts.

In the subsequent fourteen centuries, the competing faiths within this fraught and fought-over city inevitably exchanged spiritual notions. This makes the strict borders drawn among the three monotheisms as illusory as the lines nineteenth-century Europeans drew to divide up Jerusalem's heterogeneous neighborhoods.

Recent archaeological revelations also demand a major retooling of the image of not just Pontius Pilate but the Romans in general. Even the Roman emperor Hadrian, cursed for millennia by Jews for turning Jerusalem into a polytheistic city—and thereby possibly sparking the second and final Jewish revolt of 132 CE in the process—is getting a makeover. "Hadrian is actually the savior of Jerusalem, even if he was very imperialistic in imposing the Roman cosmos on a Jewish city," said Tel Aviv University archaeologist Guy Stiebel. He argues that the Roman ruler, like Pilate a century before, aimed at enhancing the city's fame, not undermining it.

Another surprise is the enormous size and scope of Byzantine Jerusalem that evolved from this modest late Roman town. Excavators have concluded that it was this city, rather than that of Herod the Great, that marked the metropolis at its most magnificent, in terms of population and prosperity.

More provocative is the growing recognition that the sacred platform in Jerusalem's heart is neither a Muslim site falsely claimed by Jews nor a Jewish site hijacked by Muslims.

Archaeological finds back up contemporary texts describing Herod the Great's major renovation of the Jewish temple and the surrounding complex starting in the first century BCE that was largely destroyed in 70 CE—in Jerusalem, not Hebron or Yemen. Yet work by a host of scholars now paints a deeper and richer story of invasions, earthquakes, neglect, and remodeling by an array of peoples worshipping a variety of deities. Judean, Roman, Byzantine, Persian, Arab, Crusader, and Ottoman rulers each subtracted or added to the sacred site, which is a product—and a fascinating record—of all these changes.

Jerusalem itself is the sacred platform writ large. Newly arrived Israelites drew water from an underground system and protected themselves with walls built by previous generations of Canaanites. A later Jewish elite dined on plates identical to those used in imperial Rome. Islamic caliphs employed Christian Byzantine workers to construct their palaces and shrines. Well into the twentieth century, British engineers channeled water from a system built by a succession of Judeans, Romans, Byzantines, Arabs, and Ottomans.

Just as Jerusalem's religions can't be split into three nonintersecting faiths or its geography neatly divided into four quarters, so too do the city's many eras exist simultaneously. Like the strange concoction of broken stone beneath the city that can, at a moment's notice, turn liquid, Jerusalem's past is too fluid for any single narrative to contain.

"I love history for its sense of humor," said Stiebel. "It is a good lesson to show you can't throw the dart and then draw the target."

◆ ◆ ◆

ACCORDING TO THE PSALMS, those ancient poems honored by Jerusalem's monotheisms, truth springs up from the earth while justice looks down from heaven. No matter what truth emerges from beneath Jerusalem, Palestinian politicians are likely to reject evidence that a Jewish temple once stood on the Noble Sanctuary, while Israeli leaders almost certainly will downplay the twenty centuries during which Romans, Christians, and Muslims dominated the city. The stones and tunnels of subterranean Jerusalem remain pawns in the struggle above.

Yet archaeologists have revealed that the Romans could not demolish all of Jewish Jerusalem, just as the Roman empress Helena failed to rid the city of all traces of polytheistic worship. Signs of the Crusader occupation outlived Muslim rule. Villas of the ancient Jewish elite survived the ruination of 70 CE and 1948, and remains of the Arab barbershop and shoemaker's shop destroyed during the nighttime demolition of 1967 were waiting to be found.

"Everyone who ruled Jerusalem did the same thing: built his tower and hoisted his flag," said Shlomit Weksler-Bdolah, the Israeli archaeologist who found the 2,700-year-old seal that Netanyahu kept in his office. "But I think it is stronger than all those who try to control it. No one can completely erase what came before."

The discoveries made by excavators, whether celebrated in popular museums or hidden away in guarded storerooms, retain a latent power to explode the myths to which Jerusalem's partisans tenaciously cling, stories easily simplified and exploited to create hardened battle lines among competing groups.

Challenging myths doesn't have to menace people of faith. "I am Orthodox," said Lieberman. "But I don't feel my scientific work is a threat to my religious belief." She, like Schick and Kenyon, has learned to live with the contradictory truths of the heart and head. As the British philosopher Gilbert Ryle noted, "to explode a myth is accordingly not to deny the facts but to re-allocate them."

It may be another millennium before that lesson can sink below Jerusalem's stony surface to seed the elusive harmony and peace long associated with the Holy City. The fragmented inscriptions and potsherds stuffed away in archives or concealed in obscure journals could, someday, provide a path for what Jewish teaching defines as *tikkun olam,* a Hebrew term for repairing a shattered world; the arduous practice has the ultimate goal of mending the divisions among peoples.

These dusty artifacts may seem inconsequential given today's harsh politics and insatiable tourism, but their power is impervious to catchy slogans or antiquated myths. The results from a century and a half of excavations will wait patiently for later and braver generations, like unexploded ordnance. What scripture fails to impart, the earth can still reveal.

Acknowledgments

It is an act of brazen arrogance or naive foolishness—or both—to tackle the thorny history of Jerusalem. Those who live in the city or pursue its study as a career are, fortunately, used to outsiders with the temerity to take on this formidable topic. I was lucky enough to find innumerable people willing to offer their time and insight to yet another such visitor.

The archaeologists of the Israel Antiquities Authority, with the cooperation of its spokesperson Yoli Shwartz, were particularly open and helpful, allowing me full access to their ongoing excavations and making time in their packed schedules to answer endless questions. The Tel Aviv University archaeologist Israel Finkelstein, who took me on my initial tour of underground Jerusalem, must shoulder a good deal of responsibility in sparking the idea to pursue the topic. Matthew Adams and the rest of the staff at the W. F. Albright Institute of Archaeological Research, an intellectual Eden just outside the Old City, provided research materials as well as the welcome company of dedicated scholars over good meals. Felicity Cobbing at the Palestinian Exploration Society's headquarters outside London kindly offered access to its extensive files.

Special thanks to Samir al-Sharif, who served as an able guide and translator, and to the photographer Simon Norfolk, who shared his acumen and wit as we prowled the Old City. *National Geographic* magazine supported several reporting trips for its December 2019 cover story, under the able direction of editor Glenn Oeland, while a storytelling grant from the National Geographic Society furnished additional travel funds. This work would not have been possible without the generous backing of the magazine and the society.

An array of individuals contributed to translating and organizing the material, including Aliza Inbari, Evan van Leeuwen, Mary Jo Padgett, and Daniel Pinelli. Thanks to David Case, Helen Finch, Marta Martin, Alexandra Merrill, Alex Sanchez, Michell Thurmond, and two anonymous archaeologists for their manuscript comments. Among the many unmentioned in the text who provided support for this venture were Atallah Ajrab, David Amber, Nathan Boniske, Betsy Brown, Paul Farago, Mark Fleming, Yonatan Mizrahi, Elias Ramer, Ed Rihacek, Yoram Sabo, Fred Schwab, and Paul Wright.

My agent, Ethan Bassoff of the Ross Yoon Agency, and my editor at Doubleday, Yaniv Soha, gave patient and clear guidance that proved essential in bringing this effort to fruition. Finally, as always, I express my deep gratitude for the forbearance—and countless cups of coffee—provided by Mahan Kalpa Khalsa.

Notes

INTRODUCTION

xxv "Jerusalem is the gateway": Mordekhai Na'or, *City of Hope: Jerusalem from Biblical to Modern Times* (Jerusalem: Yad Izhak Ben-Zvi, 1996), 145.

xxv "angels descend every night": Burhan ad-Din al Fazari, "On the Merits of Jerusalem and Palestine," in *From Haven to Conquest: Readings in Zionism and the Palestine Problem until 1948*, ed. Walid Khalidi (Beirut: Institute for Palestine Studies, 1971), 32.

xxv "is submerged and sunken": Yehuda Amichai and Robert Alter, *The Poetry of Yehuda Amichai* (New York: Farrar, Straus and Giroux, 2017), 501.

xxvi "Jerusalem is lifted on": Colin Thubron, *Jerusalem* (London: Penguin Books, 1996), 6.

xxvi "The knobbiest town": Mark Twain, *The Innocents Abroad* (Hartford, CT: American Publishing House, 1884), 182.

xxvii "There is an old": Charles Warren, *Underground Jerusalem* (London: R. Bentley, 1876), 380.

xxvii "ignites heat in the human": James Carroll, *Jerusalem, Jerusalem: How the Ancient City Ignited Our Modern World* (New York: Houghton Mifflin Harcourt, 2011), 1.

xxix "Come let us declare": Michael B. Oren, *Power, Faith, and Fantasy: America in the Middle East, 1776 to the Present* (New York: W. W. Norton, 2007), 83.

xxix "Jerusalem was, New": Robert Peel Wakeman, *Wakeman Genealogy, 1630–1899* (Meriden, CT: Journal Publishing, 1900), 96.

xxix "The Puritans did not": Hilton Obenzinger, *American Palestine: Melville, Twain, and the Holy Land Mania* (Princeton, NJ: Princeton University Press, 1999), 23.

xxx "Obeying an impulse": Rev. James Aitken Wylie, *The Modern Judea, Compared with Ancient Prophecy: With Notes Illustrative of Biblical Subjects* (Glasgow: William Collins, Sons, 1872), 43.

xxx "not a people": Barbara W. Tuchman, *Bible and Sword: England and Palestine from the Bronze Age to Balfour* (New York: Random House Trade Paperbacks, 2014), 155.

xxx "everything seems ripe": Edwin Hodder, *The Life and Work of the Seventh Earl of Shaftesbury* (Cambridge: Cambridge University Press, 1886), 167.

xxxi "the citizens of Jerusalem": J. T. Barclay, *The City of the Great King, or, Jerusalem as It Was, as It Is, and as It Is to Be* (Philadelphia: James Challen, 1857), 456.

xxxii "There is no place": Emily Todd Helm, "Mary Todd Lincoln, Reminiscences and Letters of the Wife of President Lincoln," *McClure's Magazine,* September 1898, 480, https://books.google.com/books?vid=Harvard:32044018217216.

xxxii "And had the Holy": Eliot Warburton, *Travels in Egypt and the Holy Land: or, The Crescent and the Cross, Comprising the Romance and Realities of Eastern Travel* (Philadelphia: H. C. Peck & Theodore Bliss, 1859), 231.

xxxii "How false it all": Claude Aziza, ed. *Jerusalem: Le rêve a l'ombre du Temple* (Paris: Omnibus, 1994), 1280–83.

xxxii "the color of the": Herman Melville, *Journals,* Howard C. Horsford with Lynn Horth, eds. (Evanston, IL: Northwestern University Press, 1989), 90.

xxxii "ignorant, depraved, superstitious": Frederick Anderson, Michael B. Frank, and Kenneth M. Sanderson, eds., *Mark Twain's Notebooks and Journals,* vol. 1 (Berkeley: University of California Press, 1976), 424–25.

xxxii "Christ been once": Ibid., 449.

xxxiii "It would seem at first": Karl Baedeker, *Palestine and Syria: Handbook for Travellers* (Leipzig: K. Baedeker, 1894), 145.

xxxiii "a timeless place": Issam Nassar, "In Their Image: Jerusalem in Nineteenth-Century English Travel Narratives," *Jerusalem Quarterly,* no. 19 (October 2003): 6.

xxxiii "the far-famed capital": Baedeker, *Palestine and Syria,* 145.

I. A MOMENT OF INSANITY

3 "An intact sarcophagus!": Félix de Saulcy and Evelyn Hofer, *F. De Saulcy et la Terre Sainte* (Paris: Ed. de la Réunion des musées nationaux, 1982), 378.

5 "We finally had found": Ibid., 374.

5 "It would be no advantage": Félicien de Saulcy and Count Edward de Warren, *Narrative of a Journey Round the Dead Sea and in the Bible Land in 1850 and 1851* (London: Bradbury and Evans, 1853), iv.

6 "Fellow Israelites": Acts 2:29 (New International Version).

6 "opened another room": Flavius Josephus and William Whiston, *The Antiquities of the Jews* (McLean, VA: IndyPublish.com, 2001), 15:3; Flavius Josephus and William Whiston, *The Genuine Works of Flavius Josephus, the Jewish Historian* (London: W. Bowyer, 1737), 7:394.

6 "a flame burst out": Flavius Josephus, *The Works of Flavius Josephus* (New York: New York Book Exchange 1880), 6:271.

7 "the appreciation of the emperor": Andrew H. Bellisari, "Raiders of the Lost Past: Nineteenth-Century Archaeology and French Imperialism in the Near East, 1798–1914" (honors thesis, Rutgers University, 2010), 98, http://history.rutgers.edu/dmdocuments/thesis_2010_Bellisari_thesis.pdf.

7 "I clung with all my strength": De Saulcy and Hofer, *F. De Saulcy,* 382.

8 "without making a scratch": Ibid., 379.

8 "well-preserved skeleton": Ibid., 379.

8 "He slid his hands": Ibid., 379.

8 "That was all!": Ibid., 379.

8 "of which some stitches": Ibid., 379

8 "the importance of my": Ibid., 382.

9 "take my sarcophagus": Ibid., 383.

9 "There are certain men": Mary Eliza Rogers, *Domestic Life in Palestine* (Cincinnati: Poe & Hitchcock, 1865), 133.

9   "This month, an important": *Halebanon,* November 19, 1863.

10 "he did not respect the dignity": Ibid.

10 "Even the Muslims": Ibid.

10 "a hundred whacks": De Saulcy and Hofer, *F. De Saulcy,* 408.

10 "in an atmosphere of perpetual": Ibid., 363.

10 "I did not want my": Ibid., 364.

11 "They saw how human": *Halebanon,* November 13, 1863.

11 "all the difficulties seemed": Louis Félicien J. Caignart de Saulcy, *Voyage en Terre Sainte,* vol. 2 (Montreal: Librairie Saint-Joseph Cadieux & Derome, 1889), 190.

11 "to stone any Jew": *Halebanon,* November 13, 1863.

11 "What tribulations": De Saulcy, *Voyage en Terre Sainte,* 190.

11 "It's a diabolical": Ibid., 191.

12 "I barely had time": Ibid., 192.

12 "Monsieur de Saulcy seemed": H. Wallon, *Notice historique sur la vie et les travaux de M. L.F.J. Caignart de Saulcy, membre de l'Académie des Inscriptions et Belles-Lettres* (Paris: Imprimerie Nationale, 1881), 332.

12 "As tomorrow is mail": De Saulcy and Hofer, *F. De Saulcy,* 194.

13 "I am ready to remove": Ibid., 194.

13 "always had the sword": Wallon, *Notice historique,* 361.

13 "prepared to write directly": De Saulcy and Hofer, *F. De Saulcy,* 194.

13 "Will we have to cut it": Ibid., 194.

13 "learned society in": Ibid., 219.

14 "a number of Jews": Conrad Schick, "The (So-Called) Tombs of the Kings at Jerusalem," *Palestine Exploration Quarterly* 29, no. 3 (1897): 183.

14 "throwing ourselves at your feet": Eldridge Moore letter to consuls at Beirut and Jerusalem, January 6, 1864, British Public Records Office (National Archives), FO 78/1816.

15 "We beg you to intervene": *New-York Evening Post,* February 4, 1864.

15 "no one in the future": *Halebanon,* n.d., 1864.

15 "no Jewish shrine": Moore to consuls.

15 "with trembling hands": *Jewish Chronicle* (London), January 6, 1864.

15 "evil tidings": Ibid.

15 "the misdeed wrought": Ibid.

15 "a great and distinguished man": Ibid.

15 "was routing out everything": Ibid.

15 "Woe, woe": Ibid.

15 "righteous dead kings": Ibid.

16 "French Protection of the Holy Places": *Times* (London), January 21, 1864.

16 "A credulous enthusiast": Charles Dickens, William Harrison Ainsworth, and Albert Smith, *Bentley's Miscellany,* vol. 36 (London: R. Bentley, 1854), 179.

16 "to refute the charge of rifling": *Times* (London), January 26, 1864.

16 "utterly incapable": Ibid.

16 "Desecrations at Jerusalem": Ibid., February 1, 1864.

16 "unjust attack": Ibid., February 3, 1864.

16 "A shameless profanation": Ibid., February 1, 1864.

17 "to enrich": De Saulcy and Hofer, *F. De Saulcy,* 123.

17 "well-known antiquarian": Maurice Fleury, *Memoirs of the Empress Eugenie* (London: Appleton, 1920), 398.

17 "There are people who": Ernest Vinet, "De l'archéolgie hébraïque: Jérusalem et la Mer-Morte," *Revue des Deux Mondes (1829–1971)* 6, no. 3 (May 1, 1854): 605–25.

18 "The monument, unique": *John O'Groat Journal,* April 28, 1864.

18 "pseudo-discoveries": *Morning Chronicle* (London), April 1864.

18 "marvelous assumption": Ibid.

18 "nothing less than": Ibid.

2. A FOOL'S ERRAND

21 "It rises higher": *Hamagid* (Lyck, East Prussia), October 26, 1864.

22 "the houses of this famous city": Rupert Chapman and Shimon Gibson, "The Mediterranean Hotel in 19th Century Jerusalem," *Palestine Exploration Quarterly* 127 (1995): 96.

22 "For in Jerusalem": James Finn, *Stirring Times: or Records from Jerusalem Consular Chronicles of 1853 to 1856* (London/Boston: Elibron Classics/Adamant Media, 2004), 462.

23 "The hotel-keeper talks Greek": Charles Warren, *Underground Jerusalem* (London: R. Bentley, 1876), 83.

24 "I shall never concede": Roger Owen, *Studies in the Economic and Social History of Palestine in the Nineteenth and Twentieth Centuries* (London: Macmillan, 1982), 37.

24 "And now, so many Franks": Titus Tobler, "Briefe Aus Süd und Ost," *Allgemeine Zeitung* (Augsburg), December 23, 1865.

25 "In its present and degraded": *Jerusalem Water Relief Society, Established 1864* (London: Mitchell and Hughes, 1867), 1.

25 "a monument of English": Ibid., 7.

25 "aid to the utmost": John Irwine Whitty, *Proposed Water Supply and Sewerage for Jerusalem, with Description of Its Present State and Former Resources* (London: W. J. Johnson, 1863), 337.

26 "not what could be called": Charles Moore Watson, *The Life of Major-General Sir Charles William Wilson* (London: J. Murray, 1909), 11.

26 "began the morning lessons": Ibid., 2.

26 "The conditions were so hard": Whitworth Porter, *History of the Corps of Royal Engineers* (London: Longmans, Green, 1889), 269.

27 "wild desolation": Watson, *Major-General Sir Charles William Wilson,* 44.

27 "I found the pasha": Ibid., 45.

28 "most satisfactorily": *Times* (London), November 29, 1864.

28 "complete protection": Ibid.

28 "the means by which": Ibid.

29 "made some important discoveries": *Times* (London), December 30, 1864.

29 "perfectly honeycombed": Ibid.

29 "one of the most perfect": Capt. [Charles William] Wilson, and Capt. [Charles] Warren, *The Recovery of Jerusalem: A Narrative of Exploration in the City and the Holy Land,* Walter Morrison, ed. (London: Richard Bentley, 1871), 13.

30 "I have been doing a good deal": Watson, *Major-General Sir Charles William Wilson,* 47.

30 "the inhabitants are now": Ibid., 48.

30 "towards the expense of Captain Wilson's": *Times* (London), January 28, 1865.

30 "The ancient past of Jerusalem": Katharina Galor and Gideon Avni, *Unearthing Jerusalem: 150 Years of Archaeological Research in the Holy City* (University Park, PA: Penn State University Press, 2011), 52.

31 "It has been prophesied": William Shakespeare, *Henry IV,* in *The Complete Works of William Shakespeare* (Boston: Ginn & Heath, 1880), 257.

31 "to throw much light on": "Report of the Proceedings of a Public Meeting," *Palestine Exploration Quarterly,* no. 1, supp 1 (1865): 5.

31   "what is above ground will": George Grove, "The Palestine Exploration Fund: A Society for the Accurate and Systematic Investigation of the Archaeology, Topography, Geology and Physical Geography, Natural History, Manners and Customs of the Holy Land, for Biblical Illustration; Prospectus, 1865," *Palestine Exploration Quarterly*, no. 1, supp. 1 (1865): 3.

32   "dangerous fallacy": *Guardian*, May 13, 1865.

32   "Hear, Hear!": "Report of the Proceedings of a Public Meeting," *Palestine Exploration Quarterly*, no. 1, supp 1 (1865): 5.

32   "We mean to lay down": Ibid., 3.

32   "the controversy between 'science'": Owen Chadwick, *The Victorian Church* (Eugene, OR: Wipf and Stock, 2010), 3.

33   "Palestine belongs to you": "Report of the Proceedings of a Public Meeting," *Palestine Exploration Quarterly*, no. 1, supp 1 (1865): 4.

33   "throw light upon the history": Ibid., 6.

33   "some interesting fragments": Ibid., 11.

33   "There will of course be": Ibid., 7.

34   "The best way of conducting": Ibid., 9.

34   "The Bible was transformed": Ashley M. Irizarry, *Possessing the Holy Land: The Palestine Exploration Fund and the American Palestine Exploration Society* (Williamsburg, VA: College of William and Mary, 2014), 30.

35   "not merely to map": Charles Darwin to J. D. Hooke, July 29, 1865, Darwin Correspondence Project, Letter no. 4874.

3. A MASONIC MISSION

37   "to carry out explorations": Abdul Latif Tibawi, *British Interests in Palestine, 1800–1901: A Study of Religious and Educational Enterprise* (London: Oxford University Press, 1961), 190.

38   "absurdities": Sir Henry James to Yorkshire Philosophical Society, December 9, 1867, British Public Records Office (National Archives), O.S.1.17/1.

39   "I used to spend much spare": Watkin W. Williams, *The Life of General Sir Charles Warren* (Oxford: Blackwell, 1941), 21.

39   "Many of the best soldiers": Colin Neil Macdonald, *Warren!: The Bond of Brotherhood* (Singapore: Coleman Street Books, 2007), 10.

39   "one of the most influential": Ibid., 15.

39   "the greatest achievement": Ibid., 13.

40   "still visible foundations": Ibid., 13.

40   "There is no doubt that": Ibid., 20.

40   "somewhat in the role": Ibid., 26.

41   "kept in happy ignorance": Charles Warren, *Underground Jerusalem* (London: R. Bentley, 1876), 5.

41   "warlike": Ibid., 26.

41   "such a nuisance": Ibid., 384.

41   "He was already displaying": Kevin Shillington, *Charles Warren: Royal Engineer in the Age of Empire* (Bath, UK: Brown Dog Books, 2020), 78.

41   "a lawless set": Warren, *Underground Jerusalem*, 155.

42   "For heaven's sake": Ibid., 553.

42   "Our progress through these": Ibid., 146.

42   "With full turban": Ibid., 146.

42   "I was told by Izzet": Ibid., 154.

43   "a bigoted Moslem": Ibid., 313.

43 "worse than useless": Ibid., 7.

43 "spoilt the market": Ibid., 13.

44 "The shingle would": Charles Warren to Walter Besant, June 10, 1870, Palestine Exploration Fund Archives, JER/WAR/25.

44 "descend with a crash": Warren, *Underground Jerusalem,* 153.

44 "tetanus and other infections": Williams, *General Sir Charles Warren,* 57.

45 "The strain on the nerves": Warren, *Underground Jerusalem,* 155.

45 "come to the work cool": Ibid., 156.

45 "so that natives who": Ibid., 361.

45 "and the diminutive leg": Ibid., 322.

45 "was not water": Ibid., 370.

45 "a perilous voyage": Ibid., 189.

46 "one hand necessarily wet": Williams, *General Sir Charles Warren,* 58.

46 "On lighting up the magnesium": Capt. [Charles William] Wilson, and Capt. [Charles] Warren, *The Recovery of Jerusalem: A Narrative of Exploration in the City and the Holy Land,* Walter Morrison, ed. (London: Richard Bentley, 1871), 219.

46 "very sinister mission": Warren, *Underground Jerusalem,* 151.

47 "the farthest mosque": Surah Al-Isra, 17:1, The Noble Quran, https://quran.com/17.

47 "It is a most remarkable": Warren, *Underground Jerusalem,* 391.

47 "This hall is probably": Ibid., 371.

48 "What a chaos of ruin": Ibid., 368.

48 "These Jews are constantly": Ibid., 363.

48 "an irrepressible pride": Ibid., 360.

48 "a Jewish principality": Ibid., 363.

48 "bursts of fanatical": Ibid., 359.

48 "Was I quite sure": Ibid., 375.

49 "I had lighted up magnesium": Ibid.

49 "I was very much afraid": Ibid., 376.

49 "they had prayers in their synagogues": Ibid., 377.

49 "There is danger of great injury": Ibid., 389.

50 "we were prevented": Ibid., 395

50 "The main result of": *New York Times,* May 16, 1869.

50 "Underneath the pavements": Ibid.

50 "for in one of the vaults": Warren, *Underground Jerusalem,* 378.

50 "Of course, it made us": Ibid., 378.

50 "It is hoped that the Marquis": "Rob Roy," *Times* (London), April 5, 1869.

51 "a blouse of genuine mud color": Ibid., 23.

4. THE ROOTS OF OUR PROBLEM

55 "Here was an exciting discovery": Charles Warren, *Underground Jerusalem* (London: R. Bentley, 1876), 532.

56 "proves that the foundations": Watkin W. Williams, *The Life of General Sir Charles Warren* (Oxford: Blackwell, 1941), 21.

56 "you may safely boast": Warren, *Underground Jerusalem,* 19.

56 "I had supported the excavations": Ibid., 336.

56 "who have been down his shafts": *New York Times,* October 6, 1868.

57 "our system in excavating": Warren, *Underground Jerusalem,* 383.

58 "too greedy to listen": Capt. [Charles William] Wilson, and Capt. [Charles] Warren, *The Recovery of Jerusalem: A Narrative of Exploration in the City and the Holy Land,* Walter Morrison, ed. (London: Richard Bentley, 1871), 99.

58 "working night and day": Ibid., 103.

58 "Abu Saud was indignant": Ibid., 104.

59 "immediately outside my friend": Ibid., 109.

59 "still several feet": Warren, *Underground Jerusalem,* 385.

59 "Certainly the Pasha": Ibid., 385.

59 "I told the Consul": Ibid., 386.

59 "and that our shafts were": Wilson and Warren, *Recovery of Jerusalem,* 51.

59 "refused to give anything": Ibid., 53.

59 "all of ancient date": Ibid., 52.

59 "appeared to think": Warren, *Underground Jerusalem,* 387.

59 "The houses were so insecure": Ibid., 380.

60 "For if we cannot trace": George William Speth, W. Harry Rylands, and Charles Warren, "On the Orientation of Temples," in *Ars Quatuor Coronatorum, Being the Transactions of the Quatuor Coronati Lodge No. 2076, London* (Margate: 1888), 43.

60 "For the first time": *PEF Proceedings and Notes 1865–1869,* Public Meeting, June 11, 1868 (London: Palestinian Exploration Society), 3.

61 "not only had their effect": Wilson and Warren, *Recovery of Jerusalem,* 99.

61 "By degrees I have been": Warren, *Underground Jerusalem,* 384.

61 "on the top of a palm tree": Ibid., 96–97.

62 "there is nothing contrary": Ibid., 556.

62 "a sort of Moslem Dean": "Rob Roy on the Works at Jerusalem," *Palestine Exploration Quarterly,* no. 1 (1869): 20.

62 "Down in the hollow ground": Mark Twain, *The Innocents Abroad* (Hartford, CT: American Publishing House, 1884), 202.

62 "We never dreamed": Ibid., 202.

62 "has been the subject": Wilson and Warren, *Recovery of Jerusalem,* 14.

63 "They were interested": Ehab Jallad, personal interview with author, December 2018.

63 "an overhanging mass": Wilson and Warren, *Recovery of Jerusalem,* 228.

63 "It was very exciting": Warren, *Underground Jerusalem,* 346.

63 "we had put our lives": Ibid., 346.

64 "Even the dean of Westminster": "Rob Roy on the Works at Jerusalem," *Palestine Exploration Quarterly,* no. 1 (1869): 21.

64 "the first genuine Biblical": Neil Asher Silberman, *Digging for God and Country: Exploration, Archaeology, and the Secret Struggle for the Holy Land* (New York: Alfred A. Knopf, 1982), 94.

65 "It was Warren who restored": Walter Besant, *Palestine Exploration Fund: Twenty-One Years' Work in the Holy Land (a Record and a Summary), June 22, 1865–June 22, 1886* (London: R. Bentley, 1886), 62.

65 "Most of our buildings have": Charles Warren to Walter Besant, May 1874, Palestine Exploration Fund Archives, PEF-DA-JER-WAR-50.

66 "some foundation": Secretary of State to Consul Moore, December 3, 1875, British Foreign Office, National Archives, London, F.O. 78/2418.

66 "Mr. Schick did not possess": Charles Warren to British Foreign Office, January 1, 1876, Palestine Exploration Fund Archives, PEF-DA-JER-WAR-49.

67 "or twice the breadth of the": Letter with Subcommittee Report from PEF Executive Secretary, February 8, 1876, Palestine Exploration Fund Archives, PEF-DA-JER-WAR-51.

67 "disagreeable temper": Harold E. Raugh, *The Victorians at War, 1815–1914: An Encyclopedia of British Military History* (Santa Barbara, CA: ABC-CLIO, 2004), 337.

67 "prejudiced the chances": Abdul Latif Tibawi, *British Interests in Palestine, 1800–1901:*

A Study of Religious and Educational Enterprise (London: Oxford University Press, 1961), 196.

67   "It is a pity that excavations": Amos Elon, *Yerushalayim: Shiga'on Ladavar [Jerusalem: An Obsession]* (Jerusalem: Domino, 1989), 188–89.

5. A FAITHFUL WATCHMAN

69   "Whoever is caught will": Hannah Cotton et al., *Jerusalem: 1–704* (Berlin: De Gruyter, 2010), 42.

70   "It is remarkable that this stone": Ilan Ben Zion, "A Day of Mistakes," *Times of Israel,* October 22, 2015.

70   "After a long talk": "Letters, from Lieut. Claude R. Conder, R.E.," *Palestine Exploration Quarterly* 4, no. 4 (July 18, 1872): 153–73.

70   "the most interesting question connected": Charles Warren and C. R. Conder, *The Survey of Western Palestine, Jerusalem* (Jerusalem: Committee of the Palestine Exploration Fund, 1889), 429.

70   "men, materials, and money": Ibid., 429.

72   "I think this was the moment": Holger Siegel, personal communication with author, March 2020.

72   "frequently accompanied me": "Obituary of Dr. Conrad Schick," *Palestine Exploration Quarterly* 34, no. 2 (1902): 139–42.

72   "He was always on the spot": Katharina Galor and Gideon Avni, *Unearthing Jerusalem: 150 Years of Archaeological Research in the Holy City* (University Park, PA: Penn State University Press, 2011), 47.

72   "a faithful watchman": H. V. Hilprecht, *Explorations in Bible Lands during the 19th Century: With Nearly Five Hundred Illustrations and Four Maps* (Edinburgh: AJ Hollman, 1903), 598.

72   "better acquainted than": "Quarterly Statement," *Palestine Exploration Quarterly,* no. 4 (1872): 171.

72   "everybody—except the great": Ulf Petersson, "Dr. Conrad Schick, Missionary, Architect, Archaeologist, Model Builder, City Engineer," Friends of Conrad Schick, 2008, https://conradschick.files.wordpress.com/2013/11/conrad-schick-cs301.pdf.

73   "I would leave things": Baurath C. Schick, "Letters from Herr Schick," *Palestine Exploration Quarterly* 23, no. 3 (November 1891): 121.

74   "She opened up the earth": Edward D. Hunt, *Holy Land Pilgrimage in the Later Roman Empire: AD 312–460* (Oxford: Clarendon Press, 1982), 41.

74   "After lying buried": William Gifford and Sir John Taylor Coleridge, *Quarterly Review,* vol. 190 (London: John Murray, 1899), 110.

75   "Golgotha and the Tomb": Edward Robinson, *Biblical Researches in Palestine,* vol. 1 (London: J. Murray, 1856), 407–18.

75   "I should be loath to": Claude R. Conder, *Tent Work in Palestine: A Record of Discovery and Adventure* (London: R. Bentley, 1879), 170.

75   "The Protestants alone": Lady Mary Elizabeth Herbert, "Cradle Lands," *Harper's Magazine,* vol. 36 (New York: Harper's Magazine Company, 1868), 708.

75   "With all its clap-trap": Mark Twain, *The Innocents Abroad* (Hartford, CT: American Publishing House, 1884), 573.

76   "entertained grave and serious doubts": James Fergusson, *The Holy Sepulchre and the Temple at Jerusalem: Being the Substance of Two Lectures, Delivered in the Royal Institution* (London: John Murray, 1865), 3.

76   "a geopolitical contest": Daniel Bertrand Monk, *An Aesthetic Occupation: The Imme-*

diacy of Architecture and the Palestine Conflict (Durham, NC: Duke University Press, 2002), 22.

76   "The whole Christian world": "Underground Jerusalem," *London Daily News*, July 19, 1886, 4.

76   "A great many people": Ibid., 4.

76   "numberless errors": Charles Warren, *The Temple or the Tomb, Giving Further Evidence in Favour of the Authenticity of the Present Site of the Holy Sepulchre, and Pointing out Misconceptions in Fergusson's 'Holy Sepulchre' and 'The Temples of the Jews'* (London: R. Bentley, 1880), 107.

77   "rather fanciful": "Lieut. Claude R. Conder's Reports," *Palestine Exploration Quarterly* 6, no. 3 (1874): 183–84.

77   "more sacred shams": Laurence Oliphant, *Haifa* (Books on Demand, 2018), 237.

77   "It is very nice to see": Charles George Gordon, *Letters of General C. G. Gordon to His Sister, M. A. Gordon* (London: Macmillan, 1888), 290.

77   "He rose at seven": Lord Elton, *Gordon of Khartoum: The Life of General Charles George Gordon* (New York: Alfred A. Knopf, 1955), 290.

78   "wonderfully weird": J. Murphy-O'Connor, *Keys to Jerusalem: Collected Essays* (Oxford: Oxford University Press, 2012), 176.

78   "I deluge a poor old": Lord Elton, *General Gordon* (London: Collins, 1954), 314.

78   "Russian women lined the wooden": Charles Warren, *Underground Jerusalem* (London: R. Bentley, 1876), 431.

79   "a huge museum, a catalog": Vasili Khitrovo, "The Tasks of Scholarly Research in the Holy Land," in *Report of the Orthodox Palestine Society for 1882–1883* (St. Petersburg: Ministry of National Education, 1883), 51.

79   "apocryphal texts": Ibid., 52–55.

79   "to maintain confidentiality": Elena Astafieva, "How to Transfer 'Holy Russia' into the Holy Land? Russian Policy in Palestine in the Late Imperial Period," *Jerusalem Quarterly* 71 (2017): 17.

79   "whether political, scholarly": Ibid., 10.

79   "although the excavations are": Ibid., 11.

80   "threshold of a large antique": Archimandrite Antonin, *Pravoslavnyj Palestinskij Sbornik (Orthodox Palestine Collection)* 7 (October 1884): 1–38.

80   The news was leaked: *Times* (London), April 19, 1884.

80   "the threshold of the Gate": Antonin, *Pravoslavnyj Palestinskij Sbornik*, 1–38.

80   "widely publicized in Russia": Elena Astafieva, "How to Transfer 'Holy Russia' into the Holy Land? Russian Policy in Palestine in the Late Imperial Period," *Jerusalem Quarterly* 71 (2017): 11.

80   "Jewish masonry": "New Excavations in Jerusalem," *Palestine Exploration Quarterly* 20, no. 1 (February 1888): 59.

80   "the passing of our Lord": Ibid., 59.

81   "to leave no room": Boris Mansurov, *Russkie Raskopki v Svjatom Grade Ierusalime Pered Sudom Arxeologičeskogo Obščestva [The Russian Excavations in the Holy City Jerusalem before the Court of the Society for Archeology]* (Riga, 1887), 10.

81   "Dr Schick, whose accuracy": "Quarterly Statement," *Palestine Exploration Quarterly* 37, no. 4 (1905): 240.

81   "the private conviction": "Quarterly Statement," *Palestine Exploration Quarterly* 25, no. 1 (1893): 121.

81   "which has raged': *Guardian,* November 23, 1887.

81   "the rock-cut tomb suggested": "Quarterly Statement," *Palestine Exploration Quarterly* 24, no. 2 (1892): 120.

82   "rid itself of the incubus": "Quarterly Statement," *Palestine Exploration Quarterly* 39, no. 2 (1907): 232.

83   "the stone pavement": John 19:13 (New International Version).

6. A GREAT AND POTENT FORCE

85   "worn bits of sandstone": William M. Flinders Petrie, *Seventy Years in Archaeology* (London: Sampson Low, Marston, 1932), 160.

85   "Why that is Israel": Ibid., 160.

86   "one of the most notable monuments": *Yorkshire Post,* April 10, 1896.

88   "some of the problems": "Quarterly Statement," *Palestine Exploration Quarterly* 26, no. 3 (April 1894): 1.

88   "It is to be hoped": Rev. H. Porter, "Quarterly Statement," *Palestine Exploration Quarterly* 27, no. 1 (1895): 346.

88   "Solomon in all his splendor": Matthew 6:29 (New International Version).

88   "like a good despot": Philip J. King, "Frederick Jones Bliss at Tell el-Hesi and Elsewhere," *Palestine Exploration Quarterly,* 122, no. 2 (1990): 96.

88   "sequence-dating": Margaret S. Drower, *Flinders Petrie: A Life in Archaeology* (Madison: University of Wisconsin Press, 1995), 251.

89   "He did not allow preconceived": Rachel Hallote, *Bible, Map, and Spade: The American Palestine Exploration Society, Frederick Jones Bliss, and the Forgotten Story of Early American Biblical Archaeology* (Piscataway, NJ: Gorgias Press, 2006), 181.

89   "the site of the Holy Sepulchre": "Quarterly Statement," *Palestine Exploration Quarterly* 26, no. 3 (1894): 169.

90   "Rock Scarp of Zion": Ibid.: 170.

90   "have been of much profit": Ibid.: 174.

90   "When I . . . remember": Ibid.: 175.

90   "must combine the qualities": Frederick Jones Bliss, *Development of Palestine Exploration: Being the Ely Lectures for 1903* (New York: Charles Scribner's Sons, 1906), xvi.

90   "We are especially": "Quarterly Statement," *Palestine Exploration Quarterly* 26, no. 4 (July 1894): 175.

90   "Landowners do not trouble us": P. Baurath Von Schick and F. J. Bliss, "Discovery of a Beautiful Mosaic Pavement with Armenian Inscription, North of Jerusalem," *Palestine Exploration Quarterly* 26, no. 4 (1894): 257–61.

91   "confidence and affection": Sarah Irving, "A Tale of Two Yusifs: Recovering Arab Agency in Palestine Exploration Fund Excavations 1890–1924," *Palestine Exploration Quarterly* 149, no. 3 (2017): 223–36.

91   "The eight hours' movement": "Quarterly Statement," *Palestine Exploration Quarterly* 26, no. 4 (July 1894): 175.

91   "As to the Jerusalem landowners": Frederick Jones Bliss, *Excavations at Jerusalem, 1894–1897* (London: Committee of the Palestine Exploration Fund, 1898), 369.

92   "most pungent, especially": H. Porter, "A Visit to the Excavations at Jerusalem," *Palestine Exploration Quarterly* 28, no. 4 (1896): 345–46.

92   "an inky fluid": Frederick Jones Bliss, *The Development of Palestine Exploration: Being the Ely Lectures for 1903* (New York: C. Scribner's Sons, 1906), 278.

92   "Artistic work undertaken": Frederick Jones Bliss, *Excavations at Jerusalem, 1894–1897* (London: Committee of the Palestine Exploration Fund, 1898), 357.

92   "The City of David was clearly": Ibid., 289.

92   "David captured the fortress": 2 Samuel 5:7 (New International Version).

93   "axe against axe": "Quarterly Statement," *Palestine Exploration Quarterly* 15, no. 4 (1883): 210.

93 "The very name of Palestine": Theodor Herzl, *A Jewish State: An Attempt at a Modern Solution of the Jewish Question* (New York: Maccabaean, 1904), 29.

93 "In Basel I founded": Raphael Patai, *The Complete Diaries of Theodor Herzl,* vol. 2 (New York: Herzl Press, 1960), 581.

94 "From Jerusalem came": Alfred Sidney Johnson, *The Cyclopedic Review of Current History* (Buffalo, NY: Garretson, Cox & Company, 1898), 935.

94 "The musty deposits of": Patai, *Complete Diaries,* 745.

94 "the loud clinking": Hermann Guthe, "Das Ende des Friedlichen Kreuzzuges und die Zukunft des Heiligen Landes," *Die Christliche Welt* 32 (1918), 119.

94 "The Templars were able": Muhammad Y. Muslih, *The Origins of Palestinian Nationalism* (New York: Columbia University Press, 1988), 41.

95 "the greatest living authority": Ulf Petersson, "Dr. Conrad Schick, Missionary, Architect, Archaeologist, Model Builder, City Engineer," Friends of Conrad Schick, 2008, https://conradschick.files.wordpress.com/2013/11/conrad-schick-cs301.pdf.

95 "He was beloved and desirable": Ibid.

96 "Baron Edmond de Rothschild became": "The Reform Advocate," *Reform Judaism* 41 (1911), 650.

96 "One wonders how": John MacGregor, *The Rob Roy on the Jordan: A Canoe Cruise in Palestine, Egypt, and the Waters of Damascus* (London: J. Murray, 1904), 357.

7. GONE WITH THE TREASURES OF SOLOMON

99 "resuscitated": Carew Mairéad, *Tara and the Ark of the Covenant: A Search for the Ark of the Covenant by British-Israelites on the Hill of Tara (1899–1902)* (Dublin: Discovery Programme/Royal Irish Academy, 2003), 9.

99 "There, above the cover": Exodus 25:22 (New International Version).

100 "carried to Babylon": 2 Chronicles 36:18 (New International Version).

101 "cipher": "Buried Millions," *Wanganui Chronicle,* July 11, 1911.

101 "Well, bring back the Ark": *El Paso Herald,* September 5, 1911.

102 "and [we] could have had double": Cyril Pelham Foley, *Autumn Foliage* (London: Methuen, 1935), 112.

102 "He had to have two": *Sunday Express* (London), October 5, 1926.

102 "declared that his rendering": Foley, *Autumn Foliage,* 113.

102 "This was easily done": Ibid., 113.

103 "should be seen as": Louis Fishman, "The 1911 Haram Al-Sharif Incident: Palestinian Notables Versus the Ottoman Administration," *Journal of Palestine Studies* 34, no. 3 (Spring 2005): 9.

103 "became distinguished for fine": "Called Beyond," *National Spiritualist,* October 1, 1929: 12.

103 "particularly dirty hotel": Foley, *Autumn Foliage,* 115.

103 "They were certainly the oddest": Bertha Spafford Vester, *Our Jerusalem: An American Family in the Holy City, 1881–1949* (New York: Doubleday, 1950), 211.

104 "by their complete lack": Ibid., 212.

104 "Soon the rumors were about": Valter Juvelius, *Valkoinen kameeli ja muita Kertomuksia itämailta* (Project Gutenberg, 2005).

104 "Nothing more was said": Vester, *Our Jerusalem,* 250.

104 "the harm it would do": Ibid., 251.

104 "he didn't suffer fools": W. F. Albright, "In Memory of Louis Hugues Vincent," *Bulletin of the American Schools of Oriental Research* 164 (1961): 3.

104 "that nothing should be divulged": H. V. [Louis-Hugues Vincent], *Underground Jerusalem: Discoveries on the Hill of Ophel (1909–11)* (London: Cox, 1911), 1.

105 "My sole task": Ibid., 2.

105 "We lived underground": Ibid., 1.

105 "some old Jewish flat lamps": Foley, *Autumn Foliage*, 126.

105 "Our hopes of finding the Ark": Ibid., 127.

107 "Gone with the Treasure": "Gone with the Treasure That Was Solomon's: English Party Vanishes on Yacht after Digging Under the Mosque of Omar," *New York Times*, May 4, 1911.

107 "Have Englishmen Found": "Have Englishmen Found the Ark of the Covenant?," *New York Times*, May 7, 1911.

107 "Jerusalem has been in a terror": *New York Times*, May 14, 1911.

107 "There was an awful row": Foley, *Autumn Foliage*, 127.

107 "beard and mustache": *New York Times*, May 14, 1911.

108 "Moslems in a Rage": "Recent Sensation from Jerusalem," *Evening Star* (Washington, DC), May 11, 1911.

108 "this deplorable act": Fishman, "1911 Haram Al-Sharif Incident," 14.

108 "Moslem irritation so far": Ibid., 12.

108 "the Islamic people": Ibid., 13.

108 "Zionist ambitions": Ibid., 14.

108 "the stealing of antiquities": Ibid., 15.

109 "night and day": Ibid., 15.

109 "The government covers everything": Ibid., 16.

109 "great profit for the nation": Ibid., 17.

110 "caused profound animosity": Ibid., 19.

110 "the flamboyant imagination of the Orient": *Times* (London), May 9, 1911.

110 "extraordinarily sacrilegious": *El Paso Herald*, September 5, 1911.

110 "might have provoked": *Evening Star* (Washington, DC), May 26, 1911, 15.

111 "villagers' crude suspicions": *London's Field Newspaper*, October 14, 1911.

112 "The treasure hunt by Captain": "Quarterly Statement," *Palestine Exploration Quarterly* 44, no. 1 (1912).

112 "Captain Parker's expedition": *Times* (London), May 9, 1911.

112 "we seek to obey the law": Ibid.

8. A DANGEROUS FANTASY

115 "no ideological or political": M. Pillet, "Raymond Weill (1874–1950)," *Revue archéologique* (July 1953): 3.

115 "Merely the gesture of taking a pickaxe": Ronny Reich and Hershel Shanks, eds., *The City of David: Revisiting Early Excavations; English Translations of Reports by Raymond Weill and L.-H. Vincent* (Washington, DC: Biblical Archaeology Society, 2004), 98.

116 "Excavations be damned": Chaim Weizmann, *Trial and Error: The Autobiography of Chaim Weizmann, Book One (1874–1917)* (Lexington, MA: Plunkett Lake Press, 2013), 156.

116 "was acquired and walled up": Bertha Spafford Vester, *Our Jerusalem* (Garden City, NY: Doubleday, 1950), 252.

116 "about to visit Palestine": "The Missionary Department," *A.M.F. Monthly*, vol. 20–21 (Chicago: American Messianic Fellowship, 1911): 26.

116 "strange hermit": Walter Juva, *Valkoinen kameeli* [White Camel] (Helsinki: Otava, 1916), 6.

117 "If the Jewish expedition": Ibid.

117 "French savants engaged": *Sunderland Daily Echo and Shipping Gazette,* July 20, 1912.

117 "a number of very early tombs": Ibid.

117 "Inscriptions either in Babylonian": Ibid.

117 "archaeological digging under": Amy Dockser Marcus, *Jerusalem 1913: The Origins of the Arab-Israeli Conflict* (New York: Penguin Books, 2008), 273.

117 "These funerary deposits": Reich and Shanks, *City of David,* 23.

117 "some graves and cisterns": William N. Bates, "Archaeological Discussions," *American Journal of Archaeology* 19, no. 2 (1915): 89.

119 "Starvation in Jerusalem": *New York Times,* November 2, 1917.

119 "official possession of every building": Rennie MacInnes to High Commissioner of Egypt, May 2, 1917, British Public Records Office (National Archives), FO 141/473.

119 "with favour the establishment": Jonathan Schneer, *The Balfour Declaration* (New York: Random House, 2010), 341.

120 "teeming with fertility and": "Quarterly Statement," *Palestine Exploration Quarterly* 7, no. 3 (1875): 116.

120 "The Turk can never govern": Charles Warren, *Underground* (London: R. Bentley, 1876), 452.

120 "for fear that these deadly": "Text of the Decree of the Surrender of Jerusalem into British Control," accessed January 6, 2021, https://firstworldwar.com/.

120 "for me the supreme moment": T. E. Lawrence, *Seven Pillars of Wisdom* (Project Gutenberg, 2001), 1261.

120 "the indescribable smell": Vivian Gilbert, *The Romance of the Last Crusade: With Allenby to Jerusalem* (New York: Appleton, 1923), 175.

120 "the existing customs and beliefs": Norman Bentwich, *England in Palestine* (London: Kegan Paul, 1932), 20.

121 "Tomorrow my dear general": Lawrence, *Seven Pillars,* 1266.

121 "The City Placed Under": *Times* (London), December 11, 1917.

121 "the beginning of bitterer strife": Isaac Straus, *The American Jewish Chronicle,* vol. 4 (New York: Alpha Omega, 1918), 180.

121 "invincible and unutterable": Ronald Storrs, *Orientations* (London: Nicholson & Watson, 1943), 396.

122 "in addition to Hebrew and Jewish": *Times* (London), June 3, 1918.

122 "no modern religious": "Quarterly Statement," *Palestine Exploration Quarterly* 52, no. 1 (1920): 54.

122 "When the conditions": *New York Times,* August 4, 1921.

122 "Excellent minds demand that": Reich and Shanks, *City of David,* 3.

123 "Any proved Christian or Jewish": Ronald Storrs, *Memoirs of Sir Ronald Storrs* (New York: G. P. Putnam's Sons, 1937), 94.

123 "it was not expected": Robert Alexander, Stewart Macalister, and John Garrow Duncan, *Excavations on the Hill of Ophel, Jerusalem, 1923–1925* (London: Palestine Exploration Fund, 1926), vii.

123 "One cannot know for sure": Reich and Shanks, *City of David,* 4.

124 "Look around here, and you see": Sari Nusseibeh, personal interview with author, September 2019.

125 "Palestine should become": Chaim Weizmann and Barnet Litvinoff, *The Letters and Papers of Chaim Weizmann* (New Brunswick, NJ: Transaction Books, 1983), 257.

125 "So, in 1861": Ermete Pierotti, *Customs and Traditions of Palestine: Illustrating the Manners of the Ancient Hebrews* (Cambridge: Deighton, Bell, 1864), 77.

125 "All of a sudden, a Jew": Philipp Misselwitz and Tim Rieniets, *City of Collision: Jerusalem and the Principles of Conflict Urbanism* (Basel: Birkhauser, 2006), 35.

126   "While I was praying": Ze'ev Anner, Meir Ben-Dov, and Mordecai Naor, *The West-ern Wall* (Tel Aviv: Ministry of Defence, 1983), 125.

127   "contrary to usage": International Commission on the Wailing Wall, *Report of the Commission Appointed by His Majesty's Government* (London, December 1930), section vi, subsection 5.

127   "When your feet enter": Ofer Aderet, "Prayers, Notes and Controversy: How a Wall Became the Western Wall," *Haaretz,* May 13, 2013.

127   "even the Wailing Wall is not really": David Hulme, *Identity, Ideology, and the Future of Jerusalem* (Basingstoke, UK: Palgrave Macmillan, 2006), 76.

127   "lay hands by degrees": Letter to the UN General Assembly Security Council from the Representative of Jordan, Report of the Commission Appointed by His Majesty's Government (London, December 1930), Section IV.

127   "for the purpose of devotions": Ibid., Section VI.

128   "The Temple Mount is Israel's": Meron Benvenisti, *City of Stone: The Hidden History of Jerusalem* (Berkeley: University of California Press, 1998), 78.

128   "do not arise from their": Ibid., 78.

128   "An irrepressible conflict": Ian J. Bickerton and Carla L. Klausner, *A History of the Arab-Israeli Conflict* (Milton, UK: Taylor and Francis, 2018).

128   "I would not accept the Old": Moshe Amirav, *Jerusalem Syndrome: The Palestinian-Israeli Battle for the Holy City* (Brighton, UK: Sussex Academic, 2009), 27.

129   "It is the City of God": Meron Medzini, *Israel's Foreign Relations: Selected Documents, 1947–1994* (Jerusalem: Ministry of Foreign Affairs, 1976), 220.

129   "one of the last great": Miriam C. Davis, *Dame Kathleen Kenyon: Digging Up the Holy Land* (New York: Routledge, 2016), 137.

9. EXALTING THE WALLS

133   "We entered the Old City": Selwyn Ilan Troen, Zakai Shalom, and Moshe Tlamim, "Ben-Gurion's Diary for the 1967 Six-Day War: Introduction and Diary Excerpts," *Israel Studies* 4, no. 2 (1999): 212.

133   "Aren't you ashamed?": Uzi Benziman, "What Israel Gained—and Lost—by Unifying Jerusalem," *Haaretz,* June 7, 2017.

133   "I said that first of all this sign": Troen, Shalom, and Tlamim, "Ben-Gurion's Diary," 212.

133   "the greatest moment": David Hulme, *Identity, Ideology, and the Future of Jerusalem* (New York: Springer, 2006), 111.

133   "something had to be done": Teddy Kollek and Amos Kollek, *For Jerusalem* (New York: Random House, 1978), 197.

134   "My overpowering feeling": Ibid., 197.

134   "such destruction is rendered": Roger O'Keefe, *The Protection of Cultural Property in Armed Conflict* (Cambridge: Cambridge University Press, 2006), 331.

134   "Tell the workers that they": Ze'ev Anner, Meir Ben-Dov, and Mordecai Naor, *The Western Wall* (Tel Aviv: Ministry of Defence, 1983), 163.

134   "I was sky-high": Nir Hasson, "How a Small Group of Israelis Made the Western Wall Jewish Again," *Haaretz,* June 3, 2017.

135   "because through this gate": Ibid.

135   "the settling of historic accounts": Meron Benvenisti, *City of Stone: Hidden History of Jerusalem* (Berkeley, CA: University of California Press, 1996), 82.

135   "Bulldozers pounded with": Alona Nitzan-Shiftan, *Seizing Jerusalem: The Architectures of Unilateral Unification* (Minneapolis: University of Minnesota Press, 2017), 233.

135 "Why shouldn't the mosque": Ghada Hashem Talhami, *American Presidents and Jerusalem* (Lanham, MD: Lexington Books, 2017), 106.

136 In a 1999 interview: Odeh Bisharat, "A History of Crusaders and Zionists in Jerusalem," *Haaretz,* October 5, 2014.

136 "Order of the Kotel": Hasson, "How a Small Group of Israelis."

136 "yesterday afternoon a bulldozer": *Jerusalem Post,* June 12, 1972.

136 "among those who": Ibid.

136 "that he had the buildings removed": Troen, Shalom, and Tlamim, "Ben-Gurion's Diary," 217.

138 "The dream of every archaeologist": Meir Ben-Dov, *In the Shadow of the Temple: The Discovery of Ancient Jerusalem* (New York: Harper & Row, 1985), 19.

138 "drinking steaming Turkish coffee": Ibid., 20.

139 "suffering in their homes": *Jerusalem Post,* February 14, 1972.

139 "glorify and exalt": Doron Bar and Kobi Cohen-Hattab, "Can the Two Go Together? Archaeology and Sanctity at the Western Wall and Surrounding Area, 1967–1977," *Journal of Modern Jewish Studies* 16, no. 3 (May 15, 2017): 400.

139 "Each day I made a habit": Ben-Dov, *Shadow of the Temple,* 21.

139 "turning the place into": Kobi Cohen-Hattab and Doron Bar, *The Western Wall: The Dispute over Israel's Holiest Jewish Site, 1967–2000* (Boston: Brill, 2020), 63.

140 "naked aggression": Letter Dated 23 February 1968 from the Permanent Representative of Jordan Address to the Secretary-General, *UN Monthly Chronicle* (New York: UN Office of Public Information, 1968): 16.

140 "desist forthwith from": Ibid., 21.

140 "My new strategy was to": Ben-Dov, *Shadow of the Temple,* 21.

140 "Before long the civil": Ibid., 21.

141 "followed by a stream of other": Ibid., 22.

141 "No one breathed a word": Ibid., 22.

141 "Remain in Jerusalem, money": Charles Warren, *Underground Jerusalem* (London: R. Bentley, 1876), 337.

142 "The only way to achieve": Ben-Dov, *Shadow of the Temple,* 273.

142 "Ben-Dov is the hero": Simon Goldhill, *The Temple of Jerusalem* (Cambridge, MA: Harvard University Press, 2011), 161.

142 "A bulldozer is the last thing": Ben-Dov, *Shadow of the Temple,* 28.

142 "an almost perfectly square": Ibid., 274.

144 "Mazar was home sick": Meir Ben-Dov, personal interview with author, February 2019.

144 "Then he told me, 'Look'": Ibid.

144 "I had friends in radio": Ibid.

145 "If we could leave politics": Ben-Dov, *Shadow of the Temple,* 24.

145 "Dajani's attempt to separate": Ibid., 25.

145 "vessels of extraordinary": Meir Ben-Dov, *Jerusalem, Man and Stone: An Archeologist's Personal View of His City* (Tel-Aviv: Modan, 1990), 93.

145 "a large and well-planned": Benjamin Mazar, Gaalyah Cornfeld, and D. N. Freedman, *The Mountain of the Lord* (New York: Doubleday, 1975), 35.

146 "Meir, it is good": Ben-Dov, personal interview with author.

10. THE MAGNIFICENCE OF THE METROPOLIS

149 "On the few occasions": Danny Rubinstein, *The Mystery of Arafat* (South Royalton, VT: Steerforth Press, 1995), 22.

150 "the place of the trumpeting": Benjamin Mazar, "Herodian Jerusalem in the Light

of the Excavations South and South-West of the Temple Mount," *Israel Exploration Journal* 28, no. 4 (1978): 234.

150 "where it was custom": Meir Ben-Dov, *In the Shadow of the Temple: The Discovery of Ancient Jerusalem* (New York: Harper & Row, 1985), 95.

150 "And you will see": Benjamin Mazar, *The Excavations in the Old City of Jerusalem Near the Temple Mount* (Jerusalem: Institute of Archaeology, Hebrew University, 1971), 234.

151 "the most spiritual excavations": Kobi Cohen-Hattab and Doron Bar, *The Western Wall: The Dispute over Israel's Holiest Jewish Site, 1967–2000* (Boston: Brill, 2020), 74.

151 "the magnificence of the metropolis": Mazar, "Herodian Jerusalem," 231.

151 "One of the ironies": Ben-Dov, *Shadow of the Temple*, 194.

151 "the idea is to remove": Ze'ev Anner, Meir Ben-Dov, and Mordecai Naor, *The Western Wall* (Tel Aviv: Ministry of Defence, 1983), 181.

152 "It was one of the largest": Nadia Abu el-Haj, *Facts on the Ground: Archaeological Practice and Territorial Self-Fashioning in Israeli Society* (Chicago: University of Chicago Press, 2001), 154.

152 "Whoever has not seen": Mazar, "Herodian Jerusalem," 232.

152 "one of the most perfect": Capt. [Charles William] Wilson, and Capt. [Charles] Warren, *The Recovery of Jerusalem: A Narrative of Exploration in the City and the Holy Land*, Walter Morrison, ed. (London: Richard Bentley, 1871), 13.

153 "presumably the pasha's wall": William Stinespring, "Wilson's Arch Revisited," *Biblical Archaeologist* 29, no. 1 (Feb. 1966): 33.

154 "Fear of disapproval within": Dan Bahat, *The Jerusalem Western Wall Tunnel* (Jerusalem: Israel Exploration Society, 2013), 1.

154 "he wore a black robe": Nadav Shragai, "A Rabbi, an Officer and a Mystic," *Haaretz*, July 12, 2018.

154 "He didn't like what": Isaac Hershkowitz, personal communication with author, April 2020.

155 "Every night at midnight": Yiftach Getz, "The Attempt to Find the Temple Beneath the Temple Mount, according to the Diaries of Rabbi Getz" (Jerusalem: August 4, 2014, speech), https://www.youtube.com/watch?v=QBrFc8ymNyE.

155 "The laborers and their supervisors": Meir Ben-Dov, personal interview with author, February 2019.

155 "whenever any one of the residents": Ben-Dov, *Shadow of the Temple*, 172.

155 "This secrecy created uncertainty": Dan Bahat, *The Jerusalem Western Wall Tunnel* (Jerusalem: Israel Exploration Society, 2013), 1.

156 "The Jordanians, Israelis, and Americans": Ben-Dov, personal interview with author.

156 "The gate is the most important": Randall Price, *Searching for the Ark of the Covenant* (Eugene, OR: Harvest House, 2005), 153.

158 "I believe that the archaeological": Kathleen M. Kenyon, *Jerusalem: Excavating 3,000 Years of History* (London: Thames and Hudson, 1967), 52.

158 "I wish the excavators luck": Kathleen M. Kenyon, *Digging Up Jerusalem* (London: Praeger, 1974), 94.

158 "It is an exciting": Hershel Shanks, "The City of David After Five Years of Digging," *Biblical Archaeology Review* 11:16 (November–December 1985).

158 "Kenyon thought once she": Hershel Shanks, "BAR Interview: Yigal Shiloh—Last Thoughts," *Biblical Archaeology Review* 14:2 (March–April 1988).

159 "the law forbidding excavation": Hershel Shanks, "Politics at the City of David," *Biblical Archaeology Review* 7:6 (November–December 1981).

159 "Death to Archaeology": el-Haj, *Facts on the Ground*, 263.

159 "Why don't you dig": William E. Farrell, "Israel's Ultra-Orthodox Are Battling Archaeologists Digging for the City of David," *New York Times,* August 16, 1981.

160 "was very effectively carried out": Martin E. Marty and R. Scott Appleby, *Fundamentalisms and the State: Remaking Polities, Economies, and Militance* (Chicago: University of Chicago Press, 1996), 468.

160 "What we have are really": Farrell, "Israel's Ultra-Orthodox," 3.

160 "pray, cry, scream, and tear": Marty and Appleby, *Fundamentalisms and the State,* 468.

160 "a barrage of personal threats": Nachman Ben-Yehuda, *Theocratic Democracy: The Social Construction of Religious and Secular Extremism* (New York: Oxford University Press, 2010), 65.

160 "They don't care about": Hugh Orgel, "Goren Takes Hard Line on Digs," *Jewish Telegraphic Agency,* August 9, 1981.

160 "An archaeological dig or site": Ibid.

161 "The archaeologists have to learn": Neil Asher Silberman, *A Prophet from Amongst You: The Life of Yigael Yadin; Soldier, Scholar, and Mythmaker of Modern Israel* (New York: Addison-Wesley, 1993), 362.

161 "That dig won't be renewed": Gil Sedan, "Chief Rabbinate Angered by Rulings on City of David Dig," *Jewish Telegraphic Agency,* September 25, 1981.

161 "help strengthen the people's": Farrell, "Israel's Ultra-Orthodox," 3.

161 "Until now the biggest enemies": William E. Farrell, "Rabbi's Stand on Excavation Splits Israel," *New York Times,* August 21, 1981.

162 "In our state, which is not": David K. Shipler, "Archaeologist Defends Work as Israeli Rabbis Rail," *New York Times,* September 24, 1981.

162 "What would happen": William Claiborne, "Archaeological Fight Tests Israeli Coalition," *Washington Post,* September 24, 1981.

162 "fanatic Jews": Hershel Shanks, "BAR Interview: Yigal Shiloh—Last Thoughts, Part II," *Biblical Archaeology Review* 14, no. 3 (May–June 1988).

162 "threatening to undermine": Abraham Rabinovich, "Noted Academics Blast Goren," *Jerusalem Post,* August 31, 1981.

162 "This is their problem": Orgel, "Goren Takes Hard Line."

163 "evil, wicked, abominable": Simon Goldhill, *The Temple of Jerusalem* (Cambridge, MA: Harvard University Press, 2009), 254.

163 "It was a sweet victory": Hershel Shanks, "BAR Interview: Yigal Shiloh—Last Thoughts, Part II," *Biblical Archaeology Review* 14, no. 3 (May–June 1988).

II. THE RABBI'S MCGUFFIN

165 "The Bible tells of it": Lawrence Kasdan, *Raiders of the Lost Ark,* directed by Steven Spielberg (Los Angeles: Paramount, 1981), DVD.

165 "an old dentist I went to": J. W. Rinzler and Laurent Bouzereau, *The Complete Making of Indiana Jones: The Definitive Story behind All Four Films* (New York: Del Rey, 2008), 17.

166 "He told me about an amazing": Rabbi Getz, *Kotel Diaries #9,* July 22, 1981 (Hebrew; trans. by Aliza Inbari), https://www.beitharavgets.co.il. Accessed April 17, 2021.

166 "A long hour I sat there": Ibid., 13:00.

167 "for security reasons": Ibid., 13:00.

167 "Now we will know": Ibid., 18:15.

167 "We refused, of course": Ibid., July 28, 1981, 8:00.

167 "It was clear as the sun": Ibid., July 30, 1981, 19:30.

167 "Nobody on the outside": Randall Price, *Searching for the Ark of the Covenant* (Eugene, OR: Harvest House, 2005), 155.

168 "the archaeologist gave": Getz, *Kotel Diaries #9,* August 11, 1981, 16:30.

168 "Rabbi Getz came to me": Meir Ben-Dov, personal interview with author, February 2019.

168 "undercover guards": Getz, *Kotel Diaries #9,* August 19, 1981, 15:00.

169 "in a very dramatic way": Ibid., August 21, 1981, 7:30.

169 "amazement and anger": Hugh Orgel, "Mystery Surrounds Tunnel Uncovered Near Western Wall Leading in the Direction of Second Temple Site," *Jewish Telegraphic Agency,* August 28, 1981.

169 "I fear 'invasion' from the Arabs": Getz, *Kotel Diaries #9,* August 29, 1981, 15:00.

169 "one of whom I suspect is waqf": Ibid., August 31, 1981, 8:00.

169 "I told him that I get my orders": Ibid.

170 "I stood alone in front": *The Hidden Rabbi,* directed by Arnon Segal (November 2020, in Hebrew), 29 min., https://www.youtube.com/watch?v=oL-04TUPLBU. Accessed April 18, 2021.

170 "hundreds of Arabs": Price, *Searching for the Ark,* 159.

170 "the police, including the supreme": Getz, *Kotel Diaries #9,* August 31, 1981, 21:00.

170 "Finally, I called to": Price, *Searching for the Ark,* 160.

170 "We sent ten of our Arab": Meir Ben-Dov and Issam Awwad (Jerusalem: Discussion at Albright Institute, 2015), recording courtesy Beatrice St. Laurent.

170 "I found that the Arabs": Getz, *Kotel Diaries #9,* August 31, 1981, 21:00.

170 "A border policeman had": *Guardian,* September 2, 1981.

171 "but they didn't": Ben-Dov and Awwad (Jerusalem: Discussion at Albright Institute, 2015), recording courtesy Beatrice St. Laurent.

171 "I have never felt": Getz, *Kotel Diaries #9,* August 31, 1981, 21:00.

171 "gave orders to kill Arabs": Ibid., September 3, 1981, 14:00.

171 "the discovery of the remnants": Ibid., September 6, 1981, 21:00.

171 "I heard the sound of the Arabs": Ibid., September 2, 1981, 24:00.

171 " 'God, the heathen are come' ": Psalms 79:1 (New International Version).

171 "part of the Zionist effort": Letter dated 8 September 1981 from the Permanent Representative of Jordan to the United Nations addressed to the Secretary-General (New York: United Nations, September 14, 1981), item 64 of the Provisional Agenda.

172 "the fulfillment of biblical prophecy": D. J. Berggren, "Carter, Sadat, and Begin: Using Evangelical-Style Presidential Diplomacy in the Middle East," *Journal of Church and State* 56, no. 4 (2014): 739.

172 "To stand against Israel": Jerry Falwell, *Listen, America!* (New York: Doubleday, 1980), 107.

173 "who was as usual very testy": Peter Jessup, "Interview with Ambassador Samuel W. Lewis," *Association for Diplomatic Studies and Training Foreign Affairs Oral History Project,* August 9, 1998, 171, https://www.adst.org/OH%20TOCs/Lewis,%20 Samuel%20W.toc.pdf.

173 "an internal committee to examine": Memo from Minister of Interior to Efrain Shilo, Chaim Chefez, Archaeologist Ben-Dov, "Minutes from meeting no. 4–27," September 1981.

173 "We prepared a thirty-three-page": Ben-Dov, personal interview with author.

174 "Change the last sentence": Ibid.

174 "built a structure in which": Nir Hasson, "Jerusalem's Time Tunnels," *Haaretz,* April 24, 2011.

174 "The legend of the 'Lost Ark' ": Tzvi Fishman, "Where Is the Aron Today? Three Experts Weigh In," *Jewish Press* (Brooklyn, New York), March 13, 2020.

174 "Dad was striving to find": Lily Horowitz, personal communication with author, June 2020.

175 "could lead to the chamber": Fishman, "Where Is the Aron Today?"

175 "the dig for him": Yiftach Getz, "The Attempt to Find the Temple Beneath the Temple Mount, according to the Diaries of Rabbi Getz" (Jerusalem: Speech of August 4, 2014), https://www.youtube.com/watch?v=QBrFc8ymNyE. Accessed April 18, 2021.

175 "In a struggle between": Isaac Hershkowitz, personal communication with author, April 2020.

175 "well known for his limited": Baruch Kimmerling, *Politicide: Ariel Sharon's War against the Palestinians* (London: Verso, 2003), 84.

176 "As the excavation of the tunnels": Nadav Shragai, "Raiders of the Lost Ark," *Haaretz,* April 24, 2003.

177 "They were good friends": Horowitz, personal communication with author.

177 "They all told him": Fishman, "Where Is the Aron Today?"

177 "This insect verified": Price, *Searching for the Ark of the Covenant,* 156.

177 "We believe that the Holy": Randall Price, *In Search of Temple Treasures: The Lost Ark and the Last Days* (Eugene, OR: Harvest House, 1994), 166.

177 "They were afraid that": Ibid., 168.

178 "I knew very well they would": Dan Bahat, personal communication with author, April 2020.

178 "competition with the archaeologists": Sarina Chen, personal communication with author, May 2020.

178 "Dad was able to identify": Horowitz, personal communication with author.

178 "I can confirm to you that": "Holy of Holies," *GodsSecret's Weblog,* January 5, 2010, https://godssecret.wordpress.com/category/holy-of-holies-2/.

12. SOMEONE OF GREAT IMAGINATION

181 "righteous men": Ellen G. White, *The Spirit of Prophecy* (Battle Creek, MI: Seventh-Day Adventist, 1880), 414.

182 "He was given permission": Letter by Peter Wells, Garden Tomb Director, May 22, 2000, https://en.wikipedia.org/wiki/Talk%3ARon_Wyatt. Accessed April 17, 2021.

182 "that Ron had to exhale": Mary Nell Wyatt, *The Ark of the Covenant* (Nashville, TN: Wyatt Archaeological Research, 1995), excerpt from https://www.wyattmuseum.com/arkofthecovenant.htm. Accessed April 17, 2021.

183 "enough to know for sure": Mary Nell Wyatt, "The Ark of the Covenant Special Article," Wyatt Archaeological Research, November 25, 2014, https://wyattmuseum.com/the-ark-of-the-covenant-special-article/2011-338. Accessed April 17, 2021.

184 "He came to me": Dan Bahat, personal communication with author, June 2020.

184 "the officials that Ron dealt": Mary Nell Wyatt, "The Ark of the Covenant Special Article," Wyatt Archaeological Research, November 25, 2014, https://wyattmuseum.com/the-ark-of-the-covenant-special-article/2011-338. Accessed April 17, 2021.

184 "Bahat himself does not want": William Shea to Ron Wyatt, July 20, 1986, in "Update: Ark of the Covenant," Anchor Stone International, March 28, 1999, https://anchorstone.com/update-ark-of-the-covenant-march-28-1999/. Accessed April 17, 2021.

184 "Ron heard a voice": "Archeologist Encounters Jesus While Restoring His Tomb," The Divinity of Jesus. https://sites.google.com/site/thedivinityofjesus/home/archeologist-encounters-jesus-while-restoring-his-tomb. Accessed April 17, 2021.

185 "the discoveries": "Museum #1 Closes," Pinkoski.com, April 23, 2006, https://pinkoski.com/museum-1-closes/. Accessed April 17, 2020.

185 "Mr. Ron Wyatt is neither": Russell R. Standish and Colin D. Standish, *Holy Relics or Revelation* (Rapidan, VA: Hartland, 1999), 88.

185 "a bunch of unbelievers": Ibid., 90.

185 "Ron Wyatt has never received": Ibid., 123.

186 "Members of our staff": "Update: Ark of the Covenant," March 28, 1999, Anchor Stone International, https://anchorstone.com/update-ark-of-the-covenant-march -28-1999/. Accessed April 17, 2021.

186 "has never brought anything": William H. Shea, "Statement by William H. Shea," Tentmaker, accessed January 8, 2021, https://www.tentmaker.org/WAR/Shea.html. Accessed April 18, 2021.

186 "Yes, it is very controversial": "Ark of the Covenant," Pinkoski.com, April 24, 2006, https://pinkoski.com/ark-of-the-covenant/. Accessed April 18, 2021.

186 "He vilified me": Dan Bahat, personal communication with author, June 2020.

187 "We visited the holy sites": "Address of United States President William Jefferson Clinton to the Knesset" (Jerusalem: October 27, 1994), https://www.knesset.gov.il /description/eng/doc/speech_clinton_1994_eng.htm.

187 "It was the beginning": Bill Clinton, *My Life: The Early Years* (New York: Vintage Books, 2005), 387.

187 "that if I ever let Israel": Robert E. Levin, *Bill Clinton: The Inside Story* (New York: SPI, 1992), 147.

187 "Remote sensing now": Lambert Dolphin, "Geophysics and the Temple Mount," June 22, 1995, http://ldolphin.org/tempgeophy.html. Accessed April 19, 2021.

188 "It was already obvious": Ibid.

189 "We hoped to locate": Ibid.

190 "Slouching Toward Armageddon": Louis Rappaport, "Slouching Toward Armageddon," *Jerusalem Post,* July 6, 1983.

190 "there are significant and to some minds worrisome": Ibid.

190 "the cheap attacks": Ibid.

191 "The Almighty will": Amos Elon, *Jerusalem: City of Mirrors* (Lexington, MA: Plunkett Lake Press, 2019), 169.

191 "earth has been removed": "Note from the Jordanian Ministry of Foreign Affairs," May 19, 1981. *Cultural Heritage of Jerusalem—UNESCO Director-General Report* (Paris: UNESCO, August 27, 1981), item 5.3.1 of the Provisional Agenda.

192 "the destruction of the Islamic": Ibid.

192 "some of which form": Ibid.

193 "For almost twenty years": Gideon Avni and Jon Seligman, "Between the Temple Mount/Haram El-Sharif and the Holy Sepulchre: Archaeological Involvement in Jerusalem's Holy Places," *Journal of Mediterranean Archaeology* 19, no. 2 (January 2006), 275.

193 "There was no archeological": Mike Levy, "Digging In," *Jewish Journal,* March 15, 2001.

193 "radical secularist": Dan Bahat, personal interview with author, February 2019.

193 "he was a good person": Ibid.

194 "Fresh air is pumped into the shaft": Sabra Chartrand, "A Skirmish Along the Wall Between Arab and Jew," *New York Times,* August 13, 1988.

194 "For visitors": Ibid.

195 "I decided to extinguish the fire": Bahat, personal communication with author, April 2020.

195 "I can tell you": Chartrand, "Skirmish Along the Wall."

195 "Clashes between believers": Raymond Lemaire, "UNESCO Reports/Letters from Raymond Lemaire Related to Jerusalem" (Paris: UNESCO, May 18, 1989), 5. https://unesdoc.unesco.org/ark:/48223/pf0000082709. Accessed April 19, 2021.

195 "had alarming bulges": Ibid., 6.

195   "There were nonstop": Bahat, personal communication with author, April 2020.

196   "see all the children of Abraham": Clinton, *My Life,* 387.

196   "The descendants of Isaac": Bill Clinton, *Public Papers of the Presidents of the United States, William J. Clinton, Book 1* (Washington, DC: Office of the Federal Register, National Archives and Records Administration, 1993), 436–37.

196   "Now the horns would": Clinton, *My Life,* 101.

13. A FREE PEOPLE IN OUR LAND

200   "since most researchers": "Jerusalem 3000—City of David," Israel Ministry of Foreign Affairs, June 1, 1993, http://www.israel.org/MFA/MFA-Archive/1993/. Accessed April 19, 2021.

200   "There has never before": John Noble Wilford, "From Israeli Site, News of House of David," *New York Times,* August 6, 1993.

200   "a stunning discovery": Ibid.

200   "At a single blow": Eric H. Cline, *Biblical Archaeology: A Very Short Introduction* (New York: Oxford University Press, 2009), 60.

202   "Pore over it": Eilat Mazar, "Did I Find King David's Palace?," *Biblical Archaeology Review* 32:1 (January–February 2006).

202   "I work with the Bible": Etgar Lefkovits, "Archeology: Dr. Eilat Mazar: The Bible as Blueprint," *Jerusalem Post,* September 25, 2008.

202   "There is no reason to doubt": Eilat Mazar, "Excavate King David's Palace!," *Biblical Archaeology Review* 23:1 (January–February 1997).

202   "Choosing a site": Mazar, "Did I Find King David's Palace?"

203   "during the period of monarchic": Mazar, "Excavate King David's Palace!"

203   "This, of course, would change": Israel Finkelstein, "The Archaeology of the United Monarchy: An Alternative View," *Levant* 28, no. 1 (1996): 177.

203   "Excavate King David's Palace!": Mazar, "Excavate King David's Palace!"

204   "Three thousand years of history": "Address by Prime Minister Yitzhak Rabin Inaugurating Jerusalem 3000 Festivities" (Jerusalem, September 4, 1995), Israel Ministry of Foreign Affairs, https://mfa.gov.il/MFA/MFA-Archive/1995/Pages/. Accessed April 19, 2021.

204   "They glorify occupation": Dilip Hiro, *Sharing the Promised Land: A Tale of Israelis and Palestinians* (New York: Olive Branch Press, 2002), 27.

204   "the ones who came before King": Eric H. Cline, *Jerusalem Besieged: From Ancient Canaan to Modern Israel* (Ann Arbor: University of Michigan Press, 2005), 12.

204   "Our forefathers": Ibid., 12.

205   "biblical heritage": Laura Zittrain Eisenberg and Neil Caplan, *Negotiating Arab-Israeli Peace: Patterns, Problems, Possibilities* (Bloomington: Indiana University Press, 2010), 186.

205   "martyr for peace": Bill Clinton, *Public Papers of the Presidents of the United States, William J. Clinton, Book 2* (Washington, DC: Office of the Federal Register, National Archives and Records Administration, 1994), 1723.

206   "We did not find a great deal": Ronny Reich, personal interview with author, September 2020.

206   "They had a religious": Ibid.

207   "a free people in our": Hela Crown-Tamir, *Israel, History in a Nutshell: Highlighting the Wars and Military History* (Jerusalem: Lulu.com, 2017), 12.

207   "I am a Jew but an agnostic": Reich, personal interview with author.

207   "a state of disrepair": "The Ir David Foundation," City of David, 2012, https://www.cityofdavid.org.il/en/The-Ir-David-Foundation. Accessed April 19, 2021.

208 "the City of David is a place": Israel High Court of Justice, Case 4747/91.

208 "Of course, it was all staged": Meron Rapoport, "Shady Dealings in Silwan," ed. Ehud Tagari, trans. Shoshana London Sappir (Jerusalem: dissertation, Ir Amim, 2009), 13.

208 "a serious conflict of interest": Ibid., 14.

208 "has been directly responsible": Nir Hasson, "Hidden Links Unearthed Between State, Settler Group at Israel's Most Controversial Dig," *Haaretz,* November 17, 2014.

208 "You do what I say": Reich, personal interview with author.

209 "He and his men came": Ibid.

209 "We immediately recognized": Ronny Reich and Eli Shukron, "Light at the End of the Tunnel: Warren's Shaft Theory of David's Conquest Shattered," *Biblical Archaeology Review* 25:1 (January–February, 1999).

210 "it is essential to preserve": Hasson, "Hidden Links Unearthed."

211 "guardianship and maintenance": Francesco Chiodelli, *Cities to Be Tamed?: Spatial Investigations across the Urban South* (Newcastle upon Tyne: Cambridge Scholars, 2014), 228.

212 "holding up the mountain": Meron Rapoport, "Shady Dealings in Silwan," 24.

14. THE CELLAR CRUSADE

217 Metropolitan of the Holy: "Holy Synod of Coptic Orthodox Church," Orthodox Wiki, 2009, https://orthodoxwiki.org/Holy_Synod_of_Coptic_Orthodox_Church. Accessed April 20, 2021.

217 "Who is the fucking superpower": Aaron David Miller, "The Curious Case of Benjamin Netanyahu," *Foreign Policy,* May 30, 2012, https://foreignpolicy.com/2012/05/30/the-curious-case-of-benjamin-netanyahu/. Accessed April 20, 2021.

218 "Many situations over time": Father Antonious, personal interview with author, November 2019.

218 "We knocked on their door": Gideon Avni, personal interview with author, November 2019.

219 "The construction of a new Christian church": Leah Di Segni et al., *One Land—Many Cultures: Archaeological Studies in Honour of Stanislao Loffreda* (Jerusalem: Franciscan Printing Press, 2003), 159.

220 "We knew we were working": Gideon Avni, personal interview with author.

220 "Everything exploded": Ibid.

220 "It was crazy": Reuven Yehoshua, personal interview with author, March 2019.

222 "This means that it is": "Disputes Start Small in Holy City," *Tampa Bay Times,* September 16, 2005.

222 "By Israeli law": Yehoshua, personal interview with author.

223 "We were asked": Avni, personal interview with author.

223 "People in ancient times": Yehoshua, personal interview with author.

223 "Bizarrely, I received": Nir Hasson, "Bitter Dispute Over Church of Holy Sepulchre Cellar Resolved After Two Decades," *Haaretz,* February 21, 2016.

225 "I am afraid my father": Ibid.

15. THE BEDROCK OF OUR EXISTENCE

228 "a sloping heap of rubbish": Charles William Wilson, *Ordnance Survey of Jerusalem vol. 1* (Jerusalem: Ariel, 1980), 31.

229 "wilderness of pillars": Mark Twain, *The Innocents Abroad* (Hartford, CT: American Publishing House, 1884), 582.

229 "a stunning underground world": Meir Ben-Dov, *Jerusalem, Man and Stone: An Archeologist's Personal View of His City* (Tel-Aviv: Modan, 1990), 76.

229 "I told him that I thought": Dan Bahat, personal interview with author, February 2019.

229 "Both sides emphasized": Nadav Shragai, "The IAA Authorized Waqf to Work in Solomon's Stables a Year and a Half Ago," *Haaretz,* October 10, 1996.

230 "I said don't": Bahat, personal interview with author.

230 "In the course of the meeting": Yitzhak Reiter, in Marshall J. Breger and Ora Ahimeir, eds., *Jerusalem: A City and Its Future* (Syracuse, NY: Syracuse University Press, 2002), 286.

230 "Naturally the director": Bahat, personal interview with author.

230 "the position of the Muslim": Reiter, *Jerusalem,* 287.

231 "It was very simple": Bahat, personal interview with author.

232 "He had an interest in": Gideon Avni, personal interview with author, May 2020.

232 "because this was an exclusively": Gideon Avni and Jon Seligman, "Between the Temple Mount/Haram El-Sharif and the Holy Sepulchre: Archaeological Involvement in Jerusalem's Holy Places," *Journal of Mediterranean Archaeology* 19, no. 2 (2006): 268.

232 "Drive south past": Gershom Gorenberg, *The End of Days: Fundamentalism and the Struggle for the Temple Mount* (Oxford: Oxford University Press, 2002), 17.

232 "Information reached us": Ibid., 198.

232 "In three years": Ibid., 17.

233 "prevent the site from being": Shmuel Berkovitz, "The Holy Places in Jerusalem: Legal Aspects," *Rivista Di Studi Politici Internazionali* 65, no. 3 (September 1998): 407.

233 "an internal change": Shragai, "IAA Authorized Waqf."

233 "a stone floor was laid": Jon Seligman, "Solomon's Stables, the Temple Mount, Jerusalem: The Events Concerning the Destruction of Antiquities 1999–2011," *Atiqot 56* (January 2007): 50.

234 "I was against the opening": Yisrael Hasson, personal interview with author, September 2019.

234 "It was part of his strategy": Saeb Erekat, personal communication with author, June 2020.

234 "I had a call from our": Dennis Ross, personal communication with author, May 2020.

235 "The government says": Karin Laub, "Israel Completes Controversial Tunnel Near Holy Sites," Associated Press, September 24, 1996.

235 "He was standing there": Hasson, personal interview with author.

235 "We opposed the tunnel": Danny Rubinstein, *Haaretz,* August 26, 1996.

235 "There are Islamic structures": Ibid.

235 "They started to shout": Bahat, personal interview with author.

236 "Why did they put": Rebecca Trounson, "Tunnel Opening in Jerusalem Sparks Protests," *Los Angeles Times,* September 25, 1996.

236 "It means the peace is over": Trounson, "Tunnel Opening."

236 "the Palestinian people": Nadav Shragai, et al., "Arafat Calls on the Palestinians to Protest Protests and Trade Strike," *Haaretz,* September 25, 1996.

236 "in a state of crisis": P. R. Kumaraswamy, "Chronology," *Israel Affairs* 4, no. 2 (1997): 349.

236 "has provoked outrage": Shragai et al., "Arafat Calls on the Palestinians."

236 "It should have been done": Ibid.

236 "our rock of existence": Ibid.

236 "Nothing like this had": Dennis Ross, *The Missing Peace: The Inside Story of the Fight for Middle East Peace* (New York: Farrar, Straus and Giroux, 2008), 265.

236 "a new and regrettable": Steven Erlanger, "Alarm Around the World, and Calls for Calm Talks," *New York Times,* September 26, 1996.

237 "our grave concern": "Texts of Three-Power Letters to Prime Minister of Israel Benjamin Netanyahu and President of the Palestinian Authority Yasser Arafat," London, September 25, 1996, *The Question of Palestine Developments/Peace Process Review* (New York: United Nations, 1996), 3.

237 "I deeply regret": Bill Clinton, *Public Papers of the Presidents of the United States, William J. Clinton, Book 1* (Washington, DC: General Services Administration, 1996), 1680.

237 "the Palestinian Authority has no full": Serge Schmemann, "50 Are Killed as Clashes Widen from West Bank to Gaza Strip," *New York Times,* September 27, 1996.

237 "a religious issue of fanaticism": Storer H. Rowley, "Netanyahu: Riots Aren't Israel's Fault," *Chicago Tribune,* September 28, 1996.

237 "I told them this tunnel": Schmemann, "50 Are Killed."

238 "burned up the phone": Bill Clinton, *My Life: The Early Years (*New York: Vintage Books, 2005), 1451.

238 "the Israelis had opened": Ibid., 1450.

238 "Only a dramatic step": Dennis Ross, *The Missing Peace: The Inside Story of the Fight for Middle East Peace* (New York: Farrar, Straus and Giroux, 2008), 299.

238 "Can we get Netanyahu": Dennis Ross, personal communication with author, May 2020.

238 "I invited Netanyahu and Arafat": Clinton, *My Life,* 1451.

238 "The blood is all over": Schmemann, "50 Are Killed."

239 "unjustified firing of rubber": Reuven Shapiro, "No Evidence of Live Fire Use Was Found When Scattering the Riot on the Temple Mount on September 27 Last Year," *Haaretz,* February 7, 1997.

239 "It is necessary to calm": Schmemann, "50 Are Killed."

239 "I have not seen such": Eitan Rabin and Sami Sokol, "90 Palestinians Wounded in a Violent Incident at Rachel's Tomb; 2 Soldiers Were Lightly Wounded," *Haaretz,* September 26, 1996.

239 "a monstrous decision": Nadav Shragai, "Olmert: PA Behavior—'Crazy Incitement,'" *Haaretz,* September 26, 1996.

239 "an entrance to the tunnel": *United Nations Law Reports,* vol. 30 (New York: Walker, 1995), 21.

239 "the immediate cessation": Voting Practices in the United Nations: Report to Congress Submitted Pursuant to Public Law 101–167. (Washington, DC: U.S. Department of State, 1996), 111–12.

239 "I do not regret": Serge Schmemann, "10 More Die in Mideast Riots as Violence Enters 3rd Day; Mosque Is Scene of a Clash," *New York Times,* September 28, 1996.

239 "the closing of the tunnel": "Netanyahu, Arafat to Attend White House Summit; Israel Reopens Tunnel," CNN Interactive, September 29, 1996, http://www.cnn.com/WORLD/9609/29/israel/. Accessed April 20, 2021.

240 "Arafat had felt that Bibi": Ross, personal communication with author.

240 "We can surprise the world": Ross, *Missing Peace,* 301.

240 "a much larger number": Morton Klein, "The PLO's War Against Jewish History," *Washington Post,* September 29, 1996.

240 "every visitor to the tunnel": Ibid.

241 "We have shed enough": Sami Sokol, "Dozens of 'Yesh B Border' Activists Protested Near the Western Wall Tunnel and Were Evacuated by Police," *Haaretz,* October 7, 1996.

241 "A thousand tunnels": Gideon Alon and Zvi Zarechia, "Kahalani: The Riots in the Territories Would Have Happened Even If the Tunnel Had Not Opened," *Haaretz,* November 5, 1996.

16. MILLENNIAL MADNESS

243 "We will not accept violations": Nadav Shragai and Nina Pinto, "Security Alert Following a Home Temple Conflict," *Haaretz,* August 10, 1999.

244 "What will happen if there": Ann LoLordo, "Trouble in a Holy Place; Jerusalem: The Lone Doorway to the Church," *Baltimore Sun,* June 28, 1999.

244 "We needed to prepare": Azzam al-Khatib, personal interview with author, October 2018.

244 "was clearly inadequate": Jon Seligman, "Solomon's Stables, the Temple Mount, Jerusalem: The Events Concerning the Destruction of Antiquities 1999–2011," *Atiqot 56* (January 2007), 50.

245 "accumulation of earth": Yusuf Natsheh, personal interview with author, October 2018.

245 "Both the waqf engineers": Ehad Jallad, personal interview with author, December 2018.

245 "The waqf was in charge": Al-Khatib, personal interview with author.

245 "Things were tense then": Jallad, personal interview with author.

246 "what the engineers refer": Shragai and Pinto, "Security Alert."

246 "Nobody is allowed to take": Nazmi Jubeh, personal interview with author, February 2019.

246 "There was no archaeology": Natsheh, personal interview with author.

246 "I knew what was going on": Palestinian archaeologist, speaking anonymously to author, December 2019.

247 "We didn't get wind": Jon Seligman, personal interview with author, December 2018.

247 "Barak didn't realize": Gideon Avni, personal interview with author, November 2019.

247 "The extraction of the ancient": Seligman, "Solomon's Stables," 45.

248 "The Islamic Movement didn't": Avni, personal interview with author.

248 "systematic destruction of Jewish": Gershom Gorenberg, *The End of Days: Fundamentalism and the Struggle for the Temple Mount* (Oxford: Oxford University Press, 2002), 201.

248 "The church is an extraordinarily": Shragai and Pinto, "Security Alert."

248 "The Israelis used bulldozers": Al-Khatib, personal interview with author.

249 "went beyond the bounds": Shragai and Pinto, "Security Alert."

249 "no Jewish archaeological": Ibid.

249 "I can say that there was antiquities violation": Moshe Reinfeld, "In Practice, Not Everything Is Judicious," *Haaretz,* January 23, 2000.

249 "an archaeological crime": Seligman, "Solomon's Stables."

249 "to the best of the authorities' ": Reinfeld, "Not Everything Is Judicious."

249 "is almost certain to bring": *Haaretz,* December 10, 1999.

249 "The vestiges of the Jewish people's": *Haaretz,* December 28, 1999.

249 "capitulation": *Haaretz,* December 8, 1999.

250 "It was the largest demonstration": Gorenberg, *End of Days,* 201.

250 "I knew the material": Zach Divra, personal communication with author, May 2020.

251 "The one thing I am sure": Jessica Stern, *Terror in the Name of God: Why Religious Militants Kill* (New York: HarperCollins, 2004), 139.

251 "To our surprise": Divra, personal communication with author.

252 "Within five minutes": Ibid.

252 "Everybody gathered around": State of Israel v. Zachi Zweig, Jerusalem Magistrate Court, January 1, 2003.

253 "archaeologists are not the": Divra, personal communication with author.

253 "We have been given a corpse": Nadav Shragai, "Dozens of Archaeologists Protest against the Waqf Excavations on the Temple Mount," *Haaretz,* January 7, 2000.

253 "The scholars weren't going": Gorenberg, *End of Days,* 200.

254 "You have a chance": State of Israel v. Zachi Zweig.

254 "to renew cooperation with": Shmuel Berkovitz, *The Temple Mount and the Western Wall in Israeli Law* (Jerusalem: Jerusalem Institute for Israel Studies, 2001), 65.

254 "They took all the artifacts": Divra, personal communication with author.

255 "So we called a patrol car": State of Israel v. Zachi Zweig.

255 "By now the story": Divra, personal communication with author.

255 "serious acts of vandalism": *Haaretz,* June 8, 2000.

256 "the world's highest-stakes": Massimo Calabresi, "The Man with the Plan," *Time,* July 17, 2000.

256 "the single most explosive": J. Goldberg, "Jerusalem Endgame," *New York Times Magazine,* October 3, 1999.

256 "the Archimedean point": Ron E. Hassner, *War on Sacred Grounds* (Ithaca, NY: Cornell University Press, 2010), 80.

256 "Do not budge on this": Ibid.

256 "Even the very discussion": Yitzhak Reiter, *Contested Holy Places in Israel/Palestine: Sharing and Conflict Resolution* (Oxfordshire, UK: Routledge, 2007), 34.

256 "Is it a cake": Erik Freas, *Nationalism and the Haram Al-Sharif/Temple Mount: The Exclusivity of Holiness* (New York: Springer International, 2018), 107.

256 "The Israelis and Americans": Tony Karon, "Why a Camp David Deal May Be a Bridge Too Far," *Time,* July 16, 2000, http://content.time.com/time/magazine /article/0,9171,50026,00.html. Accessed April 20, 2021.

257 "You are the bravest man": Lior Lehrs, "Jerusalem on the Negotiating Table: Analyzing the Israeli-Palestinian Peace Talks on Jerusalem (1993–2015)," *Israel Studies* 21, no. 3 (2016), 31.

257 "It was God's will": Bill Clinton, *Public Papers of the Presidents of the United States, William J. Clinton, Book 2* (Washington, DC: Office of the Federal Register, National Archives and Records Administration, 1994), 1890–93.

257 "In our Bible, the place": Clayton E. Swisher, *The Truth about Camp David: The Untold Story about the Collapse of the Middle East Peace Process* (New York: Bold Type Books, 2009), 344.

257 "almost shouted": Ibid., 344.

258 "You are leading your people": Gilead Sher, *The Israeli-Palestinian Peace Negotiations, 1999–2001: Within Reach* (London: Routledge, 2013), 84.

258 "But the ruins of the temple": Charles Enderlin, *Shattered Dreams: The Failure of the Peace Process in the Middle East, 1995–2002* (New York: Other Press, 2003), 281.

17. RUINS IN THE MIND

261 "Of the Temple proper": Joseph Patrich, "538 BCE–70 CE: The Temple and Its Mount," in *Where Heaven and Earth Meet: Jerusalem's Sacred Esplanade*, Oleg Grabar and Benjamin Z. Ḳedar, eds. (Austin: University of Texas Press, 2010), 38.

261 "No remnants of the Temple": Kamil Jamil al-'Asali, *Jerusalem in Arab and Muslim Travel Narratives* (self-pub., 1992), 39–40.

261 "The mystery of this sacred place": Shimon Gibson and David M. Jacobson, "The Oldest Datable Chambers on the Temple Mount in Jerusalem," *Biblical Archaeologist* 57, no. 3 (September 1994): 150.

262 "We seem to be a long": Charles Warren, "Lieut. Warren on the Temple of Herod," *Palestine Exploration Quarterly* no. 1 (1869): 26.

262 "He set fire to the temple": 2 Kings 25:9–11 (New International Version).

262 "Holy to the Priest": Yuval Goren et al., "A Re-Examination of the Inscribed Pomegranate from the Israel Museum," *Israel Exploration Journal* 55, no. 1 (2005): 3–20.

262 "storied structure": Ed Greenstein, "The So-Called Jehoash Inscription: A Post Mortem," Friends of ASOR, May 20, 2020, http://www.asor.org/anetoday/2016/02/the-so-called-jehoash-inscription-a-post-mortem/. Accessed April 20, 2021.

262 "the House of Yahweh": Anat Mendel-Geberovich et al., "A Brand New Old Inscription: Arad Ostracon 16 Rediscovered via Multispectral Imaging," *Bulletin of the American Schools of Oriental Research* 378 (November 2017): 113–25.

263 "Jerusalem is the capital": Clifford F. Moore, trans. *Tacitus: The Histories*, vol. 2 (Cambridge: Harvard University Press, 1962), 189.

264 "temple denial": Dennis Ross, personal communication with author, May 2020.

264 "whatever he wished": Fadel Soliman, *Bridges' Translation of the Ten Qira'at of the Noble Qur'an* (self-pub., Authorhouse UK, 2020), 34:13.

264 "in a central position in Muslim": William J. Hamblin and David Rolph Seely, *Solomon's Temple: Myth and History* (London: Thames & Hudson, 2007), 138.

264 "You have a whole culture": Sari Nusseibeh, personal interview with author, September 2019.

265 "To us, the Temple Mount": Daniel Williams, "Arabs, Jews Fired Up Over Sacred Sites," *Los Angeles Times,* April 22, 1989.

265 "let hell break loose": Clayton E. Swisher, *The Truth about Camp David: The Untold Story about the Collapse of the Middle East Peace Process* (New York: Bold Type Books, 2009), 326.

265 "I can't betray": Ron E. Hassner, *War on Sacred Grounds* (Ithaca, NY: Cornell University Press, 2010), 80.

265 "Do you want to attend": Martin Indyk, *Innocent Abroad: An Intimate Account of American Peace Diplomacy in the Middle East* (New York: Simon & Schuster, 2014).

265 "No Arab leader is": Saut Al-Haqq Wa Al-Hurriya, "The Debate at Camp David over Jerusalem's Holy Places," August 18, 2000, http://www.la.utexas.edu/users/chenry/aip/Class%20materials/israel_state_of_israel_part_3-8.29.2000.html. Accessed April 20, 2021.

265 "If there were any compromises": Swisher, *Truth about Camp David,* 345.

266 "we cannot accept any": Thomas Graham, *Unending Crisis: National Security Policy after 9/11* (Seattle: Institute of Global and Regional Security Studies, Jackson School of International Studies in association with University of Washington Press, 2012), 150.

266 "going to the dentist": Marc Lacey and David E. Sanger, "Impasse at Camp David," *New York Times,* July 26, 2000.

266 "something profound had": Dennis Ross, *The Missing Peace: The Inside Story of the Fight for Middle East Peace* (New York: Farrar, Straus and Giroux, 2008), 761.

266 "Of course, the temple": Ibid., 768.

266 "Mr. Chairman, regardless of": Ibid., 768.

267 "He was challenging not just": Ross, personal communication with author.

267 "I thought, let's create": Ibid.

267 "perfectly honeycombed": *Times* (London), December 30, 1865.

267 "I even checked with my rabbi": Ross, personal communication with author.

267 "What do you think of the formula": Charles Enderlin, *Shattered Dreams: The Failure of the Peace Process in the Middle East, 1995–2002* (New York: Other Press, 2003), 281.

268 "You have three or four": Ibid., 282.

269 "I bring a message": Joel Greenberg, "Sharon Touches a Nerve, and Jerusalem Explodes," *New York Times,* September 29, 2000.

270 "the Jewish cemetery": Ross, *Missing Peace,* 796.

270 "live with your control": Ibid., 797.

270 "Yes": Ibid., 797.

271 "I threw the paper on the table": Yisrael Hasson, personal interview with author, September 2019.

271 "recognize the sanctity of the place": Gilead Sher, *The Israeli-Palestinian Peace Negotiations, 1999–2001: Within Reach* (London: Routledge, 2013), 194.

271 "parameters": Ross, *Missing Peace,* 704–705.

271 "This is the best I can do": P. Edward. Haley, *Strategies of Dominance: The Misdirection of U.S. Foreign Policy* (Washington, DC: Woodrow Wilson Center Press, 2006), 86.

271 "Why so late?": Enderlin, *Shattered Dreams,* 339.

272 "I came up with": Ross, personal communication with author.

272 "From our side, we were clear": Saeb Erekat, personal communication with author, June 2020.

273 "both sides were close": Terje Rød-Larsen, Nur Laiq, and Fabrice Aidan, *The Search for Peace in the Arab-Israeli Conflict: A Compendium of Documents and Analysis* (Oxford: Oxford University Press, 2014), 471.

273 "This was the end of the": Ross, *Missing Peace,* 806.

273 "There were three words": Ross, personal communication with author.

273 "I am absolutely unwilling": Moshe Amirav, *Jerusalem Syndrome: The Palestinian-Israeli Battle for the Holy City* (Brighton, UK: Sussex Academic, 2009), 190–91.

273 "in anticipation of the establishment": Yitzhak Reiter, *Jerusalem and Its Role in Islamic Solidarity* (New York: Springer, 2008), 110.

274 "The brutal fact is that": Colin Thubron, *Jerusalem* (London: Penguin Books, 1996), 186.

18. REALITY IS ALWAYS STRONGER THAN BELIEF

277 "The defendant, a sophomore": State of Israel v. Zachi Zweig, Jerusalem Magistrate Court in Jerusalem, January 1, 2003.

277 "a beginner's mistake": Ibid.

278 "For the Freedom of Zion": G. Barkay and Zachi Dvira, "Relics in Rubble: The Temple Mount Sifting Project," *Biblical Archaeology Review* 42, no. 6 (January 2016).

279 "finds of this nature": Amanda Borschel-Dan, "Temple Mount Sifting Project Reboots, Aims to Salvage Ancient Temple Artifacts," *Times of Israel,* June 7, 2019.

279 "We worked hand in hand": Gabriel Barkay, personal interview with author, February 2019.

279 "black hole of history": Amanda Borschel-Dan, "Temple Mount Sifting Project Reboots, Aims to Salvage Ancient Temple Artifacts," *Times of Israel,* June 7, 2019.

279 "Our very existence reminds": Barkay, personal interview with author, February 2019.

279 "They were not interested": Ibid.

279 "Before we start pumping more": Carl Hoffman, "Temple Mount Sifting Project at a Crossroads," *Jerusalem Post,* July 20, 2017.

280 "It was very noisy": Eli Shukron, personal interview with author, July 2019.

281 "If Eli had not stopped": Ronny Reich, personal interview with author, September 2020.

281 "These must be steps": Hershel Shanks, "The Siloam Pool Where Jesus Cured the Blind Man," *Biblical Archaeology Review* 31, no. 5 (September–October 2005).

281 "gently flowing waters of Shiloah": Isaiah 8:6 (New International Version).

281 "the wall of the Pool of Siloam": Nehemiah 3:15 (New International Version).

282 "two basins constructed": F. E. Peters, *Jerusalem: The Holy City in the Eyes of Chroniclers, Visitors, Pilgrims, and Prophets from the Days of Abraham to the Beginnings of Modern Times* (Princeton, NJ: Princeton University Press, 2017), 168.

282 "the Siloam people took advantage": Frederick Jones Bliss, *Excavations at Jerusalem, 1894–1897* (London: Committee of the Palestine Exploration Fund, 1898), 159.

282 "I had to make sure that": Ronny Reich, *Excavating the City of David: Where Jerusalem's History Began* (Jerusalem: Israel Exploration Society, 2011), 226.

283 "miracle pool": "Archaeologists Identify Traces of 'Miracle' Pool," Associated Press, December 23, 2004.

283 "We know today that the Siloam Pool": Ibid.

283 "There is a road": Ibid.

283 "That was the starting point": Israeli archaeologist, communicating anonymously with author, January 2021.

284 "venture philanthropy": Steven Erlanger, "King David's Palace Is Found, Archaeologist Says," *New York Times,* August 5, 2005.

284 "Almost from the start": Eilat Mazar, "Did I Find King David's Palace?," *Biblical Archaeology Review* 32:1 (January–February 2006).

285 "not just any public building": Ibid.

285 "One cannot just *assume*": Margreet L. Steiner, "From Jerusalem with Love," in *History, Archaeology and the Bible Forty Years after Historicity* (London: Routledge, 2016), 76.

285 "when the Bible says King David": Mazar, "Did I Find King David's Palace?"

285 "Dr. Mazar's discovery": Gerald Flurry, "King David's Palace Has Been Discovered in Jerusalem," Watch Jerusalem, August 14, 2019, https://watchjerusalem.co.il/709-king-davids-palace-has-been-discovered-in-jerusalem. Accessed April 20, 2021.

286 "she certainly would find": Hershel Shanks, "First Person: The Bible as a Source of Testable Hypotheses," *Biblical Archaeology Review* 37: 4 (July–August 2011).

286 "Eilat had a hypothesis": Ibid.

286 "product of inspiration": Mazar, "Did I Find King David's Palace?"

286 "Carbon-14 is like a prostitute": Andrew Lawler, "Archaeology: Judging Jerusalem," *Science* 315, no. 5812 (February 2, 2007): 588–91.

287 "We all agree Jerusalem": Eilat Mazar, personal interview with author, December 2018.

287 "in the broad political battle": Steven Erlanger, "King David's Palace Is Found, Archaeologist Says," *New York Times,* September 5, 2005.

288 "try to link whatever they": Ibid.

19. THE REBEL DIG

292 "We were faced with a real": Ronny Reich, *Excavating the City of David: Where Jerusalem's History Began* (Jerusalem: Israel Exploration Society, 2011), 233.

292 "He pointed up at the Old City": Doron Spielman (Jerusalem: Speech at inauguration of the "Pilgrimage Tunnel," June 30, 2019).

293 "I did not believe this": Reich, *Excavating the City of David,* 236.

293 "the 'rebel' dig": Ibid., 241.

294 "They are saying they're 'only' ": Nir Hasson, "Jerusalem's Time Tunnels," *Haaretz,* April 24, 2011.

294 "Someday there may be peace": Ibid.

295 "the Republic of Elad": Meron Rapoport, "The Republic of Elad," *Haaretz,* April 22, 2006.

295 "The place I knew as an Arab": *Digging for Trouble* (Journeyman Pictures, January 14, 2008), 23 min., https://www.youtube.com/watch?v=aRNAJCHxa7w. Accessed April 19, 2021.

295 "the IAA has been lured": Raphael Greenberg, "Towards an Inclusive Archaeology in Jerusalem: The Case of Silwan/The City of David," *Public Archaeology* 8, no. 1 (February 2009), 42.

295 "Over all those years": Reich, *Excavating the City of David,* 249.

296 "evildoers": Hasson, "Jerusalem's Time Tunnels."

296 "One night the Silwan": Israeli archaeologist, speaking anonymously to author, October 2018.

296 "The claims are bogus": Michael Green, "Digging Too Deep?," *Jerusalem Post,* March 2, 2008.

297 "To dig a tunnel means": Ibid.

297 "the importance of investigating": Hasson, "Jerusalem's Time Tunnels."

297 "Tunnels allow you to": Raphael Greenberg, "A Future for the Archaeology of Jerusalem" (Chicago: Speech at ASOR annual meeting, November 17, 2012).

297 "There is a lot of trust": Meron Rapoport, *Shady Dealings in Silwan* (Jerusalem: Ir Amim, 2009), 18.

297 "I have a somewhat laid-back": Reich, *Excavating the City of David,* 248.

298 "Here it began": "City of David National Park," Public presentation (Jerusalem), December 2018.

298 "Archaeological evidence is not": Margreet Steiner, "The City of David as a Palimpsest," in Lukasz Niesiolowski-Spanò and Emanuel Pfoh, eds., *Biblical Narratives, Archaeology and Historicity: Essays in Honour of Thomas L. Thompson* (Edinburgh: T&T Clark, 2019), 5.

298 "training focused solely": Rapoport, *Shady Dealings in Silwan,* 18.

298 "Sixty percent of the Bible": Greenberg, "Towards an Inclusive Archaeology," 43.

298 "selectively exploited": Ibid., 42.

298 "crude amalgam of history": Ibid., 43.

298 "There are things archaeologists": *Digging for Trouble* (Journeyman Pictures, January 14, 2008).

298 "ideological-religious organizations": Raphael Greenberg, "Extreme Exposure: Archaeology in Jerusalem 1967–2007," *Conservation and Management of Archaeological Sites* 11, nos. 3–4 (August 2009): 262–81.

299 "What I create for them": Ronny Reich, personal interview with author, September 2020.

299 "my obligation is to show": Eilat Mazar, personal interview with author, October 2018.

299   "This was nonsense": Ibid.

299   "gimmick": Nir Hasson, "Top Archaeologist Decries Jerusalem Dig as Unscientific 'Tourist Gimmick,'" *Haaretz,* October 10, 2011.

299   "Dr. Mazar is trying": Ibid.

300   "Excavating in Jerusalem": Eilat Mazar, personal interview with author, February 2018.

300   "The whole use of archaeology": Nir Hasson, *Haaretz,* April 21, 2006.

300   "Therefore, in any negotiations": Ibid.

301   "If distinctive antiquities": Nir Hasson, "Hidden Links Unearthed Between State, Settler Group at Israel's Most Controversial Dig," *Haaretz,* November 17, 2014.

302   "to expose the layer": Raphael Greenberg, *A Privatized Heritage: How the Israel Antiquities Authority Relinquished Jerusalem's Past,* Emek Shaveh, October 2014, https://emekshaveh.org/en/wp-content/uploads/2014/11/Privatized-Heritage-English-Web.pdf, 33. Accessed April 19, 2021.

302   "We are talking about a building": Ibid., 20.

302   "immense building": Ibid., 20.

302   "I asked him to stop digging": Hasson, "Hidden Links."

302   "a grave mishap": *Haaretz,* June 1, 2008.

302   "The City of David tells": Hasson, "Hidden Links."

303   "We will cooperate with Elad": Nir Hasson, "TAU to Take Part in East Jerusalem Dig Funded by Pro-Settlement Group," *Haaretz,* October 25, 2012.

303   "an extreme political organization": Nir Hasson, "Petition Slams Tel Aviv University's Involvement in East Jerusalem Dig," *Haaretz,* December 25, 2012.

303   "a clear politicization": Hasson, "TAU to Take Part."

303   "No amount of sieving": Raphael Greenberg, "Jerusalem's 'What Me Worry' Archaeology," The Bible and Interpretation, May 2013, https://bibleinterp.arizona.edu/articles/2013/gre378006. Accessed April 18, 2021.

303   "not only deflected potential": "'Beit Haliba' and the Givati Parking Lot Archeological Excavations and Their Effect on the Status Quo in the Old City of Jerusalem and in Silwan," Emek Shaveh, September 9, 2013, https://emekshaveh.org/en/haliba/. Accessed April 20, 2021.

304   "The excavation project in the Givati": Hasson, "Hidden Links."

304   "I've since learned to appreciate": Yuval Gadot, personal interview with author, December 2018.

304   "so this can be a more neutral": Ibid.

20. RESISTANCE BY EXISTENCE

307   "Reich and Shukron began": Joe Uziel, personal interview with author, October 2018.

308   "We support continuing the excavation": Raz Kletter, *Archaeology, Heritage and Ethics in the Western Wall Plaza, Jerusalem: Darkness at the End of the Tunnel* (London: Routledge Taylor & Francis, 2020), 56.

309   "I was on a bit": Uziel, personal interview with author.

309   "This is not like any other": Uziel, personal interview with author.

310   "the shingle would suddenly": Charles Warren to Walter Besant, June 10, 1870, Palestine Exploration Fund Archives, JER/WAR/25.

311   "What they are doing is very": Experienced engineer, speaking anonymously to author, December 2018.

312   "Part of it may have been to appease": Andrew Lawler, "Road Built by Biblical Villain Uncovered in Jerusalem," *National Geographic,* October 20, 2019, https://www

.nationalgeographic.com/history/2019/10/road-built-biblical-villain-uncovered
-jerusalem/. Accessed April 20, 2021.

313   "New Archaeological Evidence": Candida Moss, "New Archaeological Evidence
Shows Pontius Pilate Not as Bad as We Thought," *Daily Beast,* October 27, 2019,
https://www.thedailybeast.com/pontius-pilate-not-as-bad-as-we-thought-new-
archaeological-evidence-triggers-reassessment. Accessed April 18, 2021.

313   "All right, but apart": Adele Reinhartz, *Jesus of Hollywood* (New York: Oxford University Press, 2007), 60.

313   "We have a lot of input": Uziel, personal interview with author.

314   "There was a point where": Archaeologist, personal interview with author, December 2018.

315   "You can't imagine": Ibid.

315   "Anyone walking from the Pool": Uziel, personal interview with author.

315   "If the next ten years": Doron Spielman, personal interview with author, October 2018.

316   "Business is terrible!": Abd Yusuf, personal interview with author, October 2018.

316   "The excavations pose many": Sahar Abass, personal interview with author, October 2018.

317   "I built this house in": Arafat Hamdan, personal interview with author, January 2019.

317   "The house was shaking": Hamdan family member, personal interview with author, January 2019.

317   "I just want to be left": Miriam Bashir, personal interview with author, January 2019.

317   "Yes, we are working under": Spielman, personal interview with author.

317   "the claims of politically": Doron Spielman, personal communication with author, January 2019.

318   "We lay down and wept": Video of inauguration in "Senior American and Israeli Officials Attend Inauguration of Second Temple Period Pilgrimage Road in the City of David," City of David, June 30, 2019, https://www.cityofdavid.org.il/en/news /senior-american-and-israeli-officials-attend-inauguration-second-temple-period -pilgrimage-road-. Accessed April 19, 2021.

319   "He told me, Abba": Ibid.

320   "the spiritual underpinnings": Ibid.

321   "What is truth?": John 18:38 (New International Version).

321   "the importance of the rule of the Roman": "Senior American and Israeli Officials Attend Inauguration."

21. HERE WE WILL STAY

323   "a biased manner": Ahdaf Soueif, "The Dig Dividing Jerusalem," *Guardian,* May 26, 2010.

324   "help us better confront": Benjamin Z. Kedar, *The Changing Land: Between Jordan and the Sea; Aerial Photographs from 1917 to the Present* (Detroit: Wayne State University Press, 1999), 41.

324   "I had no idea where": Benjamin Kedar, personal communication with author, February 2020.

325   "I had been curious about": Ibid.

325   "a medieval doorway": Benjamin Z. Kedar, Shlomit Weksler-Bdolah, and Tawfiq Da'adli, "The Madrasa Afdaliyya/Maqam Al-Shaykh 'Id: An Example of Ayyubid Architecture in Jerusalem," *Revue Biblique* 119, no. 2 (April 2012): 274.

325 "If the excavation at Solomon's Stables": Kedar, personal communication with author.

326 "He came to me and said": Shlomit Weksler-Bdolah, personal interview with author, November 2019.

326 "We researched it, and concluded": Kedar, personal communication with author.

326 "The Waqf": "Report of the Technical Mission to the Old City of Jerusalem," *United Nations* (Paris: UNESCO), 2007. https://www.un.org/unispal/document /auto-insert-206780/. Accessed April 18, 2021.

327 "the discovery of porcelain coffee": Hervé Barbé, Fanny Vitto, and Roie Greenwald, "When, Why and by Whom the Mughrabi Gate Was Opened?: Excavations at the Mughrabi Gate in the Old City of Jerusalem (2007, 2012–2014)," Guy D. Stiebel et al., eds., *New Studies in the Archaeology of Jerusalem and Its Region: Collected Papers* 8 (2014): 42.

327 "I used to lie on my stomach": Emdad Abu Khadijih, personal interview with author, December 2018.

328 "He broke the law": Israeli archaeologist, personal interview with author, December 2018.

329 "It took us eighteen years": Miriam Siebenberg, personal interview with author, October 2018.

329 "We were here": Ibid.

330 "There are a lot of mysteries": Amit Re'em, personal interview with author, October 2018.

330 "Then we reached the area": Ibid.

331 "I remember when I was ten": Yitzhak Goldstein, personal interview with author, July 2019.

331 "all the gold from King Solomon": Rod Salinger, personal interview with author, July 2019.

332 "They say it was stolen": Ibid.

332 "Indiana Jones is burned": Yehiel Zelinger, personal interview with author, August 2019.

332 "Nothing changes": Israeli archaeologist speaking anonymously with author, August 2019.

22. RETURN OF THE QUEEN

335 "I happened to notice": Rabbi Yitzhak Mamo, personal interview with author, August 2019.

336 "I have no other goal": Hekdesh of the Tomb of the Kings *vs.* French Ministry for Europe and Foreign Affairs. Tribunal de Grand Instance, Paris, exhibit 3, letter dated April 23, 1874.

337 "the words spoken": Ibid., handwritten note made by Chief Rabbi Lazar Isidor on document dated April 28, 1874.

338 "to lend a hand in carrying": Ibid.

338 "on behalf of Madame": Ibid., exhibit 4, document dated 1878.

338 "no changes will be made": Richard Rossin and Freddy Eytan, "Jerusalem's Tomb of the Kings: Did the French Hijack a Jewish Heritage Site?," Jerusalem Center for Public Affairs, December 3, 2019, https://jcpa.org/article/were-french-kings-buried -in-jerusalems-tomb-of-the-kings. Accessed April 20, 2021.

339 "This is how impossible": Theodor Herzl, *Diaries of Theodor Herzl,* trans. and ed. Marvin Lowenthal (New York: Dial Press, 1956), 290.

339 "science and the veneration": Rossin and Eytan, "Jerusalem's Tomb of the Kings: Did the French Hijack a Jewish Heritage Site?"

340   "The French gave me": Ran Shapira, "A Royal Return," *Haaretz,* October 1, 2010.

340   "There were no bones": Mamo, personal interview with author.

340   "had sunk into oblivion": Jean-Baptiste Humbert, "Can the Tomb of the Kings in Jerusalem, Attributed to the Queen of Adiabene, Be That of Herod Agrippa?" (Paris: Presentation at Academie des Inscriptions et Belles-Lettres, April 20, 2018).

341   "So I could be walking": Mamo, personal interview with author.

341   "long and strenuous negotiations": Ilan Ben Zion, "France Reopens Contested Jewish Tomb in East Jerusalem," Associated Press, November 8, 2019.

341   "Monuments from Palestine": Antoine Héron de Villefosse, *Notice des monuments provenant de la Palestine et conservés au Musée du Louvre (salle judaïque)* [catalog] (Paris: Louvre Museum, 1876): 22–35.

342   "Either they are hiding": Mamo, personal interview with author.

342   "I asked the guy in charge": Ibid.

342   "Our security officers": French official, speaking anonymously to author, December 2019.

343   "We deplore the violent": AFP and *Times of Israel* staff, "France Reseals Jerusalem Historic Site after Opening Marred by Dispute," *Times of Israel,* June 27, 2019.

343   "part of a global strategy": Ben Zion, "France Reopens Contested Jewish Tomb."

343   "The respect due": Hekdesh of the Tomb of the Kings *vs.* French Ministry of Culture. Tribunal de Grand Instance, Paris, exhibit 3, letter dated April 23, 1874.

344   "A good friend": Mamo, personal interview with author.

EPILOGUE

345   "It has been proved": Jonathan Lis, "Netanyahu: Not Jerusalem but Refusal to Recognize Jewish State Delays Peace," *Haaretz,* May 24, 2017.

345   "never-ending digging": Rafael Medoff, "Mahmoud Abbas, World's Worst Historian," *Jerusalem Post,* January 16, 2018.

345   "a land where the dead past": Brenda Wineapple, "A Land Where the Dead Past Walks," *New York Review of Books,* January 14, 2021.

346   "It is like working": Tehillah Lieberman, personal interview with author, November 2018.

346   "Jerusalem is a city of minorities": Ronnie Ellenblum, personal interview with author, November 2019.

346   "pottery emergency calls": Lieberman, personal interview with author.

347   "Every week or two": Retired Israeli archaeologist, speaking anonymously to author, November 2019.

347   "People come to Jerusalem": Lieberman, personal interview with author.

347   "we're not interlopers": Maayan Jaffe-Hoffman, "The Untold Story of Americans Unearthing Israeli Archaeology," *Jewish Journal,* June 21, 2018.

348   "We must be realistic": Yuval Baruch, personal interview with author, August 2019.

348   "We became archaeologists": Anne Pyburn, "Practicing Archaeology (and Science) in the Current Political Climate" (Asheville, NC: Archaeological Institute of America Lecture Program, September 25, 2019).

348   "I have no responsibility": Yonatan Adler, personal interview with author, July 2019.

348   "If you say you are just doing": Eran Tzidkiyahu, personal interview with author, October 2018.

349   "Archaeologists can be slaves to": Ellenblum, personal interview with author.

349   "She remembered me": Nazmi Jubeh, personal interview with author, February 2019.

350   "I went on an Elad tour": Ibid.

350   "Western civilization with its": James Carroll, *Jerusalem, Jerusalem: How the Ancient City Ignited Our Modern World* (New York: Houghton Mifflin Harcourt, 2011), 293.

351   "I know we are": Jubeh, personal interview with author.

353   "Hadrian is actually the savior": Guy Stiebel, personal interview with author, November 2019.

354   "I love history": Stiebel, personal interview with author.

354   "Everyone who ruled Jerusalem": Shlomit Weksler-Bdolah, personal interview with author, October 2018.

354   "I am Orthodox": Lieberman, personal interview with author.

355   "to explode a myth": Gilbert Ryle, *The Concept of Mind* (Chicago: University of Chicago Press, 2002), 8.

Further Reading

A list of the literature on Jerusalem could fill several volumes; what follows are selected books, most in English, that shed additional light on the city's past, both above- and belowground.

Abu-Munshar, Maher Y. *Islamic Jerusalem and Its Christians: A History of Tolerance and Tensions.* London: I. B. Tauris, 2013.

Abujaber, Raouf. *Arab Christianity and Jerusalem: A History of the Arab Christian Presence in the Holy City.* London: Gilgamesh, 2012.

Adelman, Madelaine, and Miriam Fendius Elman. *Jerusalem: Conflict and Cooperation in a Contested City.* Syracuse, NY: Syracuse University Press, 2014.

al-'Asali, Kamil Jamil. *Jerusalem in Arab and Muslim Travel Narratives.* Amman: 1992.

Amichai, Yehuda, and Robert Alter. *The Poetry of Yehuda Amichai.* New York: Farrar, Straus and Giroux, 2017.

Amirav, Moshe. *Jerusalem Syndrome: The Palestinian-Israeli Battle for the Holy City.* Brighton, UK: Sussex Academic, 2009.

Andrews, Richard. *Blood on the Mountain: A History of the Temple Mount from the Ark to the Third Millennium.* London: Phoenix, 2000.

Anner, Ze'ev, Meir Ben-Dov, and Mordecai Naor. *The Western Wall.* Tel Aviv: Ministry of Defence, 1983.

Armstrong, Karen. *Jerusalem.* New York: Ballantine Books, 2005.

Avineri, Shlomo. *The Making of Modern Zionism: The Intellectual Origins of the Jewish State.* Boulder, CO: Basic Books, 2017.

Aziza, Claude, ed. *Jerusalem: Le rêve a l'ombre du Temple.* Paris: Omnibus, 1994 (French).

Baden, Joel S. *The Historical David: The Real Life of an Invented Hero.* New York: Harper-One, 2014.

Baedeker, Karl. *Palestine and Syria: Handbook for Travellers.* Leipzig: K. Baedeker, 1894.

Bahat, Dan. *Carta's Historical Atlas of Jerusalem.* Jerusalem: Carta, 1976.

———. *The Jerusalem Western Wall Tunnel.* Jerusalem: Israel Exploration Society, 2013.

Bahat, Dan, and Shalom Sabar. *Jerusalem, Stone and Spirit: 3,000 Years of History and Art.* New York: Rizzoli, 1998.

Barclay, James Turner. *The City of the Great King; or, Jerusalem as It Was*. Philadelphia: W. H. Thompson, 1883.

Bartel, Tim. *Jerusalem in Original Photography*. London: Stacey International, 2003.

Bellow, Saul. *To Jerusalem and Back*. London: Penguin, 2012.

Ben-Arieh, Yehoshua. *Jerusalem in the 19th Century: The Old City*. Jerusalem: Yad Izhak Ben Zvi Institute, 1984.

———. *The Rediscovery of the Holy Land in the Nineteenth Century*. Jerusalem: Sefer Ve Sefel, 2007.

Ben-Arieh, Yehoshua, and Moshe Davis. *Jerusalem in the Mind of the Western World: 1800–1948*. Westport, CT: Praeger, 1997.

Ben-Dov, Meir. *In the Shadow of the Temple: The Discovery of Ancient Jerusalem*. New York: Harper & Row, 1985.

———. *Jerusalem, Man and Stone: An Archaeologist's Personal View of His City*. Tel Aviv: Modan, 1990.

Ben-Yehuda, Nachman. *Theocratic Democracy: The Social Construction of Religious and Secular Extremism*. New York: Oxford University Press, 2010.

Bentwich, Norman. *England in Palestine*. London: Trubner & Company, 1932.

Benvenisti, Meron. *City of Stone: Hidden History of Jerusalem*. Berkeley: University of California Press, 1996.

———. *Jerusalem: The Torn City*. Minneapolis: University of Minnesota Press, 1976.

Berkovitz, Shmuel. *The Temple Mount and the Western Wall in Israeli Law*. Jerusalem: Jerusalem Institute for Israel Studies, 2001.

Besant, Walter. *Palestine Exploration Fund: Twenty-One Years' Work in the Holy Land (a Record and a Summary), June 22, 1865–June 22, 1886*. London: Bentley, 1886.

Bickerton, Ian J., and Carla L. Klausner. *A History of the Arab-Israeli Conflict*. Milton Park, UK: Taylor and Francis, 2018.

Bieberstein, Klaus. *A Brief History of Jerusalem from the Earliest Settlement to the Destruction of the City in AD 70*. Wiesbaden: Harrassowitz Verlag in Kommission, 2017.

Black, Ian. *Enemies and Neighbours: Arabs and Jews in Palestine and Israel, 1917–2017*. London: Penguin Books, 2018.

Bliss, Frederick Jones. *Development of Palestine Exploration: Being the Ely Lectures for 1903*. New York: Charles Scribner's Sons, 1906.

———. *Excavations at Jerusalem, 1894–1897*. London: Committee of the Palestine Exploration Fund, 1898.

Bottini, G. Claudio, Leah Di Segni, and L. Daniel Chrupcała, eds. *One Land—Many Cultures: Archaeological Studies in Honour of Stanislao Loffreda*. Jerusalem: Franciscan Printing Press, 2003.

Breger, Marshall J., and Ora Ahimeir. *Jerusalem: A City and Its Future*. Syracuse, NY: Syracuse University Press, 2002.

Burgoyne, Michael Hamilton., and D. S. Richards. *Mamluk Jerusalem: An Architectural Study*. Jerusalem: Published on Behalf of the British School of Archaeology in Jerusalem by the World of Islam Festival Trust, 1987.

Carew, Mairéad. *Tara and the Ark of the Covenant: A Search for the Ark of the Covenant by British-Israelites on the Hill of Tara (1899–1902)*. Dublin: Discovery Programme/Royal Irish Academy, 2003.

Carroll, James. *Jerusalem, Jerusalem: How the Ancient City Ignited Our Modern World*. New York: Houghton Mifflin Harcourt, 2011.

Chadwick, Owen. *The Victorian Church*. Eugene, OR: Wipf and Stock, 2010.

Cheshin, Amir, Bill Hutman, and Avi Melamed. *Separate and Unequal: The Inside Story of Israeli Rule in East Jerusalem*. Cambridge, MA: Harvard University Press, 2002.

Chiodelli, Francesco. *Cities to Be Tamed?: Spatial Investigations across the Urban South.* Newcastle upon Tyne, UK: Cambridge Scholars Publishing, 2014.

Clausen, David Christian. *The Upper Room and Tomb of David: The History, Art, and Archaeology of the Cenacle on Mount Zion.* Jefferson, NC: McFarland, 2016.

Cline, Eric H. *Biblical Archaeology: A Very Short Introduction.* New York: Oxford University Press, 2009.

———. *Jerusalem Besieged: From Ancient Canaan to Modern Israel.* Ann Arbor: University of Michigan Press, 2005.

Clinton, Bill. *My Life: The Early Years.* New York: Vintage Books, 2005.

Cohen, Raymond. *Saving the Holy Sepulchre: How Rival Christians Came Together to Rescue Their Holiest Shrine.* Oxford: Oxford University Press, 2008.

Cohen-Hattab, Kobi, and Doron Bar. *The Western Wall: The Dispute over Israel's Holiest Jewish Site, 1967–2000.* Boston: Brill, 2020.

Conder, Claude R. *Tent Work in Palestine: A Record of Discovery and Adventure.* London: R. Bentley, 1879.

Crossan, John Dominic. *God and Empire: Jesus against Rome, Then and Now.* New York: HarperOne, 2009.

Crown-Tamir, Hela. *Israel, History in a Nutshell: Highlighting the Wars and Military History.* Jerusalem: Lulu.com, 2017.

Dalachanis, Angelos, and Vincent Lemire. *Ordinary Jerusalem, 1840–1940: Opening New Archives, Revisiting a Global City.* Boston: Brill, 2018.

Davies, Graham. *The Beginnings of "Biblical Archaeology."* Leiden, Netherlands: Brill, 2012.

Davis, Miriam C. *Dame Kathleen Kenyon: Digging Up the Holy Land.* New York: Routledge, 2016.

Drower, Margaret S. *Flinders Petrie: A Life in Archaeology.* Madison: University of Wisconsin Press, 2014.

Dudman, Helga, and Ruth Kark. *The American Colony: Scenes from a Jerusalem Saga.* Jerusalem: Carta Jerusalem, 1998.

Dumper, Michael. *The Politics of Jerusalem Since 1967.* New York: Columbia University Press, 1997.

Eisenberg, Laura Zittrain, and Neil Caplan. *Negotiating Arab-Israeli Peace: Patterns, Problems, Possibilities.* Bloomington: Indiana University Press, 2010.

El-Haj, Nadia Abu. *Facts on the Ground: Archaeological Practice and Territorial Self-Fashioning in Israeli Society.* Chicago: University of Chicago Press, 2002.

Elad, Amikam. *Medieval Jerusalem and Islamic Worship: Holy Places, Ceremonies, Pilgrimage.* Leiden, Netherlands: Brill, 1995.

Eliav, Yaron Z. *God's Mountain: The Temple Mount in Time, Place, and Memory.* Baltimore: Johns Hopkins University Press, 2008.

Elon, Amos. *Jerusalem: Battlegrounds of Memory.* New York: Kodansha International, 1997.

———. *Jerusalem: City of Mirrors.* Lexington, MA: Plunkett Lake Press, 2019.

Elton, Godfrey. *Gordon of Khartoum: The Life of General Charles George Gordon.* New York: Alfred A. Knopf, 1955.

Enderlin, Charles. *Shattered Dreams: The Failure of the Peace Process in the Middle East, 1995–2002.* New York: Other Press, 2003.

Falwell, Jerry. *Listen, America!* New York: Doubleday, 1980.

Fergusson, James. *The Holy Sepulchre and the Temple at Jerusalem: Being the Substance of Two Lectures, Delivered in the Royal Institution.* London: John Murray, 1865.

Finkelstein, Israel, and Neil Asher Silberman. *The Bible Unearthed.* New York: Simon and Schuster, 2002.

———. *David and Solomon: In Search of the Bible's Sacred Kings and the Roots of the Western Tradition*. New York: Free Press, 2007.

Finn, James. *Stirring Times: or Records from Jerusalem Consular Chronicles of 1853 to 1856*. London: C. K. Paul, 1878.

Fleury, Maurice. *Memoirs of the Empress Eugenie*. London: Appleton, 1920.

Foley, Cyril Pelham. *Autumn Foliage*. London: Methuen, 1935.

Fox, Edward. *Palestine Twilight: The Murder of Dr Albert Glock and the Archaeology of the Holy Land*. London: HarperCollins, 2002.

Freas, Erik. *Nationalism and the Haram Al-Sharif/Temple Mount: The Exclusivity of Holiness*. New York: Springer International, 2018.

Galor, Katharina. *Finding Jerusalem: Archaeology between Science and Ideology*. Oakland: University of California Press, 2017.

Galor, Katharina, and Gideon Avni. *Unearthing Jerusalem: 150 Years of Archaeological Research in the Holy City*. University Park: Penn State University Press, 2011.

Galor, Katharina, and Hanswulf Bloedhorn. *The Archaeology of Jerusalem from the Origins to the Ottomans*. New Haven, CT: Yale University Press, 2015.

Gange, David, and Michael Ledger-Lomas, eds. *Cities of God: The Bible and Archaeology in Nineteenth-Century Britain*. Cambridge: Cambridge University Press, 2016.

Geniesse, Jane Fletcher. *American Priestess: The Extraordinary Story of Anna Spafford and the American Colony in Jerusalem*. New York: Anchor Books, 2009.

Gibson, Shimon, and David M. Jacobson. *Below the Temple Mount in Jerusalem: A Sourcebook on the Cisterns, Subterranean Chambers and Conduits of the Haram Al-Sharif*. Oxford: Tempus Reparatum, 1996.

Gibson, Shimon, Yoni Shapira, and Robert L. Chapman III. *Tourists, Travellers and Hotels in 19th-Century Jerusalem: On Mark Twain and Charles Warren at the Mediterranean Hotel*. Milton Park, UK: Routledge, 2018.

Gilbert, Martin. *Jerusalem in the Twentieth Century*. New York: Wiley, 1998.

Gilbert, Vivian. *The Romance of the Last Crusade: With Allenby to Jerusalem*. New York: Appleton, 1923.

Gold, Dore. *Fight for Jerusalem: Radical Islam, the West, and the Future of the Holy City*. Washington, DC: Regnery Press, 2009.

Goldhill, Simon. *Jerusalem: City of Longing*. Cambridge, MA: Belknap Press of Harvard University Press, 2009.

Gonen, Rivka. *Contested Holiness: Jewish, Muslim, and Christian Perspectives on the Temple Mount in Jerusalem*. Jersey City, NJ: KTAV, 2003.

Goodman, Martin. *Rome and Jerusalem: The Clash of Ancient Civilizations*. London: Penguin, 2008.

Gorenberg, Gershom. *The End of Days: Fundamentalism and the Struggle for the Temple Mount*. Oxford: Oxford University Press, 2002.

Gorton, T. J., and Andree Feghali Gorton, eds. *A Jerusalem Anthology: Travel Writing through the Centuries*. Cairo: American University in Cairo Press, 2017.

Grabar, Oleg. *The Dome of the Rock*. Cambridge, MA: Belknap Press of Harvard University Press, 2006.

Grabar, Oleg, and Benjamin Z. Ḳedar, eds. *Where Heaven and Earth Meet: Jerusalem's Sacred Esplanade*. Austin: University of Texas Press, 2010.

Graham, Thomas. *Unending Crisis: National Security Policy after 9/11*. Seattle: Institute of Global and Regional Security Studies, Jackson School of International Studies in association with University of Washington Press, 2012.

Haley, P. Edward. *Strategies of Dominance: The Misdirection of U.S. Foreign Policy*. Washington, DC: Woodrow Wilson Center Press, 2006.

Hallote, Rachel. *Bible, Map, and Spade: The American Palestine Exploration Society, Fred-*

erick Jones Bliss, and the Forgotten Story of Early American Biblical Archaeology. Piscataway, NJ: Gorgias Press, 2006.

Hamblin, William J., and David Rolph Seely. *Solomon's Temple: Myth and History*. London: Thames & Hudson, 2007.

Harland-Jacobs, Jessica L. *Builders of Empire: Freemasons and British Imperialism, 1717–1927*. Chapel Hill: University of North Carolina, 2013.

Hassner, Ron E. *War on Sacred Grounds*. Ithaca, NY: Cornell University Press, 2010.

Herzl, Theodor. *A Jewish State: An Attempt at a Modern Solution of the Jewish Question*. New York: Maccabaean, 1904.

Hilprecht, Hermann. *Explorations in Bible Lands during the 19th Century: With Nearly Five Hundred Illustrations and Four Maps*. Edinburgh: AJ Hollman, 1903.

Hiro, Dilip. *Sharing the Promised Land: A Tale of Israelis and Palestinians*. New York: Olive Branch Press, 2002.

Hodder, Edwin. *The Life and Work of the Seventh Earl of Shaftesbury*. Cambridge: Cambridge University Press, 1886.

Hosein, Imran Nazar. *Jerusalem in the Qur'an: An Islamic View of the Destiny of Jerusalem Including: A Muslim Response to the Attack on America*. San Fernando, Trinidad and Tobago: Masjid Jāmíah, 2011.

Hulme, David. *Identity, Ideology, and the Future of Jerusalem*. New York: Springer, 2006.

Hunt, Edward D. *Holy Land Pilgrimage in the Later Roman Empire: AD 312–460*. Oxford: Clarendon Press, 1982.

Immanuel, Jonathan. *Britain, the Bible, and Balfour: Mandate for a Jewish State, 1530–1917*. Lanham, MD: Lexington Books, 2019.

Indyk, Martin. *Innocent Abroad: An Intimate Account of American Peace Diplomacy in the Middle East*. New York: Simon & Schuster, 2014.

Irizarry, Ashley M. *Possessing the Holy Land: The Palestine Exploration Fund and the American Palestine Exploration Society*. Williamsburg, VA: College of William and Mary, 2014.

Israel Exploration Society. *Jerusalem Revealed*. Jerusalem: Israel Exploration Society, 1975.

Jayyusi, Lena. *Jerusalem Interrupted: Modernity and Colonial Transformation 1917–Present*. Northampton, MA: Olive Branch Press, 2015.

Jeffers, H. Paul. *The Complete Idiot's Guide to Jerusalem*. Indianapolis: Alpha, 2004.

Johnson, Alfred Sidney. *The Cyclopedic Review of Current History*. Vol. 12. Boston: Current History Company, 1903.

Jones, Dan. *The Templars: The Rise and Spectacular Fall of God's Holy Warriors*. New York: Viking, 2017.

Josephus, Flavius. *The Antiquities of the Jews*. Translated by William Whiston. McLean, VA: IndyPublish.com, 2001.

———. *The New Complete Works of Josephus*. Translated by William Whiston. Commentary by Paul L. Maier. Grand Rapids, MI: Kregel, 1999.

———. *The War of the Jews*. Translated by William Whiston. Auburn, NY: John E. Beardsley, 1895.

Juvelius, Valter. *Valkoinen kameeli ja muita kertomuksia itämailta*. Project Gutenberg, 2005 (Finnish).

Kark, Ruth. *American Consuls in the Holy Land, 1832–1914*. Detroit: Wayne State University Press, 1994.

Kedar, Benjamin Z. *The Changing Land: Between Jordan and the Sea; Aerial Photographs from 1917 to the Present*. Detroit: Wayne State University Press, 1999.

Kenyon, Kathleen M. *Archaeology in the Holy Land*. London: Routledge, 2016.

———. *Digging Up Jerusalem*. London: Praeger, 1974.

———. *Jerusalem: Excavating 3,000 Years of History*. London: Thames and Hudson, 1967.

Khalidi, Rashid. *Palestinian Identity: The Construction of Modern National Consciousness.* New York: Columbia University Press, 1997.

Kimmerling, Baruch. *Politicide: Ariel Sharon's War against the Palestinians.* London: Verso, 2003.

Kingsley, Sean A. *God's Gold: The Quest for the Lost Temple Treasure of Jerusalem.* London: John Murray, 2007.

Kirsch, Jonathan. *King David: The Real Life of the Man Who Ruled Israel.* New York: Ballantine Books, 2001.

Klein, Menachem. *The Jerusalem Problem: The Struggle for a Permanent Status.* Gainesville: University Press of Florida, 2003.

Kletter, Raz. *Archaeology, Heritage and Ethics in the Western Wall Plaza, Jerusalem: Darkness at the End of the Tunnel.* London: Routledge Taylor & Francis Group, 2020.

———. *Just Past?: The Making of Israeli Archaeology.* Milton Park, UK: Routledge, 2014.

Kollek, Teddy, and Amos Kollek. *For Jerusalem.* New York: Random House, 1978.

Lagerlöf, Selma. *Jerusalem.* Stockholm: Bonnier, 2017.

Lambert, Michel Join. *Jerusalem.* London: Elek, 1958.

Lapierre, Dominique, and Larry Collins. *O Jerusalem!* New Delhi: Vikas, 2008.

Lawrence, T. E. *Seven Pillars of Wisdom.* Project Gutenberg, 2001.

Lemire, Vincent, Catherine Tihanyi, and Lys Ann Weiss. *Jerusalem 1900: The Holy City in the Age of Possibilities.* Chicago: University of Chicago Press, 2017.

Levin, Robert E. *Bill Clinton: The Inside Story.* New York: SPI, 1992.

Lewis, Jack P. *Early Explorers of Bible Lands.* Abilene: Abilene Christian University Press, 2013.

Lipschits, Oded. *The Fall and Rise of Jerusalem: Judah under Babylonian Rule.* Winona Lake, IN: Eisenbrauns, 2014.

Macalister, Robert Alexander Stewart, and John Garrow Duncan. *Excavations on the Hill of Ophel, Jerusalem, 1923–1925.* London: Palestine Exploration Fund, 1926.

Macdonald, Colin Neil. *Warren!: The Bond of Brotherhood.* Singapore: Coleman Street Books, 2007.

MacGregor, John. *The Rob Roy on the Jordan: A Canoe Cruise in Palestine, Egypt, and the Waters of Damascus.* London: J. Murray, 1904.

Mackintosh-Smith, Tim. *Arabs: A 3,000-Year History of Peoples, Tribes and Empires.* New Haven, CT: Yale University Press, 2019.

Mansurov, Boris. *Russkie Raskopki v Svjatom Grade Ierusalime Pered Sudom Arxeologičeskogo Obščestva [The Russian Excavations in the Holy City Jerusalem before the Court of the Society for Archeology].* Riga, 1887 (Russian).

Marcus, Amy Dockser. *Jerusalem 1913: The Origins of the Arab-Israeli Conflict.* New York: Penguin Books, 2008.

Mare, W. Harold. *The Archaeology of the Jerusalem Area.* Eugene, OR: Wipf & Stock, 2002.

Marty, Martin E., and R. Scott Appleby. *Fundamentalisms and the State: Remaking Polities, Economies, and Militance.* Chicago: University of Chicago Press, 1996.

Masalha, Nur. *The Bible and Zionism: Invented Traditions, Archaeology and Post-Colonialism in Israel-Palestine.* London: Zed Books, 2007.

———. *Palestine: A Four Thousand Year History.* London: Zed, 2018.

Massey, William Thomas. *How Jerusalem Was Won: Being the Record of Allenby's Campaign in Palestine.* Charleston, SC: Bibliobazaar, 2006.

Mayer, Tamar, and Suleiman Ali Mourad, eds. *Jerusalem: Idea and Reality.* Milton Park, UK: Routledge, 2008.

Mazar, Benjamin, Gaalyah Cornfeld, and D. N. Freedman. *The Mountain of the Lord.* New York: Doubleday, 1975.

Mazar, Eilat, and Benjamin Mazar. *Excavations in the South of the Temple Mount: The Ophel of Biblical Jerusalem.* Jerusalem: Institute of Archaeology, 1989.

Mazar, Eilat, Shalev Yiftaḥ, Peretz Reuven, Jonathan Steinberg, and Balage Balogh. *The Walls of the Temple Mount.* Jerusalem: Shoham Academic Research and Publication, 2011.

Mazza, Roberto. *Jerusalem: From the Ottomans to the British.* London: I. B. Tauris, 2014.

Medzini, Meron. *Israel's Foreign Relations: Selected Documents, 1947–1994.* Jerusalem: Ministry of Foreign Affairs, 1976.

Melville, Herman. *Journals.* Edited by Howard C. Horsford with Lynn Horth. Evanston, IL: Northwestern University Press, 1989.

Misselwitz, Philipp, and Tim Rieniets. *City of Collision: Jerusalem and the Principles of Conflict Urbanism.* Basel: Birkh, 2006.

Monk, Daniel Bertrand. *An Aesthetic Occupation: The Immediacy of Architecture and the Palestine Conflict.* Durham, NC: Duke University Press, 2002.

Montefiore, Simon Sebag. *Jerusalem: The Biography.* London: Weidenfeld & Nicolson, 2011.

Morris, Benny. *The Birth of the Palestinian Refugee Problem Revisited.* New York: Cambridge University Press, 2004.

Morris, Robert. *Freemasonry in the Holy Land: A Narrative of Masonic Explorations Made in 1868, in the Land of King Solomon and the Two Hirams.* La Grange, KY: self-pub., 1879.

Moscrop, John James. *Measuring Jerusalem: The Palestine Exploration Fund and British Interests in the Holy Land.* London: Leicester University Press, 2000.

Mourad, Suleiman A., Naomi Koltun-Fromm, and Bedross Der Matossian, eds. *Routledge Handbook on Jerusalem.* Milton Park, UK: Routledge, 2019.

Muhaiyaddeen, M. R. Bawa. *Islam and World Peace: Explanations of a Sufi.* Philadelphia: Fellowship Press, 2002.

Murphy-O'Connor, Jerome. *Keys to Jerusalem: Collected Essays.* Oxford: Oxford University Press, 2012.

Muslih, Muhammad Y. *The Origins of Palestinian Nationalism.* New York: ACLS History E-Book Project, 2005.

Na'or, Mordekhai. *City of Hope: Jerusalem from Biblical to Modern Times.* Jerusalem: Yad Izhak Ben-Zvi, 1996.

Nassar, Issam. *Photographing Jerusalem: The Image of the City in Nineteenth Century Photography.* Boulder, CO: East European Monographs, 1997.

Natsheh, Yusuf. *Discovering Jerusalem's Secrets: Walking Trails through the Old City and Beyond.* Jerusalem: Jerusalem Tourism Cluster, 2015.

Nitzan-Shiftan, Alona. *Seizing Jerusalem: The Architectures of Unilateral Unification.* Minneapolis: University of Minnesota Press, 2017.

Norwich, John Julius. *Cities That Shaped the Ancient World.* New York: Thames & Hudson, 2015.

Obenzinger, Hilton. *American Palestine: Melville, Twain, and the Holy Land Mania.* Princeton, NJ: Princeton University Press, 1999.

O'Keefe, Roger. *The Protection of Cultural Property in Armed Conflict.* Cambridge: Cambridge University Press, 2006.

Oren, Michael B. *Power, Faith, and Fantasy: America in the Middle East, 1776 to the Present.* New York: W. W. Norton, 2007.

Orr, Akiva. *The unJewish State: The Politics of Jewish Identity in Israel.* London: Ithaca Press, 1983.

Owen, Roger. *Studies in the Economic and Social History of Palestine in the Nineteenth and Twentieth Centuries.* London: Macmillan, 1982.

Passia. *Passia Diary 2019*. Jerusalem: Palestinian Academic Society for the Study of International Affairs, 2019.

Patai, Raphael. *The Complete Diaries of Theodor Herzl*. Vol. 2. New York: Herzl Press, 1960.

Peters, F. E. *Jerusalem: The Holy City in the Eyes of Chroniclers, Visitors, Pilgrims, and Prophets from the Days of Abraham to the Beginnings of Modern Times*. Princeton, NJ: Princeton University Press, 2017.

———. *Jerusalem and Mecca: The Typology of the Holy City in the Near East*. New York: New York University Press, 1987.

Petrie, William M. Flinders. *Seventy Years in Archaeology*. London: Sampson Low, Marston, 1932.

Pfoh, Emanuel, and Lukasz Niesiolowski-Spano. *Biblical Narratives, Archaeology and Historicity: Essays in Honour of Thomas L. Thompson*. Edinburgh: T & T Clark, 2019.

Pfoh, Emanuel, and Keith W. Whitelam. *The Politics of Israel's Past: The Bible, Archaeology and Nation-Building*. Sheffield, UK: Sheffield Phoenix Press, 2013.

Pierotti, Ermete. *Jerusalem Explored*. London: Bell and Daldy 1864.

Pressfield, Steven. *The Lion's Gate: On the Front Lines of the Six Day War*. New York: Sentinel, 2015.

Price, Randall. *In Search of Temple Treasures: The Lost Ark and the Last Days*. Eugene, OR: Harvest House, 1994.

———. *Searching for the Ark of the Covenant*. Eugene, OR: Harvest House, 2005.

Raugh, Harold E. *The Victorians at War, 1815–1914: An Encyclopedia of British Military History*. Santa Barbara, CA: ABC-CLIO, 2004.

Raz, S. *The Kotel Rabbi: The Life of Rabbi Meir Yehudah Getz*. Jerusalem, 2003 (Hebrew).

Reich, Ronny. *Excavating the City of David: Where Jerusalem's History Began*. Jerusalem: Israel Exploration Society, 2011.

Reich, Ronny, and Hershel Shanks, eds. *The City of David: Revisiting Early Excavations; English Translations of Reports by Raymond Weill and L.-H. Vincent*. Washington, DC: Biblical Archaeology Society, 2004.

Reinhartz, Adele. *Jesus of Hollywood*. New York: Oxford University Press, 2007.

Reiter, Yitzhak. *Contested Holy Places in Israel/Palestine: Sharing and Conflict Resolution*. Oxfordshire: Routledge, 2007.

———. *The Eroding Status-Quo: Power Struggles on the Temple Mount*. Jerusalem: Jerusalem Institute for Policy Research, 2017.

———. *Jerusalem and Its Role in Islamic Solidarity*. New York: Springer, 2008.

Ricca, Simone. *Reinventing Jerusalem: Israel's Reconstruction of the Jewish Quarter after 1967*. London: I. B. Tauris, 2007.

Rinzler, J. W., and Laurent Bouzereau. *The Complete Making of Indiana Jones: The Definitive Story Behind All Four Films*. New York: Del Rey, 2008.

Ritmeyer, Leen. *The Quest: Revealing the Temple Mount in Jerusalem*. Jerusalem: Carta, 2006.

Ritmeyer, Leen, and Kathleen Ritmeyer. *Jerusalem: The Temple Mount*. Jerusalem: Carta Jerusalem, 2015.

———. *Secrets of Jerusalem's Temple Mount*. Washington, DC: Biblical Archaeological Society, 2006.

Rogan, Eugene L. *The Arabs: A History*. London: Penguin Books, 2018.

Rogers, Mary Eliza. *Domestic Life in Palestine*. Paris: Poe & Hitchcock, 1865.

Rose, Pauline. *Window on Mount Zion*. New York: A. S. Barnes, 1973.

Rosovsky, Nitza. *City of the Great King: Jerusalem from David to the Present*. Cambridge, MA: Harvard University Press, 2013.

Ross, Dennis. *The Missing Peace: The Inside Story of the Fight for Middle East Peace*. New York: Farrar, Straus and Giroux, 2008.

Rubinstein, Danny. *The Mystery of Arafat*. South Royalton, VT: Steerforth Press, 1995.

Said, Edward W. *Culture and Imperialism*. London: Vintage Digital, 2014.

———. *Orientalism*. New York: Vintage Books, 2003.

Saulcy, Félicien de. *L. F. Caignart de Saulcy: Carnets de voyage en Orient, 1845–1869*. Paris: Presses Universitaires de France, 1955 (French).

———. *Narrative of a Journey around the Dead Sea, and in the Bible Lands, in 1850–1851*. London: R. Bentley, 1854.

Schnabel, Nikodemus. *Zuhause im Niemandsland: Mein Leben im Kloster zwischen Israel und Palästina*. Munich: Herbig, 2015 (German).

Schneer, Jonathan. *The Balfour Declaration*. New York: Random House, 2010.

Segev, Tom. *One Palestine, Complete: Jews and Arabs under the British Mandate*. London: Abacus, 2014.

Sekulow, Jay. *Jerusalem: A Biblical and Historical Case for the Jewish Capital*. Tustin, CA: Trilogy Christian Publishers, 2018.

Shagrir, Iris, Roni Ellenblum, and Jonathan Riley-Smith, eds. *In Laudem Hierosolymitani: Studies in Crusades and Medieval Culture in Honour of Benjamin Z. Kedar*. Aldershot, UK: Ashgate, 2007.

Shakespeare, William. *Henry IV*. In *The Complete Works of William Shakespeare*. Boston: Ginn & Heath, 1880.

Shanks, Hershel. *The City of David: A Guide to Biblical Jerusalem*. Washington, DC: Biblical Archaeology Society, 1973.

———. *Jerusalem: An Archaeological Biography*. New York: Random House, 1995.

Sher, Gilead. *The Israeli-Palestinian Peace Negotiations, 1999–2001: Within Reach*. London: Routledge, 2013.

Shragai, Nadav. *The Temple Mount Conflict (Har Ha-Meriva)*. Jerusalem: Keter, 1995 (Hebrew).

Silberman, Neil Asher. *Digging for God and Country: Exploration, Archaeology, and the Secret Struggle for the Holy Land*. New York: Alfred A. Knopf, 1982.

———. *A Prophet from Amongst You: The Life of Yigael Yadin; Soldier, Scholar, and Mythmaker of Modern Israel*. New York: Addison-Wesley, 1993.

Standish, Russell R., and Colin D. Standish. *Holy Relics or Revelation*. Rapidan, VA: Hartland, 1999.

Stern, Jessica. *Terror in the Name of God: Why Religious Militants Kill*. New York: Harper-Collins, 2004.

Stiebel, Guy D., Orit Peleg-Barkat, Doron Ben-Ami, and Yuval Gadot, eds. *New Studies in the Archaeology of Jerusalem and Its Region, Collected Papers*. Vol. 8. Jerusalem: Tel Aviv University, 2014.

Storrs, Ronald. *Memoirs of Sir Ronald Storrs*. New York: G. P. Putnam's Sons, 1937.

———. *Orientations*. London: Nicholson & Watson, 1943.

Straus, Isaac. *The American Jewish Chronicle*. Vol. 4. New York: Alpha Omega, 1918.

Swisher, Clayton E. *The Truth about Camp David: The Untold Story about the Collapse of the Middle East Peace Process*. New York: Bold Type Books, 2009.

Talhami, Ghada Hashem. *American Presidents and Jerusalem*. Lanham, MD: Lexington Books, 2017.

Thubron, Colin. *Jerusalem*. New York: Time Life Books, 1976.

Tibawi, Abdul Latif. *British Interests in Palestine, 1800–1901: A Study of Religious and Educational Enterprise*. London: Oxford University Press, 1961.

———. *The Islamic Pious Foundations in Jerusalem: Origins, History and Usurpation by Israel*. London: Islamic Cultural Centre, 1978.

———. *Jerusalem: Its Place in Islam and Arab History*. London: Islamic Cultural Centre, 1969.

Tuchman, Barbara Wertheim. *Bible and Sword: England and Palestine from the Bronze Age to Balfour.* London: Phoenix, 2001.

Twain, Mark. *The Innocents Abroad.* Hartford, CT: American Publishing House, 1884.

———. *Mark Twain's Notebooks and Journals.* Vol. 1. Edited by Frederick Anderson, Michael Barry Frank, and Kenneth M. Sanderson. Berkeley: University of California Press, 1976.

V., H. [Louis-Hugues Vincent]. *Underground Jerusalem: Discoveries on the Hill of Ophel (1909–11).* London: Cox, 1911.

Vester, Bertha Hedges. *Our Jerusalem.* Garden City, NY: Doubleday, 1950.

Vogel, Lester I. *To See a Promised Land: Americans and the Holy Land in the Nineteenth Century.* University Park: Pennsylvania State University Press, 1993.

Wakeman, Robert Peel. *Wakeman Genealogy: 1630–1899.* Meridian, CT: Journal, 1900.

Wallon, H. *Notice historique sur la vie et les travaux de M. L. F. J. Caignart de Saulcy, membre de l'Académie des Inscriptions et Belles-Lettres.* Paris: Imprimerie Nationale, 1881 (French).

Warburton, Eliot. *Travels in Egypt and the Holy Land: or, The Crescent and the Cross, Comprising the Romance and Realities of Eastern Travel.* Philadelphia: H. C. Peck & Theodore Bliss, 1859.

Wardle, Timothy. *The Jerusalem Temple and Early Christian Identity.* Tübingen, Germany: Mohr Siebeck, 2010.

Warren, Charles. *The Temple or the Tomb, Giving Further Evidence in Favour of the Authenticity of the Present Site of the Holy Sepulchre, and Pointing out Misconceptions in Fergusson's "Holy Sepulchre" and "The Temples of the Jews."* London: R. Bentley, 1880.

———. *Underground Jerusalem.* London: Bentley, 1876.

Warren, Charles, and C. R. Conder. *The Survey of Western Palestine, Jerusalem.* Jerusalem: Committee of the Palestine Exploration Fund, 1889.

Wasserstein, Bernard. *Divided Jerusalem: The Struggle for the Holy City.* New Haven, CT: Yale University Press, 2008.

Watson, Charles Moore. *The Life of Major-General Sir Charles William Wilson.* London: J. Murray, 1909.

Weizman, Eyal. *Hollow Land.* London: Verso Books, 2017.

Weizmann, Chaim. *Trial and Error: The Autobiography of Chaim Weizmann, Book One (1874–1917).* Lexington, MA: Plunkett Lake Press, 2013.

Weksler-Bdolah, Shlomit. *Aelia Capitolina—Jerusalem in the Roman Period.* Milton Park, UK: Routledge, 2019.

White, Ellen G. *The Spirit of Prophecy.* Battle Creek, MI: Seventh-Day Adventist, 1880.

Whitty, John Irwine. *Proposed Water Supply and Sewerage for Jerusalem: with Description of Its Present State and Former Resources.* London: W. J. Johnson, 1863.

Williams, Georges. *The Holy City: Historical Topographical and Antiquarian Notices of Jerusalem.* London: Parker, 1849.

Williams, Watkin W. *The Life of General Sir Charles Warren.* Oxford: Blackwell, 1941.

Wilson, Capt. [Charles William], and Capt. [Charles] Warren. *The Recovery of Jerusalem: A Narrative of Exploration in the City and the Holy Land.* Edited by Walter Morrison. London: Richard Bentley, 1871.

Wilson, Charles W. *Ordnance Survey of Jerusalem.* Authority of the Lords Commissioners of Her Majesty's Treasury, 1886.

Wroe, Ann. *Pontius Pilate.* New York: Random House, 2001.

Wyatt, Mary Nell. *The Ark of the Covenant.* Nashville, TN: Wyatt Archaeological Research, 1995.

Wylie, Rev. James Aitken. *The Modern Judea, Compared with Ancient Prophecy: With Notes Illustrative of Biblical Subjects.* Glasgow: William Collins, Sons, 1872.

Index

Page numbers in *italics* refer to maps.
Surnames starting with "al-" and "el-" are alphabetized by the following part of the name.